Black Gold

Jeremy Paxman

BLACK GOLD

THE HISTORY OF HOW COAL MADE BRITAIN

WILLIAM COLLINS

William Collins
An imprint of HarperCollins*Publishers*
1 London Bridge Street
London SE1 9GF

WilliamCollinsBooks.com

HarperCollins*Publishers*
1st Floor, Watermarque Building, Ringsend Road
Dublin 4, Ireland

First published in Great Britain in 2021 by William Collins

2

A catalogue record for this book is
available from the British Library

ISBN 978-0-00-812834-0

Typeset in Minion Pro
Printed and bound in the UK using 100%
renewable electricity at CPI Group (UK) Ltd

MIX
Paper from
responsible sources
FSC
www.fsc.org   FSC™ C007454

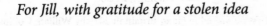

For Jill, with gratitude for a stolen idea

Contents

Prologue

The Hastings is a roadside pub in the village of Seaton Delaval, a few miles north-east of Newcastle. The pub (and village) are named after local landowners, who had been granted land by William the Conqueror and become abundantly rich, mainly on the proceeds of coal-mining. They had that instinct for survival which marks so many wealthy families with large estates. When they fell on hard times, they restored their fortunes through adroit marriage, after which they commissioned a fashionable architect to build them a massive stately home. Admiral George Delaval picked Sir John Vanbrugh, the architect of Blenheim Palace and Castle Howard, to build a magnificent English baroque pile in the early eighteenth century. These families intended to impress, and in that the Delavals were successful – Vanbrugh's designs were his last for a country house, and are thought by many to be his finest work. Seaton Delaval Hall is vast, with an enormous central courtyard of almost 2,500 square metres between two symmetrical wings. It is one of the grandest houses in Northumberland.

If they get that far, some of the 80,000 annual visitors to the Hall are entertained by the mausoleum in the grounds dedicated to a nineteen-year-old son and heir who died after being kicked in 'a vital organ' while attempting to seduce a laundrymaid in 1775. If they but knew it, there is a much more dramatic story to be found in the village outside the gates of the majestic Hall. The families of the miners who worked in the new mine, which

opened in the year of Queen Victoria's accession, lived in 360
gimcrack cottages, supplied with water which had to be carried
indoors from standpipes. There was, of course, no internal sanitation either. The village had three shops – a tailor, a butcher and
a grocer/draper. A few of the residents – the local doctor, minister, stationmaster and some senior colliery officials – had bigger
houses, but the best of the miners' homes contained two rooms
downstairs, with a ladder leading to an attic. Most of the
mine-workers lived five people to a house, and for those with
large families, conditions must have been appallingly cramped.
(The 1891 census shows Edward Ranshaw, a fifty-one-year-old
miner, living in two rooms and an attic with a wife, six children,
and two lodgers.[1])

Across the road from the Hastings pub is a branch of the local
Co-op, successor to the shop founded by the residents in 1863 as
the first miners' co-op in Britain. It nestles behind a petrol station
selling pork scratchings on the counter. In front of the pub, beneath
a plastic sign offering 'Geordie Tappaz', and live sport on the bar's
numerous televisions, a middle-aged white man walks his two
greyhounds on a leash. The pub doesn't look as if it is on a
Campaign for Real Ale pilgrimage route.

But one Sunday in 1862 the place was besieged by huge numbers
of customers. They had arrived by train, horse, carriage and on
foot. The pub was, said a witness, 'literally swarming with visitors
… passages and staircases alike being impassable; and, with a
callousness that is positively shocking, all are drinking, joking and
enjoying themselves'.[2] The local police struggled to exert some sort
of control outside the pub, by erecting temporary barriers. But it
was the weekend, the Hastings was the only licensed premises in
the area, and the sheer number of customers was simply unman-
ageable. Nothing draws a crowd like the chance to learn details of
a tragedy. The visitors had come to try to discover what was
happening literally beneath their feet.

Three days earlier, between ten and eleven on the morning of 16 January 1862, the second shift of the day had assembled for work at the colliery in the next-door village of New Hartley. The newly arrived miners were due to take over from what was called the foreshift, which had begun work in the middle of the night. Like most changeovers it was to take place underground, to save time and money for the mine operators, who did not want to pay men for the time they spent being dropped in cages down the mineshaft and then walking or crawling along underground passages to the face they were expected to chip away at. The pit had been sunk over fifteen years beforehand and had been an unlucky place from the start. Its predecessor had been closed in the 1840s, because it kept flooding. But, the mine produced good steam coal and its newly rich owner, Charles Carr – all sideburns and waistcoat and with what was said to be the tallest top hat in the county – believed that with a big enough steam pump to drain water from the pit, the coal could be extracted and sold. The machine made for him was one of the most powerful in the entire north-east coalfield, and built by one of the heavy engineering firms which had developed on the banks of the Tyne in the wake of the coal trade. The main cylinder of the beam engine was over seven feet across, pushing up and down an enormous horizontal girder over thirty-four feet long, made of cast-iron and weighing forty-two tons.

Shortly before eleven that morning, with a tremendous shattering noise, it broke in two. Part of the beam – perhaps weighing over twenty tons – fell down the shaft, which was the only way into – and out of – the mine. The accident had occurred at the worst possible time, when the maximum number of men were underground for the shift change. It would have been easier to manage a rescue had there been – as existed at other pits – two mineshafts. But the owners had followed local practice and sunk only one shaft into the earth, about twelve feet across. The shaft was divided in two all the way down by a timber partition – or 'brattice' – to allow the usual mining ventilation system, in which clean air could reach the men underground through a 'down' draught while a fire was kept burning low down on the 'up-cast' side, to draw in the foul air of the mine and release it to the surface. If the single shaft became blocked for any reason – as now happened – tragedy would surely follow.

That morning a cage was being raised to the surface. Inside were eight men who had just finished their shift, doubtless pleased to be the first to have completed their time underground. When they were about halfway to the surface they heard a terrifying crack, followed by a roar, as the broken beam careered down the hole. Debris dislodged from the walls of the shaft, and bits of lift machinery struck the cage, snapping two of its four supporting cables. Four of the men inside the ungated cage were thrown out and plunged into the darkness below, as rock, metal and timber rained down upon them. The remaining miners knew their friends would not survive the fall. The massive beam continued its descent down the shaft, dislodging rock, rubble and heavy timbers as it fell. The rocks, rubble and rubbish then jammed across the shaft, blocking access to two of the three seams of coal; 204 men and boys were now trapped underground.

The fatal accident at Hartley Colliery sounds extraordinary to the modern ear. The Hartley disaster was bigger than most, but Britain had by this time a barely satiable appetite for coal, and it was fed at a terrible price in human suffering. For over 400 years, the fuel of a nation and empire was dogged with accident. 'Close the coal-house door, lad,' sang the Tyneside radical Alex Glasgow a hundred years later, 'there's blood inside.' Perhaps there were years when no one died trying to get coal out of the ground. But they were exceptional.

After the initial paralysis caused by the shock, men on the surface at Hartley began quickly to organise rescue efforts. By midnight, rescuers had clambered down and reached the cage, where George Sharp, though badly injured, was saying that he wanted to climb down to help his son, Young George, whom he could hear lying injured and moaning on the rockfall below. One of the rescuers put a sling around the old man, but as he was being lowered, he struck an overhanging piece of timber, was knocked from the sling, and plunged to his death. He hit the ground a few feet away from where his son had fallen. Two other men from the cage were retrieved successfully, but the most heroic act that day came from Thomas Watson, a recent convert to Primitive Methodism, who had himself lowered into the darkness and stayed with the wounded men on a pile of debris part way down the shaft, leading them in prayers, and hymn-singing, until they died. Watson was the last man to be brought to the surface alive. He had been underground for eleven hours. Other miners rushed to the stricken colliery to offer what help they could. Under the leadership of William Coulson – who, with over forty years' experience was considered the finest sinker of mineshafts in the north-east – they worked on feverishly. But the obstacles were enormous. Great quantities of debris blocked their way and often they had to line the walls of the shaft with heavy timber to prevent another fall.

By now, word had spread across the north-east that a life-or-death rescue drama was taking place. Over the weekend, the trippers began to arrive and the Hastings found itself with a roaring trade. Among those despatched to the scene was Thomas Wemyss Reid, a nineteen-year-old reporter on the *Newcastle Journal and Courant*, who began to keep an hourly account of what he rapidly recognised as 'the most terrible calamity that was ever visited upon any coal mine in the country'.[3] His writing is purple in places, but for the most part remains an object lesson in how to write about ongoing drama: urgent, frank, emotional, exploitative, of course, yet dignified. On the Saturday he noted how

Around the pit buildings a crowd of men are gathered, talking to each other in undertones, speculating upon the fate of their comrades. Whenever the gin [winch] needs to be turned they volunteer for the service, for the horses are thoroughly worn out with the labour through which they have gone. At other times they stand idly and silently, apparently quite unconscious of the bitter blast which is sweeping in from the sea with chilling force. Occasionally one or two women, with tearless faces … come from the village to know if anything has transpired regarding the fate of their loved ones, and then, with fixed stony countenances, the sight of which is far more moving than any violent outbursts of passion would be, slowly return to their desolate homes. The appearance of the village itself indicates the presence of some overpowering calamity.

'Few villages are more noisy or cheerful than those connected with collieries,' he wrote with some journalistic licence, 'but here a deep and solemn silence prevails. No children are at play, every door is shut, and the one or two little shops at which the inhabitants supply themselves are partially closed. Through the windows can be seen the clean bed, which is always remarkable in the cottage of the north-country pitman, while upon the table in front of the window, in almost every case, the breakfast things prepared for the prisoners on Thursday morning are still standing awaiting them.'

Hour by hour the reporter recorded the frenzied efforts and the false hopes. Someone had seen smoke rising – the trapped men must have made a fire and could feed themselves on the dead pit ponies. 'Hope at last, thank God!' Wemyss Reid wrote in his journal at midday. 'Jowling' had been heard, which was taken for a sign of life (it turned out later to be sounds of rock and water moving). 'Helpful' suggestions were coming in from across the country. A Mr Hill of Bristol had suggested boring a small hole through the debris in the shaft and pouring soup down it to the men. 'Mr Hill and the others who propose this plan may rest assured that, had it been feasible, it would long ago have been attempted.' At nine on Monday morning he reported that digging was going better than expected, and 'another hour, or at the most two, must decide the dreadful fate of the 204 prisoners'. In Newcastle, some idiot in his newspaper's circulation department had placards painted with the words 'Glorious News At Last'.

The truth was that those who had survived the accident to the cage had been poisoned by 'stythe' or chokedamp – one of a variety of gases produced when hitherto buried coal was exposed to the atmosphere. Deep in their hearts, the wives and families of the missing miners, most of whom sat up all night in their cottages, began to realise that their menfolk were never to return alive. At the pithead, Wemyss Reid heard suspicions sweeping the crowd that the survivors of the accident had been gassed. At ten o'clock he wrote that 'the very heart sickens and the hand palsies as we write these lines, and anticipate a dreadful conclusion to our long and painful watch'. At four on Tuesday morning – almost five whole days after the accident – 'an incident of a truly appalling nature' happened. A man had run to the platform at the pithead and shouted 'All the men are alive. They've got the shaft clear. They're all safe.' No sooner had he screamed this than five of the rescuers were brought to the surface, having been gassed: it was now clear that any miner who had not been crushed had probably been asphyxiated. But the see-sawing of emotions continued. At seven in the morning, officials were said to be confident that the trapped miners could be rescued. At 11.30 on Wednesday, Wemyss Reid reported that one of the rescuers had found two axes, a saw and a back-protector belonging to the missing men. But on Wednesday afternoon a particularly bold group of rescuers forced their way into a hitherto unexplored area, a coal seam called The Yard. Here they found two bodies, and then, pushing on through the foul air, about fifty other bodies 'strewn in all directions'. Many were badly swollen, indicating they had been dead for days. The next party of rescuers found more bodies 'lying promiscuously side by side; but the boys of each family appeared to be clustered around their relatives'. Since they had food in their pockets, they could not have starved to death. It was small comfort. Now the business of the rescuers was to retrieve bodies, and leather slings were lowered into the pit. An official then decided that it was not worth risking more lives to recover the corpses. The decision confirmed what many had by now sadly accepted.

> The shock was given on Thursday morning, when the dreadful news flew like lightning through the desolate village. Gradually, bit by bit, the noble fires of hope have sunk lower and lower in every heart; and it is only the last uncertain flickering flame that has now been quenched. With a dead silence the people heard the words which told them they were widows, orphans or childless. Job, in all his calamities, could not have been more resigned than they; and the audible 'God help them all,' muttered upon the platform, was the only comment the address called forth.

Later that day two brothers braved the gas, and returned to the surface, reporting they had found over 150 bodies. 'There was a very bad smell, indeed, from the bodies. They had no appearance of having been starved; but all appeared just to have lain down and slept themselves to death. Only one or two seemed to have died hard; but it was quite discernible, from the appearance of all, that they had been dead some time.'

The entire country was now transfixed. Coal was the nation's special gift from God: however much imperial painters and writers preferred to claim otherwise. Thomas Jones Barker began work on a painting about the country's mission in the year of the disaster. It showed Queen Victoria handing a Bible to a fawning, kneeling

African potentate, as her frock-coated prime minister and Foreign Secretary looked on. Those who really knew how things worked understood this was a fable: the true secret of England's greatness was the power unleashed by coal.

This filthy rock had performed an act of magic upon a set of islands of undistinguished size in the North Atlantic. It had liberated the country's scientific and technological potential. It had enabled the people living there to make objects the rest of the world wanted. That very year, the world's biggest warship, HMS *Warrior*, was deployed at sea. As well as her three masts, she was powered by ten coal-fired boilers and clad in coal-smelted wrought iron. Coal had produced the gas which provided the illumination for the Great Exhibition and there was hardly a town in the land without gas lighting. Coal would soon drive the generators to make electricity. It was the source of England's power.

At about two that January afternoon in 1862, a telegram had reached the rescuers in Northumberland. It had been sent from Queen Victoria in her ostentatious retreat at Osborne, on the Isle of Wight. 'The Queen is most anxious to hear that there are hopes of saving the poor people in the colliery, for whom her heart bleeds,' it read. In truth, there was now no hope. But the rescuers sent a message back that there was a faint chance that perhaps some of the men might be rescued. That evening they faced reality and sent a further telegram, with the news that over a hundred men had been found dead and there was no hope of discovering anyone alive. Miners continued to try to burrow down the blocked shaft, but, Wemyss Reid thought, with less enthusiasm, now that they knew they were only in the business of recovering bodies. The anxious crowds of wives and children at the pithead started to melt away.

The gas in the mine affected the rescuers in a variety of ways. Many passed out. One came up seeming to be raging drunk, offering to fight anyone. By Thursday, though, there was another problem. The stench of decomposition was so bad that men coming to the surface after their two-hour shift underground were violently sick. All the colliery carpenters in the area were assigned to the task of building coffins. It was decided to put the bodies into the coffins before they were brought to the surface.

That night, Wemyss Reid noted that 'dreadful scenes are occurring. Fathers coming to the shaft, almost frantic, to seek their children, wives wailing for their husbands, and sons for their parents. It is a most painful scene.'[4] Soon the women had disappeared and that night some of the men on the surface became 'wickedly unreasonable'. One man, who had four sons lying dead in the pit, clambered onto the platform. 'Grief had completely unhinged his intellect,' the reporter noted, and 'had he not been restrained, he would undoubtedly have thrown himself headlong down the shaft'.[5]

There was now a sharp disagreement between those organising the retrieval of corpses and some relatives of the dead. Many of the bodies – especially those of boys who had died – were unrecognisable except by their clothes, yet many of the families wanted to see the dead with their own eyes. It was agreed, eventually, that the coffins would be brought to the surface with their lids only lightly secured, so that those who wanted to look inside could prise them open and do so.

Conditions in the shaft were now appalling. Every time there was another fall of debris, a terrible stench of decomposition was blown into the faces of those making their way down. Everyone knew that, with no pump working, the water level inside the mine was rising all the time and that soon recovery work would have to stop.

By now, visitors from further afield had flocked to the scene of the tragedy, each train disgorging more crowds of sightseers, though miners prevented them jostling too close to the shaft and getting in the way. Men selling hot pies plied their trade among the crowds. The Bishop of Durham and the mayor of Newcastle arrived, the bishop going from door to door offering what spiritual succour he could to the bereaved. He was later followed by 'men of different creeds and classes, for once bound together by the common bond of charity'. At eight on the Thursday evening the rescue committee calculated that the accident had created 103 widows and left 257 children and 47 dependent adults with no means of support. The local vicar decided there was not enough room in the church graveyard to bury the dead and asked the Duke of Northumberland for more land. It was decided to set up a relief fund, with a public meeting in Newcastle at the weekend.

The crowd at the pithead had thinned out, though people still came who had travelled great distances. Mining was an industry which attracted immigrants from across the country, prepared to descend into the depths of the earth for the sake of decent wages, so the effects of the tragedy were unconfined. 'An old man named Yule came here from Glasgow and found that he was childless,' wrote Wemyss Reid. 'Today we have seen wives and mothers, daughters and sisters wend their weary way here, from all parts and receive sentence of bereavement.'[6] On Friday the men from *The Times*, the *Morning Chronicle* and the *Mining Journal* arrived, along with a couple of artists from the *Illustrated London News*. They were in time to see horse-drawn carts deliver the first of the 200 black coffins that had been ordered. Along with barrels of chloride of lime, a hundred pairs of long-armed gloves were stock-piled at the head of the shaft for the men who would have to bring up the remaining corpses. On Saturday, the final effort to recover the bodies began in earnest. A chartered train arrived, carrying nothing but coffins. Bodies were brought up by the same impro-vised winch which had been lowering the rescuers. The men who were expected to ride to the surface with the human remains were given tots of whisky to help them cope with their grisly task.

As the end of the rope drew near the surface, one of the men was seen riding upon the little sling on which the sinkers have so fearlessly ascended and descended. Just below him, carefully attached to an iron chain, was a strange and hideous object which at first we could not recognise. In a moment however, we saw that it was the stiffened form of one of the victims of the carbonic-oxide that was dangling in mid-air before us. In a moment he was landed upon the platform. It was dreadful to look upon his skinny, attenuated form, which seemed so small beside the gigantic men around, his fleshless hands curiously marked in white and blue, and his fixed, immobile features, the closed eyes of which denoted that he had slept even while treading the valley of the shadow of Death. He was thrown down upon an open shroud, spread upon the ground, and while he was being rapidly rolled up in it, someone called out his name, which was methodically entered in a book by one man, whilst another chalked it on the lid of the coffin into which he was forthwith lifted. Thus laden, the coffin was placed upon a small trolley, and pushed along the wooden bridge separating one portion of the pit-heap from another. At the further end, the name inscribed upon the coffin was called out; someone stepped forward from amongst the dense crowd of waiters, and claiming the body as that of a relative, it was placed in a cart and conveyed to the home it left in health and strength some ten days ago … Men and boys of all sizes and ages were brought up to the surface. Some had died with a smile upon their faces, others frowning in terror or anger. There were strong men of gigantic mould, still apparently engaged in a deadly struggle with the last adversary; and there were children – weak and helpless, early doomed to toil in everlasting darkness – clasped in the arms of loving fathers, who, even in their own extremity, remembered those whom they had begotten. One after another they were dragged forth from the huge charnel-house below; and as hour by hour in unending succession they were brought forth, it seemed as if some unholy, premature resurrection were going on.[7]

This miserable work continued throughout the night, with the area around the top of the shaft lit by flickering torches, and the gruesome task of identification largely carried out by Mark Bell, a boy of about fourteen, whose role at the pit had been to collect the identity 'tallies' handed in by the men as they went down to begin work. Once the victim's name had been scrawled on the lid of the coffin, Robert Turnbull, the miners' leader – a man with dark ringlets and enormous shaggy beard – shouted it out, so that the body might be claimed by the family and carried away on a horse-drawn cart to the miner's cottage. Those bodies which could not be identified were stacked in their coffins in a makeshift morgue inside the Methodist chapel of the dreary village.

At four on Sunday morning, the last of the dead were brought to the surface. Now, the crowds of disaster tourists grew again. Throughout the morning they arrived by train, trap and cab, gawping at the wreckage, and then peering through any open cottage doors at the grieving families inside. At midday on the sloping side of one of the spoil heaps, half a dozen clergymen conducted a service for the crowd. Before the prayers a letter from Sir Charles Phipps, one of the queen's equerries, was read out. Her Majesty hoped that as much as possible would be done for the families of the dead, and would like to make a contribution herself. At one-thirty, the funeral of the dead miners began. Wemyss Reid believed that no one had ever before witnessed such a spectacle. He was probably right – there had not been a loss of life on this scale in Britain since the Battle of Culloden in 1745. The side of the slag heap nearest the station was so covered in people that it looked vaguely like a fairground or racecourse, with stalls selling tea and food. Outside the miners' cottages 'a cart seemed standing at almost every door, and was surrounded by a few men decently attired in mourning'. Wemyss Reid noted that a large number of the mourners were fellow miners, many of them 'attired in the showy garments which this class so much affects, velvet waistcoats and white feathers being very common articles of apparel'.[8] Most of the carts carried a single coffin, though the reporter saw seven coffins brought out of a single cottage. At a very slow pace, the horses and carts, white sheets thrown over the coffins, plodded their way to the village of Earsdon, four miles away. The first coffins had arrived at St Alban's Church before the last had left the pit village. It took until after dark to bury them all.

That afternoon, the men who had supervised the retrieval of the bodies opened the area around the top of the mineshaft to visitors. For a sixpenny donation to the relief fund, sightseers would be allowed up close and could even stare down the hole in the ground through which the bodies had been recovered.

The disaster had been on a larger scale than most mining accidents, but it was different only in magnitude. Think of a violent death – crushed, blown up, poisoned, gassed, incinerated, cut to pieces, even murdered – and it almost certainly happened in a mine somewhere beneath our feet. It was inevitable that the digging of coal would be political, for there were few other occupations in which the arbitrariness of fate could have such harsh consequences. The rich owned the rolling acres and the poor dug in the dark underneath them. Grubbing out the stuff that made their country function, the miners were out of sight and out of mind. But they were also beyond close control – they organised themselves and they educated each other, in anything from horticulture to power politics. The two greatest industrial confrontations of the twentieth century – the 1926 General Strike, and the miners' strike of 1984–5 – were both about coal.

In the Hartley disaster of 1862, the grandest local toff, the Duke of Northumberland, honoured his word and gave land for the local churchyard to be extended to accommodate the miners' graves. (The duke could afford it – the family estate had grown to 19,200 acres, largely on the proceeds of coal royalties.) A small number of the dead were laid in single graves, others adjacent to family members under stones recording their deaths in the 'fatal calamity'. Thirty-three of the victims, many unidentified, were buried in a communal grave. Today, the graveyard extension is as overgrown with ivy and nettles as the rest of the cemetery. In one corner of the graveyard is an obelisk stained green by the lichen growing in the shade of the slatternly sycamores which have invaded the place. On the memorial's sides you can make out the names of the dead, ranging in age from ten to seventy-one, among them eight members of the Liddle family, including seven children and teenagers. Beneath the green mould on the memorial, you can just make out the words from St Matthew's Gospel chiselled into the stone, 'THEREFORE BE YE ALSO READY: FOR IN SUCH AN HOUR AS YE THINK NOT, THE SON OF MAN COMETH', along with St Paul's stern warning that 'GOD IS NOT MOCKED; FOR WHATSOEVER THOU SOWETH, THAT ALSO SHALL YE REAP'. Victorian religious practice seems as unforgiving as the backbreaking daily labour of the time. The stonemasons might as well have opened the King James Bible and carved 'to those who hath, to him shall be given: and from he that hath not, from him shall be taken away even that which he hath'. The men who died in the Hartley disaster had been the poor of the earth, who fed themselves by burrowing underground for other men.

By the end of April 1862, the public relief fund to support the bereaved had gathered £75,000 (equivalent to perhaps £10 million at current values). But the greatest consequence of the disaster was a change in the law. Had there been more than one shaft, the airway might not have been completely blocked and the men – or some of them – might have escaped. The safety benefits of having more than one shaft had been pointed out over twenty years beforehand, but the suggestion had not been acted upon, since it doubled the cost of getting down to the coal. Now, at the inquest into the men's deaths, the jury added a rider to their verdict that 'all working collieries have at least a second shaft or outlet'. Even mine-owners now supported the idea, and a law was passed making it compulsory for all pits to have at least two entrances: it is noticeable how many safety precautions in mining only came about when legislation compelled the mine-owners to introduce them. Wemyss Reid went on to something of a stellar career in journalism and publishing: by twenty-eight he had become editor of the *Leeds Mercury*, and after moving to London established a reputation for scoops about the inner workings of the Liberal Party, of which he was an active member. In due course, a grateful Lord Rosebery recommended him for one of the first journalistic knighthoods, and he duly developed into a pompous bore, dying of pleurisy in 1905. The Hartley mine itself was abandoned and later rented to another company, which in 1900 pumped the water out of the main seam and discovered the mining gear and coal tubs exactly as they had been left thirty-eight years earlier.

We have become unaccustomed to hearing of long-gone mining disasters. But coal was bought with human life wherever it was mined. There had been numerous other fatal accidents in the coal-fields before the Hartley tragedy, and within five years of it happening, 361 men and boys were killed in explosions at The Oaks Colliery near Barnsley, the biggest single loss of life in an English mine. There was a melancholy pattern of behaviour at these disasters. The initial shock spread through the little communities like an electric charge, with anxious wives and families rushing to the pithead, or as close as they were allowed, everyone wondering whether their husband, son or neighbour, was alive or dead, or perhaps gasping, bleeding, or drowning somewhere beneath their feet, then the arrival of other miners, grim-faced and resolute, who had volunteered as rescuers, then the food which appeared from nowhere to feed the rescuers, the silence which fell upon everyone as bodies were recovered, 'Abide With Me' sung at the subsequent church services and the many appeals launched by men in dark suits and mayoral chains.

In modern times, the most horrifying of British mining trage-dies occurred not underground but in a school, when a South Wales spoil tip slid downhill and engulfed Pantglas junior school in Aberfan in October 1966; 116 children, most aged between seven and ten, along with twenty-eight adults, were killed that morning. It surely could not get any worse. By then, coal-mining in Britain was in what turned out to be terminal decline and there is something horribly apposite in the fact that the most recent victims of a great disaster were killed not by coal but by what is left after coal has been mined. Only a fool would say that there will never be another mining-related catastrophe in Britain. But since it became unfashionable to deep-mine for coal, the country has outsourced its production, and the attendant pain usually occurs somewhere else, too. It may be in Colombia, Australia, India or somewhere else out of earshot. But for sure, someone is crying somewhere.

Go to Aberfan today and the site of the school is a Garden of Remembrance. The children's graves are well kept in the village cemetery. The old coal-yard is a site for commuter homes: today's valley-dwellers do not have to walk to work. The name Aberfan perhaps rings an unhappy echo in the memory of old people, but soon the dead children will be as forgotten as William and George Fairbairn, young and old George Sharp and the three Wanless brothers, aged from fourteen to twenty who died in the Hartley disaster in 1862. In 1976, over a century after that catastrophe, a small memorial garden was opened around the capped top of the old shaft from which the bodies of the dead men had been retrieved, by the then president of the miners' union, Joe Gormley.

It takes an extraordinary effort of will to make a connection between the verdant grass, geraniums and benches and the 204 men and boys who died. Perhaps it was easier to make the imaginative leap thirty or forty years ago.

Such is the story of coal: go to an old mining village and the chances are that you won't even see the spoil heaps, let alone the winding gear. Time moves on and the things we understand change. It sometimes seems that all that really remains of an occupation which employed well over a million men are thoughtless clichés – people 'dig down' to 'mine' information, yielding a 'seam' of meaning. To get there may involve 'labouring at the coalface'. It is dead language, but we understand it. There are vaguely remembered tales of great-uncles who sat in tin baths scrubbing themselves clean in a cottage kitchen, and pit ponies which lived all their working lives underground.* But it had only been in 1842, when legislation made it illegal to employ women and children underground, that ponies became widely popular as beasts of burden. A bizarre device – a small oxygen cylinder mounted on a cage and intended to revive canaries which had succumbed to gas when taken down a mine – is occasionally shown to mesmerised children at a science museum in Manchester to show them how miners assessed the quality of the air underground. But the coal merchant, his flatbed truck piled with dirty jute sacks of coal, belongs only in period dramas. Most city-dwellers are unable to identify the acrid smell of coal smoke.

---

* The precise number of ponies working in the mines is unknown. When the mines were nationalised, in 1947, the Coal Board inherited 21,000 pit ponies. Most ponies chosen for pit work were under eleven hands tall, and some colliery proprietors became rather proud of their breeding programmes: Lord Londonderry maintained his own stud in the Shetlands. While it is true that once lowered into the mine many ponies rarely emerged into the air, stabled underground, they were generally well fed: a familiar complaint from the miners was that the owners cared more for their ponies than for their humans. A 1911 law required them to be at least four years old, and generally worked with the same handler. The last pit pony, Tony, died in 2011 at the age of forty. The story that they all went blind is untrue.

1

Dirty Heat

Newcastle upon Tyne is as good a place as anywhere to begin. For generations, the city was synonymous with the coal trade – hence the implied stupidity of trying to carry 'coals to Newcastle': it was the place coal came from.

Perhaps there was a single person who was the first to realise that some of the rocks dug from the ground would burn for longer and with greater heat than wood from the trees growing on the surface of the earth. Perhaps it was an accidental, collective discovery by people wearing animal skins who lit a fire on top of an outcrop of coal on the surface of the ground, and then watched, open-mouthed, as it burned for hours. No one will ever know. There is evidence the Romans burned coal during their occupation of Britain. Certainly the Saxons are believed to have used coal in shaping tin implements. By the Middle Ages, people were digging to get at the seams, and then widening a chamber into the coal so that, in architectural cross-section, the excavation resembled a handbell. The miners were lowered into the heart of the bell in baskets. There is plenty of evidence that by the fourteenth century, coal was being dug from the ground in Wales. The fifteenth-century Pius II published an account of a visit he had made to Scotland before becoming pope. He described a place 'wild, bare and never visited by the sun in winter'. He had noticed that poor people there were given stones as alms. Being 'impregnated with sulphur or some fatty matter', they burned them instead of wood, of which the

country was, he claimed, 'destitute'. (In both England and Scotland
the popularity of coal may have had something to do with the fact
that so many trees had been felled to clear land for agriculture.)
Certainly, by the seventeenth century, there was a coal pit 'eight
fathoms' (nearly fifty feet) deep in Somerset and other deposits
were being exploited in the Midlands, Yorkshire and Lancashire.

The north-east of England was, then, far from unique in being
gifted deposits of this strange, flammable rock. But Newcastle
contained people with the imagination to see how coal could make
them rich. The city is nearly 300 miles north of the English capital
with its wealth and hunger for heat, while coal is bulky, heavy and
dirty. The vital Geordie realisation was that significant quantities
could be delivered to the capital in much less time than it would
take for other coalfields to do so, even if the mines there were as
efficient as those in the north-east: horse-and-cart haulage was
slow, and both Newcastle and London were seaports.

Coal extracted from seams which occurred near the river Tyne
was soon being floated downstream towards the estuary on
flat-bottomed boats, to be transferred to sailing vessels for transport south to London. The trade flourished, and soon French,
German and Dutch ships were sailing across the North Sea to carry
coal to the continent as well. By the middle of the sixteenth century,
one enthusiast was claiming that Newcastle coal had become so
integral to French manufacturing that 'France can lyve no more
withowte [it] than the fishe without water'. By 1615 there were
reported to be 400 freighters carrying coal from Newcastle. Most
of it was shipped to London, which was soon acutely aware of its
dependency: coal was so important to the functioning of the city
that it had become a strategic need. In 1629 the veteran naval
administrator, Sir John Coke, recommended the creation of a dedicated squadron of warships to protect the Newcastle coal fleet from
continental navies. Soon, at any threat of aggression, the colliers
were shepherded by warships to London in protective convoys.

Once the coal had been wrested from the earth, power belonged to those who could organise its transportation to the places where it would be burned. In the eighteenth century this meant the digging of canals* and, later, the laying of railway tracks.

In Newcastle the coal trade offered a very comfortable living to a privileged group of merchant families belonging to the 'Hostmen's Company', one of those smart English coteries which in other places would be called a 'racket'. By 1771, the leading producers of coal were meeting to agree upon how to keep the price up, by deciding how much coal they would release to the market. Customers of the coal trade became increasingly fed up, an anonymous shipowner writing a pamphlet in 1842 to lambast the 'unprincipled conduct' of the Newcastle coal merchants: 'No man can set foot in an office on the quay, with one or two rare exceptions, but must prepare to be cheated or overreached', he howled.[1] The merchants would delay the loading of ships, diddle shipowners by giving short measures, overcharge and refuse to provide receipts.

The Hostmen still exist, organised by a dozen ageing men and women who enjoy dressing up in blue and red robes and exercising the right to graze cattle – or rent out the right – on Newcastle moorland. Entry is restricted to sons and daughters of Freemen of the City 'born in lawful wedlock'. It sounds a self-interested and slightly comical piece of mummery of the kind that still exists all over England, but the people of Newcastle can thank them for the fact that the city has nearly 1,000 acres of open space within its boundaries. Precisely how this clique acquired the rights to the highly lucrative Newcastle coal 'vend' is unknown, though it was well-enough established by the sixteenth century for Elizabeth I to

---

* On the other side of the country, when the third Duke of Bridgewater opened his canal from his mines at Worsley to the centre of Manchester in 1761, the cost of coal was immediately halved.

'incorporate' the company and its monopoly in 1600. This was a royal stamp of approval for a cartel: the main interest of the Hostmen was to look after their members by keeping out competition and keeping down their workers. At both these tasks they were highly effective, acquiring control of mines and controlling way leaves over land between collieries and riverside loading wharves.

The figures speak for themselves. In 1622 the Hostmen sold 14,420 tons of coal. By the middle of that century there were 900 coal vessels carrying coal out of the city, with each cargo negotiated by a Hostman. The cartel may have been the antithesis of capitalism 'red in tooth and claw' – and, like most cartels, made for corruption and laziness – but it had the advantage for officialdom of making it easier to tax the coal trade. The Hostmen's meeting place – the Mayor's Parlour – testified to their hold over the city. Some became proprietors of mines themselves, but control of the transport of coal to seagoing vessels remained the key to their power.

The best-known feature of Newcastle is its abundance of bridges: passengers high up on the train between London and Edinburgh have looked out for generations upon the river and city and their bridges. There had been a road bridge across the river since medieval times, part-owned by the prince-bishops of Durham, but its arches were too low to allow through the coasters carrying coal south to London. Then a roiling great flood brought down the bridge in 1771. An elegant new construction opened ten years later. But its architects had failed to take into consideration the needs of the growing coal trade: the nine stone arches spanned the river at a height which made it still quite impossible for sailing ships to travel upstream to take on their cargo. So for generations coal continued to be carried downstream to the seagoing vessels in flat-bottomed wherries called 'keels'. Which is bizarre, considering they hardly had one. At their peak there were said to be 500 of these boats at work on the Tyne, each approximately forty feet long, broad in the beam (nearly twenty feet across), pointed at each end, manufactured of oak and elm, powered and steered by oars. From a distance, the river must have looked as if there had been a great hatch of enormous black insects upon its surface. Each boat was usually operated by a crew comprising a skipper, two crewmen known as 'bullies', and a boy. Most of the keelmen seem to have originally been migrants from Scotland and the border areas. It was wearying work, and they were not even free agents, for each keelman was 'bound' to a Hostman – binding time was Christmas Day.

Where the Hostmen wore robes and fancy hats, the Sunday best of the indentured keelmen was a white shirt, yellow waistcoat, blue coat and a flat-brimmed black hat: like many of the miners, their 'off-duty' clothes were colourful and impractical. The bright colours could hardly have been in greater contrast to their mucky everyday wear, and have been romanticised in Tyneside culture as reminders of the origins of the city's prosperity.* Admiration rarely stooped to indulgence, for several times the town summoned the army to put down disputes by keelmen. Consigned to folk memory, Newcastle might show a greater appreciation of their existence by properly caring for the magnificent Keelmen's Hospital, which they built to look after sick and elderly members of their trade with the proceeds of a self-imposed tax of one penny each tide from every boat. It is one of the most wonderful buildings in the city.

Members of the great cartel of suppliers, the Hostmen, were blessed by the inventiveness of others. Merchants needed to waste no effort in dreaming up new applications for their product, for once this combustible rock had become widely available, scientists, inventors, engineers and manufacturers found endless

---

* The miners' holiday dress was equally colourful, if less uniform – long hair, under a hat decorated with ribbons. Their 'posey jacket' they decorated with flowers.

uses for it. By the early 1700s, coal had become essential to manufacturers of metals, bricks and glass; extractors of salt; refiners of sugar; makers of dyes; brewers of beer; distillers of gin, to say nothing of blacksmiths or those who just wanted to heat their homes. In 1730, one writer had estimated that 'there are above a Thousand Sail of Ships constantly imployed in Carrying Coals to the different Parts of England, Ireland, Spain, Portugal, Germany, France, Flanders, and Holland; and the Market at London is the Standard and settles the Price, for the most Part for all other Markets'.[2] By the middle of the eighteenth century an estimated 1 million tons of coal were being shipped to London each year.[3] Coal was making Britain's fortune. It was steam generated by coal that made possible the industrialisation of Britain, and it was industrialisation that made possible the country's world dominance.*

It is tempting to see the coasters which brought coal from Newcastle to London as somehow not 'proper ships'. But the *Endeavour* on which Captain Cook sailed to Botany Bay and then claimed Australia for Britain, had been built in Whitby in 1764 as one of these coal carriers. Sturdily constructed, broad in the beam and with a flattish bottom, the Admiralty realised that its shallow draught also meant the boat was well suited to uncharted waters with unknown rocks, shoals and reefs. Cook not only mapped the coasts of the two islands of New Zealand but claimed the east coast of Australia from his converted collier, before sailing it all the way back to England around the Cape of Good Hope. When Matthew Flinders later set out to circumnavigate the continent of Australia, he too did so in a former east-coast collier, built in County Durham. The fact that north-eastern coaling ships were reckoned safe enough to be used on voyages of discovery speaks volumes

---

* The last locally produced coal left the Newcastle quayside in 1998. By 2004, the docks were *importing* coal from Russia.

about the hazards of the east-coast coal trade, when one estimate calculates that on average two ships were lost off the Yorkshire coast each week between 1500 and 1900.

The trade was distinctive in other respects, too. In most places, miners were taken on or got rid of on a fairly casual basis. But for much of the life of the north-eastern coalfield, the terms of employment were quite astonishingly feudal. For a payment of one shilling, miners entered into a 'bond' which obliged them to be available for work whenever called upon, but did not require the employer to provide anything for them to do to earn the shilling. The bond was a hangover from the 'hiring fairs' when wandering agricultural labourers were contracted to work for the coming year and it originally ran from one autumn to the next, with breaking of the bond being a criminal offence, punishable by a fine or gaol with hard labour. (The employer faced no criminal sanction if he failed to honour the deal.) The terms were laid out in numerous clauses which might run to thousands of words, recited by the hiring agent for the benefit of illiterate miners who might then sign en masse by pushing forward to touch the pen marking an 'X'.* The miner employed under these conditions was a serf. When mine bosses tried in 1765 to make things even worse for the miners, by demanding that they produce a 'leaving certificate' from their last employer (this was almost the arrangement in Scotland, which practised a form of slavery, with miners bound to mine-owners for their entire life, and bought and sold along with the mine if it changed hands), an estimated 4,000 men went on strike. The Dragoons were made ready, but were given no opportunity to draw their swords, for the miners behaved impeccably, simply refusing to work, and after six weeks, the owners gave in and abandoned the 'leaving certificate' notion. This early example

---

* Requests to have the wording of the bond available for inspection two weeks before signing had been rejected by the owners.

of the power of collective action reverberated in the minds of miners for decades.

But, generally, there was no shortage of labour: employers believed they could hire and fire men as readily as they hauled and sold coal. There was something magical about the thought of human beings descending into the earth to become the first living things to see a layer of rock which had once – millions of years beforehand – been alive itself. But it took a supreme effort of imagination to keep that vision alive in the dangers and sheer drudgery of the harshest manual labour.

The 'hewers' who attacked the seam of coal with picks and shovels – and later with explosives – had to adjust themselves to the space they found themselves in. Often, this meant working bent double, on their knees, or lying on the ground. The coal they had won (the competitive language explains a great deal about how everyone in the industry saw their task) was hauled away from the face by small teams of two or three 'putters', who might be their sons or nephews. The putters then had to manoeuvre great 'corves' – round baskets made of hazel twigs – through tunnels to the bottom of the shaft sunk from the surface. Here, they attached the baskets to thick hemp ropes. Each of these corves could hold about 4.5 hundredweight (about 230 kilos) of coal. They were then raised up the approximately eight-foot-diameter shaft to the surface by horses made to plod in a circle, winding a winch. On a good day, the manual labour of a deep mine might produce about ninety tons of coal.

Aspects of the local coal trade like the bond are specific to Newcastle. But the pattern of development is characteristic of the business everywhere – landowners who cannot believe their good fortune, colliery proprietors who pay them a royalty for the right to extract coal, miners working in appalling conditions, rapacious merchants and entrepreneurs exploiting transport opportunities to bring it to the marketplace (where other labourers unload the vessels, and other merchants make their living from the trade). While the South Wales coalfield was one day to become the centre of the production of 'steam coal' and high-quality anthracite essential in the bellies of Royal Navy destroyers, and some of the thickest seams of the Midlands and Yorkshire would only become reachable with technology as yet unimaginable – these early days of coal exploration were as significant in their way as striking gold or other precious metal. No wonder lumps of coal acquired the nickname 'black gold'. And no wonder there were so very many fingers in the pie.

If the cleanest way to make money from coal was to be a land-owner, and the second easiest to be a middleman selling it, the keelman was only slightly better off than the men, women and children who went into the bowels of the earth to extract the rocks which made the Hostmen wealthy. Shovelling coal at all hours of the day and night (the work was dependent upon the tides), the keelman's job was a filthy one – especially when it required them to shovel coal 'uphill', because the collier's gunwale was much higher than that of the keel. After work, they returned to homes in Sandgate, their grimy slum outside the city walls, a place which so scandalised the visiting preacher, John Wesley, that he remarked in 1742 that he had never encountered 'so much drunkenness, cursing and swearing, even from the mouths of little children'.[4]

Though the coal trade began with the exploitation of seams which outcropped near to the river, ever-increasing supplies were needed for the burgeoning business. By geological good fortune, the Newcastle area was remarkably rich in deposits of coal, and those who owned the land above it became very rich. Everyone seemed to be making money; even those with no coal under their grass, but who could charge for the right of others to transport it across their land to collection points. The soft southern customers could only moan about how harsh their lives would be without the comfort of coal. 'Everybody complains of the dearness of coals, being at 4*l.* per chaldron [the standard unit of measurement, equivalent to just over 2,500 kilos],' the Londoner Samuel Pepys had written in his diary on 6 March 1667, 'the weather, too, being become most bitter cold, the King saying to-day that it was the coldest day he ever knew in England.' And there was worse to come, for the English and Dutch were at war, and the British too short of money to deploy many of their better ships, which were laid up at Chatham. In June, the Dutch fleet broke into the Medway and destroyed most of them – the worst calamity in the history of the Royal Navy. London became a place of panicky rumours, for, among other things, Dutch command of the sea cut the capital off from its source of warmth. Pepys wrote of how 'the great misery the City and kingdom is like to suffer for want of coals ... and it is feared will breed a mutiny; for we are not in any prospect to command the sea for our colliers to come, but rather, it is feared, the Dutch may go and burn all our colliers at Newcastle'. The Dutch never did so, and by the end of the seventeenth century 'staiths' or wharves had been built up and down the Tyne, to transfer coal from cart to riverboat. Soon, waggon ways were being laid, to allow horses to pull carts of coal from the mines to the wharves on wooden rails: as the gradient was generally downhill, one horse might draw four or five waggons of coal. The appetite for warmth was insatiable and the merchants knew they could sell just about all the coal that could be got from the ground: the challenge was merely to regulate the laws of supply and demand to keep the prices up.

For London's appetite for coal seemed insatiable. The more of the fuel was available, the more applications human ingenuity devised for it. London was burning more coal than anywhere else in Europe, as increasing numbers of citizens and businesses aban- doned wood and charcoal as sources of heat. Many residents became sick of the pungent, acrid smell which began to hang over much of the city. Even royal nostrils twitched in disgust. No one took greater care to appear splendid in front of his citizens (think

van Dyck's magisterial portrait of the supercilious king on horseback) than Charles I. The new king was obsessed with cleanliness,
his government passing laws about the nattiness of the streets and
waterways and about keeping poor and diseased people away from
the royal personage. Air quality was a particular bugbear. He
believed the problem was the breweries of Tothill Street in St
James's and shortly before succeeding to the throne in 1625, a bill
was introduced to Parliament attempting to prevent London breweries burning coal within a mile of the royal palaces in Westminster,
or to the west of London Bridge. In January 1637, Charles
summoned the English Privy Council, the body through whom,
effectively, he ruled the entire country. This time, before the council turned to England's endless wars, the king wished to bring to its
attention an imminent Act of State which would forbid brewers
near the court from using coal to manufacture beer.

He wasn't the first monarch to be appalled by the air quality of
the capital. In 1586 Queen Elizabeth was said to have been 'greatly
grieved and annoyed with the taste and smoke' of the breweries
near her palaces. But, in a pattern to be repeated for centuries, the
needs of business trumped worries about the environment.

For even expressions of royal disapproval of the pollution did
nothing to dent demand for coal, which was almost magical in its
capacity to encourage inventors and entrepreneurs to devise new
products. By the middle of the seventeenth century, viewing the
London smog (from a distance) was a tourist attraction, and the
writer John Evelyn complained that the filthy pall had even turned
St Paul's Cathedral into a 'loathsome Golgotha'. Clergymen were
constantly distracted by the incessant coughing and spitting during
their sermons. In 1661, soon after the restoration of the monarchy,
Evelyn produced *Fumifugium or, The Inconveniencie of the aer and
smoak of London Dissipated*. Evelyn's tract was Nimbyism in a lace
collar. In a simpering dedication to the king, the author claimed to
have been present at a reception at the royal palace in Whitehall

when 'a presumptuous Smoake' had begun to appear from nearby tunnels and filled the place 'to such a degree as men could hardly discern one another for the Clowd'. He found it offensive that 'this Glorious and Antient City' which 'commands the Proud Ocean to the Indies' should 'wrap her stately head in clouds of Smoak and Sulphur, so full of Stink and Darknesse'. Visitors to the city could smell the place before they saw it. The list of offensive industries had grown from brewers to include 'Diers, Lime-burners, Salt and Sope-boylers' whose coal-burning had between them turned the city into a suburb of hell or something like Mount Etna, a volcano Evelyn had visited during his self-imposed exile from England during the Civil War. The smoke made clothes smell, killed insects and forced ladies to clean their faces with ground almonds. The stink of coal smoke made people fall ill: how often, he asked, had we heard people talking about a dead friend or neighbour that 'he went up to London and took a great cold which he could never afterwards claw off again'?

Evelyn also claimed that bad air was 'a potent and great disposer to rebellion'. His solution was to move all the polluting industries downwind, to distant suburbs in the east beyond Greenwich, and to plant lots of fragrant shrubs around the rest of the city. The perfumed garden never happened, but Evelyn's tract was deemed sufficiently powerful to be cited even in the 1930s, during discussions about where to build Chelsea Power Station. The National Smoke Abatement Society went on to produce no fewer than five editions of his pamphlet.[5]

But demand for coal did not abate and, inevitably, mining was as affected by the transformative power of coal as any other industry. The first difficulty to overcome was simply to find the coal in the ground, which was easy enough, once the extent of the coalfields had been established. The second challenge was to dig it out, which was just a matter of sinking a shaft and then hiring miners. Problems of ventilation, replacing foul air with fresh, appeared to have been solved. That they required young children to sit all day in pitch darkness, opening and closing trapdoors to direct the air, was not an issue. Once the West Country blacksmith Thomas Newcomen had developed a reliable steam pump in 1712, proprietors could continue to extract coal from mines which were previously closed by flooding.* As time went by, there would be developed more and more ways of overcoming the third obstacle, of getting it to market – waggons meant new roadways, barges meant canals, and eventually, coal would drive steam railways all across the countryside.

As the Londoner Daniel Defoe wrote in stage astonishment, on his visit to the Newcastle area in the 1720s, 'when we see the prodigious heaps, I might say mountains, of coals which are dug at every pit, and how many of those pits there are, we are filled with equal wonder to consider where the people should live that can consume them'.[6] Most of the coal was being shipped to his home town. And, for all the smoke it produced, it was the Newcastle coal trade which gave the capital its most beguiling building. When a bakery in Pudding Lane caught fire in September 1666 and strong winds swept the Great Fire through the city, great numbers of wood-framed slums burned to the ground. Over eighty churches, the Royal Exchange, Guildhall and several livery companies were also consumed, along with the medieval St Paul's Cathedral. Christopher Wren was chosen to design a replacement, but how was his magnificent creation to be paid for? In 1670, Parliament reached for the usual solution of deciding to put their hands into the pockets of the public. A surcharge was added to the tax on coal brought from Newcastle by sea. Inevitably, the surcharge was increased three times. It was the proceeds of this tax – and the freedom it allowed St Paul's to borrow further money – which paid for the cathedral to be completed. The wonderful building which

---

* Being able to drain the mines was a mixed blessing, since it enabled pits to be sunk further into the earth, which in turn made accumulations of gas more likely.

resulted never escaped the clutches of coal and soon was stained black by the smoke which had paid for it.

Just as the Hostmen in Newcastle got control of the export of coal, so wood merchants and the owners of wharves and lighters in London tried to manage the importation of coal to their advantage. The seventeenth-century gadfly pamphleteer, William Prynne (he had already had his nose slit and ears cut off for sedition), accused 'a confederacy of woodmongers' of conspiring to drive up the price of coal. Within a few years, though, the wood merchants had lost out to the barge operators, who established an effective monopoly on much of the trade, through the Lightermen's Company. Complaints about how the lightermen drove up coal prices became so strident and numerous that a few years later Parliament legislated to try to open up the market.

It would be very hard to exaggerate the importance of coal to the capital; there was, simply, no alternative. Towards the end of the eighteenth century, trading was formalised in a Coal Exchange next to the fish market at Billingsgate, where most of the coal vessels unloaded. The coal brokers, or 'crimps', were soon taking their trade and themselves seriously enough to feel they needed a new purpose-built trading floor, and in the early nineteenth century they acquired one.

By the middle of the century, the trade had become so vast, with over 3.5 million tons being shipped from the north-east to London each year, that the business felt it had outgrown its exchange. The merchants now demanded, and in October 1849 got, a place of business which matched their self-esteem. To allow their enormous heads to pass through the door the Doric columns beneath the classical pediment were done away with and the new Coal Exchange building was an astonishing edifice, constructed – years before the famed Crystal Palace housing the Great Exhibition – on the north bank of the Thames around an ornate cast-iron skeleton with a soaring glass dome atop three circular galleries where the merchants had their offices. On trading days, the place thrummed to the sound of hundreds of factors, merchants and proprietors doing business. The building had been designed as much as a temple as a business centre, with twenty-four panels depicting carboniferous plants, more showing north-eastern collieries and wharves, others glorifying grandees of the coal trade. All were set off by decorative ironwork shaped and cast as coils of rope. The floor of the exchange was inlaid with 4,000 fragments of wood from around the world, arranged in the shape of a mariner's compass. Commemorative medals showing off the architecture were struck to mark the opening by Prince Albert, and Coal Exchange Quadrilles, or square dances, were specially composed for the occasion.

The *Illustrated London News* described the building as 'the most striking which has been erected in London for a long time past'.[7]* In the *Dictionary of London,* a piece of hack work thirty years later, Charles Dickens' son (also called Charles) waxed excitedly about the fact that the exchange was an 'open market, established by Act of Parliament, to which anyone can seek admission'. Like much Victorian capitalism, while this may have been true on paper, in practice, once officials had skimmed off the taxes payable by the traders, the exchange became the preserve of a sort of cartel.†

---

* The closest we can get to it now is from period illustrations and an architectural model in the Victoria & Albert Museum: the exchange was pulled down to make way for a traffic jam in 1962. The barbarian booby responsible, the chairman of the City of London Streets Committee, set the tone for the demolition project, declaring the building 'dingy' and claiming the exchange would not have been accepted by his committee as a public lavatory. The architectural historian Sir Nikolaus Pevsner, who was slightly more knowledgeable, considered the Coal Exchange to be one of the twelve irreplaceable buildings of Victorian Britain.

† The exchange was damaged by German bombs during the Second World War, but what really finished it off was the post-war nationalisation of the industry and the creation of the National Coal Board: for all its architectural exuberance, the building no longer had a function.

Once the trade had its own building, consumers were less than welcome.

The whole supply chain of coal from the hewer's pick to the Tyneside wharves, passage via 'keel' and coastal trading fleet, might all seem to end tidily in an opulent London urbanite's counting hall. But there were always men who kept their hands cleanest of the dirty business of salesmanship, or mining for that matter, and through the sometimes inexplicable rights of birth claimed some of the largest levies on the industry. What was it like to be one of the families who owned the very ground of the north-eastern coal deposit? Landowners from under whose acres coal was being extracted were the luckiest beneficiaries of the lot, for they were paid a royalty on each ton of coal, yet had generally contracted out the hard work to others, who hired the miners who did the sweating work. The Londonderry dynasty amply demonstrated the way that to those who hath, shall be given. Over the generations, the family grew prodigiously wealthy and much loathed. They are the embodiment of a conundrum: how can you be right and wrong at the same time?

The second marquess is better known to history as the Foreign Secretary, Lord Castlereagh, who was simultaneously the most successful British diplomat and the most reviled politician of his day.* Castlereagh's support for reactionary regimes and his defence of the Peterloo Massacre did nothing for his popularity (Percy Bysshe Shelley famously remarked that he had a face like murder; William Cobbett greeted the news that he had cut his own throat with a penknife as a 'consolation'). His successor as Marquess of Londonderry was his avaricious half-brother Charles, who had enhanced the family fortune by marrying as his second wife the haughty, but fabulously rich, Frances Anne Vane-Tempest, who

---

* Byron's epitaph was: 'Posterity will ne'er survey / A nobler grave than this: / Here lie the bones of Castlereagh: / Stop, traveller, and piss.'

brought to their marriage vast estates in north-eastern England and the north of Ireland (she was nineteen, he was forty-one). The new marquess was a martinet who preferred commerce to international relations. His second marriage had ensured that he became Vane by name as well as vain by nature. A twice life-size equestrian statue of the marquess in his favourite Hussar uniform, commissioned by his widow in the year of his death and unveiled by Benjamin Disraeli, stands in the middle of Durham. It is known locally as 'the man on the horse', which proves something, if not exactly what the family had intended.

In 1821, two years after his marriage, Londonderry had bought the estate of Seaham on the County Durham coast, twenty miles south of Newcastle, where he developed a harbour at the village for exporting coal. Big docks and a lighthouse were built and deeper mines sunk. He recruited John Buddle, the best mine manager in north-east England (he claimed to know his home county better underground than on the surface) as his colliery 'viewer' or managing engineer. Within twenty years, Londonderry was one of the richest men in England, and saw the world as a balance sheet of assets or liabilities.* (At the height of the Irish Famine, in 1847, he made himself a pariah by giving only £20 to a local relief committee and the following year spent £15,000 renovating the couple's imposing Irish house, Mount Stewart, in the north of the island. So it confounded his critics when it emerged that he had given all his Irish tenants a holiday from rent for over three years.)

The principle that 'by their fruits shall ye know them' makes the Londonderrys extremely hard to read. The much underrated Victorian feminist, Harriet Martineau, said Londonderry 'was always ingenuous, always brave, always meaning to be kind'.

---

* The family has had its share of both tragedy and dislike. The seventh marquess, known as 'The Londonderry Herr' for his anti-Semitism and enthusiasm for appeasement, did little to enhance the family's reputation.

Charles Dickens regarded him with contempt. And well into the twentieth century the family were still cast as pantomime villains by much of the population of the north-east coalfields. Emanuel 'Manny' Shinwell, the first Cabinet minister in charge of the nationalised coal industry, recalled that he only had to mention the Londonderry name during a speech in County Durham to set off 'derisive applause'. The mining industry was an activity with long memories, because its history was so harsh.

There was no denying there was something feudal about life in the north-eastern coalfield. The 'bond', which tied miners to pits by yearly contract, was an outrage to anyone who believed in freedom of association, organisation and employment. Inevitably, when the Combination Acts forbidding trade unionism had been repealed in 1824, Londonderry's lands emerged as a hotbed of union activity. Thomas Hepburn, a Primitive Methodist lay preacher who had begun working in the mines at the age of eight, formed an Association of Durham and Northumberland pitmen, which in the spring of 1831 organised concerted action against the bond. There was great alarm among owners and managers, some of whom believed their homes would be burned to the ground – John Buddle was reported to have summoned sixty-four special constables and barricaded himself indoors. The arsonists never came. Instead, the bosses tried to maintain a united front, locking the men out from the mines, but when Lord Londonderry had a face-to-face meeting with Thomas Hepburn, he gave him just about everything he asked for, including a reduction in the hours worked by boys in the mines to a mere twelve hours per day.* Londonderry was not the worst of the proprietors, but he knew how to make money. By being the first of the owners back in business, he made a killing from the inflated prices caused by the unrest.

---

* Hepburn paid for his activities by being blacklisted from employment by the owners and their agents and was forced to become a wandering tea-vendor.

The truth is Londonderry does not fit the easy categories of the good or bad capitalist. He seems most of all to have been a confused, old-fashioned, anti-union paternalist who made much of his devotion to 'his' miners – employing doctors to provide medical care, providing pensions for the disabled, and schooling for children. He was willing to pay out £2,000 in compensation to dependants when his Plane Pit caught fire, killing over fifty people, and was still paying regular annuities twenty years later. But when asked to contribute to a relief fund after his competitors' pit at Haswell burned in 1844 he replied that there was a 'sacred Duty on their part alone to support those left behind'.[8] In the end, we can only judge by actions. He expected loyalty and obedience, and in return sometimes clearly felt he owed his workers something.

The same year as the fire at the Haswell pit, almost all the miners of Northumberland and Durham agreed to demand half-yearly contracts in place of the annual bond. The miners were not fools and had favoured the schedule by which new contract negotiations would come around in October, when demand for coal rose as the seasons turned. But letters to Londonderry seeking 'amicable adjustments' to the current arrangements went unanswered. The miners knew that striking was risky, since their bosses would immediately look around to import substitute labour from else-where – frequently from poor estates in Ireland – offering accommodation in the cottages from which their 'candymen' had evicted the strikers. As the multiple roofs over his own head demonstrated, coal had made Londonderry more than comforta-bly off, with a mansion on Park Lane as well as his seat in County Durham and his neoclassical pile in County Down.

This time, Londonderry warned the shopkeepers and trades-men of Seaham they would lose all his business if they gave credit to any of his 3,639 'unreasonable pitmen'. After twelve weeks of strike his manager sent around a handbill threatening to evict one hundred miners each week, and to replace them with one hundred

Irishmen from the Londonderry estates across the Irish Sea. The
threat was followed by a strange entreaty in which he begged them
to return to work to save their jobs.[9] Though his letter warned of
'foreigners' taking local work it was Londonderry himself who was
bringing them over. It is true that he devoted some of the proceeds
of his vast coal wealth (by this time the harbour at Seaham was
yielding Londonderry an average of £33,400 a year) to maintain
doctors and schools for his workers. But he is reckoned to have
spent over £2.5 *million* on himself and his family. It is tempting to
conclude that more than anything, Londonderry became a pantomime villain because he was too dim, too blinkered and too
arrogant to escape the role.

Once the strike was over, Londonderry drove a coach and horses
through the coal-producers' cartel. First, he demanded the voting
system be weighted in favour of the bigger, more efficient mines
like his own, and then he refused to pay the recommended
compensation to those collieries most badly affected by the strike.
The cartel, by which the mine-owners of the north-east had kept
up coal prices at fortnightly meetings, collapsed. A benign examination of Londonderry's business career applauds his dedication
and single-mindedness, concluding that 'Unbridled, Londonderry
would most probably have taken his family headlong into the
court of Chancery. By risking all, he left a town and a harbour and
the memory of a colourful career.'[10]

His widow, whose wealth had, after all, made his career as a coal
tycoon possible, took up many of his enthusiasms and moved into
a mansion among the smokestacks of Seaham. Other pit-owners
at the time were trying to get as far as possible from the noise and
filth they had inflicted on the countryside, but when she was asked
if she minded the smoke from the four blast furnaces and 120 coke
ovens she had built, she is said to have replied that they weren't a
nuisance as 'they were making money for her'.[11] There spoke a true
Londonderry.

Ownership of the Seaham Colliery passed to George Henry Vane-Tempest, fifth Marquess of Londonderry and son of the man who had built Seaham Harbour. Soon after two in the morning of 8 September 1880, when the mine was packed with colliers who had swapped shifts so they could attend a local flower show (to this day, competitive gardening remains a working man's pastime in the north-east), there was a great explosion deep underground. Sixty-seven miners were brought to the surface alive, but 136 had been blown to pieces, burned or gassed – including two fourteen-year-old boys; 181 pit ponies had also been killed. An estimated 30,000 people attended the mass burial at Seaham Colliery church. *The Times* reported that 'During the whole time the Marquess of Londonderry, who is suffering badly from gout, sat in the churchyard, surrounded by members of his family'.[12] The spectacle is touching. When one of the seams caught fire again, it was decided that the only thing to be done was to wall it up, with any survivors inside. According to messages later recovered, a number of the trapped miners passed the time waiting to be rescued 'singing hymns', praying and getting 'ready for heaven'.

Owners like the Londonderrys often claimed that the toiling done for them underground was a family trade, and that boys were bred to the job. If the owners' claim was ever true, it was the product of circumstance – the fact that mining communities were often isolated, with few other jobs available, and that if you've grown up watching someone perform a particular task, then it can seem perfectly natural that at some stage you may have to do it yourself. It was rarely the sort of job that careers advisers attempted to encourage their most able students to contemplate. And yet a curious inversion took place. Because it would always be 'the hardest work under heaven', by the early years of the twentieth century miners were increasingly seen as the aristocracy of the labour movement: resilient members of a trade that scared others.[13] On top of that, they confronted hard-faced employers. And because people would always need the energy under their feet, they were in a job for life.

2

Invisible Underground

Coal was the means to refinement, and a statement to all.

To have smoke coming from your chimney was to proclaim to the world that those within had escaped the mere brutish battle to survive, for their house was heated, their food was cooked, and they had warm water to wash in. Heat from coal transformed animals into sophisticates. Those whose houses were heated by it (and lit – for gas was produced from coal) knew little, and generally cared less, about how it was got from the ground. In 1861 a writer declared that 'of miners, the mass of mankind knows no more than if they were Hottentots; born, bred and buried, for the most part out of sight of the highly civilised and educated people around them'.[1] But what was life really like underground?

The scavenging of coal followed a predictable pattern, in which the seams nearest to the surface were the first to be plundered. These could often be so wet and muddy that men were soaked-through all day. As shafts were sunk to reach the deeper coal, the temperature in which miners had to toil rose: the rule of thumb was that the temperature rose one degree Fahrenheit for each 46 feet of descent or one degree Celsius for every 83 feet. Some shafts eventually became thousands of feet deep. By the time they had reached the face where they were working, the heat was often sweltering. Miners eased the discomfort by removing clothing, to work naked or semi-naked, their bodies encased in sweat and dust. The smell in the pit could be appalling, with men and horses perspiring, excreting and urinating all day. Men had to eat the food and drink the cold tea or water they had brought from home wherever they found themselves. As a result of the sordid conditions there was an enormous population of rats in some pits. 'You could hear them,' said a miner, 'scurrying all over the place, making a sound like a flock of sheep' rattling across a farmyard.[2] Furthermore, you couldn't see anything much. In the early days of coal-mining, men had used candles, until the mounting casualty list from explosions of the various 'damps' or gases which naturally occurred in coal seams made the search for a safety light a matter of urgency. The lamps developed in the early nineteenth century by gifted men like Humphry Davy and the railway pioneer, George Stephenson, allowing air to enter through tiny holes in a mesh screen and preventing flames from leaping out, were much safer than candles.* But they were pretty poor illuminators, which brought on eye conditions in many a miner. When, as sometimes happened, a section of roof collapsed, burying miner and lamp, the suffocating darkness was terrifying.

After hurtling from the surface at ear-popping speed to the bottom of a mineshaft in a steam-wound cage, you still had to reach the coal. This might involve a walk of several miles underground. The constantly unsettling thing about the 'roads' to the coalface was their irregularity. *Charity Main*, a novel by a former miner, Mark Benney, published at the end of the Second World War, imagines what would happen if 'Johnson', a middle-aged temporary civil servant, found himself having to go down a mine even after battery lights on helmets had replaced safety lamps, and

---

* Davy (1778–1829), a working-class Cornishman, was awarded a baronetcy, rose to become president of the Royal Society, and was one of the founders of London Zoo. He invented his safety lamp in October 1815. It transformed nineteenth-century mining, thus making possible much of the Industrial Revolution. He refused all efforts to get him to patent the lamp.

a mechanical conveyor belt had done away with pit ponies and wheeled tubs. First there was the commute to work, on foot and underground.

An occasional jar on his helmet warned Johnson to keep his head down, that the height of the roof was becoming very uneven … The floor, too, was becoming very uneven, with pools of deep mud between the sleepers; he had to vary his pace from step to step … the electric battery hanging on his hip became a weight to reckon with. His kneepads hampered him. The air was warm and stale, an unchanging current that only half-dried the sweat on his forehead and produced a sticky discomfort. He was glad when another line of tubs came along, and they had to withdraw into a recess while it passed. 'Is it much further?' Johnson gasped. Norman laughed. 'Man, ye're only just startin'.' They came to a cross-roads where the roof heightened and they could walk upright for a precious half-minute … Now they left the road where the tracks ran, and turned into a gallery where the conveyor belt ran alongside them with a rustling sound like a shadowy underground stream. The average height of the roof here was three feet, although at places it dropped to two feet six. On the floor was anything from three to twelve inches of thin soft sucking mud. Bent double, Johnson found himself slithering at every pace; and each time he slithered, he grazed his back-bone against the steel straps supporting the roof. They were now travelling through the actual coal-seam itself; coal formed the side walls of the gallery … it seemed to go on interminably, this 'gate' as Norman called it, and it took ten minutes of this desperate scrambling on all fours before Johnson saw lights ahead. By that time he was feeling that, if the gallery went on for another twenty yards, he would faint. Every muscle in his body was shrieking in protest. His head was one dull ache from incessant banging of his helmet against the roof. The skin had been rubbed off his spine all the way down his back … 'How far have we come?' 'Aboot three an' a half mile.'[3]

In earlier days, men had no helmets and only home-made body protection: descriptions like this are almost enough to make you understand the coal-owners' argument that miners were born to the trade, but could rarely be made.

Little pieces of this coal got between Johnson's kneepads and his knees, causing excruciating pain … once he passed a man, naked save for his shorts and kneepads, lying on his side hammering a prop into place: in the dim circle of light his eyes stared wildly out of red rims in an otherwise completely black face … By some habitual cunning of his burly limbs, the miner seemed able to shovel away comfortably in a kneeling position, and yet keep his head and back so low that neither scraped the roof … after ten minutes Johnson was so utterly exhausted that he had to lie down full-length in the black slime … He had always considered himself a hardy man. But this – this was different. It was like trying to do any other job while chained down by heavy manacles … He found himself feeling grateful for the dust and darkness; they at least hid something of his weakness from the other men.[4]

The unfortunate Johnson reflected that at the end of his shift:

He had stayed for five hours in that two-foot slit of earth. He had shifted between one and two tons of coal. He had done it, and he would never have to do it again. The other men had each shifted an average of ten tons. In seventeen hours' time, after two more shifts of men had brought forward the conveyor, undercut and fired another length of coal, and finished a number of ancillary tasks, these same men would return and shift another ten tons of coal each. Day after day, month after month, year after year.[5]

Fortunate miners might find themselves in tall belts of coal like the nine-foot-high Barnsley Bed in South Yorkshire, but elsewhere, the thinness of the seams would mean digging on your hands and knees or lying down. 'Those who work above ground,' said a Somerset miner recalling his early days in the 1890s, 'would do well to consider what it would be like to get under the chair at home, and work with shovel and pick.'[6] But the rest of the world preferred to remain oblivious, leaving the mines to produce the enormous quantities of fuel which powered forges and lathes, rolling mills and presses, burned in grates from Buckingham Palace to industrial tenements, warmed the clerks on their stools in counting houses and those taking tea in comfortable parlours. If snug folk thought about miners at all, they did so with a shudder. In 1898 the long-forgotten Victorian poet Robert Williams Buchanan described the mines as 'sinister caverns of Night ... where the Hell-fires are glowing', and 'gnome-like' miners breathed the 'Stifling and thunderous vapours of Hell'.[7] Pitmen toiled under the earth, beyond the reach of civilisation: they were clannish, physical, frightening. Those who laboured there had moral values as black as their faces. Their communities were nests of violence and sexual licence.

Since the men who made the laws of the land largely belonged to 'respectable' society, they left the mining industry to get on with it, unless some compelling tragedy forced them to act. Sixty years before the Somerset miner invited us to imagine what it could be like to crawl under a kitchen chair and then to spend the day trying to hack coal, the country's lawmakers were obliged to pay attention to conditions in the industry. They passed a law which changed mining forever.

On the warm Wednesday afternoon of 4 July 1838 a group of miners had been hewing coal down the Huskar pit at Silkstone in South Yorkshire. The mine was owned by Robert Clarke of Noblethorpe Hall, whose family had made a fortune as wire-makers and, in the characteristic English way, used the proceeds of heavy industry to become local lords of the manor. At about two that afternoon, a freak thunderstorm broke out, during which hailstones and an estimated two and a half inches of rain fell in a torrent. The fire heating the boiler which worked the steam engine which powered the winch which pulled coal to the surface was put out. The winch was also the mechanism which might have lifted any underground miners to the surface. So a man shouted down the hole that the miners below should stay put for a while. But the shift had been working underground for almost nine hours already, and about forty of the more young and agile decided to try to escape by climbing up the ventilation shaft.

As bad luck would have it, there was an old watercourse near the mouth of the pit, dry for nine months of the year. The sudden downpour first flooded the dried-out streambed, which then burst its banks. The onrush of water poured down the ventilation shaft, knocking the miners off their feet and trapping them under the water which accumulated against the door at the bottom of the shaft.

One of the first rescuers to go down into the mine was James Garnett. Among the bodies he discovered at the bottom of the shaft was that of his own daughter, Catherine. She was eight years old. The greatest horror of the Huskar Colliery accident that afternoon was that all of the victims were children. Twenty-six of them died, aged from seven to seventeen.

The corpses of these children, bearing first names like Amos, Eli, Hannah and Ellen were carried from the pithead, and taken to a nearby farmhouse, where their faces were washed so that they could be identified. Then they were loaded onto horse-drawn carts for delivery to the family homes they had left that morning. Mr Badger, the local coroner, arrived to look at the bodies, before beginning an inquest, held at the local coaching inn. When it ended, the jury returned a verdict of accidental death. The twenty-six children 'suddenly summoned to appear before their maker' were buried in two mass graves in the graveyard of the local parish church, where a memorial sternly warned of the moral to be drawn from the disaster:

REMEMBER … REMEMBER

Every neglected call of God will appear against Thee
At the Day of Judgement
Let this solemn warning then sink into thy heart &
So prepare thee that the Lord when he cometh may find thee

WATCHING

Though it came very close to blaming the children for their own deaths, the admonition seems to have been readily accepted as a way of giving meaning to the event. The courtiers of the recently crowned Queen Victoria let it be known that she had taken a deep and sympathetic interest in the disaster. As it happened, her prime minister, Lord Melbourne, was an uncle by marriage of Anthony Ashley Cooper, the seventh Earl of Shaftesbury, who remains one of the greatest social reformers who ever lived. A handsome, slightly haunted-looking man, he had entered Parliament in 1826 representing Woodstock, a pocket borough in the gift of his uncle, the Duke of Marlborough. Deeply held Christian beliefs led him to propose in 1833 that children be prevented from working more than ten hours a day in factories. The employment of children in mines – a subject which polite society seems to have preferred not to think about – was an obvious topic for him to be asked to investigate.*

The task he was given in 1840 was to discover the extent of child labour in mines and factories: how many collieries like Huskar existed, and how young were the children in them? Four men were appointed to a Royal Commission, and the entire country divided into regions where a sub-commissioner was expected to visit each mine. It turned out that the problem of child labour was so large as to be almost impossible to investigate properly – the sub-commissioner for Yorkshire, for example, had to visit 200 collieries. (Another problem was that evidence was not given under oath and some of the children were expected to testify in front of their mine managers.) But even so, children's testimony to the commission was horrifying. Though a good proportion did not know how old they were, some were definitely as young as five. Great numbers had started working underground at the age of ten or younger. Sarah Gooder told the commission about her life at a pit only a couple of miles from the scene of the Huskar tragedy. 'I'm a trapper,' she said, meaning she spent her working day squatting alone in the darkness of the Gawber pit in South Yorkshire, occasionally

---

* Shaftesbury was one of the very greatest Victorians. As a young parliamentarian he campaigned for mental hospitals to be regarded as something more than a circus where Sunday-afternoon tourists could gather to laugh at the antics of the patients. He fought for a maximum ten-hour working day for children in wool and cotton mills. His later achievements, in fighting to stop small boys being sent by sweeps up chimneys, and setting up the 'ragged schools' initiative for children who would otherwise not be educated at all, endeared him to a public who, when he died, poured into the streets in their thousands to see what they could of the funeral of 'the poor man's earl' at Westminster Abbey. Like all passionate campaigners he was an obsessive (Florence Nightingale is said once to have remarked that had he not been so devoted to reform of the asylum system he could have been in one himself). Few, if any, of the tourists licking ice cream around the art nouveau 'Eros' (actually his brother, Anteros, the god of love requited) in Piccadilly Circus have any idea that the statue is a memorial to this handsome, slightly austere man.

opening and closing a wooden door to allow air and coal waggons to pass. 'It does not tire me,' she said, 'but I have to trap without a light and I'm scared. I go at four and sometimes half past three in the morning, and come out at five and half past [in the afternoon]. I never go to sleep. Sometimes I sing when I've light, but not in the dark; I dare not sing then. I don't like being in the pit … I would like to be at school far better than in the pit.'[8] She was eight years old.

Controlling the doors which directed the flow of fresh air to men working underground and allowed dangerous gases to escape was a vital, if immensely tedious job, requiring little strength or skill. It could easily be entrusted to the youngest children in the mine. Though there are some stories of three-year-olds being employed as trappers, most seem to have begun work at around the age of five. The commission's investigator for Lancashire and Cheshire summarised the trappers' work: 'Their whole time is spent sitting in the dark for twelve hours … Were it not for the passing and repassing of the waggons, it would be equal to solitary confinement of the worst order.'[9]

Slightly older boys and girls were employed on the 'rolley[rail]-way', where they existed, leading the pit ponies used to drag waggons where the passageways were tall enough. It could be a dangerous job: it was pitch-dark and the ponies might shy at any sudden noise. From the age of about ten children were judged strong enough to work as 'trailers' pushing trucks (which could weigh about a third of a ton) in the 'roads' too low for ponies. In the lowest passageways of all, pulling waggons loaded with coal was left to the women and children who worked as 'hurriers', with a leather belt around their waist and chains between their legs attached to a truck behind. Artists' woodblock impressions of this work provided some of the more sensational images to emerge from the inquiry and were later printed in pamphlets designed to enlist public sympathy. A commissioner described how in one

Yorkshire mine every hurrier was expected to draw twenty-four loaded trucks each day. In the very thinnest seams, the trucks had to be pushed rather than pulled, the 'thrusters' having to use their heads to push the waggons. Many of them developed bald patches just above their foreheads. The hardest job of all, though, was that of the 'bearer' who carried baskets of coal on their back in places where it was impossible to use trucks. These were usually women and girls. A commissioner in Scotland took evidence from a miner who had ruptured himself when he tried to lift the coal he had hewn onto the backs of women, boys and girls. The children were expected to perform all these miserable jobs not as emergency or short-term help, but on shifts which lasted for twelve or fourteen hours. At the surface, other children worked as gin-drivers, leading heavy horses on the winches, or as 'skreeners' or 'wailers', hand-picking impurities from the coal. It was filthy, torturous work.

It is important to recognise that this was not what would today be called 'child abuse', or calculated brutishness. The truth was simpler, harsher, yet arguably less malign. In the rural communities from which miners came it was common for entire families to work together when there was much to be done. Harvest-time is the most obvious example. But some children had jobs throughout the year, milking cattle, scaring away birds from seeded fields, or tending flocks of sheep. As work in the fields was replaced by clattering looms and seams of coal, working customs took time to change. For most of the first half of the nineteenth century it was common for children to be sent to work in the mines, to carry or push away in a trolley coal which had been hewn by their father. But the ways of the countryside – attempts by poor rural families to see that earnings stayed under one roof – had little bucolic charm in the more brutal industrial age.

The commission's report was vital in convincing Parliament and the people that the custom of employing entire families now appeared brutal. The verbal testimony needed no rhetorical embellishment. Seventeen-year-old Patience Kershaw, described as 'an ignorant, filthy, ragged, and deplorable-looking object, and such an one as the uncivilised natives of the prairies would be shocked to look upon', was one of ten children – all five brothers worked as colliers. She was employed as a 'hurrier', dragging or pushing 'corves' (in her pit, the woven baskets had been replaced by trucks with coal by the hewers). She was illiterate.

> I go to pit at five o'clock in the morning and come out at five in the evening; I get my breakfast of porridge and milk first; I take my dinner with me, a cake, and eat it as I go; I do not stop or rest any time for the purpose; I get nothing else until I get home, and then have potatoes and meat, not every day meat. I hurry in the clothes I have now got on, trousers and ragged jacket; the bald place upon my head is made by thrusting the corves ... I hurry the corves a mile and more underground and back; they weigh 300 cwt; I hurry 11 a-day; I wear a belt and chain at the workings, to get the corves out; the getters that I work for are naked except their caps; they pull off all their clothes; I see them at work when I go up; sometimes they beat me, if I am not quick enough, with their hands; they strike me upon my back; the boys take liberties with me sometimes they pull me about; I am the only girl in the pit; there are about 20 boys and 15 men; all the men are naked.

Reading the report, you can almost sense Victorian jaws dropping. The British Empire was sending ships across the world to redeem natives from sin and nudity and to suppress slavery, yet here, Britain's own people were being used as beasts of burden. In Lancashire, Betty Harris described how she worked at a pit near Bolton:

I have a belt round my waist, and a chain passing between my legs, and I go on my hands and feet. The road is very steep, and we have to hold the rope; and, where there is no rope, by anything we can catch hold of. There are six women and about six boys and girls in the pit I work in; it is very hard work for a woman. The pit is very wet where I work, and the water comes over the clog-tops always, and I have seen it up to my thighs: it rains in at the roof terribly; my clothes are wet through almost all day long … I am not so strong as I was, and cannot stand my work so well as I used to do. I have drawn till I have had the skin off me: the belt and chain is worse when we are in the family way. My feller [husband] has beaten me many a time for not being ready. I were not used to it at first, and he had little patience: I have known many a man beat his drawer. I have known men take liberties with the drawers, and some of the women have bastards. I think it would be better if we were paid once a week instead of once a month, for then I would buy victuals with ready money. It is bad to live on 7s., and rent 1s. 6d.

Another woman described how she had given birth underground and brought the baby to the surface at the end of her shift hidden in her skirts. There were frequent tales of miscarriages and still-births brought on by working conditions. The report was the first that many of the beneficiaries of coal knew of its human cost.

When Parliament came to debate the report, Shaftesbury did not hold back. It was impossible, he said, for any person with a heart 'to read the details of this awful document without a combined feeling of shame, terror, and indignation'. He listed the ages at which children began work in different parts of the country. 'In Shropshire some begin as early as six years of age; in Warwickshire the same; in Leicestershire nearly the same. In Derbyshire many begin at five, many between five and six years, many at seven ... Near Oldham, children are worked as low as four years old, and in the small collieries towards the hills some are so young they are brought to work in their bed-gowns. In Cumberland, many at seven; in South Durham, as early as five years of age, and by no means uncommonly at six.' In some of the collieries, for example in the east of Scotland, the seams of coal were only twenty-two inches high, 'so that in such places the youngest child cannot work without the most constrained posture. The ventilation, besides, in general is very bad, and the drainage worse.' Doctors had seen much evidence of deformity and scrofula as a result of children being bent double for most of the day crawling around dragging heavy weights. Shaftesbury quoted an old miner who said 'I went into the pit at seven years of age. When I drew by the girdle and chain, the skin was broken, and the blood ran down. If we said anything, they would beat us. I have seen many draw at six. They must do it or be beat. They cannot straighten their backs during the day. I have sometimes pulled till my hips have hurt me so that I have not known what to do with myself.' Of all the coalfields, those in eastern Scotland seem to have been the worst, where most of the carrying of coal buckets appeared to be done by women and girls.

Shaftesbury believed that British employment practices would be 'disgusting in a heathen country, and perfectly intolerable they are in one that professes to call itself Christian'. He proposed a total ban on all females in mines. 'I think that every principle of religion – I think that every law of nature calls for such a step.' There was one simple explanation for colliery-owners wanting to employ girls and women. They were cheaper. One assistant manager had confessed to the commission 'a girl of twenty will work for 2s. a day, or less, and a man of that age would want 3s. 6d.' It was clearly understood that women could never graduate to becoming hewers working at the coalface, and therefore, 'When a lad gets to be half [that age], he is all for getting coal; but a lass never expects to be a

coal-getter, and that keeps her steady to her work.' The practice
was not merely unfair, but immoral. He quoted one of the
sub-commissioners that 'the chain passing high up between the
legs of two girls, had worn large holes in their trowsers. Any sight
more disgustingly indecent or revolting can scarcely be imagined
than these girls at work. No brothel can beat it.' Salaciousness ran
riot at these tales – though no comment was made at the time
about what the chafing must have done to the skin beneath. And
despite the gossip there is no evidence that the women who worked
in the mines had 'looser' morals than any of their contemporaries.

Respectable opinion had been disgusted by the revelations
about life underground. The poet Elizabeth Barrett Browning was
moved to tears, producing 'The Cry of the Children' – described
by one critic 'as one long sob':

> Do ye hear the children weeping, O my brothers,
> Ere the sorrow comes with years?
> They are leaning their young heads against their mothers,
> And that cannot stop their tears.

But it was the nudity rather than the physical violence to children
which troubled some members of the House of Lords. The Bishop
of Norwich presented a petition about the fact that boys and girls
were working semi-naked 'which but too frequently engenders
habits of the most loathesome and disgusting sensuality. It exhibits
a state of physical toil and moral degradation that few will consent
to believe exists in their country in this age of enlightened philan-
thropy.'[10] Practical arguments were made about how the end of
child labour would make things better for adult miners: since
women and children were employed as beasts of burden in
passages that were too small for men, banning them would result
in better conditions underground. There would also be fewer accidents in the mines if responsible jobs, like supervising winding

gear, were not left to children. But it was the examples of abuse which had the most impact. Stories were told of how miners starved their apprentices or lost their tempers and attacked the boys supposed to be assisting them with pickaxes and other weapons. An account was given of a Rochdale boy who had been beaten so many times that 'his back and loins were beaten to a jelly; his head, which was almost cleared of hair on the scalp, had the marks of many old wounds'. He had been forced to continue working for weeks after his arm had been broken by an iron bar in an attack. 'Is all this cruelty necessary?' asked one MP.[11] Quite apart from the horror of seeing children scarred and maimed by their work, 'practical' arguments were made that allowing miners' wives and children to augment the family income from the mine encouraged the men to work less, and spend more time 'drinking, cockfighting and gambling'.

Not all readers of the commission's report were horrified by its contents or relieved that Shaftesbury's suggestions might soon become law. Mine-owners who gave evidence had predictable objections to do-gooders trying to interfere in their industry. Some protested that it was often the miners themselves who begged for their children to be given jobs. Within a week of publication of the report, Shaftesbury produced a bill to make it illegal to employ women and children in the mines. Prominent among the mine-owners, the third Marquess of Londonderry exploded when he read about the lives of boys and girls working underground. Londonderry wrote a 145-page pamphlet not in support of the inquiry but vigorously objecting to sentimental attempts to make judgements about business. Charles Dickens laughed at the noble lord's outrage, reserving especial scorn for Londonderry's argument that 'men are not all born to read and write, but that they must obtain by the sweat of their brow food for the mouth as well as the mind'. Dickens observed that it was certainly a profound truth that 'men are not all born to read and write'. Indeed, 'there be

Lords who are not born to write one correct sentence in the language of the country they have represented abroad'.[12]

In response to the troubling disclosures about child labour in the mines, the government appointed a deeply conservative clergyman-cum-lawyer as its first inspector of mines. It cannot have been an easy job, for he had responsibility for about 2,000 working pits and, according to one of his contemporaries, never went underground. He once said that he wanted to convince the miners of the virtues of capitalism and to discourage any subversive ideas from 'agitators'. But Lord Londonderry detested him anyway, saying he was welcome to go down any of his pits, and stay there.

Parliament ignored much of Londonderry's braying, and Shaftesbury said he was prepared to sacrifice some of his safeguards for children 'to save the females'. And so it came to be. The Mines and Collieries Act took effect on 10 August 1842 as a total prohibition on the employment of girls and women underground, and of children under the age of ten. Though there would doubtless now be protests about the denial of equality of opportunity (and there is no denying a strong sense in Parliament at the time that women really ought to be confined to the chores of domestic life), there was widespread popular enthusiasm for the new law from a shocked population.

But even as the bill limped towards the statute book in its maimed form, some people were still infuriated. There had been predictable opposition in the House of Lords, where landowners objected to government interference in their businesses. *The Economist*, the free-market magazine founded the following year, later cited the law as expressing 'the sickly sentimentality of the drawing room presuming to regulate the world'.[13] In particular, the banning of women from working underground was a 'foolish, premature and cruel act which has arbitrarily deprived these women of their labour and driven them underground by stealth'.[14]

Victorian sensibilities were denying women use of their labour –
but in a workplace that really was thoroughly detestable.

Today we might have drawn up the laws differently to address
the root of the problem, which was the actual conditions of work
and the need for education, but there is no denying that
Shaftesbury's Act did prevent a great deal of suffering – especially
amongst the nation's youngest children. And the new law did have
flaws – as *The Economist* suggested would happen, some
colliery-owners defied it for the simple reason that the chances of
being caught were slight, and the possible penalties easily afford-
able.

Until 1850 there was only one mines inspector. Even in 1866, an
inspector candidly admitted he would not bother enforcing the
fines unless a child had died – and few inspectors ever 'went below'
as they feared being killed by the miners themselves. Decades later,
the fines of £10 or so would still fall 'not upon the colliery-owner,
but upon the father or the guardian of the boy' – because children
could technically be said to be employed by their own parents.[15]

Still, Shaftesbury's Act was the first attempt by Parliament to
demonstrate that what was out of sight was not necessarily out of
mind.

In truth, only a small proportion of the underground population
had been female – perhaps about 5,000 all told. And now all were
nominally deprived of an income. In areas such as Lancashire,
which had had a high proportion of women working at the pits,
the loss of income was predicted to be sudden and severe. The
agent for the Earl of Crawford and Balcarres, who owned enor-
mously profitable mines near Wigan, said that the law should only
be phased in gradually, because otherwise it would produce more
'misery' than 'the vice and immorality' it was supposed to prevent.

The Lancashire area does seem to have had many more women
working in the mining industry than other places, and inevitably,

some of them broke the new law. In November 1846 – four years after the Act had been passed – an explosion caused by 'firedamp' (methane) in a mine at Chorley, Lancashire killed three girls under the age of fourteen. The owner of the pit, John Hargreaves, was a local magistrate, who told the colleagues trying him that the girls normally worked at the pithead and had been sent underground by his manager to help remove debris from a new tunnel. The fact that they were wearing men's clothing at the time was not to conceal their gender but because of the job they had to do. The *Preston Guardian* was disgusted by his acquittal, which would, it said, 'astonish' any man 'of common decency and generous feeling'.[16] A second trial was ordered, at the end of which he was fined a total of £20 for putting the three children in harm's way.

But in most places the 1842 law making it illegal for women and young children to work underground seems to have been respected. Modern gender politicians have claimed that men wanted to keep women out of the mines to preserve their jobs. At the time, there were arguments that allowing women to do heavy work underground encouraged them to behave like men and to get drunk instead of going home to prepare their husband's tea. Lord Londonderry discharged his blunderbuss in support of traditional family values when he argued in the House of Lords that colliery women were 'unfitted to be good wives or mothers, the habit beings wholly inconsistent with those domestic duties'.[17]

Though the new law prevented women and children from working underground, where they were often replaced by pit ponies, it did not remove them from the mines altogether. At the 'pit brow', whether pushing waggons of coal, standing alongside giant oscillating mesh trays picking out extraneous rock from the coal, and sorting good coal by size, women were a common sight – at least in parts of Yorkshire, east Scotland and South Wales, where the colliery women were famous for their enormous earrings. In the Black Country, they talked of 'Wednesbury Wenches' in long skirts and – in an attempt to keep coal dust out of their hair – cotton bonnets.

Most famously, they were to be seen – and advertised their presence – in the Wigan coalfield, Lancashire. Here, local photographers began producing *cartes de visite* – small picture postcards which were soon being collected by enthusiasts. Most of them show women in trousers, aprons, clogs and headscarves, posing with shovels, sieves or lumps of coal. Lady Blundell, wife of the proprietor of Blundells Collieries – some of the biggest mines in Britain at the time – even went to the extent of designing a uniform for 'her' women workers. In blue serge, it consisted of a loose jacket, presumably intended to allow the women to work easily, a turban-like headdress, trousers and clogs. It must have been intended as a sort of Sunday best.

The most assiduous seeker-out of pit-brow lasses was, inevitably, a man. Arthur Munby, a lawyer, civil servant and not particularly good poet, travelled all over Britain in search of poor women whom he could watch in manual labour. His diaries, which he ruled should be locked up until he had been dead for forty years, record a tireless appreciation of acrobats, charwomen, coster-girls, fisherwomen, labourers, milkmaids, 'mudlarks' and dozens of other working women. From Prime Minister William Gladstone downwards, Victorian society was replete with middle-class men who made secret night-time visits to 'fallen women' (though few seem to have recorded the acts of self-flagellation Gladstone found necessary after his acts of 'rescue'). There is no evidence that Munby died anything other than a virgin – though his accounts record meetings with prostitutes, he is more interested in the brawn than the sexual allure of the working women he approaches. What he seemed to enjoy was the strength and energy of the women he watched, and the dirt and grime on their skin. In the studio of a Wigan photographer, in 1873, Munby was able to persuade one of his favourite female colliers, Ellen Grounds, to pose beside him for a picture. He wears a luxuriant beard, hat, tweed suit and pocket handkerchief. She is in a scarf, cotton jacket, apron, her right hand resting on a shovel. At the time, Munby was a forty-five-year-old bachelor and something of a High Church snob. He was also clearly a voyeur and possibly a fetishist. Perhaps he was a pervert – it would be most interesting to know what the women in whom he took an interest thought of him. Certainly, that year he secretly married a Shropshire woman, Hannah Cullwick, who had been 'in service' since the age of eight. The two lived out a bizarre master–servant relationship (she is said to have been particularly devoted to cleaning his boots).

The pit-brow lasses were as much survivors from an earlier age as they were standard-bearers for feminism – relics from a time when paid employment was a family occupation involving children as well as their parents. Polite society, which had already decreed that there were some occupations – hewers of wood and drawers of water – that were 'male' and others – nurturing and caring – that were necessarily 'female', regarded the pit-brow lasses as hoydens – noisy, boisterous exceptions to the normal order of things. In September 1891, the *Wigan Observer* could not hold back from a purple carnival, describing them as 'weird, swarthy creatures, figures of women, half clad in men's and half in women's attire, plunging here and there, as if engaged in some bedlamish saturnalia'.

The First World War's need for labour would give a breath of life to the employment of women in the collieries, but once the war was over, the men wanted their old jobs back. Though the National Union of Mineworkers did the absolute minimum for the pit-brow lasses, they lost their role not through legislation but because machines were invented which could wash and grade coal more cheaply. Out of sync with their times, they had been a curiosity in a male-dominated world and if there were men who could not imagine women performing such work without also being sexually available, that was their problem. Photographs exist of female surface workers in the 1940s, but by the mid-1950s only two collieries in Lancashire still had women working 'bankside'. One of the last of the pit-brow women reflected – is there an undertone of anger in her voice? – on how, for all the grubbiness of their job, they washed their hair every night, protected their complexions with Snowfire cream and make-up before going to work, and tried (unsuccessfully) to protect their clothes from coal dust with brown paper worn beneath their shawls. It was almost impossible to get the coal dust out of their hands. But they scrubbed them hard before going out.[18]

From a twenty-first-century perspective, the banning of women from underground work seems as absurd as trying to prohibit them from bringing in the harvest, picking hops, milking cows, becoming doctors or, come to that, mining engineers. In fact, if coal-mining had survived in Britain it would have required more mechanisation and less brute force. The modern mine will be operated by buttons rather than by picks and shovels. Equality laws would prevent discrimination against the employment of women.

3

To Those Who Hath Shall Be Given

If the human beings who cut coal had one of the hardest jobs on earth, those who owned the mines had one of the easiest. Coal really was 'the gift that kept on giving'. Once someone had dug a hole in the ground, you received a royalty on each shovel-load of coal extracted from it until the seam was worked out, which might be in a hundred or more years' time. Inheriting a coalfield made you one of the luckiest people alive; a man might 'jog along on £40,000' a year, as the first Earl of Durham put it in 1821, after he came into the family mines in County Durham.* That is about £4.5 million a year at today's values.

The thing about coal was that unless you, or your workers, were unlucky, you didn't have to do much to continue to benefit. You had done nothing to put the stuff into the ground, and you could usually let others get it out for you: people desperate for a job would beat a path to your door. It stood to reason that coal supplies would run out one day, but why not make hay while the sun shone?

---

* This florid, bad-tempered man at least gave the rest of us the consolation that money isn't everything when he moaned in 1822 that it was 'damned hard that a man with £80,000 a year can't sleep!' Politically, he turned out to be on the side of the angels, though, working hard to promote the great 1832 Reform Act, which began the process of making Parliament representative of the people. Few owners were shrinking violets. He is commemorated by a huge smoke-stained monument in the shape of a Greek temple at Penshaw Hill looking out over the Durham coalfield.

Lord Londonderry kept a close eye on his mines. Others just enjoyed the money they provided.

Hugh Cecil Lowther, for example, had been twenty-five when his elder brother, the fourth Earl of Lonsdale, died in February 1882, and he was saved from penury and became one of the richest men in England, largely on the proceeds of the family's coal mines in the west of Cumberland. The wealth of the new fifth Earl of Lonsdale meant he could now devote himself to a life of pleasure. He was a man of simple, if not inexpensive, tastes: one of his four mansions and castles was devoted solely to fox hunting. The greatest compliment his biographer could summon was that he 'was not handsome or sophisticated but he had an energy and a taste for self-advertisement'. In the way that others might be described in one word as 'politician' or 'farmer', he is summed up in the *Dictionary of National Biography* as a 'sportsman', which is accurate enough, though 'chancer' might have done as well. He chased actresses and other men's wives, often successfully. He trekked across Alaska. He was master of two of the smartest hunts in Britain. He became a good friend of George V (a man of comparable intellectual talents and similar modesty). At the age of twenty, he had heard that a champion American road-walker was in Britain, accepted a £5 bet, and challenged him to a hundred-mile race up the Great North Road. He walked it in seventeen hours and twenty-one minutes at an average speed of almost six miles an hour, and won. Soon afterwards, he travelled to New York to go into the ring against John Sullivan, the world heavyweight boxing champion and (according to an account he later wrote for *The People*) knocked him out in the sixth round. The earl's enthusiasm for boxing is commemorated in the Lonsdale Belt trophy. An obsession with yellow led to his having all his carriages painted in the colour and earned him the nickname 'the yellow earl' (it survives in the Automobile Association's yellow livery, from the days when he was the organisation's president). He had a specially recruited orchestra of twenty-four musicians travel with him from house to house, and even though he had entertained the kaiser as his house guest more than once, when war broke out with Germany in 1914 he attempted to raise his own Pals' Battalion with a poster headed 'ARE YOU A MAN OR ARE YOU A MOUSE?', which continued:

> Are you a man who will be handed down to
> posterity as a Gallant Patriot
> or
> are you to be handed down to Posterity as a
> Rotter and Coward?

By now, the earl – who would occasionally appear at inspections of men who had volunteered for military service, while smoking a cigar – was too old for active service. On the Somme, the Lonsdale Battalion climbed out of their trenches and into German fire with some of them singing, to the tune of 'John Peel', 'Do ye ken Lord Lonsdale that sportsman true?' The assault reduced twenty-eight officers and 800 men to three officers and 280 men.

When he died in 1944 *The Times* remarked that 'he personified an English type now fast disappearing – that of a wealthy, genial, well-dressed gentleman, a gallant devotee of sport in all its healthiest forms, respected and admired by all classes for his sportsmanlike qualities and his goodness of heart'.[1] This was taking the convention of not speaking ill of the dead to extremes, for the earl was not even 'admired' by those who inherited his title. The seventh earl thought him 'decadent', and the entire family had to live with the consequences of his mismanagement of the family business. 'Almost an emperor, not quite a gentleman' was a less partisan judgement. He was a feckless individual and an appalling businessman. While he frittered away the fortune his miners had made him, their prospects went from bad to worse. A new deep coal mine – the last in Cumberland – was sunk on Lonsdale's land near Whitehaven and named Haig Pit in honour of the field marshal who had sent so many of the Lonsdale Battalion charging to their deaths. The mine closed in 1986, reopening a few years later as a mining museum. After persuading charities to donate millions to it, it closed for lack of business. By then the nation had not only lost the taste for coal, it had lost almost all interest in it.

Of course, the coal-owners had done nothing to create the coal: how much money was to be made had been determined by events millennia beforehand. After that, it was just a question of getting at it. Ownership of the mines therefore reflected ownership of land and was dominated by aristocratic families. (In 1920s Nottinghamshire, there was even a 'Dukeries Coalfield', so named because no fewer than four dukes – the highest rank of nobility – had their 'seats' in the locality: here the bosses built 'model villages', but behaved almost feudally, dominating every aspect of the miners' lives, including where and how they worshipped and the sort of education their children received.*) Mine-owners across the land who did not already have a title knew that if their miners brought enough coal to the surface, then, sooner or later, the British honours system would reward them with some handle or other. Once a shaft had been sunk, men to hew the coal were relatively easily found and, paid on a piecework system, the reward for their labour was directly related to the amount of coal produced: miners who had many mouths to feed knew they needed to cut plenty of coal, which meant the pit-owner had more to sell.

By comparison with the men who went down the mines, the Stuart family of the Isle of Bute in the estuary of the river Clyde were some of the luckiest people on earth. Their origins were impeccably Scottish, claiming descent from one of King Robert II's

---

* Some of the companies to whom they leased the mines even employed private police forces.

thirteen illegitimate children (in addition to the fourteen legally recognised offspring sired by the first Stuart king). In the eighteenth century, under George III, the third Earl of Bute had become Britain's first Scots-born prime minister.

His son was both socially ambitious and commercially astute. In November 1766 he married the famously rich and ugly Charlotte Jane Windsor, deciding that the first adjective more than compensated for the second. Ms Windsor brought to the marriage great tracts of Wales, including the ownership of Cardiff Castle, which had come to her through her ancestors, the Herbert family, earls of Pembroke. Her new husband then parlayed a position as an incompetent British ambassador in Madrid into a marquessate. When his wife died of a stroke in 1800, the fifty-six-year-old Bute – by now also titled 'Baron Cardiff of Cardiff Castle' – waited nine months and then married the young daughter of the banker, Thomas Coutts. Two marriages and he was free from any danger of pauperism. The greatest security came from owning much of South Wales: even at the end of the twentieth century almost a quarter of the Welsh population was living on land which had once belonged to the Bute family. But it was what lay beneath the surface of much of this land that would secure the family fortune. In 1814, when the first Marquess of Bute died, a catalogue of the family art collection was published. It included a Raphael, a Rembrandt, four works by Rubens, a Velázquez, a couple of Titians, two Cuyps, five by Reynolds and many other pictures by less distinguished artists.

John Crichton-Stuart, the second marquess, who inherited the family estates in 1814, was a humourless man afflicted with a serious eye condition, which meant that he found reading and writing a terrible chore. When out walking or riding, he was accompanied by a guide, and spent the first six years after succeeding to the marquessate living quietly on the Isle of Bute. Here he nonetheless managed to woo and marry Lady Maria North, granddaughter of

George III's prime minister, Lord North, 'the man who lost the American colonies'. She, too, was something of an invalid. But she also happened to be extremely wealthy. Quite apart from her large dowry, the marriage settlement entitled the second marquess to all of Maria's income from the family estates when she died. This she did, childless, at forty-eight. Four years later, he married again, to the thirty-six-year-old Lady Sophia, daughter of the Marquess of Hastings. She was a short-tempered woman with literary pretensions who, to the delight of the Marquess of Bute, at half-past five on the afternoon of 12 September 1847 provided him with an heir. Like others before him – and since – the baby was christened John Crichton-Stuart.

The child's proud new father was a dull man, who took the business of estate management very seriously (so seriously, in fact, that he sometimes wondered whether his energetic preoccupation with the subject had contributed to his first wife's death). Much of his life was passed in a restless progress from one of his houses to another, from the Isle of Bute to Dumfries House, to their pile in Newcastle upon Tyne, to their house at Luton Hoo in Bedfordshire, to South Wales and back to Scotland. In his wake flew endless letters – sometimes a dozen a day – full of instructions for improving buildings and developing businesses. He was a rotten orator, but the success of his enterprises had a direct political consequence, in changing him from a protectionist to a free-trader. He acquired none of the traditional interests of the very rich in gambling, horses, field sports or seduction, but kept his attention relentlessly focussed on the development of the family business: anyone who wanted to mine coal on his land paid handsomely for the privilege. He promised to make Cardiff, then no more than a small provincial town, into 'a new Liverpool', and he did so. By the late nineteenth century, Cardiff had become the biggest coal port in the world and its ornate Coal Exchange was alive with buyers and sellers. (In 1904 the world's first million-pound cheque is said to have been signed there.) By then, he was long dead, his title and massive fortune having been inherited by his infant son, the eternal John Crichton-Stuart, in 1848. He was the richest baby in the world and though he also died young (at fifty-three) in 1900, he was never to fall on hard times: by adulthood, he was the biggest receiver of mineral royalties in Britain. He also had many colonies of bats in his belfry.

When Benjamin Disraeli, the Conservative titan who stalked through mid-nineteenth-century British public life, lost the 1868 general election to his rival Gladstone, he consoled himself by taking to his writing desk to produce *Lothair*, a novel about a handsome, well-bred young man of exquisite taste. The eponymous hero was, unambiguously, modelled on the young Marquess of Bute. Despite its great length (it originally appeared in three volumes), *Lothair* sold out in two days and was followed by eight new editions later in the year. Waltzes, racehorses and a perfume were all inspired by the book. Its success is rather baffling, since the novel is pretty hard-going.

People who do not need to work are attractive heroes to authors of fiction because, unlike the rest of us, who must spend our lives in the more-or-less tedious toil necessary to keep a roof over our heads, the otherwise idle rich are free to be tormented by passion or prejudice. Like Lothair, the young Marquess of Bute found the torment which he could now indulge to be exquisite. As a dutiful Scottish toff, he had been brought up a Presbyterian. But the moment he got to Oxford he flirted with Judaism, Islam, the Orthodox Church and Buddhism. In 1870 he began translating the Roman Catholic breviary into plain English.

Lothair, like the Marquess of Bute, is an orphaned Scottish aristocrat who spends an eternity choosing between three young women, representing differing political and religious fashions of the time. After sauntering about the Holy Land, admiring the 'agreeable' views and discussing the nature of belief with assorted mystics, Disraeli's hero returns home, and like a sensible chap, joins the Church of England. But as soon as he could do so, the real-life third marquess converted to Roman Catholicism – an act described in the press as a 'perversion'. The *Glasgow Herald* feared 'priestly influences acting upon a weak, ductile and naturally superstitious mind'.[2] Disraeli, who had been born Jewish, was kinder to an outsider and when, in 1872, Bute married Gwendolen Mary Anne Fitzalan-Howard – a granddaughter of the thirteenth Duke of Norfolk, Britain's premier Catholic aristocrat – 'Dizzy' was happy to act as a witness as they signed the wedding register.[3] Gwendolen was eighteen, late growing out of her puppy fat, and short, with brown hair and beautiful eyes. Bute worried that she was perhaps too uninterested in art to play much of an active role in the questions of design which were beginning to obsess him. But he loved her.

And however much Lothair may have been modelled on the Marquess of Bute (indeed, when the marquess died in 1900, a number of obituaries referred to the 'death' of Disraeli's creation), as so often, real life was much more exciting than fiction. One example had been the massive parties in 1868 to celebrate the marquess's coming of age. On the hills overlooking Cardiff Bay, celebratory bonfires blazed. A choir of 8,000–9,000 local school-children had been assembled to sing the national anthem and 'God Bless Lord Bute'. The organist at the main city centre church composed a piano suite in his honour. A full-length portrait of the young man was unveiled. A new steamer named the *Marquess of Bute* nodded at anchor in the bay. A regatta was held in the estuary of the river Taff. The local theatre staged special performances to mark the event and there were numerous concerts. A balloon took to the skies, watched by a crowd described by the local newspaper as being more people than had 'ever before assembled'. The *Merthyr Guardian* went on to fawn that 'We are satisfied that were it possible Lord Bute would invite all Cardiff under his roof; but as this cannot be, he sends into the streets and alleys and courts, and into the highways and byways, and graciously, kindly, and nobly wishes the needy to eat of his bread and drink of his cup – to cast no thought upon the morrow, and to bask for a while – a little while – in the sunshine of life.'[4] At a 'workmen's banquet' for 3,700, the band of the Grenadier Guards played 'The Roast Beef of Old England', while guests downed plates of bread, meat and plum pudding, and pints of beer. There were numerous further dinners, toasts, oxen-roastings, balls, and the opening of the Glamorganshire Agricultural Show. Sadly, the highlight of the after-dark celebrations, a pyrotechnic display of fireworks which had 'never before been introduced into the Principality' was spoiled by thunderous rain.

Almost everyone loves a party, but the adulation accorded the young marquess was exceptionally lavish. The *Merthyr Guardian* suggested – almost certainly rightly – that had it not been for the business activities of his family, Cardiff would have remained a provincial backwater:

> Twenty years ago Cardiff numbered a few thousands of inhabitants. Today her settled population is at least sixty thousand! Then, two or three dingy streets were all she could boast of: now, her streets are measured by miles. Cardiff now sends ships and steamers, laden with native produce, to the ends of the earth ... Very few of the great peers of the realm have ever at so early an age inherited such vast wealth as Lord Bute ... all the good fairies of fable could hardly shower more fortune or favours upon a terrestrial being.[5]

The good fairies were said to have made the young marquess into the richest man in the world. And what did he do with his astonishing good fortune? He sallied into fairyland. He was cultivated and scholarly, certainly, and he took literally the modern cliché about 'living the dream'. His hagiographers claim the third marquess spoke, or at least understood, twenty-one languages. Perhaps he did. He certainly learned Welsh and inherited thirteen titles and vast estates in England, Wales and Scotland. But he is remembered not for the new additions to the docks during his lifetime, but for his medieval fantasies. Cardiff Castle had been in his family for just over one hundred years before the third marquess came of age. Now, like some other beneficiaries of Victorian industrial inventiveness, he scorned the coal dust lying on his wealth and turned to pre-industrial times as being a much happier period to celebrate. Bute engaged the eccentric and myopic architect William Burges, who was twenty years his senior and the outstanding designer of the age, to turn the castle into what he would like it to have been, allowing him what seems to have been almost total freedom to follow his instincts. The product of the relationship between the richest man in Britain and the talented designer was astonishing, and in its magnificence almost enough to compensate for the fouling of the South Wales valleys which had yielded the wealth to make it possible. 'I wish I had been born in the Middle Ages,' he asserted.[6] When invited to become rector of St Andrews University, he designed his own robes, in the style of a Middle Ages divine.

For nearly two decades, Burges let his imagination run riot, in a way only possible when you have a patron with bottomless pockets. The marquess was obsessed by the passage of time? There would be rooms in which the seasons were picked out in gold leaf. He admired oriental and ancient languages? There would be legends chiselled into the walls in Greek, Assyrian and Aramaic. He was a conscientious Roman Catholic? There would be a chapel. He also believed in astrology? There would be models of planets and figures of the zodiac scattered everywhere. The marquess was intrigued by Arab culture? Very well, there would be an Arab room, decorated in gold leaf. The roof garden was styled after the gardens of Pompeii, and there were both winter and summer smoking rooms. Sculpted animals were everywhere. Cardiff Castle is one of the most exuberant buildings in the world.

But, despite lavishing unimaginable amounts of money on medieval fantasies at Cardiff Castle and at his personal folly, Castell Coch, just outside the Welsh capital, the Bute family hardly lived in the places – a few weeks each year at Cardiff Castle, while Castell Coch was little more than a place to entertain visitors on picnics.* Both castles pulse with a mad energy. Asked whether he worried that Burges was taking a long time to finish, the third marquess answered with the dilettante's response that 'I have comparatively little interest in a thing after it is finished.'

It would be unfair to suggest that all he did with his money was to wallow in a bogus medievalism – striking though the contrast is with the source of his wealth – for Bute was twice mayor of Cardiff and donated money generously to causes in which he believed. That was what the ruling class did. And the Butes were indisputably members of the ruling class. Though their origins were Scottish, they had inevitably acquired the style and manners of British toffs, which is to say that they dressed and sounded as plummy as any privately educated Englishman.

The third marquess died in 1900, stricken by kidney disease, leaving instructions that his heart was to be cut from his body and buried in the Holy Land. Two years later, he was succeeded, as fourth marquess, by his son – yet another John Crichton-Stuart – a shy, sickly man with a weak heart. He was still fabulously wealthy, of course, having inherited mines, docks, and much of Cardiff. In 1905, he married a baronet's daughter, Augusta Mary Monica Bellingham in a lavish ceremony in glorious sunshine at her

---

* For living, the marquess had his house on the Isle of Bute, Mount Stuart, which he also had redesigned as a Gothic fantasy, but in which he had taken care to install central heating (and a heated indoor swimming pool). The hall was large enough for the children to play badminton.

father's seat in County Louth, the record of which is one of the very first wedding films in Britain. The film ends with the bride and groom being rowed away by white-uniformed estate retainers, followed by the marquess's personal bagpipers in another barge. After that his steamer took the guests (and pipe band) across the Irish Sea to his seat at Mount Stuart, on the Isle of Bute. He shared his father's obsession with art and architecture (though he much preferred classical architecture to his father's medievalism) and was an early supporter of the National Trust for Scotland. He was also periodically convinced the world was going to hell in a hand-cart. Bute was one of the very few peers to enlist as a private in the First World War, and spent much of his service as an observer in balloons. He had perhaps come to appreciate the bitterness of feeling against inherited wealth among ordinary soldiers. In 1919 he wrote to his brother about his fear of 'a bloody revolution or general strike' and the following year offered Mount Stuart for sale, to be rebuilt elsewhere (since he couldn't find a buyer, nothing came of the plan).

The attitudes of the Bute family reflect the way in which 'the coal question' became increasingly a matter of politics. In few industries was the contrast between the 'haves' and the 'have nots' starker, and what had begun as the exploitation of mineral reserves developed into an argument about social justice. By the turn of the century, the trade unions were convinced that the mine-owners had to be dispossessed and their reserves made the property of the state. Early in 1938, the Conservative government would come to the very unconservative conclusion that the best way to ensure the nation had a reliable supply of coal was to do precisely that and set aside over £66 million (about £4.5 billion at today's values) to compensate the Butes and their ilk. The marquess was so unnerved that he decided his time was up. 'Peer sells half of a city' was the *Daily Herald* headline in May, as he put shopping streets, residential suburbs, docks, theatres, cinemas and 250 pubs in Cardiff on the market. From then on, the marquess devoted his life to pottering about preserving traditional Scottish buildings and crafts.

Within four months of his death from cancer in 1947, his son, the newly created fifth marquess, ditched the family's last significant property in the Welsh capital. Newsreel cameras recording the event show a parade of top hats, mayoral chains, aldermen's robes, military uniforms, judges in full-bottomed wigs and a herald in black tricorn hat crossing the castle drawbridge. They are led by a thin man in a dark suit with a tightly furled umbrella, hair slicked to his skull and a luxuriant moustache encrusting his upper lip. In the patrician drawl of the gently born English the marquess handed over the fantasy on which great-grandfather had lavished so much of the fortune cut from the ground by Welsh labourers. As a massed choir of schoolchildren sang 'Men of Harlech', the Bute fascination with the Celtic twilight vanished like a phantasm.

The sixth marquess emulated his grandfather, running the Edinburgh Tapestry Company and attempting to preserve buildings in Scotland. As you might expect, his son and heir, the seventh marquess, dropped out of school and devoted himself to driving fast cars as 'Johnny Dumfries' and later 'John Bute'.

Were the Butes brutes? It depends which member of the dynasty you're talking about. How could anyone think that a man as away-with-the-fairies as the third marquess was a monster, when all he wanted to do was to create some imaginary medieval kingdom? Yet his wealth was a pure accident of geology. In the middle of the nineteenth century if anyone had suggested to any one of this privileged family that their cosseted, artificial way of life was the consequence of an unjust system, they would have been denounced as one of those seditious, newfangled communists. The Butes had just been born lucky. That was how God planned it – in the words of the British hymnodist's response to the *Communist Party Manifesto*, 'God made [men] high or lowly / And ordered their estate'. Here, in the good fortune of the coal-owners; the urgent energy and vision of capitalist endeavour; the readiness to take advantage of those who had only brute strength to make their way in the world; and the owners' final relinquishing of a fortuitous source of unearned income to the state, is the tale of coal until twentieth-century politics barged in.

4

Full Steam Ahead

The main use of coal was to make steam, the alchemy which created Britain's wealth and power. Indeed, it had been the heat of coal and the force of steam which made it possible to get the stuff out of the ground in usable quantities at all.

Quite apart from the dangers of rockfalls, explosions and poisonings, there were natural obstacles to be overcome, notably water, which had a nasty habit of sinking through the porous rocks above and flooding mines. Some mines required an endless procession of men with buckets to slop liquid up from the 'sump' at the bottom of the pit: if water levels rose, work became impossible. In other pits, horses could be used to drive pumps on the surface, but horses cost money: first, the price of the animal, and then constant supervision by adults or children as well as frequent feeding. Then in July 1698, a Devon man, Thomas Savery, took out a patent for 'a new Invention for the Raiseing of Water … by the Impellent Force of Fire'. Savery was one of those restlessly energetic inventors willing to try to find a better way of doing almost anything.* After excitedly demonstrating his primitive steam engine to the Royal Society, he published a book called *The Miner's Friend; or, An Engine to Raise Water by Fire*. Owners of coal mines

---

* Among his previous inventions had been a double paddle-wheel contraption for manoeuvring becalmed sailing vessels. Even though the king was keen, the Admiralty was unenthusiastic.

eagerly trooped along to his workshops – just off Fleet Street in London – to see the solution to their problems demonstrated.

But the Miner's Friend was a temperamental beast, which could become positively hostile at times, due to its tendency to explode when the great heat needed to raise water from the bottom of a mine melted the soldered joints of the machine. Savery's device had the advantage of being extremely simple by comparison with later steam engines, having neither a piston nor heavy moving parts. He is generally credited as the first man in Britain to apply heat and steam to the problem of flooded mines. There were, of course, similar inquiries and experiments being conducted in other industrialising nations: the development of an effective way of using steam was the province of no single nation. Soon after the death of Christ, the Greek mathematician Hero of Alexandria had played about with steam, as had Leonardo da Vinci and Taqi al-Din in the sixteenth century. In the following century Evangelista Torricelli, Denis Papin, Otto von Guericke, Edward Somerset, Christiaan Huygens and Jerónimo de Ayanz y Beaumont had all noted the phenomenon generally ascribed in Britain to James Watt watching his aunt make tea, that a boiling kettle produces power. Their names disclose the universality of the challenge: how could the force be put to work?

No doubt human ingenuity would have harnessed the power of steam sooner or later, somewhere or other. But Britain was blessed by having had its political revolution a century or more earlier than some other countries, had a fluid class system, a great army of labourers looking for work (and the food to feed them), and a number of financial institutions willing to encourage enterprise. It seems a fanciful thing to say – though there are probably right now people saying it in China – that material success feeds on itself, and soon begins to free the imagination. The visionary strength of Victorian engineers – the reason that Britain has lived in the shadow of the Victorians ever since – is that they never saw a problem without imagining a possible solution, however unlikely it might appear to others. Let the late Victorian Tower Bridge in London, and the 1876 revolving Swing Bridge in Newcastle, stand as their monuments. But let us recall, too, that without the possibilities unleashed by coal the engineers who designed these bridges (Horace Jones and William Armstrong) would have remained mere doodlers.

The refinement of steam power took as a given the ready availability of coal. In the course of his business, Thomas Newcomen, a speak-as-you-find West Country ironmonger and Nonconformist lay preacher, had visited Cornish tin mines, selling picks and shovels. As early eighteenth-century tin reserves became depleted and mines had to be sunk deeper, owners increasingly complained to him of the cost and inconvenience of trying to keep the pits dry by drawing water to the surface with human or horsepower.

Savery's patented 'Miner's Friend' lifted water by means of a vacuum. He was barking up entirely the wrong tree by trying to defy the laws of physics: even if he had managed to develop a perfect vacuum, it would only have been able to raise water 33.9 feet at sea-level atmospheric pressure. Newcomen became obsessed with refining Savery's machine and ingeniously decided that the answer lay in using vacuums for more suitable tasks, like filling and emptying a cylinder which would push water past a non-return valve. Though Newcomen's machine was quite different, Savery was a disputatious man, and the two engineers eventually went into partnership to avoid a patent wrangle. By 1712, the first Newcomen engine had been installed at a mine in Staffordshire and soon, colliery-owners across the land wanted their own 'surprising machine for raising water by fire'.[1] In 1726, one was installed to lift water from the Seine to supply Paris, and the following year a Newcomen engine was pumping water out of the most important iron-ore mines in Sweden. Within a decade, there were one hundred of them installed at mines across Europe.

Remarkably, given the vast quantities of coal to which they had access, some of the colliery-owners began to resent the cost of raising steam to drain the pit.

In just about the only story of the Industrial Revolution that you can guarantee every child may know, this was when James Watt entered the story. Watt was the son of a wealthy Scottish shipowner from Greenock. Legend has it that, as a teenage boy, Watt had been sitting in his aunt's house one day in 1751, when she turned on him with the accusation that he had done nothing but watch the kettle boil for an hour. According to a letter written by James Watt's cousin and sold at Sotheby's in 2003 for almost £16,000, his aunt exclaimed 'I never saw such an idle boy, take a book or employ yourself usefully.' Being a well-mannered lad, James did not respond to his aunt that he had been doing something useful. He had been trying to figure out the power of steam. The story is as well known as those of Newton and the apple or Robert Bruce and the spider. The Sotheby's auctioneer of course claimed it to be true. But it suffers from some innate plausibility problems. How many kettles could produce steam for 'an hour' without boiling dry? Why do some accounts attribute the scolding not to his aunt, Jane Muirhead, but to his own mother?

The Watt legend goes on to describe how he was given a model of a Newcomen engine to repair. He soon recognised that Newcomen's machine wasted tremendous amounts of energy by heating, cooling and then reheating the same cylinder: his experiments seemed to show that perhaps three-quarters was frittered away. There is no exaggerating the importance of James Watt's insight. The recognition that the key to a more efficient engine was not to let energy go to waste ensured his place in history. His efficiencies of design and refinements in creating a vacuum enabled human artifice to harness natural forces. Watt's engine condensed the steam in a separate chamber, while the steam cylinder itself stayed hot. His new machine was much more powerful than its predecessor and was one of the greatest advances in energy generation ever made. Once again, it took little more than a decade for these new engines to appear at mines across the country, lifting water out of the pits.

As an adult, this clever, nervy, often diffident man had moved south from his native Renfrewshire, to become one of the most distinguished engineers in England,* where he went into partnership with Matthew Boulton, one of the more influential men who turned Birmingham into the 'city of a thousand trades'. James Watt was as hopeless at business as Boulton was noisy in his marketing. In a letter to a friend Watt confessed 'I am extremely indolent, cannot force workmen to do their duty, have been cheated by undertakers and clerks, and am unlucky enough to know it.' He was, he knew, temperamentally unsuited to striking deals, admitting 'I would rather face a loaded cannon than settle an account or make a bargain.'[2] The different temperaments of the two men have inevitably meant that the relationship was characterised as a man with creative ideas meeting a man with money and drive. In fact, Boulton was a creative engineer in his own right, and as energetic as the machines he championed. Having no capital to turn his inventions into machines, Watt had previously formed a partnership with John Roebuck, a doctor with a massive ironworks about a mile from Falkirk in the Scottish Lowlands. The partnership did not last, for while Watt may have been full of ideas but short of cash, Roebuck was overfull of optimism, but defective in judgement. By the early 1770s the Carron Company was in financial trouble. Matthew Boulton, who had inherited his father's metal-trinket business in Birmingham, and then married two heiresses in succession, was one of Roebuck's creditors and was happy to take Watt's patents off him.

---

* Bored with the need to copy invoices by hand, he also developed a copying machine, an example of which was still being used by the Great Western Railway in the early twentieth century.

The partnership between Watt and Boulton was one of the most successful in industrial history. By 1800, the two men enjoyed a virtual monopoly on steam engines and had sold 470 of them. On every one they received a royalty calculated at one-third of the amount mine-owners had saved in the cost of coal by not using the more fuel-hungry Newcomen engines. Watt seized the opportunity to plunge into further research and devised a rotary-motion steam engine which could be used to drive machinery. Watt also devised the term 'horsepower' as a way of judging the power of engines. He noted in his 'Blotting and Calculation' book that a 'standard' draught horse could lift '33,000 lb. 1 foot high p. minute'.[3] The modern international unit of power is named a 'Watt' in his honour. Doubtless, someone, somewhere, would have been bound eventually to harness the power of steam effectively. As it is, the wherewithal for the Industrial Revolution – and therefore the invention of the modern world – owes the greatest debt to the brains of Savery and Newcomen, Watt, and Boulton.

It is hard, in a shallow, cynical age, to imagine the thrill which must have passed through the minds of men and women able to feel they were bending the world to their will, rather than having it act upon them. When Dr Johnson's biographer, James Boswell, visited Boulton's 700-worker factory in March 1776, Boulton declared to him 'I sell here, sir, what all the world desires – Power.' Boswell thought this self-regarding bombast worthy of 'an iron chieftain, [who] seemed to be a father to his tribe'.[4]

Both Watt and Boulton became members of the group of 'Lunar Men' so prominent in the Midlands Enlightenment. Even though the general body of knowledge was much smaller than today,* it is still hard to comprehend the breadth of enthusiasms shared by the

---

* The polymath Thomas Young, who died in 1829, was described as 'the last man who knew everything'. After that, the volume of knowledge was simply too vast for a single person to acquire.

Lunar Men, under the leadership of Erasmus Darwin (grandfather of Charles), a brilliant doctor, poet, conversationalist, inventor, evolutionist, botanist, social reformer, agricultural technologist, physicist and psychologist. Erasmus Darwin was both sexually voracious and successful with women, though it is hard to understand his physical appeal – Anna Seward, a poet known as 'the Swan of Lichfield', describes a big, fat shambling man, in large wig and with a face scarred by smallpox. The cartoonist James Gillray lampooned him as an ape. But, though he stammered badly, he was said to be an exceptional conversationalist, even if his listeners often found him fearsomely bossy. He shuffled about with a bad limp after an accident riding in a home-made carriage, in whatever clothes had been nearest to hand when he woke up. Just for good measure, the *Monthly Magazine* noted in its obituary in 1802 that he was in the habit of walking about 'with his tongue hanging out of his mouth'.[5] Darwin attributed his success with women to the fact that he had become a teetotaller.

Erasmus Darwin had settled in Lichfield, twenty miles north of Birmingham, to practise medicine. Though badly knocked about by Parliamentarians during the English Civil War, Lichfield was comfortable enough by Darwin's time for Dr Johnson to invite his friend James Boswell to visit the place, in order to see 'genuine civilised life in an English provincial town'. Johnson was naturally prejudiced in the town's favour, having been born there, and described the place as 'a city of philosophers'. By now, Boulton and Watt had established their own 'manufactory' at Soho in Birmingham and there occurred among those living in the area an extraordinary effervescence of ideas, like steam escaping from one of the cylinders in their manufactories. The astonishing growth of industries which was to earn Birmingham the title of 'The Second City' was made possible by the abundance of ideas, initiatives, projects and processes in turn made feasible by coal and its products. The intellectual bubbling-up can be readily seen in the 'Lunar

Society', whose members met on the Sunday closest to the full moon each month. Among the botanists, clockmakers, doctors and geologists who were fellow members of the Birmingham Lunar Society alongside Darwin, were William Murdock, a massively built Scottish engineer hired by Boulton and Watt and who was soon out-earning them through valve and gearing inventions which made it possible to apply steam power to all manner of mechanical devices. Other members included Joseph Priestley, the man who discovered oxygen; Josiah Wedgwood, who mechanised pottery production; Richard Lovell Edgeworth, a pioneer of telegraphy; and James Keir, glassmaker and chemist. What did these men have in common? Many of them were friends. But, more than anything else, the Lunar Society exulted in possibility: 'what if?' must have been the most frequently asked question. (Murdock, for example, not only developed coal-gas lighting but worked to harness tidal power.) The Birmingham Lunar Society was a quintessential Enlightenment institution. Nothing was off-limits – chemistry, climatology, double-glazing, engineering, ethics, geology, language, mechanics, papermaking, philosophy, physiology and politics were all argued over. Similar questions were being asked and addressed at the Royal Society in London, but the Birmingham gatherings had the additional quality of being moored in practicality. Coal had freed man from the need to worry about energy and in the process had turned everyone into alchemists.

Steam made it possible to mechanise almost anything, from spinning and weaving, through the manufacture of wire, ships and needles, to the threshing of corn, the tanning of leather and the folding of envelopes. Its apostles claimed that steam set workers free from the drudgery of repetitive tasks. Too often, the reverse was true: it prevented people working at their own rate and made human beings slaves to a relentless machine. A poem by Edward Mead, published in the *Northern Star and Leeds General Advertiser* in February 1843 and reprinted by Friedrich Engels in his *Conditions of the Working Class in England*, captures the resentment at the despotism of steam:

> There is a king, and a ruthless king,
> Not a shade of the poet's dream,
> But a tyrant fell, white slaves know well,
> And that ruthless king is Steam

Among the things made possible by coal power was socialism.

Steam made speed paramount, and the acceleration in the pace of life finally finished off medieval trades, the Newcastle keelmen among them. The elegant Georgian bridge which had spanned the Tyne in Newcastle was torn down to meet the ever-increasing demands of the Victorian coal business. A new swing bridge – an astonishing, once unimaginable invention – was designed, manufactured and paid for by William Armstrong, who had a vested interest in enabling ocean-going ships to reach his shipyard upstream of the heart of Newcastle, at Elswick. The replacement of the Georgian bridge meant that at a stroke, the physical obstacle which made the keelmen's trade necessary was gone: coal-dealers built wharves, or 'staiths' up and down the river, the best of which towered high over the water, allowing the coal to be tipped directly into the holds of ships which would carry it to the estuary and south to London. The development of steam power brought steam-fired tugs to work on the river, which was soon also being dredged, to allow colliers to travel further upstream. No one needed keelmen any longer.*

'The world goes on at a smarter pace now than it did when I was a young fellow,' George Eliot's self-made – and self-important – businessman, Mr Deane, remarks in her 1860 novel, *The Mill on*

---

* They live on in the jaunty tune 'Keel Row', the 'trot' music of the Life Guards.

the Floss. 'It's this steam you see, that has made the difference. It drives on every wheel at double pace, and the wheel of fortune along with 'em.'[6] Engineers were the new heroes of the age – 'the most illustrious followers of science and the real benefactors of the World.'[7] Samuel Smiles, author of the quintessential Victorian tract *Self-Help* ('It is idleness that is the curse of men – not labour. Idleness eats the heart out of men, as of nations, and consumes them as rust does iron'), produced five biographical volumes of the *Lives of the Engineers* in the 1850s and 60s, glorifying the men who invented steam engines, built roads, lighthouses, harbours, locomotives, railways and bridges, drained swamps and designed safety lamps. The books sold by the thousand. At Robert Stephenson's death in 1859, 3,000 mourners packed Westminster Abbey. Isambard Kingdom Brunel – who did not feature in Smiles' works – was glorified in a stained-glass window in the abbey depicting the Bible's description of the building of the Temple in Jerusalem. Fortunes were being made by engineers. Watt had bought a country estate near the spa town of Llandindrod Wells in mid-Wales. As a modest man, he had requested in his will the quietest of burials. He was instead rather over-memorialised: a larger than life-size commemorative marble statue was commissioned for Westminster Abbey, which turned out to be so large that the plinth had to be split into three to get it inside one of the abbey chapels, smashing the lid of the tomb of one of Henry V's standard-bearers as it was dragged in. The statue's enormous weight then caused it to sink through the floor. In the 1960s, various fashionable clergy at the abbey decided it no longer fitted the mood of the times, and sent the edifice to the Transport Museum. After years of being shifted from place to place like some marble Flying Dutchman, the thing eventually found a home in the Scottish National Gallery.

Coal was midwife to genius. To those with vision, it seemed to make almost anything possible. Many of the entrepreneurs who got rich were brash, brassy figures, who gloried in their new-found wealth. But in Newcastle there arose a fabulously wealthy engineer who appeared the polar opposite – a bit shy, mild-mannered and courteous.* The career of William Armstrong, a corn merchant's son, demonstrates the capacity of coal to open minds. What had initially caught his imagination was the energy to be generated by harnessing water power, which soon led to a broader interest in hydraulics. His timing was lucky, for ports around the country needed new wharves and cranes and so did the rapidly growing railway network.

But by the middle of the nineteenth century, Armstrong had diversified into using steam power to make artillery and developed ever more effective ways of killing people, which in turn meant that governments beat a path to his door. He was soon supplying armies across Europe and South America, and both sides in the American Civil War. Armstrong warships were supplied to China, Japan and Italy, and when, in the 1880s, he launched the *Esmeralda* for the Chilean navy, a new type of 'protected' cruiser with armoured decks and a pair of powerful, rotating ten-inch guns, admiralties around the world decided they needed them too. By then, Armstrong had largely retired and was living at Cragside, the mansion he had built north of Newcastle (the first domestic house in the world to be lit by hydroelectricity) and was devoting himself to good works and benefactions, in stark contrast to the source of his wealth. He eventually had 60,000 people working for him at Elswick, just up the Tyne from the centre of Newcastle, and had become one of the grandest examples of how the exploitation of coal unleashed ingenuity and made fortunes. The institutions of

---

* A four-month strike by engineers in 1871 showed how deceptive appearances can be. The sixty-year-old Armstrong, by now the biggest employer in the area, refused demands for a nine-hour day, locking out the strikers and importing strike-breakers from elsewhere. However house-trained they appeared, Victorian industrialists did not like to be jibbed at.

state would always rather black the boots of success than enquire whose soul hangs from his watch-chain, and Armstrong duly collected a barony and numerous official genuflections. Despite becoming fabulously rich by designing ways of killing fellow human beings, he successfully presented himself as a mild-mannered philanthropist whose main interests lay in the countryside.

Few places in Europe exulted more in Victorian industry and science than his home city. At the height of railway mania in 1845, the Newcastle and Berwick Railway had obtained parliamentary approval for a spectacular bridge in the heart of Newcastle. As they travelled between Edinburgh and London, passengers clattering across the Tyne on Robert Stephenson's magnificent High-Level Bridge (the first in the world to carry a railway on one tier, and a road on the other) could look down on the old walled city and see how completely it had been surrounded by heavy industry. No city in Britain has ever truly rivalled London for significance, but in terms of enterprise, energy and achievement, late nineteenth-century Newcastle could make a plausible claim. The multiple bridges across the deep valley – five in the space of a single mile* – were like box-kites soaring in celebration of the city's inventiveness.

George and Robert Stephenson and William Armstrong are the best-known engineers to have emerged from the north-east. Armstrong's armaments factory stretched for nearly a mile along the banks of the Tyne, and the National Trust preserves the stately home he built twenty miles away. Armstrong's genius for ballistics was only one example, though. By 1845, South Shields, at the mouth of the Tyne, was making most of the plate glass in England, as well as many of the chemicals used in the country's manufacturing. In Gateshead, they spun wire, manufactured underwater telegraph cables, and Joseph Swan invented the electric light bulb.

---

* Now seven, since the completion of a Metro bridge in 1978 and a rather magical pedestrian crossing in 2001.

There were shipyards and there were factories producing alkalis for use in detergents and dyeing. There were pharmaceutical plants, and later, plastics manufacturers.

In the short term, steam power gave the Tyneside coal business a shot in the arm. Railway lines were laid from collieries, so locomotives could bring coal from much further out in the Northumberland coalfields and deliver it direct to the purpose-built quays on the riverbank, the largest of which – Dunston Staiths in Gateshead, an almost 2,000-foot-long quay, opened in 1893 – is still standing, and is claimed to be the biggest timber structure in Europe.

5

The Right Side of the Tracks

Coal was the future. On hillside pathways, alongside bustling turn-pikes and on wooded lanes, entire families carried all their worldly goods away from the settlements of their birth towards new villages, towns and cities announcing their energetic presence with belching smokestacks and the promise of employment. In the early eighteenth century, for example, there had been nothing much to distinguish Merthyr Tydfil from many other Welsh farming villages. But it was blessed – or so it seemed at the time – not only with nearby deposits of coal and iron ore, but with plentiful water power. One of the many enterprises sited nearby, the Dowlais iron-works, was to become the biggest in the world. By 1801, the time of the first census since the Domesday Boke, the population of the little village of Merthyr had grown to 7,700. Fifty years later, it was reckoned that every year about 10,000 people made their way to this Klondyke hoping for work. (So unknown and frightening was the 'new frontier' town at Dowlais that many made their wills before setting off to get rich quick.[1]) The Dean of Llandaff, the celebrated fossil-hunter William Conybeare, described this enormous, unplanned and unnatural expansion as a 'condensation of people'. By the middle of the nineteenth century it was the biggest town in Wales.

One of the most successful of these incomers was the Shropshire-born John Guest, appointed as manager of the growing Dowlais ironworks. By the time he died in 1787, he had handed the place over to his son and son-in-law. It was a wonderful time to be an industrialist: in the letters, journals and lectures of the time you can almost smell the sense of wonder at the possibilities of trans-figuration of the natural world by the application of human ingenuity. It was to continue for another hundred years or more. Thomas Guest increased rates of production at Dowlais again, by introducing one of James Watt's steam engines to the site to blow air into the furnace.

In 1804, the people of Merthyr witnessed something sensa-tional. A moving black chimneystack, with an eight-foot-diameter flywheel at its side, rattled, clanked and hissed into the town, piston pulsing and waggons trailing behind, filled with coal and seventy cheering men. Legend has it that the world's first steam locomotive was built after two of the famously argumentative South Wales ironmasters – Samuel Homfray of the furnace at Penydarren, and Richard Crawshay of the Cyfarthfa works – a man of immense arrogance and very little patience – had each wagered 500 guineas on whether it could be done.

Crawshay's ironworks were the biggest in the land and he was well familiar with welcoming visitors like the most famous man in Britain, Admiral Nelson, to admire his furnace. His rival iron-maker approached the engineer, Richard Trevithick, a ruddy-faced Cornish giant (pub fable claimed he could lift half a ton, or throw a ball over the tower of Camborne Church) asking him to design a coal-burning steam engine for his plant. Not much of a scholar, Trevithick was one of those whose natural inventiveness had found a purpose in the magic of steam. Before the end of the eighteenth century he had designed a road-going locomotive which had so terrified local Cornish folk on its maiden journey from Camborne that they had assumed it was driven by the Devil.

Learning from his Cornish experience, Trevithick made some-thing quite revolutionary in South Wales. In the late eighteenth century Britain had been seized by a fashion for digging canals, to transport raw materials to factories and finished products to market. The significant disadvantage of canal transport was the need to negotiate inclines, a problem which was overcome with the use of locks. The canal from Merthyr Tydfil to Cardiff docks required the opening and closing of the gates of almost fifty locks. The Glamorganshire Canal had opened in 1794, at the height of 'canal mania'. But steam transport promised better. The legislation authorising the canal had also envisaged horses pulling trucks along rails, nearby.[2] Homfray cunningly offered Trevithick the use of the length of track running from Merthyr to the canal basin at Abercynon, on which horses drew supplies for his foundry.

On 21 February 1804, the Cornishman's invention made the demonstration run of over nine miles, pulling five laden waggons and seventy men at an average speed of five miles an hour. There is little evidence that Richard Crawshay ever paid his debt.* But the run on that single-lane track was the beginning of steam railways, which in turn would mean an apparently endless demand for iron rails from the South Wales foundries. Messages were soon arriving asking for rails for planned routes all over Britain and Europe – from the Netherlands, from the Dublin and Drogheda Railway Company, the Saxony and Bavaria Railways, the Leipzig and Dresden Railway Company, as well as colossal orders destined for Russia. With better public relations, Trevithick could perhaps

---

* In the graveyard of a little church on a windswept hillside outside Merthyr – carefully separated from other occupants by a metal fence – is a nine-ton slab of stone laid flat upon the ground. It is Crawshay's grave. Of his crest, 'a mastiff guarding a pyramid of cannon ball', there is no sign. The only words set in the stone's polished surface read 'GOD FORGIVE ME'. For what? For not settling his bet, for his implacable pursuit of production, for condemning his workers to live in squalor? The furnaces of the Iron King had enabled him to grow fat and wealthy, and as his brass band in their blue uniforms played solemn music, his enormous coffin was lowered into the grave he had designed, fourteen feet deep and eight feet long. Like all funerals, that of Crawshay demonstrated the emptiness of much human endeavour. But he and his ilk had changed British life forever.

have become known as the father of railways, instead of Stephenson. But he set off for South America, where there was much talk of installing steam engines as part of the reopening of silver mines in Peru. This turned out to be a bad idea, for political rather than engineering reasons, and ten years later he returned to England a veteran of Simon Bolivar's revolutionary army and a pauper. He died while staying in a pub at Dartford in 1833 and was buried there in an unmarked grave.

By then, the Dowlais plant had twelve blast furnaces producing iron. In another dozen or so years, there were eighteen of them, burning over 1,500 tons of coal each week. The spectacle at night was astonishing. An 1848 visitor described 'the vivid glow and roaring of the blast furnaces near at hand – the lurid light of distant works – the clanking of hammers and rolling mills, the confused din of massive machinery – the burning headlands – the coke hearths, now if the night be stormy, bursting into sheets of flame, now wrapt in vast and impenetrable clouds of smoke – the wild figures of the workmen'.[3] Once upon a time, the area must have been beautiful. The description is hellish.

It was even worse for those who lived there: the rapidly increasing population needed housing, and no one wanted to spend money on it. It was not the fault of the residents. One of Brunel's engineers wrote – also in 1848 – that 'the colliers are much disposed to be clean, and are careful to wash themselves in the river, but there are no baths or washhouses or even water pipes'.[4] Houses had been thrown up wherever a speculator wished, with no regard to whether there were drains in the area. Inside the houses, people might sleep up to sixteen to a room. Such 'streets' as existed were unpaved, no sewers had been laid in most places, there were no dustbins or rubbish dumps or lighting. Because the door sills had been laid level with the road, every time there was heavy rain, water poured into the houses. For supplies of drinking water, inhabitants had a choice between the river, which by the time it reached them had already passed through Richard Crawshay's ironworks upstream and was running black, or queueing up with dozens of others at one of the town's polluted water spouts, half of which dried up in summer anyway. The rector of Dowlais said he regularly saw people standing in line all night. Mothers of small children often had to leave them at home, where, he said, several had been burned to death in accidents.[5] According to the local minister, the graveyard drained into one of the wells.

The graveyard itself was so jam-packed that decomposing bodies were exposed, and the minister noted 'I have seen pigs nuzzling among the graves.'[6] The Back o'Plough district of Dowlais was said to be the ugliest place in England and Wales, with houses largely built of rubble, four rooms apiece, each about eleven feet square, and floors made of small stones 'up from which the black ooze squelches when the foot falls unevenly on them'.[7] One report into conditions in the area was judged so horrifying that it remained unpublished. It was later deemed to be 'factually correct and a model of restraint'. The author, Dr Holland, wrote that he had previously inspected 'the worst parts of the worst towns in England' but 'never did I see anything which could compare with Merthyr', which had no roads or drains.[8] Unsurprisingly, Merthyr Tydfil soon had the highest mortality rate in Wales.

A great number of the dead were young children: between 1848 and 1853, two out of every five children born there died before the age of five, most of them before even their first birthday. One consequence of the appalling rate of infant mortality among coal and iron families was to reduce average life expectancy. In 1851 it was calculated that the newly born child of a miner or ironworker might live seventeen and a half years, and even among the trades-people of Merthyr life expectancy was only thirty-two. A visitor to the community claimed that only once before, 'in the lowest suburb of Liverpool', had he seen a place 'where humanity had actually become putrescent'.[9] Yet when the Merthyr town surveyor put a scheme for a drainage and sewerage system before the local Board of Health in August 1852, the necessary £33,000 could not be found. The partners in the Dowlais plant had been withdrawing double that amount from the company every year.

In such squalid living conditions, outbreaks of cholera were inevitable. In 1849, an epidemic lasted over five months, and at its peak was carrying off over thirty people each day. Inevitably, the casualty rate was highest amongst the poorest inhabitants: two-thirds of the 1,430 fatalities occurred in the Tydfil's Well district, where the most poverty-stricken lived. Lady Charlotte Guest, the young wife of the Dowlais ironmaster, wrote in her journal that eight men were 'constantly making coffins'.[10] Another outbreak, in 1854, killed over 400 people. Yet another in 1866 killed a further 115.

For those on the top of the heap, though, life was good and followed the usual British pattern: first escape the countryside, next make your fortune, and then pass yourself off as a landed aristocrat.

By the time John Josiah Guest died in 1852, his company was the biggest manufacturer of iron in the world. Each roaring furnace produced one hundred tons a week. He had been made a baronet in the splurge of honours at the coronation of Queen Victoria in 1838, by which time his wife had died. He remarried into the English aristocracy. Together he and the accomplished Lady Charlotte Elizabeth Bertie,* daughter of the Earl of Lindsey, first lived in the mansion he had built at Merthyr, from where at night they could watch the flames of the furnaces. They then bought a home more befitting their status, a substantial manor house well

---

* Lady Charlotte, who had earlier been pursued by Disraeli, was a highly energetic, talented woman. She had mastered seven languages by the time of her marriage, including Hebrew, Arabic and Persian. She now set herself to learning Welsh and translated the *Mabinogion* into English. For a century, her translation was considered the standard work.

away from the smoke, at Canford in Dorset. He was by now also established as the first MP for Merthyr Tydfil, a seat he held until his death. By then, the town had become renowned worldwide, a place of pilgrimage for the awestruck and the envious. There was something inevitable about the marriage of John Josiah's son, Ivor, to the Duke of Marlborough's daughter, Lady Cornelia Henrietta Maria Spencer Churchill. Gonged as the first Baron Wimborne and nicknamed 'the paying Guest', he devoted less and less attention to the Dowlais plant, and then merged it with that of a Birmingham nut-manufacturer Arthur Keen.* After Eton and Cambridge, his son – another Ivor – went into politics, and eventually became one of Asquith's stage-army of newly created peers in the House of Lords. An unpopular figure memorialised in the couplet 'One must suppose that God knew best / When he created Ivor Guest', he devoted his career to opposing votes for women and was appointed to a political post way beyond his competence, as Lord Lieutenant of Ireland, when it was plain that the union could not survive much longer.

The plant that had made their fortunes was nationalised, privatised and nationalised again during the course of the twentieth century, until eventually what had been the biggest concern of its kind in the world, produced one final ingot for display on a memorial plinth, closed its doors and unleashed the wrecking balls.

A corn merchant had remarked in 1824 that it was cheaper to bring grain 6,000 miles from the Cape of Good Hope to Newcastle than to carry it the fifty or so miles across England from Newcastle to Carlisle. Fifteen years later, there were five trains a day between the cities and you could make the journey in three and a half hours.

Coal set inventiveness free almost anywhere it was found. The world's first steam locomotive may have made its debut in South

---

* The beginning of the engineering giant, GKN.

Wales. But steam power was ideal for transporting bulky cargo, and what is now the world's oldest surviving steam locomotive, the *Puffing Billy*, had been constructed between 1813 and 1814 to draw coal at the colliery at Wylam about ten miles west of Newcastle. ('Wylam is the very worst colliery village that we have yet beheld', according to a local paper in 1874.[11]) George Stephenson, who had been born in the colliery village, found his fortunes transformed by the capacity of coal. The ingenuity of the 'father of the railways' may have been his own. But it was ignited by coal. It was his son, Robert Stephenson, who built the steam engine *Locomotion No. 1*, for the Stockton and Darlington railway line. The name of the company makes plain what would turn out to be the danger posed by steam railways: Stockton and Darlington are Teesdale towns. Steam trains manufactured in Newcastle upon Tyne were soon attracting business away from the town and towards the developing ports of the river Tees and further south in the north-eastern coalfield, like Middlesbrough and Hartlepool.

The world's first mainline railway service, between Liverpool and Manchester, opened in 1830, when a train drew the prime minister – the Duke of Wellington – and a claque of dignitaries and hangers-on from Liverpool to Manchester.* Steam travel was almost magic. The train companies had not only given Britain a universal 'railway time' – before 1840, different localities had operated on their own mean times – but by reducing the significance of distance, steam seemed to be collapsing time and space. In the process, a certain drab uniformity was laid everywhere. From the English Channel to the north coast of Scotland, steam locomotives drew waggons laden with 'black diamonds', as firemen fed the

---

* One of them, the Liverpool MP William Huskisson, did not complete the journey, having got down from the train when it stopped to refuel and been hit by the *Rocket*, which was travelling on the track alongside.

furnaces driving metal wheels forged in coal-heat on metal rails forged in coal-heat to other places, so that almost nowhere was free from the whiff of coal smoke.

It was the sheer speed of railway travel which was most astonishing. Robert Louis Stevenson caught the awe felt by many adults at trains when he talked in a children's poem of careering through the countryside:

> Faster than fairies, faster than witches,
> Bridges and houses, hedges and ditches;
> And charging along like troops in a battle,
> All through the meadows the horses and cattle:
> All of the sights of the hill and the plain
> Fly as thick as driving rain;
> And ever again, in the wink of an eye,
> Painted stations whistle by.

Even the historian Thomas Carlyle, usually seen as one of the great sobersides of Victorian Britain, was captivated, writing descriptions of the sheer thrill of train travel in a letter about a journey to Lancashire. 'To whirl through the confused darkness on those steam wings was one of the strangest things I have experienced – hissing and dashing on, one knew not whither. We saw the gleam of towns in the distance – unknown towns. We went over the tops of houses … snorting, roaring – we flew – likest thing to a Faust's flight on the Devil's mantle; as if some huge steam night-bird had flung you on its back and was sweeping through unknown space with you.'[12] Queen Victoria herself – who asked train drivers to please limit their speed to a respectable thirty miles per hour – made rail travel socially acceptable, by travelling from Slough (the nearest station to Windsor Castle) to Paddington in June 1842, and arriving in a mere twenty-five minutes.[13] In the twelve years before she came to the throne, a grand total of 500 miles of railway track had been opened. Within ten years of her journey from Slough to London, the country had 7,500 miles of track.

Every single sleeper, every length of rail, each bolt holding one to the other, to say nothing of rolling stock and stations, had to be paid for somehow. Parliament would look after the business of seeing that no man could claim his house was a castle and stand in the way of lines drawn on maps: once approval had been granted in Westminster, the companies just had to raise the necessary capital, which was generally done by offering shares, of which only a small part had to be paid at once, and the rest as it might – or might not – be called upon. Investors fought to give their money away, seduced by the prospect of unprecedented profits. By the 1840s, building a railway line looked a sure-fire investment, with would-be investors drawn in by the need to pay only 10% up front and the rest when asked, competing for a slice of the promised action. Tracks were soon being announced to run all over the country. In 1845 Parliament authorised the laying of 4,500 miles of railway line, which was over four times what they had consented to less than a decade earlier. No one seemed to give a damn: even the celebrated Whig historian and apostle of English sophistication, Thomas Babington Macaulay, moaned at having his time wasted by having to attend Parliament to scrutinise railway legislation. In May 1845 he complained in a letter that 'I am detained at Westminster every day and all day long by three railway bills. May he-asses defile the mothers, sisters, wives and daughters of the parties, counsel, solicitors, and witnesses in all three!'[14] The government of the day did little or nothing to stop an almost textbook capitalist bubble taking hold. Everyone succumbed: Disraeli, Gladstone, Peel, even thoughtful figures like Charles Darwin, John Stuart Mill and Charles Babbage were investors. The architect of the Crystal Palace, Joseph Paxton, made his fortune from speculating in railway stock. The philosopher Herbert Spencer, a former railway engineer, gave his father the advice that led him to sell his shares almost at the peak of the market. For a while, the entire newspaper industry seemed to be kept afloat by advertisements for railways.

But not everyone was taken in. In 1845, William Aytoun, an Edinburgh lawyer and poet, wrote in *Blackwood's Magazine* of the Glenmutchkin Railway, a line planned by Augustus Reginald Dunshunner and Bob McCorkindale (who 'abhorred work with a detestation worthy of a scion of nobility' and who had once compiled *A Tour Through the Alcoholic Districts of Scotland*). The line would, they told investors, be twelve miles long, take six months to build and eventually carry 4 million cattle each year, to say nothing of all the other cargo. They promised they would 'set their face AGAINST ALL SUNDAY TRAVELLING WHATSOEVER'. The plan only foundered when seventy-three errors in the company surveyor's report were pointed out. The scheme thereupon collapsed, with sixpence per share returned to investors.

Aytoun's railway had been a satirical figment of his imagination, and not even very funny at that. Perhaps that was because life was too busy imitating art. It was just so easy to set up a railway – a committee of local stuffed shirts, registration of the company, a survey of the route, an application for parliamentary approval of the new line, a few advertisements to beguile investors willing to part with an initial 10% of the total cost of the shares they wanted. Between 1843 and 1845, the number of railway securities listed on the London Stock Exchange roughly trebled. As the mania progressed, promoters found it easier and easier to sell subscriptions. Then the bubble burst. On 14 October 1845 a man walked into Hyde Park and shot himself. 'From papers found on the unfortunate gentleman's person', the papers reported, 'there is every reason to suppose that his name is Elliott, and that his residence is Porchester Terrace, Bayswater. A large quantity of papers connected with several railways in different parts of the kingdom was found in his pockets.'[15]

Inevitably, it turned out that some of the proposed schemes had been as well planned as William Aytoun's Glenmutchkin Railway. The newspapers, which had been happy to pack their pages with advertisements for railway investments, began to probe. It wasn't long before they were crowing, *The Times* pronouncing magisterially that 'the dismal mockery of intelligence and discretion serves only to reveal the inward void. A mighty bubble of wealth is blown before our eyes, as transient, as contradictory to the laws of solid material, as confuted by every circumstance of our actual condition, as any other bubble which man or child ever blew before.'[16]

George Hudson, a fat little farmer's son from Yorkshire, whose enthusiasm for train travel had earned him the moniker 'The Napoleon of the Railways', was the most notorious of the swindlers involved. Hudson had begun as a legitimate railway entrepreneur, and it is fair to say that York would never have developed as a railway town had Hudson not persuaded George Stephenson to route the London to Newcastle line through the city. Somehow Hudson had become a wealthy man (he attributed much of his riches to an unexpected legacy from a great-uncle) and became the biggest shareholder in the York and North Midland Railway, joined the Conservative Party and rose to become lord mayor of York. By 1844 he controlled 1,000 miles of track and was known as 'the railway king'. Full-length portraits of him in crisp evening waistcoats and fur-trimmed gowns, together with wax effigies in Madame Tussaud's, followed. When William Gladstone, then president of the Board of Trade, became sufficiently worried by railway mania to prepare an Act of Parliament to regulate them, it was Hudson who led the proprietors' opposition, while at the same time planning the mergers which would make him, by a long way, the biggest railway boss in England. In 1846, at the peak of his powers, Hudson laid plans for no fewer than thirty-two different pieces of railway legislation – costing £10 million – before Parliament. Hudson had acquired the arrogance which so often comes to people who make a fortune and then believe that rules are for other, less wealthy, people. He also did not control either the crops or the weather. In the summer of 1846, the harvest failed, leading to massive imports of food, which in turn doubled the trade deficit and drained the Bank of England's gold reserves, making it unwilling to lend. The depression continued into the following year, meaning that railway shareholders could not meet their liabilities to the companies. Investigations discovered that Hudson had been using his companies as if they were his personal bank accounts, paying dividends out of existing capital (a variant of the racket later known as a 'Ponzi scheme'), and inventing trading figures. His Yorkshire bluster was enough to carry him through most of it, and even after the day of reckoning had come, he still managed to be re-elected as a Tory MP – evidence, if ever it was needed, that often enough the world takes you at your own estimation of yourself. While Parliament was sitting he could not be charged with debt, and he spent the intervals between sessions on the continent. In the end, his wealth disappeared as quickly as it had come, and the estates he had bought were shed. When he lost his seat – and parliamentary immunity – Hudson hid from his creditors in France, while his mansion on the edge of Hyde Park, where once some of the best-connected people in Britain had come to fawn upon him,* was rented out to the French ambassador and later became the French Embassy. He died of heart trouble at his much more modest house in Pimlico in December 1871.

Unlike later fraudsters, he did at least leave something behind, his *Times* obituary remarking that despite defrauding investors, 'it

---

* 'Came the nobles of the land, humbling themselves on their gartered knees, and pressing the earth with their coroneted brows, and calling him King of Men, that he might give them shares,' was the way the frequently drunk and always argumentative journalist George Augustus Sala described their obeisance. Unlike Hudson, Sala did not escape the debtors' prison, though when someone had the temerity to mention that he had been in gaol, he still had the nerve to sue him for libel.

is impossible to deny that he did great things to develop the railway system in the North of England', which was true.[17] And
'railway mania' was the making of the accountancy trade, after a
young man called William Welch Deloitte was invited to audit the
books of the Great Western Railway in 1849.* The craze is still
cited by some economists in much the same way as people talk
about the dotcom bubble of the end of the twentieth century.
Railway mania was the product of the intersection of numerous,
often apparently unconnected, yet hugely powerful forces – an
intense excitement in science, an almost religious belief in
'progress', a growing class of clever entrepreneurs, lax regulation
(the scams had been made very easy indeed by the recent repeal of
the 1720 Act, passed after the South Sea Company fraud), and the
perpetual desire to get rich quick. It had all been made possible by
coal. And, as with all revolutions, there was no telling how it might
end.

Throughout the second half of the nineteenth century, the
volume of coal shipped to London from the north-east grew enor-
mously. But the development of railways raised a more corrosive
question: why bother to transport coal by sea when you could have
it delivered to the capital by train from Wales, Yorkshire, Scotland,
the Midlands, Lancashire, or any other coalfield? Demand was
rising furiously and while steam-driven coasters might be quicker
than sail, new mines were being sunk all over the country, whose
coal could be delivered by train to the capital in a matter of hours.
At King's Cross station alone, there was a vast complex where coal
brought in by train could be swiftly transferred to canal barges and
horse-drawn carts. Ingenious three-tier unloading warehouses
allowed waggons full of coal to be pushed onto an elevated siding,
where the floor of the carriage could be released to allow the coal

---

* He made a better job of it than the firm which bears his name did of auditing the
books of the Royal Bank of Scotland before it crashed in 2008.

to fall through to a level below where it was sorted and then carted away by local merchants.* By 1867, more coal was being sent to London by train than by sea.

The growth of coal-mining in the nineteenth century had been astonishing. In 1800, about 13,000 men are reckoned to have worked as miners in Northumberland and Durham, producing between them about 2.5 million tons of coal each year. By 1911, there were 200,000 men sweating in the mines there.[18] Across the land everyone seemed to be at it. Great quantities of coal were also being either prospected for or 'won' in coalfields from Cumberland to Kent, Denbighshire to Derbyshire, Lancashire to Leicestershire. The nineteenth century was the century of combustion and it was midwife to genius all over the place. The fruits of this frenzied activity could be found on every high street, in shops which sparkled with new, mass-produced enchantments. There was hardly an area of human activity, from bookbinding to warfare, that was not affected by the burning of coal. The clothes that people wore, the meals they ate, the conversations they enjoyed, were all enabled by the heat from these burning rocks.

While the public enjoyed what they made possible, they never inspired affection. In Charles Dickens' *Hard Times*, the most forceful of his denunciations of the inhumanity of Britain at the height of Victorian capitalism, he imagines Coketown, one of the northern settlements at the heart of this revolution, 'a town of machinery and tall chimneys, out of which interminable serpents of smoke

---

* Of course, steam power was also applied to the vessels which carried the Newcastle coal south, until steam had virtually supplanted sail. The screw-colliers (propeller-driven coal transports) eventually changed the location of shipbuilding, too. Because the northern rivers and estuaries had an abundance of coal and iron, an experienced workforce and sheltered waters, it was easier to build ships in places like the Tyne than to try to continue doing so in the south of England. The centre of gravity in the industry moved north – the origin of so many shipyards in the north-east.

trailed themselves forever and forever, and never got uncoiled'.[19] Throughout the novel, the town appears as a malevolent, fire-breathing monster, big enough for any human to be swallowed up and never seen again. The picture of the grime and dirt of industry came to stand for towns all over Victorian Britain. The smoke came from the furnaces heating water to produce power 'where the piston of the steam-engine worked monotonously up and down, like the head of an elephant in melancholy madness'.[20] Yet it was coal which made it possible for Dickens' books to be printed and bound, and which warmed his readers' feet. Every trinket and milk jug, every inch of railway track, every tin-tack, each horseshoe or belt buckle, required the energy produced by coal. But it remained unlovely and unloved.

6

Smoke on the Water

In 1736, a thirty-seven-year-old Gloucestershire clockmaker by the name of Jonathan Hulls had a flash of inspiration: was it possible that steam might solve a problem which had troubled mariners since the dawn of navigation? Could it allow boats to be manoeuvred when there was no wind, tide or current to move them? By comparison with the great vessels that were built later, his ambitions were modest: he planned a tugboat powered by a steam-driven paddle. Hulls knew how ready dullards are to sneer at visionaries and his first patent application for steam propulsion is almost the only thing that stands as his memorial. Inventors, he wrote, rarely got the benefit of the doubt: people were far more ready to go in for 'Ridicule and Contempt' than for 'unprejudiced Estimation of Things'.[1] So it proved with his plans for an atmospheric-pressure steam tugboat. The patent application survives, but no boat or even prototype was ever built, and Jonathan Hulls retreated to the Cotswolds, where he died five years later in poverty. But he had been prescient: on the accession of Queen Victoria, a century after that first patent application, there were steam-powered ships providing regular passenger services across the English Channel to France, and HMS *Comet* was serving in the Royal Navy. The following year, the *Great Western*, the largest passenger ship in the world, sailed under steam paddle from Bristol to New York. By the time Queen Victoria died in 1901, steam-driven ships had completely eclipsed sail power.

Of the many things made possible by the use of coal – anvils and artillery; cannonballs and church bells; pins and pans; costly microscopes and cheap tin trays – perhaps none was more politically significant than its effect upon British ships. Steam transformed the Royal Navy, which had become pre-eminent in Europe because of Nelson's tactical genius at the Battle of Trafalgar in 1805. But it was dirty old coal that then turned it into the most formidable navy on earth. War with Russia in the Crimea had shown how vulnerable wooden ships were to shore artillery, and France – with whom Britain was allied – soon began to clad its ships with iron plates. The British followed suit, and then recognised that because they could forge metal in almost any shape, there was no need for an interior wooden hull at all. Once it was realised that steam power could replace wind energy entirely, the nature of naval warfare was revolutionised.*

Sail-driven warships of the type that fought at Trafalgar in 1805 had been equipped with cannon pointing out of their port and starboard sides, and the basic design had not changed for generations: a captain's ambition was to manoeuvre his ship into a position from which he could fire a broadside into the enemy. Very often this also involved exposing yourself to a broadside. When, in the 1860s, the Admiralty realised that since a warship powered solely by steam engines made sails, masts and the attendant rigging unnecessary, guns could be mounted on top of the hull instead of

---

* There was even a coal-fired submarine, *Resurgam*, designed by a Lancashire clergyman, George Garrett. Built in 1879, it sank off Rhyl the following year. Coal-fired submarines were horribly hot and suffered from the operational inconvenience that before diving you had to take down the funnel and damp down the furnace. They nonetheless managed to inspire a series of oil-fired steam turbine submarines, which entered service in 1916. Crewed by volunteers they were still stuck with funnels which were supposed to be retracted when the diving klaxon sounded. Three of the subs were sunk in collisions, one sank in harbour and another just vanished. The 'K' class to which they belonged was known in the navy as the 'Kalamity' class.

inside the ship. This made it possible for the guns to rotate and to be aimed at a target almost anywhere. The naval architect, Sir Edward Reed, set to work designing HMS *Devastation*, the first major warship to be solely powered by steam. On a wet July day at Portsmouth in 1871, with a Royal Marines band playing the national anthem and sailors on other vessels cheering noisily, *Devastation* (her sister ship, launched later, was named *Thunderer* – the British navy was never knowingly under-threatening) took to the water. She had a 280-degree arc of fire from each of her twin-barrelled twelve-inch guns. The gun turrets were protected by armour over one foot thick. So emblematic did *Devastation* become of British naval power that an image of the ship found its way into every smoker's pocket, as the trademark on each box of 'England's Glory' matches.

No longer powered by the wind, the ship was fast and manoeuvrable. But at full power *Devastation* burned 150 tons of coal in a day, which meant she could carry enough coal to travel at full speed for only twelve days. If the British Empire was to rule the waves, *Devastation* and her successors needed ready access to huge quantities of coal. Without ammunition for the guns a ship could turn tail and hope to fight another day, but without coal for the boilers, she was a sitting duck. The solution to the problem was to establish fuel depots ('coaling stations') across the world.

The British Empire was fortunate in already having seized possessions across the globe, which gave the navy a head start, and soon it established coaling stations on most continents. But did they work? 'Coal rules the destinies of nations,' sermonised Sir Archibald Hurd in 1898. Hurd, a Conservative prig who had been given a pulpit in what was to become the party's favourite newspaper, was not a man to whisper his opinions on nautical subjects and held forth with the specialist correspondent's customary repetition of conventional opinion. 'Coal is the source of our commercial prosperity and the secret of our naval supremacy,' he wrote from the comfort of the *Daily Telegraph*. 'Coal is the first requisite of empire.'[2] The Royal Navy's 450 warships were, he opined, the British Empire's equivalent of the life insurance policy bought by a prudent man. 'We have more coaling stations than any other Power, but have we enough?'

On a map, the network certainly looked impressive. In the Atlantic, Royal Navy steamships might take on coal in Halifax, Nova Scotia, in Bermuda, in Sierra Leone, and at Ascension Island, St Helena and the Falkland Islands. In the Caribbean, there were depots at St Lucia and Jamaica. In the Mediterranean ships could refuel in Gibraltar, Malta, Cyprus and Port Said. The coal bunkers of Simons Town naval base at the Cape of Good Hope were available. In the Indian Ocean there were coaling stations in Mauritius, Zanzibar, the Seychelles, Bombay, Karachi, Colombo, Trincomalee; and Singapore in the Straits of Malacca. In the Bay of Bengal, Calcutta was available. In Australia, warships could refuel at Melbourne, Sydney, Newcastle and King George Sound; in New Zealand at Wellington or Auckland. In the Pacific, there was Port Hamilton in Korea and Fiji. Esquimalt in British Columbia and Valparaíso in Chile were also available. In the South China Sea, coal bunkers had been established in Hong Kong and at Labuan Island, north Borneo. Almost all these places had mountains of Welsh coal deposited by British cargo vessels. Even so, alarmists like the man from the *Telegraph* worried: he wanted to see new coal depots on the west coast of Africa and on the north Australian coast. Hurd particularly hoped that the port of Weihaiwei, controlling sea access towards Peking and reluctantly leased to the British in 1895, 'may be developed into a second Hong Kong'.[3] A quick glance at the map shows that some of the areas coloured pink on the imperial map, like Aden at the entrance to the Red Sea, really only mattered to the empire because of their strategic location. In the event of unexpected deployments beyond the range of usual coal stocks, captains might be supplied from a growing network of commercial ports. Nonetheless, at the back of the mind of every warship's captain was always a worry about where and when he might take on the coal to remain at sea.

Furnishing the biggest navy on earth with fuel was clearly a highly lucrative business, which led to much competition: Britain was fortunate in harvesting plentiful supplies of coal. The problem was that not all coal had the same properties. Since Newcastle and the Northumberland area were well known as the place from where coal came, the first ships of the steam navy were powered by coal from the north-east of England. But there turned out to be a number of problems with north-eastern coal, one of them being that when shovelled into the boilers of warships it produced a heavy black smoke which could be so thick that it made signalling between ships almost impossible. Sometimes it even made it difficult for navigating officers to see where they were going. The smoke additionally rendered it virtually impossible to make a stealthy approach on the enemy: the great black clouds belching from their funnels were visible for miles.

Throughout the middle years of the nineteenth century, the Admiralty sponsored at least twenty-one trials of the various types of coal available, attempting to meet the requirements later set out in the 1904 Royal Commission on Coal Supplies; to be dangerous, ships had to be able to travel at speed. But 'if you use a coal that burns quicker without producing the same calorific effects and power, you would burn out the coal sooner than you otherwise would, and the consequence would be that a ship instead of running her 10,000 miles at a certain speed, would be reduced probably to 8,000 or 9,000 miles'.[4] There were additional considerations, too: in order not to damage the engines and compromise effectiveness the coal should burn with as little smoke as possible, be relatively clean and hard, be easy to stoke, burn freely and not produce great quantities of 'clinker' – the stony deposits left after burning some lower-quality coal.

Welsh steam coal was judged to burn best and to give off the least smoke. Any colliery hoping to get a contract to supply the fleet had first to be included on the Admiralty List, which was only possible if their coal had been tested by naval engineers in boilers at Portsmouth, and then on warships. Even though getting onto the Admiralty List was in itself no guarantee of business (merely that should the need arise, the colliery would be entitled to sell coal to the navy), it became an internationally recognised stamp of excellence: getting onto it was a thing to boast about. John Nixon, a commercially astute Durham mining engineer who freely admitted that he had moved his business to South Wales because he had seen the superior qualities of Welsh steam coal, filled his boots. Nixon's Navigation trumpeted in the 1890s that its coal was also 'supplied to the Russian, German, Austrian, Italian, Swedish, Dutch and Egyptian governments for royal yachts and special naval purposes'.[5]

As might be imagined, proprietors of collieries elsewhere in Britain grumbled noisily. When the subject was debated in the House of Commons, T. E. Smith, a North Country MP who did as the colliery proprietors told him, simply asserted that there was 'no evidence' to support the claim that Welsh steam coal was superior. Northern coal would raise steam much more quickly, which was essential in an emergency. By contrast, he claimed, when Welsh coal was exposed to the tropical sun it 'turned into dust, which was perfectly useless'.[6] (The truth is that all coal deteriorates if left exposed to the elements.) Unsurprisingly, Richard Fothergill, a South Wales ironmaster and mine-owner, did not agree. He told the House of Commons that Wales had the finest steam coal in the world – indeed coal was finest of all in his own constituency. This point-scoring was a childish political reflection of the decision reached by Her Majesty's naval officers. Admiral Napier's dispatch from the Baltic had been succinct: 'Send me out Welsh coal, or I cannot be responsible for the safety of the fleet.'[7] The level of civilian political debate did not much improve.

Welsh steam coal was undeniably expensive and during public spending crises there were constant attempts to save money by mixing it with other types of fuel. Gladstone was no great friend of the navy, and his Admiralty Secretary from 1868 to 1871, a smug, Dundonian businessman named William Baxter, decreed that Welsh coal be mixed with cheaper fuel from northern collieries. The practice did not last long. Naval captains complained that their ships were less efficient, and that their engines had been designed to burn Welsh coal and so were being damaged by the mixture. By the 1880s the British navy was using the more expensive Welsh steam coal exclusively, even when refuelling its ships on the China station. Still, in 1914 Welsh coal dominated the naval station in Vancouver, over 14,000 miles from where it had been mined. The government had heaved a sigh of relief when in 1883 Westport coal from the South Island of New Zealand was judged to be good enough for Royal Navy ships, which would otherwise have to be replenished with coal brought all the way from home. New Zealand coal was not quite as good as Welsh coal, but immensely superior to Australian coal, which drove warships more slowly, produced much more smoke and damaged the boilers.* Even in 1913 Westport was almost the only other type of coal used by British warships.

It would be years before the government had either the means or the inclination to go into coal production itself, and in the early twentieth century bought from collieries and their agents, secure in the 1907 prediction that the navy's wartime needs would be about half a million tons a month, which could easily be obtained

---

* The boring detail. In tests on HMAS *Australia*, it was demonstrated that to keep the propellers turning at 186 revolutions a minute required sixteen tons of coal from New South Wales, 12.5 tons of Westport coal, but only ten tons of coal from Wales.

on the open market. It was carried to overseas ports by civilian tramp steamers. These coaling stations, by all accounts, were polyglot places, with a population which had migrated from all over the globe drawn by the promise of work. In the wake of the 'heavers' or 'lumpers' came an ever-shifting mass of bar-owners, cooks, merchants, thieves and prostitutes. Few of them stayed long.

Within the navy, the sailors who had most to do with coal, the stokers, were considered the lowest of the low – stupid, vulgar, brawling, heavy-drinking, ignorant, dirty and so full of moaning that they might drown out the engines. With many recruited from the slums, it was generally acknowledged that they were not necessarily built like prop forwards. A good proportion were illiterate and innumerate. The job of the 'clinker-knocker' (the stokers were so called because they used a nine-foot steel bar to clean the furnace of 'clinker' or fused residue left by burned coal) was unskilled and filthy, and the men who performed it were – oddly, since everyone else on the ship depended on the power they produced – resented and sneered at. Feeding and tending a roaring fire in a heaving sea was a highly dangerous occupation, made worse by the possibility of pipes jamming, boilers exploding or fumes building up in confined spaces. In the tropics, there was the added danger of heatstroke for those working in an already over-heated environment. A few outsiders, like Midshipman Alexander Scrimgeour, overcame the general contempt for stokers after spending a few months on the Falklands veteran, the battlecruiser HMS *Invincible* in early 1916: 'The engine and boiler rooms at sea are hell; one cannot realise the life of the stokers and other "saints who toil below" until one actually experiences it. These men's work can vie with any, trenches and deserts not excluded; their whole life in wartime is a vivid succession of discomforts and hardships, unparalleled in severity and monotony.'[8]

A pithead, *c.*1800. You could find a coal mine anywhere a landowner had happened to get lucky.

Two illustrations from the Report of the Children's Employment Commission of 1842. (*Above*) A teenage girl acts as an underground beast of burden, as younger siblings push the coal wagon. (*Right*) Children are lowered into a mineshaft, where they might spend the next twelve hours underground.

J.M.W. Turner captures both the romance and the grim reality of loading coal on the River Tyne. A flood of moonlight illuminates the sky, the water and the smog.

The Japanese artist Yoshio Markino's *Constitution Hill in the Evening* (1910). The London smog created an entirely new aesthetic.

Dowlais Ironworks (1840). This steelyard in South Wales became the biggest steel producer in the UK during the nineteenth century.

Miners prepare to try to rescue colleagues trapped underground at Seaham Colliery in County Durham. The explosion occurred at 2.30 a.m. while two hundred and thirty-one men were in the pit.

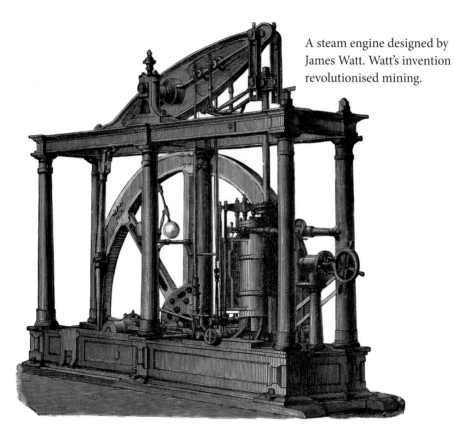

A steam engine designed by James Watt. Watt's invention revolutionised mining.

Chimneys define the view of Sheffield's rooftops in 1879. Factories and steel works sprang up side by side.

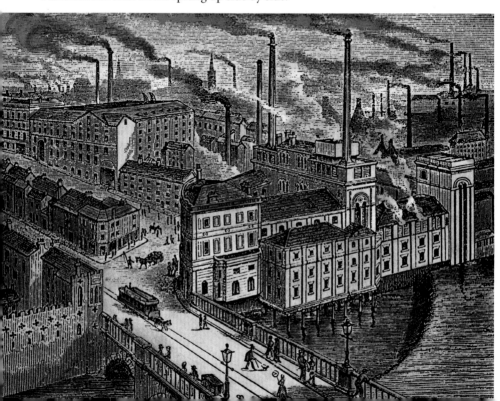

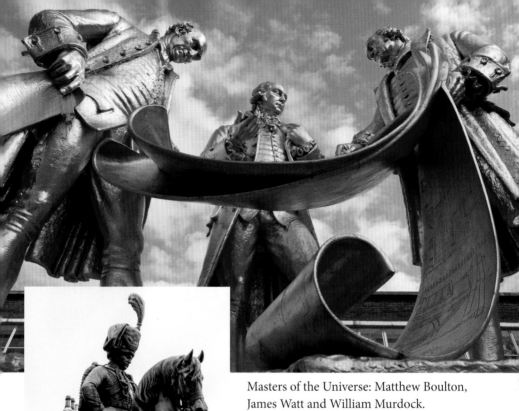

Masters of the Universe: Matthew Boulton, James Watt and William Murdock.

The Marquess of Londonderry Charles Vane, Durham's 'Man on a Horse', in his favourite uniform.

The great Victorian reformer, the Earl of Shaftesbury – plenty of reasons for the long face.

Lord Bute, unhappily removed from Fairy Land, in 1872.

A nicely scrubbed-up Ellen Grounds with A.J. Munby at a Wigan photographers in 1883.

Ellen's colleagues, armed with their working equipment.

Wigan women moving and sorting coal, on site at Moss Hall in the early 1900s.
The railways killed the Newcastle coal trade.

Nautical coal's last hurrah. The *Turbinia*, the first vessel to be fitted with steam turbines, photographed in 1894.

You had to buy pit ponies – the boys came (nearly) free.

But one major change wrought in all sailors' lives by the switch from sail to coal was the fact that because their vessels travelled so much faster and then had to stop and refuel, ships spent less time on the high seas, and more time at a quayside somewhere. Warships might need to take on fresh coal every week or ten days and once sailors had tired of watching local labourers heave tons of coal on board,* there were usually swimming, football, cricket or golf tournaments, concerts or fancy-dress dances organised to mark their arrival, as well as traditional Jack Tar activities like drinking and whoring (in 1868, one-tenth of British navy personnel were reckoned to have syphilis, though the figure had been cut to one in 200 by 1913).

The moment a ship finished bunkering brought nearer the day when the whole thing would have to be repeated. Even in 1914 most coal was still being loaded by hand, but the quantities of coal required to keep the navy at sea had escalated prodigiously. HMS *Dreadnought*, the fast and mighty battleship which had been commissioned by Admiral of the Fleet 'Jackie' Fisher to revolutionise naval power, entered service in 1906. Even though she was driven by very efficient steam turbines she still burned an average of 300 tons of coal a day. It was not just that the powerful new warships wolfed down more coal. There was also the size of the navy itself. In 1889, scare stories had persuaded Parliament to instruct the navy to maintain a fleet of at least as many battleships as those of the next two biggest fleets combined. To keep the expanded fleet operational, vast quantities of coal had to be moved around the globe.

---

* Techniques varied from place to place, but were often accompanied by rhythmic chanting or singing. Port Said was described in some ships' logs as a model of efficiency, Zanzibar and the British-leased Chinese territory of Weihaiwei as appalling. The Chinese 'coolies' at Singapore were exemplary. In St Lucia and Zanzibar, most of the heavers were women. In Australia, the heavers were so heavily unionised that they were considered to be the best-paid casual labourers in the entire continent.

Often, the fact that a warship was too big to enter a port, or needed quickly to take on coal directly from a freighter, required sailors to do the refuelling themselves. It was a filthy, hugely unpopular job, which might even have to happen at a recognised shore coal bunker if there was a shortage of local labour because of a strike or public holiday. Transporting coal from a barge or even directly from a collier might be more efficient, but it could be even more filthy work. Sailors from the warship would shovel the coal from the collier's hold into two-hundredweight sacks, which would be winched up by steam-driven 'donkey engine' winches. By the late nineteenth century, various patent devices were attached to coal vessels to make it easier to raise the coal buckets into the much bigger warships. The most famous of these was the 'Temperley Transporter', a sort of crane-cum-single-track aerial railway, designed by John Temperley, in which loads of coal could be raised and then slid across to the waiting ship. But even here, any sailor below risked being injured by falling lumps of coal. Thomas Cooper, a former coal miner who joined the navy as a stoker, because it was 'damn hard work down the pits', thought that when compared to mining, a day coaling a ship, was 'far harder'.[9] A naval surgeon noticed how, during coaling everything 'tasted, smelt and felt, like coal'.[10]

Almost everyone on the warship's crew was involved in these hated coaling duties – including officers, chaplains and cooks. The ship's band was on hand, expected to play jaunty tunes throughout. Rules were relaxed and no one was expected to wear uniform; many took the opportunity to wear fancy dress – one ship's log records a rating in sombrero and cricket whites (at the start of the day, presumably). Some men would appear in women's underwear. However hard they tried to keep the warship clean, the deck was almost always quickly covered in coal dust. The men working in the hold of the collier alongside were soon no more than the occasional red mouth and eyes. After they had filled the sacks to be lifted to the warship, the coal was tipped into the vessel's various bunkers. There, the half-naked stokers levelled the piles of coal, sometimes by lying on top of it and using their feet to push lumps into the corners. The sailors worked all day, getting only an occasional tot of lime juice, until a bugler sounded 'ceasefire'. Great pride was taken in how fast a ship could refuel, with competitions organised to try to keep up the rate, even at the risk of fatal accidents during the process (of which, between 1910 and 1912, there were sixteen, with twenty-three other sailors being seriously injured). For almost everyone, coaling was a misery: black dust got everywhere and when the filthy business was finished, the ship (and the men) were washed down with seawater. Even with the promise of a beer issue afterwards, one sailor recalled that 'a shadow would come over the ship as soon as you heard you were coaling'.[11] 'I wish I could get hold of that man who first found coal,' muttered another.[12]

While they were taking on coal, warships were sitting ducks. Winston Churchill was once asked what had been his most anxious moment during the entire two world wars. He replied that it had been the occasion when, as First Lord of the Admiralty (political head of the navy) in 1914 he had been handed a badly drafted telegram from the governor of the Falkland Islands which seemed to say that the German Admiral Maximilian von Spee had attacked the great British battlecruisers *Invincible* and *Inflexible* 'while they were coaling'. If so, they would almost certainly have been sunk.*

But the message was garbled. The British had already suffered their worst naval defeat for over a century at Coronel, off the coast of central Chile, when, outnumbered and outgunned by Spee's ships, they had lost the cruisers *Good Hope* and *Monmouth* with

---

* The German navy – also coal-fired – suffered the same inconvenience of regularly refuelling. Admiral Spee wrote to his family on 27 October 1914, 'The eternal worry about coal, coupled with the total lack of fixed bases, is ghastly, If our needs should once prove impossible to meet, then I am done for.'

all hands. The British, brought up to believe they were protected by the greatest navy on earth, were stung. Churchill had ordered Admiral Doveton Sturdee to leave England for the British base at the Falkland Islands in the South Atlantic, with a force containing the two battlecruisers, to be joined off Brazil by five lighter cruisers in support. Sturdee planned to refuel at the British coal depot in the Falkland Islands, and arrived there on 7 December 1914, anchoring in Port Stanley harbour. The following morning, look-outs spotted German warships approaching the islands. Unaware of the presence of Sturdee's ships, Spee had decided to seize what coal he could and then to destroy the British base on the islands. 'There is no question that Stanley [the capital] would have been burned to the ground,' the Falkland Islands Company manager wrote to his head office later.[13] The first two German attackers had been ordered to destroy the radio station.

The first shots fired in the battle came from HMS *Canopus*, on about the only occasion in the ship's life when it happened to be in the right place at the right time. *Canopus* wasn't an especially bad ship. Just unlucky. She had been built in 1897 for service on the China station and was on her way there when news came through that Japan and Britain had signed a treaty, making her presence redundant. So she returned for service in British waters, and was on manoeuvres in the English Channel in 1904 when she collided with HMS *Barfleur*. She had a brief excursion to the Mediterranean, and then was put into the reserve. When the First World War broke out she was sent to help hunt down Spee's battle group off South America. The officer commanding the British force, Admiral Kit Craddock, had been told that although HMS *Canopus* was supposed to be able to travel at eighteen knots, a leaky piston meant that she could only limp along at a maximum of twelve knots, which was far too slow for chasing Spee's group of raiders at sea. (What Craddock did not know was that the ship's first engineer, William Denbow, was suffering from depression and had probably misled the ship's captain – in fact the *Canopus* might have managed sixteen or seventeen knots.) Craddock decided to leave *Canopus* – and its twelve-inch guns – behind. This meant that Spee was at an immediate advantage in gunnery terms and the engagement, though heroic, doomed. Craddock's flagship, HMS *Good Hope*, was repeatedly hit by German shells, exploded and sank, killing the admiral and over 900 men. The death of Kit Craddock, a strikingly handsome man with an immaculately trimmed beard who had been in the Royal Navy since the age of thirteen, was felt deeply in the navy. Admiral David Beatty, commander of the 1st Battlecruiser Squadron and future Admiral of the Fleet, wrote 'He was a gallant fellow, and I am sure put up a gallant fight, but nowadays no amount of dash and gallantry will counterbalance great superiority unless they are commanded by fools.'

The next deployment orders received by *Canopus* instructed the ship to head for the Falkland Islands, to defend them from German attack by mooring in the harbour at Port Stanley, with guns able to command the entrance. She was also to 'extemporise mines outside the entrance'. The captain was to hide the ship by taking down her masts and to prepare to be shot at by the Germans. A few days later a member of the crew was astonished to see that the upper parts of the ship were being painted 'all the colours of the rainbow' – perhaps an early attempt at the contour-breaking 'dazzle camouflage' which became common on naval vessels later in the war. A couple of weeks later, the captain, worried that if the *Canopus* fired her twelve-inch guns she might shift in the water, ran the ship into a mudbank, where she stayed for the duration of the battle to come.

At 7.30 on 8 December, her lookout spotted enemy warships, soon identified from their outline as being the German cruisers *Gneisenau* and *Nürnberg*. *Canopus* fired five shells at the two warships – all of which missed their target. They were the first shots the ship had fired in anger and the first in the battle which would end the danger from Spee's marauders. Being told of the sighting, Admiral Sturdee immediately ordered his other ships to raise steam for full speed. Hidden behind the hillside, the Germans mistook much of the smoke from the ships for the British burning things on land that they did not want to risk falling into enemy hands. But as soon as Spee realised the size of the British naval presence, the German ships turned and fled. Now it was the turn of Sturdee's fast battlecruisers, *Invincible* and *Inflexible*, to do the chasing. The German ships had a fifteen-mile head start, but the main British ships were both faster and carried heavier guns. By lunchtime the British had the Germans in range of their twelve-inch guns and Spee recognised his only hope was to use the fact that smoke was making signalling and sighting of guns very tricky ('Nothing could be observed here, due to smoke', said a semaphore signal from *Gneisenau* to Spee's flagship, *Scharnhorst*, towards the end of the battle) and to try to land sufficient shells on the British ships to make them back off. *Invincible* was hit several times by German shells (German gunnery seemed to be more accurate than that of the British) but her armour was so thick that most of them did little or no damage. The British continued to pour shells at the German flagship. At just after 4.15, *Scharnhorst* sank, taking all hands with her. Both Spee and his two sons perished. *Gneisenau* fought on, though it had been hit many times, and as late as 5.15 was seen to land a shell on *Invincible*. But within minutes, the German ship was ablaze and dead in the water. Sturdee ordered a ceasefire, but the men on *Gneisenau* were told to scuttle the ship, and it capsized and sank. The British rescued 187 of them from the water.

Admiral Sturdee had ordered his slower and less powerful cruisers to continue chasing the lesser German warships, *Nürnberg* and *Leipzig*. *Nürnberg* was being chased by *Kent*, which in its sea trials had never managed to achieve its promised speed. But now, with the stokers throwing anything which would burn into her boilers, *Kent* reached twenty-four knots and closed to within 1,100 yards of the German vessel. Soon after 5.30 that evening two of *Nürnberg*'s boilers exploded and then British shells set the ship on fire, too. An hour and a half later, *Nürnberg* struck her colours, the internationally agreed signal of surrender. Meanwhile, the cruisers *Cornwall* and *Glasgow* had chased down *Leipzig*, which had run out of ammunition. She fired two flares, so *Glasgow* ceased fire. Then, just after twenty past nine at night, she capsized and sank. There were eighteen survivors, from a crew of almost 300. *Kent* limped slowly back to Port Stanley, conserving what little coal the ship had left.

It would be wrong to suggest that the need to maintain coaling stations overseas, like the one on the Falkland Islands, had made life more dangerous for the navy (though any enemy intelligence department could predict roughly how long it might be before a seaborne squadron would need to take on fresh supplies, and approximately where it might happen). But there were inherent problems with using coal as the main power source for the fleet. It had one obvious advantage, in that if you filled a warship with coal, you automatically reinforced the protection of its armour-plating: it was lining the interior of much of the hull with rocks. Against that, coal was a logistical nightmare, and required the constant attention of stokers to see that an even fire burned in the boilers, until the need to be resupplied dragged ships back to friendly ports. The Admiralty had to keep an up-to-date record of precisely how much coal of which variety could be obtained from dumps on the shores of every ocean on earth, and the stores themselves had to be protected from enemy attack.

One of the advantages for the British of coal-fired navies had been tactical. In the 1904–5 war between Russia and Japan, Britain was able to refuse the Russians permission to use the Suez Canal – and yet to allow their Japanese allies access to the nation's coaling stations. When Moscow attempted to send the Russian Baltic Fleet to the Far East they had been obliged to undertake an additional 3,000-mile journey via the Cape. The British refused them the use of any coaling stations they controlled en route. 'Coal! It is our weak spot,' the engineer-in-chief to the squadron, Eugene Politovsky, had exclaimed, 'Our comings, our goings, our voyage, and even our success depend on coal.' Another officer commented that 'coal had developed into an idol, to which we sacrificed strength, health, and comfort. We thought only in terms of coal, which had become a sort of black veil hiding all else, as if the business of the squadron had been, not to fight, but simply to get to Japan.'[14]

When the First World War broke out, both Germany and Britain had powerful warships which could travel great distances. But only the British were able to be sure of replenishing their vessels' coal bunkers for the return journey. Without secure refuelling bases abroad, the German navy could never really claim to be a high-seas fleet. Indeed, it spent most of the war in German waters. Even the emerging world power of the United States was hostage to coal: US coaling abilities were so poor that they constantly had to rely upon British coaling ships. The Spanish–American war had proved this in 1898, when the US was forced to purchase Australian coal for its fleet in Manila and to employ British colliers to help deliver it. President Roosevelt's 'Great White Fleet' that in 1907–9 circumnavigated the globe was plagued with similar problems: 90% of the coal consumed by the fleet was American, thanks to growing steam-coal mines in North Virginia and Pennsylvania; but these were far from the coast, and there was no coaling fleet. So, American colliers only delivered 7.5% of it, and British colliers ended up delivering 70% of the larger nation's coal stocks.[15] The power of coal gave navies strength. But it made them dependent.

* * *

Coal had one more moment of naval significance. If James Watt was the human bookend at one end of the Age of Steam, the other was Charles Algernon Parsons. As his middle name suggests he was more gently born than most Victorian engineers – unusually, he was the son of an Irish peer, the third Earl of Rosse. Parsons grew into a shy man and a brilliant engineer, considered by many to be as great in the history of steam power as the fabled Watt. Parsons began his career as an apprentice in the vast factory which Sir William Armstrong had built on the Tyne, until in 1884 he was made a partner in another local company, where he was asked to engage with the new obsession of the age, electricity. Other engineers had developed coal-fired, steam-driven generators, but Parsons was charged with developing a high-speed version. All great ideas begin with a vital insight and Parsons' inspired idea was that much more energy would be generated than could be produced from a steam-driven flywheel, by firing steam directly into the blades of a 'turbine'.* Critically, he discovered that the speed of the turbine could be controlled by moderating the power of the expanding steam produced from burning coal by directing it through a series of channels. He had uncovered the method which still drives turbines well over a century later. Parsons quickly set up on his own, built a power station in the heart of Newcastle and, by 1890, was producing electricity from turbines. Other cities quickly followed suit, and Parsons turned his mind to how to drive ships by steam turbine.

His first experimental ship, the hundred-foot *Turbinia*, was built on the Tyne and had three turbines and nine propellers. To demonstrate the revolutionary nature of his vessel, Parsons organised a stunt. He knew that most of the Royal Navy would be present at a

---

* The word had been coined in the early nineteenth century by a French mining engineer, Claude Burdin, who had taken it from the Latin *turbo*, meaning 'something that whirls'.

Review to celebrate Queen Victoria's Diamond Jubilee. Sure enough, on 26 June 1897, 165 warships lay at anchor at Spithead in the Solent in four five-mile lines. The elderly queen herself was too ill to attend, her duties undertaken by the Prince of Wales. The Review took the form of an 'inspection', in which the prince cast his eyes over the most powerful navy on earth. Once the royal yacht had taken him on his tour between the lines of warships, Parsons staged his advertising caper. His boat suddenly burst on the scene and stormed at high speed between the lines of battle-ships, cruisers and destroyers. It caused a sensation: witnesses watched in amazement as the *Turbinia*'s speed lifted her bow out of the water and flames spouted from her funnel. Not a vessel in the most powerful navy in the world could catch her. The *Turbinia* was said to have reached speeds of well over thirty knots: as the reporter from *The Times* put it, 'the patrol boats which attempted to check her adventurous and lawless proceedings were distanced in a twinkling'.[16] Visiting foreign admirals and princes were as open-mouthed as the Royal Navy officers.

Charles Parsons could not have chosen a better place to mount an advertising display. With the British determined to maintain the Royal Navy's pre-eminence, his invention was too revolution-ary to be ignored. By 1899 the Admiralty had ordered two turbine-driven destroyers, *Cobra* and *Viper*.* In later life Admiral Jackie Fisher, who was to rebuild the British navy before the First World War, liked to appear sniffy about Parsons' turbines, calling them 'a box of tricks' on 'penny steamer[s]'.[17] Yet it was civilian vessels which provided working examples of what the new tech-

---

* Neither ship lived to ripe old age. In fog off one of the Channel Islands in August 1901, *Viper* was driven by Lt William Speke onto the rocks and sank. A few weeks later, *Cobra* broke apart in heavy seas, on the journey from her Tyneside shipyard to Portsmouth. A court martial – the findings of which were kept secret for fifty years – decided the ship had had a structural fault. The Royal Navy soon gave up naming its ships after land snakes.

nology could achieve, and the lessons were unignorable. Parsons' engines later drove two pleasure-steamers, *King Edward* and *Queen Alexandra*, which carried tourists up and down the river Clyde. There was the shipping magnate Lord Furniss' elegant 800-ton yacht *Emerald*, whose turbines drove it across the Atlantic.* And, by 1906, there would be full-scale ocean liners, *Lusitania* and *Mauretania*, in which first-class passengers could pass the journey to and from the United States amid oak panelling, mahogany pilasters, ornate tapestries and marble floors, with lifts available for anyone who didn't like the chore of using the grand walnut staircases. For twenty years RMS *Mauretania* held the record for the fastest crossing of the Atlantic.

British shipyards were already producing warships for navies all over the world: three of the six Japanese battleships which had crushed the Russian fleet in the war of 1904–5 had been built on the Tyne. To a nation determined to maintain naval dominance, the turbine was now irresistible. In 1906, Parsons supplied the Admiralty with turbines to power the monstrous HMS *Dreadnought*. The ship carried a crew of up to 800 men, had ten twelve-inch guns, eighteen four-inch guns, torpedo tubes and armour plating up to fourteen inches thick. Parsons' turbines enabled this floating behemoth (nearly 20,000 tons) to achieve over twenty-one knots, a hitherto unheard-of speed for a battleship. In total, Britain built twenty-nine of these ships, and another nine dreadnought battlecruisers. Though in truth the dreadnoughts turned out to be more of a red-white-and-blue virility symbol than anything else, they made the old piston-driven warship engine obsolete.

*   *   *

---

* This splendid toy met a less than glamorous end in 1913 when it caught fire while moored in a sheltered sea loch in Argyll and Bute. The flames which consumed her polished teak decks had hardly been extinguished before the disaster was blamed on Suffragette arson.

Parsons' turbine engines were fired by coal. But the fuel's days were numbered. Admiral Fisher was no great fan of it, talking in 1912 about life on a coal-powered armoured cruiser as 'worse than in any ship in the service, owing to the constant coalings … It's an economic waste of good material to keep men grilling in a baking firehole at unnecessary labour and use 300 men when a dozen would suffice.'[18] It was a strong argument, and by the early years of the twentieth century, there was an available alternative to coal. But since the second half of the nineteenth century the persistence of prospectors like Pennsylvania's 'Colonel' Edwin Drake (he just liked the title, though he had never served in the military) had delivered another fossil fuel. By 1865 John D. Rockefeller had become the first oil baron, forming Standard Oil. Pound for pound, this new hydrocarbon could produce four times as much energy as coal and was a great deal easier to transport, needing only pipes and storage tanks, in which you could easily measure reserves with a dipstick or gauge. Possibilities of amassing great wealth in oil were limited, though, by the fact there were so few uses for it. All that changed with the First World War, after which sales of petrol for motorised vehicles outstripped everything. Heavier, less volatile, 'fuel oil' became the energy choice of the navy.

Coal-powered warships not only required armies of stokers to tend to the boilers, but also 'trimmers' who were constantly shovelling coal, so that the vessel stayed on an even keel as the mountains of coal for the boilers were reduced by burning. It would take many fewer men to tend an oil-fired furnace. The navy began by using oil and solid fuel together, with oil sprayed over the coals. This had the advantage of spreading the fire, increasing the steam generated and quickening the ship's pace. The attraction of this combined fuel for navies was immediate, even if a suitable mechanism was hard to discover. Both British and French developers attempted to produce effective methods of spraying oil onto coal to make it burn more efficiently. The French were said to have equipped the yacht of France's imperial Walter Mitty, Napoleon III, with oil-spraying equipment, and Germany, Russia and Italy all also tried to devise effective ways of using oil to get more heat from the coal of their warships' bunkers. The universal problem was that the usual method for dispersing the oil was to use steam or compressed air, which required more storage space for water or air than was generally available, and without an efficient dispersal mechanism, nozzles became clogged with carbon. It was the sort of mechanical challenge that was bound to be settled sooner or later.

And it was. By 1903, engineering officers and others were being trained how to run ships by burning oil which had the great advantage of being liquid and therefore needing nothing more than pipes to take it from storage tanks to engine room. By now, Jackie Fisher, a relentless self-publicist with unquenchable ambition, was on the cusp of becoming the most senior admiral in the navy. A squat, arrogant man with a slight resemblance to a pug,* he had been recommended for the navy by Nelson's last surviving captain, had lived through the transition from sail to steam and regarded coal as, at best, a necessary evil. In 1904, he was made First Sea Lord, and then Admiral of the Fleet with a licence to ensure the British retained the most overwhelmingly powerful navy on earth. (He immediately purged it of 150 ships he thought inefficient.) The creator of the dreadnought navy was wise enough to recognise that as well as firepower, his ships needed to have a turn of speed. Here was an opportunity to get rid of coal. Like most armed forces,

---

* 'My mother was a most magnificent and handsome, extremely young woman,' he once said. 'My father was six feet two inches ... also especially handsome. Why I am ugly is one of those puzzles of physiology which are beyond finding out.' By the time he had risen to the top of the navy, the weight of the stars, sashes, aiguillettes and medals on his front was matched only by the increasing blubber beneath his skin. He boasted in his memoirs of how he had become 'the most hated man in Germany' long before the First World War.

which prepare for the next battle as if it will be a rerun of the last one, the Royal Navy was awash with old salts who distrusted oil, as their predecessors had moaned about the introduction of steam power and breech-loading guns. Fisher, though, soon liked to boast that he was an 'oil maniac'.

It took years, though, for oil fully to supersede coal, and when Winston Churchill became First Lord of the Admiralty in 1911, coal was still the main source of power for British warships (though spraying with oil was now pretty common). But oil was clearly the future. As what became nicknamed the 'Kalamity' class had demonstrated, there were very obvious chimney difficulties in trying to drive submarines, of which Fisher was a keen advocate, by coal. In the rest of the navy, oil offered immediate economies: the turbines of the coal-fired battlecruiser HMS *Lion*, launched in 1910, required 600 men in the engine room, whereas HMS *Hood*, a battlecruiser commissioned ten years later – whose turbines were oil-powered – needed half as many.[19] To very few tears, the number of stokers recruited for the Royal Navy was deliberately reduced. Some diehards (doubtless with poor memories) still argued that the loathed task of taking on coal supplies was 'healthy exercise' and 'first-class drill' for the ship's company.[20] The harrumphing of a few old men could safely be ignored by the Admiralty. The strategic implications of not being the chief supplier of naval fuel to the world were another question. But in 1908 all that changed.

Seven years earlier, a British socialite, William D'Arcy, who had made a fortune from gold-mining in Australia, had persuaded the magnificently moustached but cash-strapped King of Persia, Mozaffar ad-Din Shah Qajar, to grant him rights to prospect for oil, in exchange for £20,000, some shares in the company and a small proportion of any subsequent oil revenues. It was a deal which would make future generations of Iranians grind their teeth. But in the short term it must have seemed like money for nothing, as, pipe clamped between his teeth, D'Arcy's geologist George

Reynolds strode about the desert in a tweed Norfolk jacket, braving intense heat, smallpox and bandits. To his frustration, he discovered that mostly what lay beneath the rocks were more rocks. By 1908, seven years after the deal with the king, D'Arcy's funds ran out. He instructed Reynolds to sack his workers, salvage or sell what he could of his equipment, and to come home. In late May, Reynolds decided to have a last throw of the dice, had one final drill, and, it is said, at four in the morning struck oil. Five days later, the telegram reached D'Arcy in England. 'If this is true,' he said, 'all our troubles are over.'

Understandably, William D'Arcy took the money and retired, aged fifty-nine. The Anglo-Persian Oil Company was founded the following year with the British government as a majority shareholder. The world's biggest oil refinery was built at Abadan and in 1913 the company signed a contract with the Admiralty to supply oil to the Royal Navy. Anxiety about the security of oil supplies – the last remaining argument in favour of coal – vanished. An order soon went out from the Admiralty that henceforth, more sophisticated 'stokers' were to be hired to look after the engine room. 'Time' was being called on the coal-fired Royal Navy.

7

All I Want is a Room Somewhere

For those who burned it, coal raised life from being a matter of mere survival into something that might even be enjoyable.

One of the most popular musicals of all time captures the seductive appeal of what this filthy rock could do. When Alan Jay Lerner sat down to write *My Fair Lady*, he first of all threw out the tedious aphorisms with which that great Irish crank, George Bernard Shaw, had larded the play *Pygmalion*, on which he was basing his script. Shaw's play had been about language, accent and class. Lerner was a commercial wordsmith and more concerned, inevitably, with love. It opens on a wet evening in Covent Garden. Before getting to grips with Eliza Doolittle's lack of a lover, what does the flower girl really want? Lerner has her answer in a song. All she wants is 'a room somewhere, far away from the cold night air', with

> Lots of choc'lates for me to eat
> Lots of coal makin' lots of 'eat
> Warm face, warm 'ands, warm feet
> Aow wouldn't it be loverly?

The Manhattan mockney words are a brave attempt to imagine life before we could take winter heating for granted. In an age which takes the ability to call up warmth as an entitlement, it is easy to overlook the importance of heat and light to our ability to function.

Without them, civilised life becomes impossible. Warmth is the precondition for comfort and culture.

At a practical level, when people are cold, they spend time trying to get warm. And time spent hunting for more to wear is time not spent doing something else. The artist shivering in a garret is a cliché, but who can write a symphony when their fingers are frozen? There are physiological factors, too. Trying to keep warm consumes glucose, meaning that there is less of it available to power the brain.

Not only did coal free men and women from the cold of the seasons, it also freed them from darkness. By the middle of the nineteenth century, great numbers of British citizens were for the first time able to see what they were doing after sunset. London, Liverpool, Preston and Exeter had installed street lights burning coal gas by 1816. By 1821 there was not a decent-sized town[1] in the country that did not have gas lighting. Two years later, London alone had 40,000 lamps, running along 215 miles of street.

Before gas lighting was available, people either accepted the dark or depended upon candlelight and lanterns. Candles provided a poor light, which could only be improved by increasing their number, and they were anyway easily blown out. Lanterns burning kerosene were not available until the latter half of the nineteenth century and were sooty if the wick was not properly adjusted. Those burning whale oil or spermaceti oil (which burned brighter and cleaner and was taken from the skulls of sperm whales by the bucketload) could have a bad smell.

That coal gas burned and gave off light had been apparent for centuries. The problem was managing it – how to extract, store and deliver it: there are records of experiments in France, Belgium and Germany as well as in Britain. As with so many inventions, the Chinese claim to have solved the problem millennia ago, and delivered natural gas through bamboo pipelines. In the late

seventeenth century, Reverend John Clayton filled ox bladders*
from a gas spring near Wigan with what he called 'the spirit of
coals'.† He then pricked the bladders and set alight the escaping
streams of gas. At around the same time, a German chemist
discovered that he could produce combustible gas from heating
coal in the absence of air.

The British man who basks in the eyebrow-raising epithet 'the
father of gas' is William Murdock, a burly Ayrshire engineer who
worked for Matthew Boulton and James Watt. Murdock is said to
have borrowed his mother's teapot, covered the spout with a thim-
ble, and heated coal inside it to produce gas. By the time he was
forty, Murdock had built a big retort in the backyard of his house,
from which he could pipe gas through a hole in the window frame
to a light in his living room. He went on to install lighting at his
employers' Birmingham factory, and then, in 1806, to begin an
enormous array of gaslights which lit up one of the biggest cotton
mills in the country. Elsewhere, other engineers were also engaged
in attempts to manufacture and distribute gas – in France, Philippe
Lebon is said to have made gas from wood, and when the German
Friedrich Albrecht Winzer heard of the technology he left
Brunswick to move to England in 1803. Here, under the name
Frederick Albert Winsor, he obtained patents for manufacturing
gas from coal. Winsor was a showman who strutted around
London enthusiastically promoting schemes for gaslit streets in a
heavy German accent. Some of these projects were commercially
viable and some – like the New Patriotic Imperial and National
Light and Heat Company (predicted annual profits £229 million,

---

* He had experimented with the bladders of various animals, but if he tried to store
the gas in bladders he had taken from calves, he discovered that within twenty-four
hours it lost its flammability.

† The term 'gas' is believed to have been coined by a Flemish scientist at the turn of
the seventeenth century.

most to be devoted to reducing the national debt) – were just ludicrous. All were attended with much hoopla, including public demonstrations of gas lighting on the walls of Pall Mall in 1807. Unfortunately, the show attracted the attention of local yobs. Winsor's response was to take space in the *Morning Advertiser* to offer cash rewards for the conviction of those responsible for attempting 'to injure the Lamp-Posts and Lamps in Pall Mall'. Winsor had not learned the art of punchy, or even grammatical copy, and rambled on about 'Fiends of darkness, who escape from justice by the glow-worms dazzling lenses that grace our streets, will strive to hinder Gas Lights that must prevent or detect crime. By the cries of "Stop thief!" and the watch-rattle, villains may be apprehended … A child or an assassin can do harm with a pocket pistol! Asses, heads and ears may be cut off with a fruit knife! Owls may be killed with pure oxygen, hydrogen, coal and tobacco smoke', by which time every sensible Londoner must have understood him to be more than a little unhinged.[2]

But Winsor was right in his conviction that gas lighting was the future, and Murdock in his belief that it would be most effectively provided by a few, efficient companies. Where Winsor, the flamboyant visionary, saw the future in a blaze of light illuminating entire cityscapes, Murdock, the practical engineer, had a tighter focus on individual workplaces. He described to the Royal Society the manufacture and distribution of gas from the point at which it was 'distilled in large iron retorts', and 'conveyed by iron pipes into large reservoirs', or 'gazometers' and thence through more and smaller pipes, throughout the Manchester mills. Not only was the system much cheaper than alternative sources of light, it also gave a 'peculiar softness and clearness'.

Though Murdock was a more practical man, it was the eccentric German vision of lights all along city streets which prevailed. Legislation allowing an apparently endless right of utility companies to dig up the streets was first granted to the Gas Light and

Coke Company in 1810, and by 1813 they had installed lighting in the Palace of Westminster and on the bridge outside. By 1815, thirty miles of gas mains had been laid in London.

The awestruck visitor to the gas plant in Westminster's Great Peter Street was especially intrigued by twenty structures he had never seen before and introduced readers to the vast circular metal drums like great upended barrels (they were forty feet in diameter and up to forty feet high), which were soon to become a familiar feature of cityscapes across the country – gasometers. An ingenious piece of telescopic engineering allowed the top of the barrel to rise and fall, depending upon how much gas was stored inside. The company had also devised methods of separating ammonia and tar, which they sold separately to chemical companies. Every hour or two, men would rake the coke from the retorts and, in clouds of hissing and steaming, throw buckets of cold water over it. The gas was piped away beneath a motto on the company's pressure indicator on the gas main: 'Fumo dare lucem' ('Light from smoke').

Scotland's most famous writer, Sir Walter Scott, is supposed to have dismissed the idea of lighting London 'with smoke' as the work of 'a madman'.[3] If he indeed said so, he soon changed his mind, and when he built his palatial house, Abbotsford, on the south bank of the river Tweed, Scott installed gas lighting, powered by his own gas plant, which could be tended 'by an ordinary labourer, under the occasional inspection of the gardener'. He concluded that gaslight gave him ten times as much light as oil lamps and wax candles. 'Besides, we are entirely free from the great plague of cleaning lamps, &c ... I never saw an invention more completely satisfactory in the results.'[4] Others were just as enthusiastic. The wit Sydney Smith was so impressed by the availability of light that he wrote to a friend 'Dear lady, spend all your fortune in gas-apparatus. Better to eat dry bread by the splendour of gas than to dine on wild beef with candles.'[5] Queen Victoria's first visit to see the exhibits of the Victoria & Albert Museum was purposely arranged for 9.30 at night to make the point that it was the first museum in the world to illuminate its exhibits by gaslight. On two days each week, ordinary people could visit until 10 p.m. The director, Henry Cole, hoped to 'furnish a powerful antidote to the gin palace'.

The most immediate, and unwelcome, consequence of the development of gas lighting was the lengthening of the working day. Labour which might have ended at sunset could now be continued more-or-less indefinitely. For the middle classes, it was the illumination of public spaces which changed the feel of the country most. In 1821 the chemist Colin Mackenzie recalled the bad old days, when you could hardly tell a watchman from a foot-pad after dark and those who could afford it might only venture out at night with one servant carrying a flaming torch and another armed with a cudgel. Now, he said, 'the gas-lamps afford a light little inferior to daylight, and the streets are consequentially divested of many terrors and disagreeables'.[6] (The men obliged to light the lamps by hand every dusk, in snow, sleet or rain may have taken a different view.*)

Producing gas for lighting and heating was the main business of dozens of companies which were established in the first few decades of the nineteenth century. But it's perhaps worth a quick look at the manufacture of the by-product of the process – coke – which enabled the gas companies to bolster their profits. Coal turned into coke when it was heated in a sealed vessel, as comparatively volatile products like water and mineral oils were driven

---

* It was a pretty miserable job. In October 1812 a lamplighter on Blackfriars Bridge was caught by a gust of wind and blown into the river 'in the presence of his son, a child of ten years old, and, before assistance could be procured, sunk to rise no more'. The surviving 1,300 gas lamps in London, the oldest of which are on Birdcage Walk, are today tended by four lamplighters who ride the streets of London on light motorcycles.

out. The black lumps that were left at the end of the process were dry and porous and had a high carbon content. Since the previous fuel for smelting – charcoal – had been made by heating wood in similar fashion, it took little or no time to realise that coke was an excellent fuel. It burned with more heat than coal and was easier to light. It was therefore perfect for metalwork. As early as 1590, the Dean of York, John Tornborough, had been granted a patent for a process of 'cooking' (coking) coal, to drive out the gas and other impurities; what interested the dean and other early manufacturers was the coke, not the gas, which seemed to them a useless by-product. (In the late eighteenth century, specialist coke ovens, looking to curious foreign visitors rather like beehives, vented waste gases to the air.) By the nineteenth century, the fact that manufactured coke could be burned in railway locomotives to produce heat, without also producing great clouds of smoke, convinced companies like the Great Western Railway to build their own ovens, first in west London and then in Bristol.

There was a certain irony about the desire to use coal to manufacture gas as a source of light, for the appalling visibility in many cities was itself the consequence of burning coal. At the turn of the twentieth century William Nicholson, Sheffield's first official smoke inspector, reckoned that in the worst-affected areas of Britain, 45% of available light was blocked by the muck in the atmosphere.[7] In 1910, another study calculated that in each square mile of central London, 426 tons of soot fell from the sky in a year. In central Glasgow – where most of the smoke was believed to have come from industrial furnaces – the figure was 820 tons of soot per square mile.[8] Some people evidently lived their lives in perpetual gloom. The easy availability of gaslight changed everything.

A few enthusiasts apart, initially, gas lighting had been confined to public highways. It was only after some well-known buildings, like the Palace of Westminster, burned gas that the safety of indoor lighting became accepted among those who could afford it. The Chamber of the House of Commons had had no gaslights, but the ceiling was made of glass, above which were gently glowing lamps. When it became gloomy, the Speaker had a handle by his chair which pulled a wire, which rang a bell above the glass ceiling, where a flunkey would open the valves and the place would be better lit.* Having seen the illumination of the Palace of Westminster and a few other grand public buildings like the National Gallery, wealthy households were soon festooned with lights. Contemporary accounts speak of the 'warm' or 'golden' light of gas lamps, although, until a way was discovered of making gaslights burn with a downward flame, much of the illumination produced by the early incandescent mantles in the home was thrown upward, where it did little more than brighten the ceiling.

It would be hard to exaggerate the way that the illumination of homes and cities changed people's attitudes. Of course it altered working patterns and gave more hours for reading and new forms of leisure activity, assisted the growth of literacy and made it easier to organise trade unions in meetings after dusk. But, above all, it offered a feeling of mastery and refinement. Heat from coal offered freedom from the ravages of frost and cold, which amounted to freedom from the calendar. Gas lighting promised freedom from time itself. It symbolised a hope for a brighter, cleaner future, making after-dark streets available to respectable people and allowing everyone to see where they were going. But there was something more profound. 'I am the light of the world', Jesus had said in William Holman Hunt's allegory – soon, through endless reproduction, to be the most famous modern painting in the world

---

* The heating and ventilation arrangements in the rebuilt Palace of Westminster had also been thought through and argued over by the architect, Charles Barry and the 'grandfather of air conditioning', David Boswell Reid. They were also fired by coal: air was drawn in by steam-fired fans, and if it was thought necessary to warm it, passed through a 'tempering chamber', across coal-heated pipes.

– and gaslight seemed to offer something almost biblical in its implications. Conjured by man from rock, pumped at will and sold at a price, gas epitomised the Victorian grip on the natural world, freeing the human being from enslavement to circadian cycles.

But the power continued to be bought at a terrible price.

There is nothing much to distinguish Senghenydd from any of dozens of other dour mining villages which lie on the map of South Wales like a rash of melanomas spreading out from Cardiff. Before the exploitation of coal, the rivers bustling down to the Bristol Channel from the Welsh hills were clear and fresh, alive with trout and salmon. Like many other villages in the mining valleys, Senghenydd has a war memorial – in this case a clock tower of pink granite on Commercial Street, topped with four improbable street lamps – listing the names of the dozens of young men killed in the First World War and buried in places from Amiens to Mesopotamia. But what is most remarkable about the village is its other place of public remembering.

A little way out of town, beyond the old railway line, the council have built a primary school. It stands on the site of Britain's worst mining disaster. Is there anything more exuberantly alive than the noise of a playground? Yet over the mesh fence from the school is a memorial to a much larger number of men than those who died in the Great War. Hundreds of them were killed, without even leaving their home parish, the year before the war began. Their names are inscribed on small ceramic tiles around a garden. The addresses speak the language of commerce which led to their deaths: the victims' homes were in places like 'Commercial Street' and 'Universal Huts'. Those who built their thin-walled dwellings had had neither the time nor the inclination to find a sympathetic feature or story to give a building a sense of place. Among the numerous Joneses and Davieses are bardic names that speak their land's misty past – next to seventy-three-year-old Gwilym Williams is commemorated Glyndwr Williams, who was only fourteen when he was killed.

On a raw November day it is hard enough to invest the place with the restrained dignity of a war memorial, especially since the site is overlooked by a grotesque wooden statue chainsawed into a tree, and as the whole site has been co-opted for a Welsh National Mining Memorial dominated by a kitsch, much larger-than-life-size bronze of one miner helping another out of the pit. There were no visitors when I called, but a few weeks earlier someone had laid flowers at the feet of the memorial plaque. The petals had long gone and all that remained were a few stalks on the ground.

Had there not been coal beneath the earth the village would not exist. Less than thirty miles north of Cardiff, Senghenydd was developed in the 1890s, when the Lewis Merthyr Consolidated Collieries Group sank shafts to lift coal from below the bleak hills above the valley of the river Rhymney. The company was owned by William Thomas Lewis, soon to be ennobled as Baron Merthyr. With his enormous bald head and bushy beard, Lewis was endlessly compared to Father Christmas. It was very inappropriate: in reality, he was about as hard-nosed a mine-owner as you could find: fable has it that Father Christmas gives lumps of coal to naughty children, but Lewis was not in the habit of giving coal to anyone. As leader of the owners' organisation, he was implacably hostile to attempts by miners to organise trade unions. In the Victorian tradition, he worked furiously, understood the relationship between muck and brass and did not like to be contradicted. This pantomime character could be generous to charity, just as long as no one dared to question his inflexible prejudices. Sidney and Beatrice Webb, socialist contemporaries who founded the London School of Economics, reckoned him the most hated man in Wales.

No one acquires such status easily, and Lewis single-mindedly devoted his entire life to turning rocks into money. He had begun his mining career working for the third Marquess of Bute, who, as we have seen, had more interest in archangels than anthracite. Lewis gilded his credentials as a miner by marrying the grand-daughter of Lucy Thomas, the woman known as 'the mother of the Welsh steam-coal trade', from a widowhood spent selling coal at the pit-mouth.[9] Before he was thirty, Lewis had been promoted to be Bute's chief mining engineer and within sixteen years he was running all the Bute family businesses in Wales, while the marquess fussed about the curlicues in his castles. By now, Lewis was also running his own mining businesses and had become the greatest panjandrum in his industry, repeatedly called upon to testify before parliamentary inquiries and to give his opinions to Royal Commissions. His businesses grew – by 1913, he owned seven collieries and employed a workforce of 7,000 men, about 1,700 of them at Senghenydd. He soon found himself chairman of the Coalowners' Association and no one was more implacable in facing down miners' demands for better pay: in 1875 he had strongly supported a lockout of miners (after five months of unem-ployment, the owners allowed the men to resume work, on condition they took a 12.5% cut in wages and accepted that future pay was dependent upon the market value of the coal they hewed). A baronetcy inevitably came his way, and then a peerage.

Under the direction of Lewis's son, and with share capital of £10,000, in 1891 Lewis's Universal Steam Coal Company had begun sinking a mine at Senghenydd, a tiny farming community in the scrubby wilderness about five miles from the local market town of Caerphilly. By the turn of the century, the miners were lifting out nearly 200,000 tons of coal a year. In comparison with some other mines, it wasn't a bad place to work. Several of the seams of coal were tall enough for a short man to work standing almost upright and were roughly horizontal, whereas at other pits, seams undulated and jinked in awkward directions. There was decent ventilation – as required by safety regulations, it had two shafts dropping into the ground, one of them (the 'Lancaster') drawing in fresh air, and the other (the 'York'), about fifty yards away, discharging stale air. It was a dry mine in most working areas. The main problem, though, was coal dust, which accumulated in great quantities on the paths along which the waggons ran carrying coal from face to shaft.

On Friday 24 May 1901, while other owners of the coalfields were still harrumphing over the recent impertinent decision of the House of Commons to approve a new tax on coal, the future Baron Merthyr was holidaying on the Côte d'Azur. It was, he insisted, for the sake of his health. At five in the morning he was in bed as the 240 men of the night shift at Senghenydd finished their work, and trudged to the bottom of the shaft to ride in the cage to the surface. Eighty-two of them were still down the mine when there was suddenly an enormous explosion. It was followed by two more roaring eruptions. Everyone who heard the sound instantly recognised a terrible calamity.

It took several hours to work out how to mount a rescue operation. One of the cages which had recently brought men to the surface had been blown straight out of the shaft and into the pit's winding gear. But the colliery manager assembled a group of volunteers and they descended into the pit. They knew that eighty-two men were missing and quickly discovered the first body, that of William Harris, one of the ostlers who looked after the pit ponies. The horse was dead and Harris's head, face and hands very badly burned. But as they looked at the man's body, he moved his arm and groaned. Though few of the rescuers expected William Harris to survive, he was brought to the surface and bandaged. He lived, and, when he had recovered sufficiently, even posed in a local photographer's studio in a head bandage.

As the rescuers made their way into the pit, they came across more evidence of the force of the blast – ventilation doors torn from their hinges, coal waggons thrown over, the gruesomely mutilated bodies of other miners. On the surface, great crowds of off-shift miners, relatives of men not yet brought to the surface and Salvation Army volunteers milled about. A shipment of forty coffins arrived on the 7.30 train from Cardiff. Many of the bodies could only be identified by clothing and personal effects, like pocket watches. Families were advised to bury what was left of their loved ones without ever opening the coffin, so terrible was the disfigurement.

William Harris and two horses, named Tenby and Radnor, were the only living things to emerge from the scene of the explosion, and most of the dead brought out were in such an awful state that three days after the accident the coroner conducting the hastily arranged inquest absolved the jury of the need to see any more corpses. The body of one young man had still not been recovered by the time the inquest had finished. The condition of the last dead bodies to be brought out of the mine, nearly two months after the disaster, does not bear thinking about.

As to what had caused this carnage, the theory of Professor William Galloway, the respected mining authority called to give an expert opinion to the inquiry, was that an attempt by Thomas and Joseph Fullerlove, a father-and-son team, to raise the height of one of the tunnels with gelignite had set off an uncontrollable blast, which engulfed the mine because of the great quantities of coal dust in the air. The flames had made the air expand suddenly, causing an airwave that swept along the tunnels, picking up coal dust and setting off further explosions. The mine-owners put on public display a number of toadies to claim the mine was 'well watered', which, while dampness would not necessarily have prevented the explosion, was considered an important measure to limit the scale of the blast. But the coroner's jury found the professor's argument persuasive, ruling it was the coal dust which had spread the explosion. They decided the arrangements for giving out explosives were slipshod and requested Parliament to pass laws requiring pit-owners to have the tunnels so 'well watered' that coal-dust explosions became impossible. The tragedy did nothing to curtail demand for high-quality South Wales coal. By the time of Eliza Doolittle's first appearance on stage in 1913, the mine at Senghenydd was producing half a million tons of coal a year.

If anyone had needed further evidence of the dangers of coal dust in the atmosphere it had come in March 1906, when over a thousand miners had been killed in an explosion at Courrières in northern France – the worst accident in the history of European coal-mining. Three months after the Courrières catastrophe the British government established a Royal Commission, which plodded along at a very slow pace producing three separate reports, many of whose life-saving recommendations were incorporated into the Coal Mines Act of 1911.* The Act, which was sponsored by Winston Churchill, instructed mine-owners to organise daily inspections and reports on accumulations of coal dust; to see that roadways inside the mines were kept damp, to prevent dust building up in the air; to establish rescue stations and teams of trained rescuers; to bring in strict controls on the use of electricity in mines to prevent sparks; and to make it possible for the fans which drove air through the mines to be instantly switchable, so that in an emergency like a fire, the air current could be immediately reversed, to blow gas and flames away from those trapped underground. Like most mining legislation, you could almost attach 'in memoriam' notices in the names of dead miners to specific clauses of the new law.†

---

* As A. P. Herbert observed, 'a royal commission is generally appointed, not so much for digging up the truth but for digging it in; and a government department appointing a royal commission is like a dog burying a bone, except that the dog does eventually return to the bone'.

† The Act also banned the employment underground of boys younger than fourteen (and girls and women of any age) and established an eight-hour working day for miners. It also banned employers from paying men their wages in pubs, though they were only compelled to provide pithead baths for miners if two-thirds of the workforce requested them and agreed to pay half their running costs. If the cost of the baths came to more than threepence a miner per week, the owners were exempt.

The legislation had stipulated that collieries with mechanical ventilation system fans were to make them reversible from 1 January 1913. At Senghenydd that had not happened, for the colliery-owners had applied for a delay, to 16 September that year. They had then applied for another extension to the deadline, until 30 September. But even this third deadline was ignored. The pit also had an inadequate water supply and seems to have had no sets of emergency breathing apparatus.

On 14 October there were about 900 men underground when, at ten minutes past eight in the morning, there was an enormous explosion. As had happened in the 1901 accident, the metal cage from one of the shafts, the 'Lancaster', had been blasted up from deep below. The cage weighed over three tons, and on reaching the surface it tore through a wooden platform before lodging in the headgear above. One of the dislodged timbers knocked the head off the man working there, John Mogridge, from whose neck spouted gouts of blood.

The mine manager, Edward 'Teddy' Shaw, who was later to be held partly responsible for the accident, soon bravely descended down the second mineshaft, the 'York', with a companion to see if they could establish the scale of casualties. Most men working in the east side of the pit seemed to be safe. But the west side of the mine was an inferno. Fires can be terrifying in the open air – a fire underground was something altogether more horrific. The blaze inside the mine was so bad that when rescuers tried to reach one of the communication tunnels 'it was exactly like looking into a furnace'. Men trapped in the dark on the other side of the burning timbers told later of how – their lamps blown out by the blast – they groped their way to what they hoped might be safety. Those who had descended into the pit to try to rescue colleagues fought the blaze with hand-held extinguishers. They could only endure the heat for a couple of minutes before retreating.

On the surface, other miners and the wives and children of those caught underground tried to comfort each other, while worried sick by the clouds of smoke billowing up from underground. Rescue squads from nearby mining areas began to arrive, followed by a police contingent to control crowds, along with members of the Salvation Army and Red Cross, local doctors, reporters and union representatives. Opportunistic undertakers began piling up coffins as far out of the sight of anxious families as possible. The mine's proprietor, the recently created Lord Merthyr, was on the train from London, as were Britain's most senior officials in the industry, for it was already clear that this was a very serious accident indeed.

It was not unrelieved gloom, though, for the day after the explosion came news that eighteen men had been brought out of the mine alive. As the rescue party stepped out of the cage which had brought them to the surface there was no applause, no cheers, no congratulations. As the crowds parted to let them through, every man took off his cap in silent admiration. Some fell to their knees in prayer. Those among the survivors who could speak talked of a tremendous bang, followed by a blast of air and dirt punching through the tunnel, extinguishing the lights and blowing men off their feet. They were aware that elsewhere in the mine, fires were raging.

Despite the encouraging fact of the rescue of survivors, the decision of the committee which had gathered at the pithead was that the priority now was to extinguish the fire and retrieve as many bodies as possible. By the evening fifty-six corpses had been brought to the surface, including that of one of the rescuers. That evening, the colourless 'nearly man' of Edwardian politics, the Home Secretary, Reginald Mckenna, visited the scene of the tragedy at the request of King George V: it wasn't much of a gesture, but it was some indication that London had at least heard about the calamity. When William Brace MP, a brilliant orator and former Welsh miner,[10] made a public statement that there were unlikely to be any more survivors rescued, in their hearts the entire village knew the disaster was far worse even than officialdom accepted.

For days afterwards, groups of men were sent into the mine to try to control the blaze. Some went underground wearing smoke masks and attached to breathing lines, while others cut turf in the valley above, to fill sandbags, which would be taken underground to build temporary walls to contain the fire. That weekend the first of the funerals took place. There were said to be 150,000 people in the crowds of mourners and sympathisers. In the cemetery, space had been set aside for 350 new graves. It wasn't enough.

Below ground, teams of volunteers fought their way through falls of rock to retrieve the bodies of the dead. It took weeks and weeks. On 13 November, the politically congenial *Western Mail* newspaper founded by the third Marquess of Bute, reported that 439 miners had been killed in the explosion, and one rescuer. All hope was now gone, and 440 became the official casualty figure for the disaster, a quarter of them aged twenty-one or younger and eight aged only fourteen. Two hundred widows had been created, one of whom had lost not only her husband, but four sons and three brothers. It was the worst accident in the history of British mining.

The corpses were now in a terrible state. After weeks underground, many were horribly decomposed. The effects of blast or fire had made others unrecognisable – in the worst cases, the bodies were simply wrapped in a winding sheet and personal effects recovered from the body left on top of the corpse, in the hope someone might recognise them. One of the unidentified bodies came with the single descriptive detail – '5ft 8in long'. One boy, most of whose clothes had been blown off by the blast, could be recognised only by the patches on his singlet and the notches on his boots. There were other boys of fourteen who had died crying underground and there were weeping widows of twenty at the surface; 542 children had been left without a father. According to the handwritten records, Lewis Merthyr Consolidated Collieries paid £75,855 in compensation.

The inquest into the Senghenydd calamity called almost fifty witnesses (though not Lord Merthyr) and found that most of the victims had died of suffocation or burial. It heard that on the morning of the accident, no one had read and recorded the barometer as they should have done (it might have mattered – though the coroner was dubious – since the pressure of the atmosphere affected the volume of air in the mine). The coroner avoided gruesome accounts of the horror underground and kept proceedings as restrained as possible. He commented that the pit was 'a comparatively modern colliery', and that the only legal obligation to spray water on the most dangerous coal dust on the roofs and sides of the underground roadways was to do so 'as far as practicable', and he had been told it had not been entirely feasible.

The jury found that the deaths were accidental rather than the result of negligence, and concluded that the explosion and fire had been caused by a naked flame at the 'lamp station' where the miners checked their lights. The jury was unanimous. An official inquiry, replete with expensive lawyers for the employers, sat for fifteen days under the chairmanship of the former manager of Seaton Delaval collieries, Richard Redmayne (now Britain's chief inspector of mines). The inquiry put thousands of questions to a similar number of witnesses and concluded it was most likely that the cause had been a fall of rock releasing a sudden cloud of gas, which was then ignited either by electrical signalling equipment or by sparks struck by the falling rocks. The mine manager, Teddy Shaw, was quite unrepentant about using electrical signalling equipment and admitted to a possible technical breach of the law. The question soon arose, 'whose fault was it?'

In early May 1914, seventeen charges were laid against the manager of the colliery and four against the company which operated the mine, Lewis Merthyr Consolidated. The case was heard by a bench of out-of-their-depth magistrates in Caerphilly. The manager was cleared of nine of the charges against him. The company was ruled to have failed to provide an adequate ventilation system. The total cost of fines imposed was £24. A local newspaper, the *Merthyr Pioneer*, calculated that the court had valued the life of a miner at one shilling, one penny and a farthing, or about sixpence in post-decimalisation currency. It amounts to about £6.50 at current values. A public appeal raised £126,000, including £500 sent by the king and two contributions of £100 by Lord Merthyr.

The company was fined £10. By then, Lord Merthyr had passed away in his bed at his stately home in Hampshire.

Simply because of the lengthy casualty lists, it was the disasters which caught the attention of a nation made comfortable by the warmth of coal. But most deaths occurred individually or in small numbers, when, for example, a section of roof collapsed. The coal-owners were accustomed to referring to the men who made them rich as superb physical specimens. In 1908 they asserted that 'their vital statistics are superior to those of every class in the country'.[11] This seems so much bluster, though to embark upon a life of unremitting manual labour would inevitably require physical strength, and in the short term, hard physical toil must have made them even stronger. But it was an astonishingly punishing and dangerous job. A 1914 calculation showed that a miner was severely injured every two hours, and one killed every six hours.[12] And for each victim of a fatal accident there were dozens who suffered non-fatal injuries: a Department of Employment analysis suggests that between 1900 and 1950, 100,000 miners were permanently incapacitated through injuries at work.[13] 'Progress' did not necessarily make things better: coal-cutting machines generated even more dust than the old picks and shovels. As late as the middle of the twentieth century, Britain had the worst rate of pneumoconiosis in Europe. In 1936, a writer with the *News Chronicle* reported from mining communities in the north-east of England and in South Wales that 'this is the country of premature old men. You see them everywhere – bent double, shuffling, panting for breath, at any age between 35 and 50.'[14] In the 1970s, government figures revealed that 85% of all people receiving benefits for occupation-related lung diseases were miners. None featured in flower-girls' dreams.

8

The People's Flag

It was only a question of time before the separate interests of mine-workers and mine-owners came into open conflict. The proprietors were aggressive capitalists, prepared, if necessary, to leave their mines unworked to keep the prices up.[1] Some of them married each other, sometimes as much to form commercial alliances as for love. Because the miners who made their fortunes were mainly working underground, the owners could not supervise them at all closely. But the miners were natural co-operators; it was their only source of strength. Coal-mining was a wholly natural crucible for conflict.

It was only a short step to the realisation that, when they acted together, the miners could replace their weakness with strength. Most of their trade unions were local. But in the autumn of 1842 some of them formed their first national organisation. It was led by a Newcastle publican, and by the following year was claiming 30,000 members, almost all of them in the coalfields of north-east England. The organisation had very simple ambitions – to reduce the hours worked and to raise the wages paid – and resolutely rejected formal links with other trade unions and political organisations, even turning its nose up at an offer from the most combative radical orator of the day, the Chartist Feargus O'Connor, to speak to their delegates. Members paid a subscription of one penny a week, and the thing seemed to grow energetically.

The all-male world of underground work, with its camaraderie, unquestioning loyalties and clannish initiation rituals,[2] was fertile ground for trade unionism. It had always been an occupation which attracted migrant workers: disappearing below ground offered the chance of a new life, often at better wages than could be obtained elsewhere. The 1851 census in Merthyr Tydfil shows that only a quarter of the population had been born in the town and by the late nineteenth century, in virtually every coalfield, you could hear voices from all over England, as well as Welsh and both Lowland and Highland Scottish accents.[3] There was also a smattering of people – often dismissed as 'trampers' (later 'tramps') – who had fled the potato famine and travelled across the Irish Sea to find work. From the miners' point of view, the only way to safeguard their jobs was through a trade union which could stop the coal-owners from breaking local strikes by bringing in 'blackleg' miners from other areas.*

By the late nineteenth century, miners had organised themselves into local trade unions in many coalfields. But because the owners insisted that each mine was a separate business, pay deals were struck pit by pit. When colliery proprietors in Yorkshire rejected a pay demand, plans were laid for the formation of a national trade union, which was finally agreed at a meeting in a temperance hall at Newport, South Wales, in November 1888. By 1910, the Miners' Federation of Great Britain had almost 600,000 members and was the biggest trade union in the country.

The miners knew that if there were ever to be a determined, drawn-out confrontation in which violence occurred, the forces of 'law and order' would be on the side of the employers. It was ever thus. The resources of the state are not limitless, but they always

---

* The term is said to originate from the claim that miners who continued to work could be identified if you rolled up their trouser legs and discovered they had black legs. It is also said to originate with the fact that rooks – birds freighted with unhappy symbolism – have black legs.

tend towards the protection of property, as the miners learned in July 1893, when the extremely wealthy machinery magnate Lord Masham and his neighbouring proprietor, John Shaw at Featherstone near Wakefield, demanded that their men take a 25% pay cut, since the price of coal had fallen by over one-third in the previous three years. Unsurprisingly, the miners refused. The mine-owners, and other proprietors then locked the men out of the pits and by the end of July, hundreds of thousands of men were without work. The chief constable was away on his holidays, having foolishly decided before-hand to send a quarter of the police force to Doncaster racecourse, 'looking for pickpockets' at the St Leger race meeting.

There being no 'reserve' police force, when Lord Masham's colliery manager asked for police protection from the mob he said was menacing the colliery buildings, the only thing to be done was to wire to Bradford for troops to be despatched. A Captain Digby Barker arrived at the pit with a detachment of twenty-six men from the South Staffordshire Regiment. A local magistrate recited the phrases of the Riot Act telling the mob at the pit to go home. He then seems to have panicked, giving the captain written permission to open fire, but asking verbally if they could use blank cartridges. The soldiers had not been issued with blanks, so the magistrate then asked the captain if his men could please shoot as little as possible. A reporter for a local newspaper claimed later to have heard him say 'For God's sake don't hit anybody.' The captain ordered two of the soldiers to fire at the ground in front of the crowd, but no one seemed to be injured, which gave some of the mob the idea that the soldiers were indeed firing blanks. Stones began to rain down on the troops. Captain Barker ordered eight of his men to fire two shots each and the stone-throwing stopped at once. Two colliery workers, James Gibbs, a part-time Sunday school teacher, and James Duggan, who had been perched on scaf-folding watching the trouble, had been hit. An inquest jury later returned a verdict of justifiable homicide.

Duggan's funeral was something of a political stunt, a theatrical affair involving an open coffin, a procession led by local MPs and 500 representatives of local organisations, the Featherstone brass band, a column of mourners stretching for hundreds of yards, and at the cemetery, fellow members of the Oddfellows friendly society shaking hands across the grave, which was next to that of James Gibbs, the other victim. When the funeral was over, many of the miners gathered at a meeting in a field behind the local pub, where they were harangued from the back of a waggon by Robert Cunninghame Graham, an Old Harrovian adventurer and charlatan who numbered Peter Kropotkin, Joseph Conrad, John Galsworthy and Buffalo Bill among his friends and who claimed to be the rightful king of Scotland. He told the mourners to see the deaths in the context of the titanic struggle between capital and labour.

Few seem to have taken him seriously, but with the killing of British working men by British soldiers in England, a line had been crossed. Most of all, perhaps, it showed how unsuited the army was to domestic peacekeeping: the soldiers' Lee Metford rifles, which fired .303 bullets, had a range of 3,000 yards. The South Staffordshires, who had fired the fatal shots, were a relatively new regiment, one of whose predecessors had been part of the humiliating British defeat at the Battle of Isandlwana only fourteen years previously. As the general secretary of the Yorkshire Miners Association remarked, 'It appears to me that although they [the army] could not beat the Zulus they seem to be desirous of showing that they can shoot down colliers.' The official inquiry ended in a fudge, saying the army had been right to open fire, with the families of the dead men given compensation of £100 each. The ship of state sailed on. In Yorkshire mining villages they nicknamed the Home Secretary, who had ordered the inquiry, 'Bloody' Asquith.

* * *

Coal-mining was an activity in which periodic unrest was inevitable – an industry in which people with nothing much were required to risk their lives every day to make more money for those who already had plenty. The rise of steam power had made this brutal business integral to the national economy and it was only a question of time before the men who extracted it from the ground realised what power they had if they could only act together. It was a filthy, sweaty job in which all the physical dangers were faced by the men underground, with the financial risks – such as they were – borne by the proprietors. There was mutual incomprehension between the landowners and the pitmen, who could not have been drawn from more distant parts of the class structure. Enquiring minds began to ask if it needed to be like this. Under the deceptively dully titled *The Miners' Next Step*, a group of radical South Wales trade unionists (members of the Plebs' League) argued that 'all leaders become corrupt, in spite of their own good intentions', by becoming 'big men' in their community. This looked like a deliberate attack on William 'Mabon' Abraham, the mountainous, bearded Methodist lay preacher who had become the miners' chief advocate in South Wales. The miners, said the Plebs, needed a single national union to fight for them, but it should never again allow the leaders to portray its members as 'the mob'. As for the industry, it should be under the control of the workers, with elected managers. Political theorists could immediately identify this formula as 'syndicalism', a French political manifesto then increasingly popular across continental Europe. When South Wales miners were given the opportunity to vote on the proposed reorganisation of their union, they rejected it soundly.

Most of all, the commodity about which the entire industry was built had no constant value. The price of coal was entirely determined by what someone would pay for it. When the prices they were willing to pay went up, there was money for everyone. When prices went down it became just another rock, while the costs of operating the mine remained the same, and the easiest thing to do to balance the books was to reduce the amount they paid the miners. From an employer's point of view, the fluctuation was like being expected to pay the same for a shovelful of gravel as a shovelful of silver. For the miner, the calculus was different. He had to work just as hard, whatever the price. And he had the same number of mouths to feed. Small wonder he felt aggrieved when the mine companies suggested lowering what he got paid.

The 'Featherstone Massacre' had been the most notorious of the events in the coal strike of 1893. Those who stopped work were members of the newly founded trade union, the Miners' Federation of Great Britain, the first national miners' organisation. Local miners who had already accepted the sliding scale of payment which the mine-owners now wished to impose on everyone – like those in Northumberland and Durham – were unable to join the federation. The Featherstone miners agreed to return to work for the old rate of pay for the next couple of months. Many trade union histories tout this as a 'victory' for the miners. If so, it was an empty one, for the minimum-wage issue remained unresolved for over a decade.

What workers were paid and what trade unions were entitled to expect had now entered the bloodstream of politics. When the six Tolpuddle Martyrs had been transported to Australia in 1834 for the crime of organising a union, it had seemed a fringe issue. Within sixty years, the rights of working men and women were a commonplace in political discussion. The professed beliefs of the unions were spelled out in the slogans on the banners which pits had adopted from medieval trade guilds at events like the Durham Miners' Gala, an annual fiesta which had begun in 1871.

The pictures on these banners were generally unsophisticated and their slogans simple. (Historically, most were executed by manufacturers in the south of England, the best known being the company of George Tutill, whose fairground connections had encouraged him to develop ways of painting on silk.) The banners often depicted heroes of the labour movement or the colliery from which the marchers came. What was most striking about them was the mildness of the slogans and quotations, whether they were home-grown or lifted from Bunyan, Milton or Shakespeare. It would be little surprise to learn that a lodge banner advocated 'peace and love'.

For by the turn of the twentieth century something quite significant had changed. The miners were not on their own any longer, and the conditions under which they worked were no more the exclusive preserve of their bosses. Governments would not allow it. An Inspectorate of Mines had been established after the horrors revealed by the 1842 inquiry into child and female labour underground and by the end of 1910, no fewer than twenty-nine more laws affecting the mining industry had been passed by Parliament, which now had to pay attention to a broader electorate. Although women and poorer men were still denied the franchise, by 1900 nearly 7 million people were entitled to vote in elections, and the rapidly rising levels of literacy in the country made them hungry for newspapers, which loved nothing more than a decent tragedy incurred in the extraction of a commodity increasingly taken for granted. The cost of protecting miners made it more expensive to extract coal, and many of the owners were unhappy. But they had to put up with it.

And the nature of union leadership was changing, too. Old Liberals, like the first president of the South Wales Miners' Federation, William Abraham – 'Mabon' was his bardic name – were elbowed aside by a new, more radical generation, like William John, chapel deacon and local councillor, and John Hoopla, who both later went to prison for incitement. Organised labour had tended to support Liberal policies, and the party liked to promote compromise – a 'we're all in this together' approach. This inevitably made trade union leaders inclined to seek a way out of confrontation, but it was all a bit feeble for anyone who saw the mining industry as expressing a fundamental clash of interests. In February 1900 a Labour Representation Committee was formed, with the Scottish former miner, Ramsay MacDonald – only forty-three, yet already beginning to be seen as Labour's 'Grand Old Man' – as its secretary. The committee managed to get two MPs into Westminster in the parliamentary elections that autumn, including the former child 'trapper' or 'pony boy', James Keir Hardie, voted in for Merthyr Tydfil. It marked the effective end of the link between trade unions and the Liberal Party. Legal judgements like the following year's Taff Vale Railway case, which held that unions taking industrial action were liable for any employers' loss of profits, sufficiently enraged trade union members that at the next election, in 1906 – a crashing Liberal victory – the Labour Representation Committee (soon renamed the Labour Party) found themselves with twenty-nine MPs. The same year, the Liberal government gave unions immunity from prosecution for damages caused by a strike. Two years later they stipulated that miners should work no more than an eight-hour day. None of which did anything much to dent the wealth of the future Lord Rhondda of the Cambrian Combine.

There was something about mining which seemed to make the men who worked with coal more restless – the words 'militant' and 'miners' running easily together. Was it the dangers of their occupation and the familiarity it gave them with sudden death? Perhaps it was the fact that they tended to live in self-contained, often isolated communities. Perhaps there was something about the hard physical toil of their work and the life-and-death importance of trust between workmates. Was it the influence of religion? Was it that though the industry had rented their bodies for the working day, their minds were their own? Was it that their occupation left few illusions about the class struggle and that their managers seem often to have been brutish figures and their ultimate bosses parodies of privilege? Partly, perhaps, it was because they considered themselves an elite, answerable with their lives for their job, but owing nobody else anything.

It is easy to see why politically conscientious miners should have come to consider a sliding scale of pay to be a sell-out. It was accepting the bosses' rules – the price determined in coal markets did not make much difference to the sweat and risk of a miner's job.

In the summer of 1910, the owners of the Cambrian Combine in South Wales decided to have a new seam of coal dug out at the Penycraig pit for one of their subsidiaries, the Naval Collieries. The Combine was an enormous concern, employing about 12,000 miners in 1910 (it would grow bigger, as it took over even more of its competitors: the owners planned to gain total control of the hugely profitable South Wales Steam Coal trade). The company sent a preliminary group of eighty miners to discover the quality of the coal and how easy it was to extract. The men repeatedly reported that it was a difficult seam to work, narrow and wet, and with many 'abnormal places'. The South Wales miners were bound by the sliding scale agreed by their union leaders over a quarter of a century previously, in which wages were dependent upon the price of coal. The miners complained that the harsh conditions meant they could barely earn enough to live on. The company responded that they were deliberately working slowly. The miners said that since their pay depended upon what they extracted, that wasn't much of an argument: do the maths.

The owners now set a rate of pay for the miners of a shilling and ninepence per ton of coal they each dug. The men demanded two shillings and sixpence a ton. There was deadlock. On 1 September 1910, the general manager of the company, Leonard Llewellyn – a man with a reputation for great bravery, but also for ruthlessness – locked out the mine's 950 workers. Miners at other collieries then stopped work. By November, the strike had spread not only to the 12,000 miners working for the Combine, but throughout the South Wales collieries. Picket lines were established at many Combine pits, to prevent the owners trying to resume production by shipping in strike-breakers.

Llewellyn turned out to have a talent for public relations, informing newspaper reporters that the miners had abandoned 300 horses underground at the Glamorgan Colliery. Newspapers reported that King George was worried about them. In response, Keir Hardie commented that 'a dead pit pony is a £20 loss. A dead collier costs nothing except heartache to those left behind.' Feelings were soon running high and the mood was volatile. Late in the afternoon of 7 November 1910, striking miners pelted the homes of colliery managers with stones and bricks, and police provided an escort for officials going into the pumphouse of the one colliery still in action, a vital support system that stopped nearby mine-workings flooding. There has always been something especially alarming about strikes by miners; it now set off fear among the law-abiding about the unknown dangers emerging from underground and night-monsters prowling the streets. As George Dangerfield described the strike at the Cambrian Combine, 'There was terror in the air, which never quite appears to have taken shape. Rumours flew up and down. The miners were armed with revolvers, they had looted quantities of high explosives, they planned to blow up the manager's house.'[4]

The Glamorgan constabulary was already seriously stretched, by a separate strike, at Aberdare in the neighbouring Cynon Valley. Here the colliery was operated by another huge South Wales mining conglomerate, Powell Duffryn, also intent on dominating the market by aggressively taking over possible competitors: by 1908 their operations were spread over 15,000 acres. The Powell

Duffryn miners were irritated by the owners' insistence on trying
to bring to the surface ever increasing amounts of coal from deteriorating seams, at ever lower costs. So when the manager at the
colliery stopped a man taking home a block of waste timber from
the mine, to use as household fuel, there was uproar. The miners
said they had been allowed to do it for years. It was a piddling
issue, but in an atmosphere of distaste and distrust, it was enough
to set off a strike and soon thousands of men had walked out. The
strikers were led by Charles Stanton, with a reputation as the greatest firebrand in South Wales (in a confrontation with the police
during an earlier dispute he had been charged with firing a gun
and sentenced to six months in prison). Stanton, the first secretary
of the local Socialist Society, was a vain man rather in love with his
image as a rabble-rouser: he believed in confrontation. (As luck
would have it, he looked a little like Arthur Scargill, the man who
led the miners through their disastrous strike in the 1980s.) The
dispute quickly got quite ugly. Anyone who did not support the
strike was in danger at least of serious abuse, and there were
numerous incidents in which people seen as strike-breakers were
beaten up. Some were attacked and had clothes torn off by gangs
of women loyal to the strike. On the same evening, strikers stopped
a train, smashed its windows and dragged out passengers. On 29
October, Stanton telephoned the mine manager with the message
'if there is going to be any blacklegging over this there is going to
be murder. My God, I mean it.' Though he claimed it was not a
threat, he did not deny saying the words, which were widely
reported in the newspapers. The mine manager requested a heavy
police presence in the area. Unsurprisingly, the chief constable of
Glamorgan took the dangers of unrest – and possibly worse – seriously.

   As ever, so much depended upon the characters of those
involved. The chief constable, Lionel Lindsay, was an unimpressive
man who had found his way into his starting rank of superinten-

dent much eased by the fact that his father had been chief constable at the time. Confronted now with a strike at the Cambrian Combine, he panicked and requested military support. Winston Churchill was Home Secretary, and his name is still reviled in parts of South Wales for deploying soldiers against the strikers. The accusation was pressed by Keir Hardie, who made capital out of claiming – with no evidence – that Churchill had said 'If the Welsh are striking over hunger, then we must fill their bellies with lead. Churchill is also accused (though the source is again never cited) of having told the army their job was to 'drive the rats back down their holes'. The remark is an excellent example of how a lie can be halfway round the world before truth has got its boots on, for he never said the words. It was, anyway, the secretary for war, Richard Haldane, who ordered infantry and cavalrymen to the area: when Churchill heard of the decision at about 10 a.m. on 8 November, the infantry train was ordered to stop at Swindon, while the detachment of the 18th Hussars got no further than Cardiff.* Churchill instructed that troops were not to be used unless and until police had been deployed beforehand. He sent instead 200 Metropolitan Police, who proceeded in an orderly direction towards South Wales, and arrived too late to be much use to anybody.

By now the local police had already clubbed one miner to death and an emergency purchase order had been made for 300 new truncheons to replace those broken or lost. There was rioting in Tonypandy, in which over sixty shops were ransacked – according to local legend, a chemist's shop belonging to local hero and Welsh international rugby captain and winger, Willie Llewellyn, was deliberately spared. The local police seem to have been absent because they had been sent to protect the property of the coal-

---

* Did anyone comment on the fact that soldiers could be deployed at short notice because the railway had been built to service the mines?

owners. The Metropolitan Police detachment deployed when the trouble had subsided.

Throughout that winter, the soldiers stayed in the area – not, as legend has it, as hated oppressors, but quite well liked. By the time they left, in March, it was said that every Lancashire Fusilier who had been deployed there could sing at least two verses of 'Cwm Rhondda'. The soldiers had organised football matches with local children and the *Rhondda Leader* remarked of their leaving from the station that 'many regret the departure of the Fusiliers as they had become very popular during their stay ... After the boarding of the train the Fusiliers crowded round the windows shaking hands with their many friends.' The strikers had been fortunate (or the authorities wise) that the military commander, General Nevil Macready, was a man of sensible views, who believed in the right to strike, declined to get stampeded into violence by nervous local magistrates, and found the employers high-handed and unreliable ('information from the managers was in practically every case so exaggerated as to be worthless', he reported afterwards to the Home Office).[5]

The Cambrian Combine miners held out until September 1911. The Powell Duffryn men had returned to work at the beginning of January that year, having achieved nothing much.* Sensible men had done what sensible people usually do, and come to a compromise. The two South Wales disputes were not the first time that soldiers had been sent into coalfields when local police feared they would be overwhelmed. But it poisoned the air for generations.

*   *   *

* Their leader, Charles Stanton, became a 'hang the kaiser' jingoist during the First World War and when Keir Hardie died in 1915 ran against the Labour Party and miners' candidate in the by-election which followed. He won. He ended his days managing a pub in north London.

The first national strike by miners began at Alfreton in Derbyshire on 26 February 1912, with the objective of winning a minimum wage. *The Times* believed that it was 'the greatest catastrophe that has threatened the country since the Spanish Armada', and proclaimed loftily – and wrongly – that a national strike was 'too monstrous a thing to be possible in the circumstances'.[6] The archbishops of York and Canterbury produced a prayer to be read in churches, begging God to 'allay all danger and bitterness'. Assorted newspaper columnists told the miners they had achieved a great victory just by persuading employers of the need for a minimum wage and that they should return to work. Instead, nearly a million miners came out on strike and vital industries across the country began to close for lack of fuel. The government panicked. Unable to find any obvious quick negotiated settlement (it did not exist), it presented Parliament with its own Minimum Wages Bill, which, while it did not give the strikers exactly what they had been demanding, did steal some of their clothes. Just before Easter and hardly a month after the *Times* declaration, Asquith's government passed a Coal Mines Act, introducing a minimum wage. Though it stuck in the craw of some trade unionists to acknowledge it, the villain of Tonypandy, Winston Churchill, as president of the Board of Trade, had been the person who introduced legally enforceable minimum wages in various low-paid industries like chain and paper box manufacturing in 1909.* In 1912, the legislation was extended to include coal-mining.

Individual employers had argued that there was no justification for a minimum wage, since conditions varied from mine to mine: the strike was bringing misery to the poorest workers in the land, thus strengthening their approach to the minimum wage with a

---

* As late as 1950, when campaigning as leader of the Conservative Party in that year's general election, Churchill found that Labour candidates in South Wales were attacking him for what they claimed to be his role in the Tonypandy 'massacre'.

suddenly discovered social conscience. Churchill had already explained to Parliament the need for a legally binding wage by saying that the laws of supply and demand did not work properly in industries where one side was much more powerful in wage negotiations than the other. But the involvement of government recognised that industries like mining were simply too important to the nation to be left to the market. Miners were not the only manual workers to be locked in disputes – Southampton seamen, Liverpool transport workers, Clydeside sewing-machine employees, employees at the Lancashire cotton mills and at jute mills in Dundee, to say nothing of strikes in London and other big cities, indicated there was a new spirit abroad. In the economy produced by steam power, everything was interdependent. Without miners, there was no coal, and without dockers and transport workers, it could not be moved, anyway. The 1912 coal strike had thrown nearly 200,000 railwaymen out of work and foundries, factories and shipyards all ceased to function.

The early years of the twentieth century are often portrayed as a long Edwardian summer, all parasols and cordials on the terrace. But among the less privileged, there was something in the air. Wages in most industries were static, while prices rose. Discontent was spreading. Trade union leaders fingered their waistcoats nervously. In 1911, no fewer than 872 different strikes had broken out. Even schoolchildren were at it: that September, when school students at Llanelli protested against the caning of a pupil, they were followed by others in over sixty towns across the country. When in January 1912 miners voted by a margin of four to one for a national strike, with the miners in Durham – which had been long considered an outpost of increasingly unfashionable Liberalism (their leader was even a Liberal MP) – coming out in favour of industrial action, the government abandoned its previous decision not to get involved. A minimum-wage bill was rushed through Parliament. It wasn't precisely what the miners had been fighting for (because wages were to be set locally, rather than nationally), but a precedent had been established.

The *British Socialist* drew a deeper lesson. 'It is absurd, truly, that a mere handful of plutocrats should be masters and owners of the mineral wealth of our country; of the coal which is the very foundation of our national life. Without coal, our industries are idle; our navy is helpless; our food supplies are cut off, and we are stricken with national paralysis', it said. 'Therefore, nationalise the mines.'[7] It would be the miners' dream for years to come.

The 1912 publication of *The Miners' Next Step*, with its argument for 'open hostility' between miners and their employers, was as close as Britain came to a revolutionary text of its own. The influence of the book spread – the communist author, Robin Page Arnot, later claimed that it became a 'household word' among miners. It would be exaggerating to claim that this now scarcely-heard-of tract achieved anything like the success of Samuel Smiles' *Self-Help*, but the mood had changed. The most powerfully subversive book was *The Ragged Trousered Philanthropists*, published in 1914. No other book – and certainly not Oscar Wilde's 1891 essay 'The Soul Of Man Under Socialism' – captured the new political spirit as effectively. In the 1950s – forty years after its publication – a writer in *Marxist Quarterly* claimed that you could go into any meeting room of the British working class and find at least one man present who would say of *The Ragged Trousered Philanthropists* 'that book brought me into the movement. That book made me a convinced socialist. That book altered the whole course and direction of my life.'[8] The story, written by 'Robert Tressell' (real name Robert Noonan, an Irish house-painter), depicts exploited workers as the 'philanthropists' of the title, willing to work for a pittance so their employers can become richer whilst remaining resistant to the notion that their lives are as worthwhile as those of their 'betters'. The novel's hero, Frank Owen, attempts to convince other workers that they have to stop making excuses for their lot. In the chapter 'The Great Money Trick', he satirises capitalism by cutting up slices of bread into small squares which the workers endlessly swop for tokens. When the game stops, the capitalist is well fed and the workers on the brink of starvation. It was a picture immediately recognisable to most miners.

9

Does Your Country
Really Need You?

In 1913 there were well over a million men working as miners. Between them that year they extracted from the ground 292 million tons of coal, about a third of which was exported overseas. In the north-east of England alone, about a quarter of a million men worked as miners, but the locations of the coalfields meant that mining was spread right across the country.

That was the year that D. H. Lawrence published his unforgettable picture of life in a mining village in *Sons and Lovers*. There are few surviving postcards of what the colliery villages were like – they were not, by any stretch of the imagination, 'picturesque'. Lawrence described Eastwood, the place of his birth, as 'an ugly little town in an ugly little county'. As he saw it, 'the great crime which the moneyed classes and promoters of industry committed in the palmy Victorian days was the condemning of the workers to ugliness, ugliness, ugliness'.[1] His fictionalised miner father in *Sons and Lovers* is an uncivilised thug, who approves of one of the other characters in the book because 'Er's like me ... Er canna see what there is i' books, ter sit borin' your nose in 'em for.'[2] You did not need to read books to hew coal. Like other sensitive young people in tough communities since, Lawrence was appalled by the way that inner landscapes could become as bleak as the world around.

But it was coal that produced the warmth and light by which books might be read, and the wherewithal for people to buy them. Britain was powerful and prosperous in part because of the ugliness of the pit villages. And it was because of the country's power and wealth that it could not stand apart from the catastrophe that overwhelmed Europe and the world a year later, when the teenage Gavrilo Princip murdered Archduke Franz Ferdinand and his wife and so set off the First World War.

War presented the miners with a dilemma. Their concerns about pay and conditions were as real as ever, yet they were quite obviously as much part of the national war effort as many of those wearing uniforms. But, unlike those in khaki, they were neither under military discipline nor the King's Regulations. They were, in ideological theory at least, bound by a doctrine of international class solidarity. At what point – if at all – did the demands of country override those of class, community and occupation?

The British government was under no illusions about the importance of coal, and soon began to restrict supplies, while warning darkly about the unpatriotic nature of hoarding. The government had been warning of imminent coal shortages almost since the announcement of hostilities, and by the winter of 1914 coal supplies were restricted and street lamps dimmed. On 30 January 1915, the Black Country newspaper the *Dudley Herald* reported local coal merchants' apologies that they were unable to promise deliveries. 'Every day we are either without coal or without men. The collieries are in the same position. Two factors are making for shortage – the rolling stock on the railways, owing to the demands of the government, and the scarcity of labour.'[3] Since virtually every household in the land depended upon coal for heating and cooking, the consequences were soon felt everywhere. Within days a 'Coal Famine' was reported, with dark stories of people hoarding coal in cellars and coal merchants profiteering. The coal queue was soon to become a familiar sight and all social classes were affected by the problem of how to keep warm, a 'young married woman' recalling 'I shall never forget the worry about coal ... My mother was old and ill, our house large and old-fashioned, with a huge kitchen range and no other apparatus for cooking or obtaining hot water. Then came a day when my mother was worse and we had no coal, and I drove round London in a cab with a laundry basket begging just a few lumps from this friend and that.'[4] In areas where they could do so, families scavenged on the beaches for something to burn, and the newspapers were full of instructions of how to make burnable 'briquettes' from tar, sawdust and clay. By October 1916, coal would be rationed according to the number of rooms in a family house. The following year was, for civilians, the worst of the war, with almost everything in short supply and lengthy queues for anything worth having.

Politically, the war was the opposite of the doctrine of international fraternity which underpinned the labour movement. In August 1914 – the very month that Britain joined the war – the increasingly infirm miners' leader and founder of the Labour Party, Keir Hardie, had delivered an electrifying speech in Trafalgar Square telling his supporters 'You have no quarrel with Germany. German workmen have no quarrel with their French comrades. The French worker has no quarrel with his Austrian comrades. If that be so, why are we on the verge of the greatest calamity Europe has ever seen? We are told there are international treaties which compel us to take part. Who made those treaties? The people had no voice in them.'[5] A statement issued in his name argued that 'the workers of all countries must strain every nerve to prevent their governments committing them to war. Hold vast demonstrations against war ... There is no time to lose. Down with the rule of brute force!'

In South Wales, where a quarter of a million miners had raised 57 million tons of coal in 1913,[6] the leading figure in the Miners' Federation, Arthur J. Cook, wrote angrily in the *Porth Gazette* about how sickening it was that government could find funds to supply the military, but would not help the poor.[7] But he was wailing in the wind. Enthusiasm for war was undimmed and flag-waving crowds were not to be denied. Within a short time of being summoned to London to become War Secretary, the imperial hero, Kitchener of Khartoum, pronounced that the war would not – as some misguided optimists shouted – be 'over by Christmas', but would last for years and be won by the last million men. The immediate challenge, therefore, was that Britain did not have a big enough army. Unlike its European neighbours, most of which had vast conscript forces, the British army was one that you joined by choice: the nation did not trust great standing armies. With superior training and motivation, the performance of the British army in combat was better than most others. But its numbers were tiny in comparison with its potential enemies. Kitchener ('a poor general but a wonderful poster', the prime minister's wife, Margot Asquith, is supposed to have said, through clenched teeth[8]) frantically appealed for volunteers to join up. It was easy enough to satisfy the entry standards for the army, but critically, it left enlistment in the hands not of the state, but of the individual citizen.

Miners were the biggest group of industrial workers in Britain, and as swept up in the fervour of war volunteering as many other citizens. Soon many mines found too few men turning up for work because they had taken the king's shilling. By March 1915, four in ten of the miners of military age – 191,170 men – had already joined up.[9] Inevitably, most of them were the youngest and fittest in the industry and as the war went on, coal production fell, because they had left the mines. Women began to be employed in surface jobs at the collieries like sieving and sorting.[10]

In the industry the enlisted miners had left behind, the great liberal historian, A. J. P. Taylor, liked to claim that Britain adopted what he called 'war socialism' – amounting to a truce between workers and employers, in which miners agreed not to go on strike, in return for limits on the profits of companies engaged in war work and government arbitration in any disputes. This was partly true, but it took time to develop and by early 1915 the price of food had risen by almost a quarter from what it had been before the war began. Engineers in Glasgow – vital to the war effort – went on strike for better pay, eventually agreeing to have their case go to arbitration. The Red Clydesiders were followed in March 1915 by miners from South Wales, whose rising at Tonypandy five years earlier had already established a reputation for militancy.

The South Wales strike was not against the conduct of the war, or in support of their leaders' views that the conflict was no concern of theirs. They struck for the usual reason: they wanted to be paid better. The Miners' Federation had demanded a 20% pay rise, to compensate them for the inflation which had seized the country and made their wages worth less. The miners were well aware that the war was terrific for the coal-owners' profits, but oddly unconfident about their own potential power: this was the first full-scale war of the industrial age. The mine-owners were as cussedly individualist as ever and rejected a national agreement, point-blank. In most coalfields, unions and management haggled over local arrangements and managed to agree deals. The big exception was South Wales, where the Monmouthshire and South Wales Coal-Owners' Association refused to offer more than a 10% raise; 200,000 men stopped work, believing that there was more or less nothing the government could do about it. They were right. Suddenly, the nation was confronted with the truth that there was nothing to be gained by having the most powerful navy in the world if it couldn't go anywhere. The nation stared into an abyss. Yet the miners were oddly reticent. 1915 was to teach them that in future they were better off with Labour. Most of the leaders of the miners' unions were Liberals and they appealed to the Liberal prime minister, Herbert Asquith, but he was distracted by one thing after another – the fiasco of the Gallipoli campaign, the resignation of the First Sea Lord 'Jackie' Fisher and the *Daily Mail* holding Asquith's War Secretary, Lord Kitchener, responsible for the 'Tragic Blunder' which had resulted in a shortage of shells on the Western Front. Forced into a corner, Asquith invited Labour politicians to join a wartime coalition and made Lloyd George minister of munitions. A Munitions of War Act prohibited private interests from obstructing or imperilling the safety of the state and made strikes in the armaments industry illegal.

The recently appointed president of the Board of Trade, Sir Walter Runciman,* the son of a millionaire Tyneside shipping magnate and a great personal friend of Margot Asquith, reached for the reassurance of the new law. The cross-party coalition, hoping to draw on new reserves of sympathy from their Labour-supporting voters, decided to make one last concerted effort to break the miners' will. Newspapers began to scream for mining areas to be put under military rule.[11] The *Illustrated London News* suggested the South Wales strike was the source of 'utmost rejoicing in Germany and Austria'. The *Western Mail* contented itself with an unsubtle cartoon showing a Welsh miner sitting in a sewer of greed and treachery. It did not take long for the king to sign the proclamation drafted for him. Soon, a copy had appeared at the gates of every colliery in South Wales, warning miners that if they did not report for work, they would be committing an offence and fined £5 a day until they returned to work. Many – especially those prevented from entering the army because the government had judged it was more important that they kept mining – were furious at suggestions they were unpatriotic and semi-criminal.

But the miners' real strength lay in their numbers. It was clearly impossible to arrest 200,000 men, and the government knew it. On 19 June, four days after the strike began, Lloyd George, Runciman and Arthur Henderson, the Scottish foundryman who had become the first Labour Cabinet minister, rushed to Cardiff to try to

---

* Runciman, a teetotal Liberal who came across as the archetypal capitalist, later acted out the megalomaniac's dream and bought the Hebridean island of Eigg. After his death, the island was sold again, to various eccentrics. It is now 'community-owned' and powered by renewable energy.

persuade the miners to return to work. Despite government threats, press insults and employers' rejections, they failed. It then took less than twenty-four hours for them to agree a deal with the miners which gave them just about everything they wanted, including a pay rise of 18.5%, to keep just ahead of vicious wartime inflation. From now on, David Lloyd George was a regular wild-haired spectacle in the coalfields. He had the ear of many of them (he had grown up speaking Welsh as his first language) and beseeched them with flattery ('you are the best organised trade union in existence ... Your men always follow their leaders') and fear ('I need hardly tell you that a strike in the coal mines would be worse for us than a German victory'*).[12]

Lloyd George was successful in persuading miners with a series of speeches in which he argued that 'In peace and war King Coal is the paramount lord of industry. It enters into every article of consumption and utility. It is our real international coinage. When we buy goods, food, and raw material abroad we pay not in gold, but in coal. We pay in diamonds, except that they are black, and not in gold. Coal brings meat and bread, say, from the Argentine, and brings it all the way ... We cannot do without coal. In war-time it is life for us, and death for our foes. Coal is the most terrible of enemies, and the most potent of friends.'[13] Asquith had decided he really preferred the stick to the carrot, wondering whether strikers shouldn't be charged with treason.[14] Had his ideas become public, there might have been violence on the streets, especially since everyone knew the mine-owners were making vast profits from

---

* A strike in the mines would be more serious than disruption by engineers, because it would stop the production not only of coal, but of trinitrotoluene (TNT), which was manufactured from toluol (toluene), which had itself been distilled from coal. The British mitigated the danger of a loss of coal by staging a daring raid in 1915 on the Netherlands, which was neutral in the war, but where a plant had been developed to produce TNT from oil. They took the plant to pieces and reassembled it in Britain.

the wartime demand for coal.[15] But with the country in the midst of a war for national survival and their own family members at the front, their sympathies were mixed. After hearing Lloyd George's entreaties, the president of the Miners' Federation of Great Britain moved a resolution that 'every effort should be made by owners and workmen alike to secure the greatest possible output of coal in the interests of the nation'.[16] Nine days later, a law took effect limiting the price of coal.

But inflation was all the time destroying the value of money and successive wage claims continued to break down the government's pay and conciliation machinery. In November 1916 there was another strike in Wales over pay. At the end of the month, the whole South Wales coalfield was brought under state control, and when Asquith resigned a few days later, his successor Lloyd George let it be known that from now on, the entire British mining industry would be controlled by the state. Some of the miners' leaders were, anyway, thoroughly disenchanted by the war. The enormous number of lives being lost was obvious and when the government decided to take a further 20,000 men from the mines and to put them in the army, it was the last straw for some. The young radical A. J. Cook, later to serve as general secretary of the Miners' Federation during the General Strike, went out of his way to obstruct the recruiting effort, posting notices at South Wales collieries advising men to ignore instructions to report for military service. In a speech in April 1917 Cook explained that 'I am no pacifist when war is necessary to free my class from the enslavement of capitalism … But the interests of my class are not benefitted by this war … War against war must be the workers' cry'.[17] This was clearly seditious talk. Cook had escaped arrest for fear of provoking a miners' strike. But the following year he taunted the government once too often, with 'I have two brothers in the army who were forced to join, but I say No! I will be shot before I go to fight. Are you going to allow us to be taken to the war? If so, I say there will not be a ton of coal for the navy.'[18]

By the end of 1917, revolutionary Russia had abandoned the war after mass desertions in the army, and numerous occasions on which peasant soldiers preferred to fraternise with the enemy than to shoot at them. When the new Bolshevik government made peace with the Germans, opponents of the war in Britain, including Cook, had been emboldened. Our old friend Lionel Lindsay had by now risen to become chief constable of Glamorgan. For years he had wanted to have Cook prosecuted for subversion, but balked through fear of widespread unrest if he did so. Now he got his way. Cook was arrested under the Defence of the Realm Act and sentenced to three months in prison for inciting disaffection. More or less exactly as had been predicted, South Wales miners threatened to go on strike and he was released a few weeks later. Cook made no bones about being a syndicalist* who believed in strikes. He became a romantic figure to the left for his open opposition to the war, the long periods under (not very competent) police surveillance and the months in prison for sedition.

Quite apart from the digging of coal, there was one area of the fighting in which the miners were indispensable. No one had expected that the front lines would become so stationary so fast, but by 1915, both sides had decided that the main way to take advantage of the stalemate was to burrow forward under the enemy front line and to detonate explosives from tunnels beneath it.† In the British army most men recruited for the task were

---

* French in origin, a philosophy which generally believed in the power of strikes to reform a capitalist system – and possibly to overthrow capitalism in its entirety.

† The first use of mines had been just before Christmas 1914, when the Germans tunnelled beneath the British front lines near Festubert and detonated hundreds of pounds of high explosive; 800 men of the Indian Corps were lost in the explosion and subsequent attack.

miners, railway tunnellers and sewer diggers. One of the men sought out was 'Empire Jack', Major John Norton-Griffiths who had tunnelled for gold in South Africa and the Ivory Coast, before returning to Britain to build seaside piers, underground railways and municipal drainage systems. He also got himself elected to the House of Commons, and when war broke out, raised his own regiment, the 2nd King Edward's Horse, which included plenty of other 'colonials'. 'Empire Jack' recommended enlisting some of the 'clay kickers' who had been digging parts of the London Underground network. They were soon joined in over twenty specialist Royal Engineer tunnelling companies by miners who had been recruited particularly for their underground experience and were often paid better than other soldiers, because of their specialist skills. The maximum age for soldiering was raised for miners who wanted to work as tunnellers and basic training reduced to a mere week. The 25,000 tunnellers were supported by 50,000 infantry, often drawn from the 'bantam' battalions made up of men too short to meet the army's usual height requirements. Canadian, Australian and New Zealand forces also had tunnelling units.

'Clay kickers' seems to have often been a general term for men who worked underground. But in its original sense it was a specialist technique used in front-line tunnelling. The tunnellers worked by candlelight and in silence, for each side knew that the other was doing the same thing. When occasionally a tunnel under construction broke through into an enemy tunnel, the underground close-quarter fighting, with knives, bayonets, spades, or even lengths of wood, was appalling. The 'clay-kicking' technique was judged to be quicker and quieter than digging by pick and shovel. It required one man to lie on his back on a wooden cross and use his legs to work a sharpened spade into the earth or rock ahead and to twist it, to extract the spoil. A second man loaded the spoil into a bag, which would then be removed by a third member of the team rolling a trolley with rubber tyres on wooden rails. The further they dug, the longer the wood-supported tunnel they left behind: the tunnellers knowing that the enemy were probably listening for noises underground as intently as they were. (British listening devices included modified stethoscopes, and 'vibration detectors', one end of which was sunk into the ground, while the other was held between the teeth.)

It was slow, painstaking and dangerous work. But it yielded results, most spectacularly at Messines in June 1917, where the British had spent months laying nineteen mines in tunnels beneath the German front line. When they were detonated, an estimated 10,000 German soldiers were killed. Lloyd George claimed to have heard the explosion from his country house in Surrey. Miners who had been recruited into tunnelling companies by an army desperate to find some way of breaking the deadlock on the Western Front had their reward when the fighting eventually stopped, and they were demobilised faster than many other troops. One can only imagine their joy when they discovered this was to enable them to return to the British hole in the ground from where they had been taken, there to remedy the coal shortage which had developed at home. Their contribution was acknowledged by their commander-in-chief, Douglas Haig, with the words that 'they have earned the thanks of the whole army for their contribution to the defeat of the enemy', which sounds pretty nugatory, but words were generally inadequate to cope with the scale of what had just happened during the war.[19]

The mine proprietors had had a more tangible reward, and could well afford to pay the 50% rate of tax which had been brought in to deter profiteering.* The war had been excellent for the coal business. The remark of the future Conservative prime minister, Stanley Baldwin, about much of the new intake of MPs in 1918 – 'a

---

* It was later raised to 80%.

lot of hard-faced men who look as if they had done very well out
of the war' – suited them down to the ground.

And beneath it.

10

Not Quite What We'd Hoped For

Eventually, the 'war to end war' spluttered to its conclusion, with funerals, medals and sonorous phrases about 'never again'. But it did not bring peace at home. The conflict had revealed to everyone the thinness of the claim of national unity. The tensions within the most important industry in Britain were bound to resurface once the laws and duties of wartime passed.[1] Before the war began, two-thirds of the entire world coal trade had come from British mines, and the industry's dominant place in the life of the nation affected everyone. The worldwide pre-eminence of the British coal industry before the war encouraged the mine-owners to believe there was no other way of doing things than the way they had been done before. So, even though it was already becoming clear that the only mechanism for the business to survive internationally was by amalgamating pits and becoming more efficient, the proprietors preferred to stick with lots of small collieries. They knew, they said, how to run their business. When times were hard they lowered prices (and wages) and when trade was good they could easily hire more men. Private enterprise was what had made Britain great and only they could judge when, for example, it was a good idea to introduce an underground conveyor belt. To the irritation of the owners, who by and large wanted to keep officialdom out of the pits, the eminence of the industry also demanded increasing regulation. It seemed to MPs as if they were forever passing legislation about how coal-mining should conduct its affairs. Between 1900 and 1926, they were asked to agree no fewer than twenty Acts of Parliament regulating the industry. There were laws about wages, about how many hours could be spent underground, about safety, about rescue arrangements, about compensation. There was a problem with trying to achieve unanimity for many of these laws, though. The miners might now be united in a national union – and one which had an increasingly socialist complexion – but there was no true unity among the coal-owners, who, by definition, were competitive capitalists. The additional complication was that a wage agreed in one colliery with generous seams of coal was simply unaffordable in another which had mean, twisted deposits: it was geology that made the rules of extraction and international economics that determined the price achieved on sale. The miners had a one-word solution to the problems of their industry – nationalisation, on both economic and moral grounds. The owners had a huge variety of specific concerns and were united only in their belief in free enterprise and the mixture of affection and contempt in which they held the miners.

Once the war was over, London was keen to divest itself of the responsibilities it had assumed for running the mines when Lloyd George's government had effectively nationalised them. The obvious answer was to return the 3,000 mines to the 1,500 owners, who were already anticipating the substantial amounts of money to be made from business as usual. The Miners' Federation of Great Britain had clung to its three ambitions – a minimum wage, cross-country agreements, and nationalisation of the industry. Of the three, nationalisation was the outstanding unfinished business. The coal-owners, naturally, loathed the idea. The miners called for the support of railway and other transport workers. Confrontation looked inevitable.

There was by now an established pattern of government behaviour when presented with serious problems in such an important industry. So in 1919 the victorious prime minister, David Lloyd

George, ducked below the parapet and asked a High Court judge, John Sankey, to chair a team of twelve commissioners to investigate the industry, promising to abide by whatever recommendations they came up with. The buck could not have been passed more quickly. The commissioners appointed to Sankey's investigation were chosen for political balance, a predictable guarantee of heated meetings and ultimate fruitlessness. Sankey himself was a mild conservative, though he found the mine-owners one of the most annoying groups of people he had ever come across and sympathised with the miners. He became a convert to nationalisation. The three economists on the commission, R. H. Tawney ('freedom for the pike is death for the minnows'), the Fabian Sidney Webb and the Liberal and serial groper* Leo Chiozza Money, were broadly sympathetic to the three trade unionists on the inquiry. But they were offset by the businessmen on the commission, most of whose instinctive sympathies were with the proprietors. Also on the committee was the former prime minister, Arthur Balfour, and the up-and-coming Tory, Allan Smith. In the end, most of them accepted that the royalty system, under which landowners were paid by the operating companies for coal raised from beneath their soil, was absurd. But beyond that, some preferred wholesale nationalisation and others wanted things left as they were. The sole engineer on the investigation, Arthur Duckham, produced his own report, only to find it dismissed as 'Duckham and water'. Because the group could not agree on a unanimous report, they issued four separate reports in the summer of 1919. It was the worst of all worlds, with both sides feeling betrayed. The commission had been a waste of time.

---

* It may be that when he was later arrested for indecent behaviour in Hyde Park with twenty-two-year-old Irene Savage, he was indeed merely giving her 'career advice' – as he claimed. But another arrest, when caught in a railway carriage with a shop girl named Ivy Ruxton, led to a £2 fine, with an additional ten shillings for 'interfering with a passenger's comfort'.

The Russian Revolution, deposing the tsar, had electrified politics throughout Europe and the end of the war had set off a spate
of strikes in Britain, two of which had even involved the police.
Detachments of soldiers were sent to collieries. The whole of
government was on edge, with the Deputy Cabinet Secretary, Tom
Jones, writing in early 1920 that 'ministers have the "wind up" to
the most extraordinary extent … From a meeting today I came
away with my head fairly reeling. I felt I had been in Bedlam. Red
Revolution and blood and war at home and abroad.'

Now, more than ever, the coal industry, with its swarms of men
toiling underground and royalties paid to lucky landowners, looked
especially old-fashioned and unjust. When the post-war economic
boom collapsed the following winter, and demand for coal plummeted, the time seemed ripe for revolution. Suddenly, Lloyd
George's government couldn't get rid of the industry quickly
enough: the mines would be returned to their pre-war owners on 31
March 1921. The bosses had achieved their overwhelming ambition
of getting their collieries back, and they reacted to the slump in their
trade in the only way they knew how. Miners' pay accounted for
most of the cost of extracting coal, so the owners proclaimed a drastic reduction in wages (in some collieries, notably in South Wales,
the cut amounted to almost half). The unions reacted with outrage,
things being made even more unappealing to them by the proprietors' announcement that they intended to return to the system of
locally agreed rates of pay, which the miners had fought – successfully – to abolish. The prime minister panicked, and called up 80,000
special constables to reinforce the police. He declared a state of
emergency. Soldiers were seen setting up machine-gun posts at
some collieries. The *Dundee Courier* reported that 'the mining areas
of Fife are in the hands of the military. Sturdy Seaforth Highlanders
are guarding the safety men at the pits', and that 'at dawn a large
force of naval ratings and military, fully equipped with machine
guns were de-trained at Wemyss Castle Station' near Kirkcaldy.[2]

The owners rejected what looked a rather sensible union suggestion of a national pool, in which more efficient pits would subsidise
those which could not afford to pay higher wages. Proprietors
preferred the rigours of the marketplace, declaring that production
had risen from 50 million tons in 1850 to almost 300 million tons
at the outbreak of war entirely by private enterprise, not by government action. If the miners didn't like their plan for the future, the
only alternative was the closure of less efficient pits. They decreed
that from 1 April 1921, the miners would have the choice of
accepting pay cuts – and longer hours – or losing their jobs. The
gates of the collieries would be locked until they did as they were
told. The other members of the so-called Triple Alliance – the rail
and transport unions – said they would show their support for the
miners by calling out their members on strike, on 15 April. In the
event, the day passed into the history of the trade union movement
as 'Black Friday'.

The leader of the Miners' Federation of Great Britain, Robert
Smillie, had already quit the struggle, to return to his cottage in a
hardline Protestant village in the Scottish coalfield.* He had been
replaced by Herbert Smith, a bluff, bespectacled Yorkshireman
who had spent part of his childhood in a workhouse. He was much
given to thunderous pronouncements such as 'Get on t'field. That's
t'place.' The words were loud, but the meaning often opaque.

The afternoon before the Triple Alliance was due to paralyse the
country, a group of worried Unionist MPs invited representatives
from the mine-owners (the Mining Association) and representa-

---

* His village of Larkhall clings to its loyalties. When a branch of the American
fast-food chain Subway opened there early in the twenty-first century, it did so without its usual green storefront: the colour is too associated with Celtic, the
traditionally Catholic soccer club. The antipathy is said to date from the use of Irish
immigrants, brought in as strike-breakers by pit-owners. In the early twenty-first
century, hundreds of green traffic lights had also vanished, and municipal green
railings been repainted red, white and blue.

tives of the Miners' Federation to separate talks. The MPs were not much impressed by the bullying tone of the owners, but at about 11.30 at night they understood Frank Hodges, the union secretary, to say that the miners would waive their demands for a subsidy pool and a national wages scheme, in the interests of a temporary deal, as long as wages did not fall below the cost of living. This was in flat contradiction of the policy of the Miners' Federation, and Hodges later admitted he had got the wrong end of the stick when talking to the MPs. Some of the MPs rushed to Downing Street, and woke up the prime minister. Sitting in his pyjamas, Lloyd George wrote a letter inviting the miners' leaders to talks the next morning. The miners failed to show up. By a majority of one, their leaders had voted to repudiate Hodges' statement of the night before. The railway workers' leader, J. H. Thomas, who was privately as lukewarm as possible about striking in support of the miners, had already written to Lloyd George, warning him the railwaymen would take action from 10 p.m. on Friday 15 April. Now, as miners, railwaymen and transport workers shouted at each other in the corridors of 'Unity House', the comically named Euston headquarters of the railwaymen, Hodges, the miners' secretary, was seen sitting at a desk, weeping.* At three that afternoon, the railway union leader, Jimmy Thomas bounced out into the daylight and cheerily told waiting reporters 'It's all off, boys.' His relief was more than evident.

So 15 April came and went without the rail or transport workers lifting a finger to help the miners. Miners' meetings across the country pilloried both Frank Hodges and the transport workers. Hodges understandably offered to resign as secretary. He was talked out of it. When word of the failed settlement attempt

---

* Hodges carried the can, earning the undying hatred of his fellow miners, for his behaviour on the eve of Black Friday. After testifying to another commission that the miners should work longer hours, he decided to clamber over the barricades and feather his own nest by becoming a successful businessman.

reached the transport leaders, they felt they had been used by miners who had not tried hard enough themselves to get a settlement. (In their defence, organising a picket line to enforce action was much easier in a mine than on a railway.) The Triple Alliance was quickly renamed 'the Cripple Alliance' and expired.

Whatever its pretensions, the government was now quite clearly taking the owners' side in the dispute, with Lloyd George claiming that the miners were using industrial muscle to achieve political objectives and making untrue accusations that the union was threatening safety workers (who had to continue working, to pump water out of the mines).

The lockout lasted three months until, at the end of June, the deeply disillusioned Miners' Federation decided to accept the offer of a deal endorsing the owners' role, and cutting members' pay by an average of 34%. It was a worse deal than they could have had before the Triple Alliance fell apart on Black Friday.

By March 1923, membership of the Miners' Federation of Great Britain had fallen by 200,000. Hodges stood as a Labour candidate for Parliament and was briefly First Lord of the Admiralty. But in December 1924, the miners elected the radical Arthur 'A. J.' Cook as secretary to succeed Hodges. He brought revolutionary zeal and great rhetorical gifts to his new position. He made no bones about being a revolutionary and gave the plodding local police watching his passionate speeches plenty to worry about. (According to the deputy chief constable, he was 'an agitator of the worst type'.[3]) He was, naturally, committed to ending private ownership of the industry. He was a mesmerising speaker, whose slogan 'not a penny off the pay, not a second on the day' was guaranteed to raise a roar at any union gathering. Unsurprisingly, he was pilloried in the newspapers.

* * *

In late 1923, Stanley Baldwin, who had inherited the Conservative prime ministership from a sick Andrew Bonar Law in May, made the catastrophic mistake of trying to seek a personal mandate by holding a general election. The result was a disaster for his party, which lost dozens of seats in Parliament and then had to watch as – with the help of Liberals – the South Wales MP, Ramsay MacDonald, set about forming Britain's first Labour government. But, when it came to the seemingly never-ending problem of seething unrest in the coalfields, the Labour government worked from the same handbook as everyone else. Yet another congenial lawyer was asked to hold an inquiry into miners' pay and conditions. Lord Buckmaster, whose humble origins did nothing to limit the bombastic self-confidence of a King's Counsel, was given the job. Buckmaster was baffled by the peculiarity of British property rights which determined ownership of coal reserves in the ground, and not just because they predated the knowledge that the world revolves in space. As he later told the House of Lords, 'the idea that people, if they own land, own it to the very molten centre of the earth and up to the top of the universe, is one of those strange legends of the law which have become an integral part of our constitution, which is extraordinarily difficult to comprehend. If it were true it would follow that every individual in the course of the spinning and rotating of the earth owned the whole universe because he owns every bit that is above his piece of land right up to the highest heights of the heaven and he goes on owning that throughout the twenty-four hours of the day and the 365 days of the year.' The notion was 'absurd'. The only undiscovered thing in the ground that was reserved to the Crown was gold, because everyone agreed it had value, whereas at the time these legal conventions had been formulated no one imagined coal to have any value at all. He found the miners 'some of the finest citizens in this country', whose courage, loyalty and patriotism 'are beyond all dispute'.[4]

But his inquiry was largely a waste of time. The miners repeated their assertion that they were now effectively earning less than they had before the First World War and, despite everything, life was as dangerous as ever. In 1923, over 200,000 miners had been injured badly enough to be off work for a week, and an additional 1,200 had been fatally wounded. 'This,' he was told, 'is part of the miners' wages; part of the price he pays in the struggle with natural forces, that the people may have coal, and that he and his family may have bread. This part of his wages never gets into a balance sheet; is never seen in a quotation; is never allowed for, or even thought of, by the consumer.'[5] Buckmaster was moved, and recommended a wage rise. But he heard from the employers that they simply could not meet the miners' request for higher wages; if they did so, they said, they would be bankrupt and the mines would close. The miners pointed out that if employers were obliged to pay higher wages, they'd have to reform their businesses. As for working hours, Buckmaster heard it had been nonsense to claim that in a seven-hour working day miners would hew more coal because they would be 'fresher': since the report of the Sankey Commission, output per man had in fact fallen. Buckmaster shied away from recommending detailed pay scales, suggesting instead that if only both sides would get together and talk a bit more, he was sure they'd sort something out. This was as useful as a wooden toothpick on a coalface.

The Labour government tottered on until the autumn of 1924 with the report of the Buckmaster Inquiry quietly gathering dust. Then, the official decision not to prosecute a communist agitator, John Ross Campbell, for publishing an open letter inciting British soldiers not to turn their guns on British workers, led to a parliamentary vote of 'no confidence', which MacDonald lost. Another election was now necessary, while the British political class was still walking on hot coals over the possibility of communist subversion. The extreme nervousness set off by the red scare was made clear four days before the imminent election. The *Daily Mail* published what it claimed was a letter from Grigory Zinoviev, the head of the Executive Committee of the Communist International (the Comintern) – whose mission was to promote revolution anywhere and everywhere – to the British Communist Party. The *Mail* – then, as now, never knowingly less than omniscient – declared that 'Moscow issues orders to the British Communists … the British Communists in turn give orders to the Socialist Government, which it tamely and humbly obeys … Everything is to be made ready for a great outbreak of the abominable class war which is civil war of the most savage kind.'[6]

The letter was a forgery. But it had the effect of helping to enlarge the Conservative vote. The Labour Party was haemorrhaging potential support anyway and the letter finished its chances. The Conservative leader, Stanley Baldwin, resumed his tenancy of 10 Downing Street. Less than a year later, in June 1925, the colliery operators gave one month's notice that existing working conditions in the mines would end. The miners would have to work an extra hour a day and take a pay cut. There could not have been a gesture more likely to infuriate the trade union, which pointed out that in the past four years the proprietors had made profits totalling £58.4 million. By contrast, said the miners' president, the brave Yorkshireman Herbert Smith,* 'we have nowt to give'. Faced with intransigence, yet again, the government reached for the magic they thought would come from appointing another eminent barrister (and notorious bore) to hold an inquiry. Hugh Macmillan, a son of the manse from Glasgow, never felt he was taken quite as seriously as he deserved, and was to spend many of his middle years collecting honorary degrees and chairing inquiries of one sort or other – examining lunacy, street prostitution, shipbuilding,

---

* An orphan who had been adopted by a miner and his wife, Smith claimed never to have been to school.

income-tax law, the Canadian dollar, medicines, royal memorials, London University and Great Ormond Street Hospital. Eventually and inevitably, he presided over the committee on political honours. This great panjandrum was just the man for the job.

The owners did have a genuine problem. Almost all coal was still being gathered by pick and shovel, because collieries had not invested enough in heavy machinery. As a result, coal continued to be costly to extract. But the industry was enjoying something of a boom, caused by France's 1923 decision to march troops into the mining areas of the Ruhr, which meant that British coal was protected from German competition. When coal production in the United States was disrupted by a strike in 1924, there was another excuse to increase production. It could not last. And it did not.

Yet it was hard to keep up with Stanley Baldwin's management of the economy: one minute he was saying there would be no subsidy to the coal industry, the next he was granting one. And one of the biggest problems of all had been invented by the government. Baldwin had invited Winston Churchill to join his government as Chancellor of the Exchequer. Though a flamboyant politician, Churchill was no economist (indeed, the pre-eminent economist of the day, John Maynard Keynes, advised him to do precisely the opposite of what he now did). Taking the advice of officials in the Treasury, in his first big judgement as Chancellor, Churchill declared that Britain would rejoin the gold standard – the mechanism by which the international value of sterling was linked to the value of gold, an arrangement which had been abandoned in 1914. The attraction was pretty obvious, for the gold standard had been an excellent way of imposing discipline upon national governments: if your currency was pegged at a set rate to the value of an ounce of gold, you couldn't devalue it, in order to make your products more competitive. Unable to go around printing extra banknotes, prices stayed stable. To Churchill, the value at which sterling could be traded for gold was the key question in management of the economy. He decided that Britain would re-enter the gold standard not at a level determined by the market, but at the value at which the country had quit at the start of the First World War, when one ounce of gold was worth £3.83 and £1 sterling was therefore worth $4.86. The immediate effect now was to make British exports – notably coal – much more expensive. 'Why did he do such a silly thing?' asked Keynes.[7] He answered his own question by saying that the Chancellor had been seduced by bankers and misled by his experts in the Treasury. Along with Churchill's enthusiasm for the Dardanelles shambles, which had killed tens of thousands of Allied soldiers at Gallipoli during the First World War, this ranks as one of the most stupid decisions of his long political career. (It has to be admitted that he wasn't alone. Britain's former enemy, Germany, together with former allies, like France and Belgium also rejoined the gold standard. But they did so at lower rates, allowing their exports to undercut those of Britain.) In the eyes of the trade unions, Britain's miners had been sacrificed to benefit the financiers of the City of London.

The boom for the coal trade had ended, and the industry had fallen back into its familiar weapons-drawn industrial relations. The owners terminated their 1924 agreement and told the miners they would have to knuckle down, agree to work a basic eight-hour day and agree to local wage deals. The miners were outraged and said they wouldn't accept. Ernest Bevin, the general secretary of the Transport and General Workers' Union, promised that his members would support the miners in any confrontation, and a few days later they were joined by the railway workers. The unions' umbrella organisation, the Trades Union Congress, was deter-mined there would be no more embarrassments like 'Black Friday' and plans were laid to bring the country to a halt.

The government was the first to blink. On what the Labour-oriented *Daily Herald* called 'Red Friday' – 31 July 1925 – Stanley

Baldwin offered the owners a subsidy to continue paying the miners their unaffordable wages for nine months while he reached for the familiar smelling salts of a Royal Commission to investigate the industry. The *Daily Mail* screamed about a 'Victory for Violence'. In fact, 'Red Friday' was neither victory nor defeat, just a feeble gesture by a desperate government, which would end in nine months anyway. This new commission of inquiry would be chaired by the former Liberal Home Secretary, Sir Herbert Samuel, just returned from a controversial stint administering the British Mandate territory in the Holy Land. He was to be assisted by the usual mixture of successful businessmen and academics. Quite what Baldwin thought Samuel would discover is unclear – though some indication of how he thought things might turn out can be gained from the fact that he asked the head of the Home Office to organise groups of volunteers who would run an Organisation for the Maintenance of Supplies (the OMS) if a strike began: this was the basis of the fabled collection of clerks, clergy, middle-managers, pipe-smoking students and others, noisily deployed in the General Strike to drive lorries and buses. The Communist Party dismissed them as fascists, who'd jump at the chance to suppress the workers' right to strike. But, when it came to it, the bogeymen turned out to be mainly concentrated in the south of England, well away from mines, and the replacement services they offered were either unused or inadequate.

Samuel's team, meanwhile, set off on a series of mine visits and hearings, by the end of which they had discovered that most of the coal brought out of the ground in 1925 had cost more to mine than it was worth on the open market; that Baldwin's subsidy had cost twice as much as had been predicted; and that the miners were right when they claimed the entire industry was in urgent need of rationalisation, mechanisation and overhaul. There was much good sense in their findings, for the bare economics of coal-mining were simple. Overall production had fallen by fifteen tons in every hundred, yet there were more men working in the industry than there had been when the war began. There were understandable reasons for this – isolated mining villages were the enemy of the open labour market so beloved of free-market economists. But there was no arguing with the fact that seven men were now trying to live off the product that had previously fed six miners. The commission took the trouble to try to collect some facts and discovered that even in the period from 1913 to 1924, miners were having to go further underground to locate coal, and that the seams were getting thinner. 'MUST THE MINERS STARVE?' asked a flyer printed by their supporters. It admitted that they were paid about 66% more than they had been in 1914, but claimed that the cost of living had risen by 81%. There were over 45,000 miners in South Wales who, under the owners' pay offer, would find their earnings falling by nearly eighteen shillings.[8] The colliery-owners claimed that because the miners were led by 'syndicalists' they were deliberately restricting the amount of coal brought to the surface. The commission judged this was nonsense. They decided the state should buy out owners' rights to coal, and then use its power to force mines to amalgamate. Since pre-war wages and conditions had been the product of a boom, Samuel unsurprisingly also concluded that the miners should accept wage cuts. Most unhelpfully from their point of view, Jimmy Thomas, the railwaymen's leader, declared the report a 'wonderful document'.

The report was a lot better than most investigations into the coal business; it was published in March 1926 and was said to have sold over 100,000 copies, which was an indication of the public's interest in how Britain's premier industry might be reformed. The proprietors didn't much care to hear that they were running an antiquated, inefficient business, and issued new terms of employment for the miners, including local wage agreements and a pay cut of between 10% and 25%. After the taxpayer subsidy which had kept their wages at what the owners had claimed to be an impossibly high level, there was not the slightest chance the miners would accept the pay cuts, which the owners declared had become urgently necessary. If the miners did not accept the new terms by 1 May – the day after the public subsidy ended – they would be locked out from the pits. Since the miners could not suddenly reduce the number of dependants they had to feed, confrontation was inevitable. It might have been A. J. Cook's moment. The miners' secretary, as we have seen, was a man of explosive energy. Unfortunately, it was not matched by any great political canniness. He wore himself out, travelling from one mass meeting of miners to another, striding about the podium, exclamatory, rousing and increasingly hoarse. Cook lived on his nerves, endlessly repeating his slogan about 'not a minute on the day' and 'not a penny off the pay'. He was a short, slightly stooped figure, regularly pilloried in the right-wing press as an evil agent of foreign powers. But even 'friends' had doubts about whether sheer energy was quite enough: you could scarcely have found a more potentially sympathetic member of the middle class than the prominent member of the Fabian Society, Beatrice Webb, who devoted her life to The Cause. Her nose twitched with Senior Common Room disdain. She found this 'loosely built ugly-featured man' looked like a farm labourer, with a 'large-lipped mouth, glittering china-blue eyes, set close together in a narrow head with lanky yellow hair'. She wailed to her diary that she found him a man of 'no intellect and not much intelligence – he is a quivering mass of emotions, a mediumistic magnetic sort of creature – not without personal attractiveness – an inspired idiot, drunk with his own words, dominated by his own slogans'. She doubted 'whether he even knows what he is going to say or what he has just said'.[9] Cook talked of 'beating the strongest government of modern times', and 'the end of capitalism', which did little to console Beatrice Webb and her friends. She lamented 'it is tragedy to think that this inspired idiot, coupled with poor old Herbert Smith [the trade union president], with his senile obstinacy, are the dominant figures in so great and powerful an organisation as the Miners' Federation'.[10] Reading her diaries, it is hard to resist the feeling that Cook would never be either posh or clever enough to satisfy her tastes. She misunderstood a man described by a sympathetic Red Clydesider as addressing crowds 'like a Salvation Army preacher', with no interest at all in possible compromises. 'He was an agitator, pure and simple … He was a flame.'[11] Cook was a tonic to the strikers; where others spoke at them, he seemed to have an ability to say what was in many of their hearts. Relations between owners and workers were so bad, it was more or less inevitable, anyway, that negotiations to avoid a strike would fail. If the miners did not accept the new deal, they would be locked out of the collieries from 1 May.

The Trades Union Congress decreed that the General Strike 'in defence of miners' wages and hours' would begin at one minute to midnight on Monday 3 May. It was intended to bring the country to a standstill. This was the most powerful weapon the trade unions could deploy. The leadership of the Labour Party was now notable by its silence, with its leader, Ramsay MacDonald writing in his diary that the strike seemed to be occurring 'to save Mr Cook's face': a man he considered a 'fool'.[12] The railwaymen's leader, Jimmy Thomas, organised negotiations with Stanley Baldwin, which he later claimed were approaching success when the prime minister was called away by a dispute in Fleet Street. Cometh the hour, cometh the *Mail*. Under the headline 'For King and Country', the *Daily Mail* constructed an editorial declaring that 'A general strike is not an industrial dispute. It is a revolutionary movement intended to inflict suffering upon the great mass of innocent persons in the community and to thereby put forcible constraint upon the government … We call upon all law-abiding men and women to hold themselves at the service of King and country.'[13] Technical staff refused to print the column, causing the paper's editor to phone the prime minister. Unsurprisingly, Baldwin saw red at what he considered a gross interference with the freedom of the press.

The Trades Union Congress called the first – and only – General Strike in British history from one minute to midnight, on 3 May 1926. A. J. Cook continued as the voice of the strikers, travelling the country, stomping the stage at one mass meeting after another, until he had no voice left. His health collapsed. (He was already suffering from emphysema and bronchitis and at one of the meetings an old mining injury had been aggravated when he was kicked by an opponent. He refused medical treatment.) His physical condition seemed a metaphor for the miners' strength, as men drifted back to the mines, unable to afford not to work. After seven months of dispute, the union had been comprehensively broken. Membership fell, and shortly before Cook's death at the age of forty-seven, he had to have his damaged leg amputated. He was back at work – on a cork leg – within six weeks, but he was the union's only full-time official, and frequently vilified in the newspapers for the failure of the 1926 dispute. Within six years of the end of the strike, he was dead.

Most of the headlines about the strike itself are well known: the miners' refusal to discuss having their pay cut; the government's bias towards the owners; their determination to maintain vital services through the deployment of police; the despatch of warships to the Clyde, Newcastle and Liverpool; the camps of soldiers in London parks; the censorship of news and Churchill's editorship of the *British Gazette* propaganda sheet; the fantastical scare stories about revolutionaries' plans to chloroform the guards at Buckingham Palace and to create a 'Soviet' to sit in the Palace of Westminster; the coming of age of the BBC (in its own eyes at least – it was never commandeered by government because, as John Reith admitted to his diary, it was never really impartial[14]); the cricket and football matches between strikers and police; armoured cars escorting food lorries from the docks to the distribution centres in Hyde Park; the derailment of the *Flying Scotsman* train. Others – like privileged young men relying upon nothing but a tally-ho enthusiasm to keep the public transport system going – are exaggerated: the government had no need to call upon the hundreds of thousands of volunteers at its disposal. However much A. J. Cook might rail against reports of crumbling support in the few regional papers still being printed (in 'the scab capitalist press'), the plain fact is that the General Strike failed.

Without even informing the striking miners, the TUC negotiators held a meeting with Herbert Samuel of the Mining Commission. The two sides – which did not, of course, involve either the employers or the strikers – agreed a return-to-work arrangement, under which there would be a national wages board and a minimum wage. The TUC snatched eagerly at the suggestion, not caring that Samuel was not speaking on behalf of the government, and hung out the miners to dry. They were no better off than they had been when the dispute had begun. Under the plan – such as it was – the government subsidy would continue, although Samuel believed it was inevitable that there were wage cuts to come. He was right, and the miners would have none of it. But on 12 May – only nine days into the action – a TUC delegation visited 10 Downing Street to say the strike was over, as long as the Samuel Commission proposals were implemented and there was no victimisation of men who had refused to work. The government maintained it couldn't force the employers to take back all those who had been on strike, but Stanley Baldwin said he was willing to provide a subsidy for six weeks. Walter Citrine, the TUC general secretary, was no supporter of the General Strike and the TUC rolled over.

The miners continued their action, though, despite hunger and crumbling support. Nottinghamshire miners signed a deal with local employers at the height of the strike, and there were increasing fears that similar decisions would follow elsewhere. (In the final agreement between the Durham miners and their bosses, the men accepted that their pay would be determined by the price of coal on the market, a principle previously anathema to the union.) The Samuel Report was thrown away. The ramshackle settlement set a familiar pattern which later governments would also follow: it demonstrated a recognition that the coal industry was too important to the nation to allow normal rules to apply, and showed the vastness of the chasm between the two sides. But the agreement didn't even satisfy the owners, who felt government had no role meddling in their business. Some of the miners who had been called out for what was effectively a nine-day demonstration of fatuousness felt they had been betrayed, and were still on strike seven months later. Walter Citrine confessed to his diary that at meeting after meeting, miners stood up and said they couldn't go back to work for lower wages. 'Was all this sacrifice to be in vain?' they asked.[15] But within six months, most of those who believed they had been betrayed had given up, too, returning to work at lower rates of pay and for a standard shift which was an hour longer than it had been. In 1921 they had been driven back to working at pre-war wage levels. Now they had been starved back to work again. Some mines could have to close anyway: all the coal in Northumberland would continue to be produced at a loss, ninety-seven out of every one hundred tons in Durham would also be loss-making, as would 90% of coal in South Wales and Monmouthshire. In Scotland, they said, already only eighty-eight tons out of every hundred were profitable. The figure must have come originally from the mine-owners, who were clearly not as efficient businessmen as they liked to claim. The Samuel Commission had recommended nationalisation, and just before the General Strike, the government's Secretary for Mines, Colonel George Lane-Fox, a Yorkshire Conservative MP, had produced a stinging secret report (stamped, in case there was any doubt about it, 'TO BE KEPT UNDER LOCK AND KEY') concluding that the cost of nationalisation would be £100 million, to be paid to the mine-owners, which would assuredly draw a lot of political flak, and set a terrible precedent for businesses like shipbuilding, steel-making and agriculture. 'Who will believe us,' he asked, 'when we say we will die in some ill-defined ditch, rather than accept the nationalisation of the coal industry, and, inferentially, the nationalisation of every other distressed industry? I shall be only too glad if my confidence can be restored, but the moral basis of the government seems to me to have dropped out.'[16]

As in the strike which drove the final nail into the coffin of the industry, in 1984, the miners had not held a national ballot before the General Strike. On the other hand, they could reasonably claim that it was not they who had prevented coal being mined, but an employers' lockout.

Trotsky described the General Council of the TUC as an 'agency of the English bourgeoisie'.[17] The credibility of the organisation was terribly damaged, but not, surprisingly, that of the Labour Party. Although it had let down the miners, the party gained seats at the next election. The main lesson for the miners – that you don't get into a fight with the government, because if it is determined enough, you are bound to lose – had still not been learned by 1984, when the then miners' leader, Arthur Scargill – a man who rather fancied himself a reincarnation of A. J. Cook – made much the same mistake as the strikers of 1926.

11
Oops!

The country was in the midst of a political crisis and everybody knew it. Even Stanley Baldwin's less than dynamic slogan 'Safety First' in the election held at the end of May 1929 had not deterred over 8.2 million people from voting for the exhausted Conservative Party which had presided over the General Strike. But a further 8 million had voted for the Labour Party, under the leadership of Ramsay MacDonald, who had stumped the country uttering the even more empty slogan 'We are going to win.' He was right: under Britain's idiosyncratic electoral system, Labour won 287 seats, which was less than an overall majority in Parliament, but twenty-seven more seats than the Conservatives (who had won a bigger number of votes on ballot papers). The Labour Party were therefore entitled to try to form an administration if they could. The once-mighty Liberal Party, which had been elbowed aside by Labour, attracted less than a quarter of the voters – just over 5 million – taking only fifty-nine seats in Parliament and confirming that Liberalism was now a spent force. But, provided the newly elected Liberal MPs (whose slogan had been 'We Can Conquer Unemployment') voted with them, Labour could muster a majority of seats in Parliament. Ramsay MacDonald became prime minister.

He reaped a whirlwind. Less than six months later, the Wall Street stock-market crash set off the Great Depression. Unemployment in Britain was soon spiralling and by the end of

1930, 2.5 million people had been thrown out of work. The Depression hit the coalfields hard – with less trade, there was a reduced need for furnaces, smelting and transport: in some areas, one in three of the workforce now had no job by which to feed themselves. In the mining areas of South Wales, which were particularly dependent upon exports, unemployment was to reach over 40% by late 1932: 150 years of economic growth were suddenly reversed, and the roads which had once been alive with people making their way to the coalfields in search of a job, were now carrying great traffic in the other direction. The damage to the public finances was also predictable: when fewer people were working, there was less tax being paid. Unemployment insurance (introduced in 1911) meant that at the very same time the government was having to spend more and more issuing 'the dole'. There have been subsequent occasions when Labour governments have wrecked the economy. But in this case, it was not Labour's fault. Economically, Britain was in a mess, with the gold standard ensuring that its exports were unnecessarily expensive and British coal and industrial manufactures simply uncompetitive. The pressure to reduce both government spending and wages paid in export industries was formidable.

MacDonald's Chancellor of the Exchequer, Philip Snowden, despaired to his diary less than a year later: 'The trade of the world has come near to collapse and nothing we can do will stop the increase in unemployment.'[1] There now arose the problem that faced almost every Labour government of the twentieth century: how much pain could the people who had voted for them withstand? By January 1931, Snowden could only think about trying to save the country's finances by cutting unemployment benefit. In February came the inevitable, when MacDonald tried to square the circle by appointing a committee to investigate the state of the nation's finances. The man he appointed was the soon-to-be ennobled George May, who had begun his working life as a clerk at the

Prudential Assurance Company, and risen to become company secretary of one of the biggest firms in Britain. A tall, thin man who wore a monocle in his one functioning eye, May had already done the government a favour in the First World War, when he clandestinely arranged for his company to sell them many of its American securities and had 44,000 bonds quietly delivered to the Bank of England in six buses. May was to be assisted on his committee by a couple of trade unionists, who would be outnumbered two to one by successful capitalists – an accountant, a governor of the Hudson's Bay Company, a shipbuilder and a shipping magnate. Six months later, the committee reported that the country was poised on the edge of catastrophe, which could only be averted by cutting £96 million from public spending, mostly from benefit payments. This was the complete opposite of the advice being given by John Maynard Keynes, who was not only the best-known economist in Britain, but probably the world. Keynes argued that a depression was the time to increase government spending, which would create demand. The two trade unionists refused to sign the committee's document, endorsing instead a load of ideas from the TUC. Keynes declared the May Report 'the most foolish document I have ever had the misfortune to read',[2] thereby confirming the essential difference between economics and politics, that one is about theories and the other about beliefs. Keynes wrote to MacDonald saying the ideas would result in 'a most gross perversion of social justice'. He recommended leaving the gold standard and devaluing the pound. But Philip Snowden was determined to cut public spending instead. There was a certain irony in the fact that this cadaverous weaver's son had begun his political career denouncing capitalism and predicting a socialist paradise. Now he proposed a socialist purgatory.

No fewer than nine members of the Cabinet told MacDonald that they would resign rather than accept spending cuts. That evening, MacDonald went to see the king, who had become convinced that the economic crisis facing Britain was so grave, he would have to abandon the protocol which decreed that he could not interfere in politics. He asked MacDonald if he would act as prime minister of a 'National Government', including the leaders of the Conservative and Liberal parties. MacDonald knew that accepting the invitation would be an act of political hara-kiri – the Labour Party would condemn him as a traitor and his political career would be over. Yet he returned to Buckingham Palace and accepted the job. The only members of his Cabinet he could persuade to serve in a National Government were Philip Snowden; the railway union leader, Jimmy Thomas, still seen as the villain of Black Friday and now the Colonial Secretary; and John Sankey, of the inquiry into the coal industry and now serving as MacDonald's Lord Chancellor. There would be four places in Cabinet for Conservatives, including their smug leader, Stanley Baldwin, and two places for Liberals, one of whom was the party leader Sir Herbert Samuel, the rather colourless leader who thought he knew all about the coal industry, and whose inquiry had so disappointed the miners. He now became Home Secretary.

The British coal industry was on the verge of bankruptcy. What a fall was here! From world dominance to imminent unviability in less than twenty years. Britain dug less coal in 1929 than it had in 1913, and much of it was being raised from the ground at a loss. Miners had lost their jobs. Pithead prices of coal had fallen, as had the wages of those miners who managed to cling on to their jobs. By this stage, everybody thought they knew what was wrong with the industry. Officialdom seeks explanations in structures, and the diagnosis was that there was something wrong with the way the industry was organised. In the carving up of responsibilities which followed the creation of the National Government, the job of Secretary for Mines had been given to the Liberals' Isaac Foot. He told Parliament in the spring of 1932 that 'this year, the potential production of coal … is over 300 million tons a year. Last year we produced about 220 million tons, and in that difference you have the problem which will arise if you ... leave [the industry] to chaotic unrestricted competition.'[3] It was the sort of sparkling, apparently plausible analysis that could only have come from a Plymouth solicitor. The 'potential production of coal' was no more than an estimate, but no matter, the clever officials at the ministry had worked out what had gone wrong and decided the Liberals were right when they said that what was needed was more reorganisation and less competition.

MacDonald decided to deal with the coal problem by socialist governments' favourite mechanism and introduced a new law. A Coal Mines Act created local boards which would decide how much coal could be mined, and the price at which it would be sold, a racket which protected inefficient mines at the expense of the consumer. It was doomed to fail, but for a moment or two, before the Depression took full hold, it seemed to offer promise. When the market shrank, colliery companies resorted to all sorts of scams, setting up bogus subsidiaries, overpaying agents or deliberately misidentifying the grade of coal being supplied, to undercut the minimum price. A new law in 1932 later attempted to enforce the quota. But the plain fact was that government did not understand how the market worked, and Britain was geared up to produce far too much coal. If it ever achieved its full potential, there would be cut-throat competition, the Mines Secretary who had succeeded Isaac Foot told Cabinet,* the price of coal would fall, while unemployment soared.

As he suspected might happen, by agreeing to serve at the head of a National Government, Ramsay MacDonald had signed his

---

* The Mines Secretary was the boom-voiced Liberal MP Ernest Brown. Stanley Baldwin was once disturbed in 11 Downing Street by a great shouting. When told it was Ernest Brown 'talking to Scotland', Baldwin asked 'Why doesn't he use the telephone?'

own death warrant with most of his party.* When the National
Government's plans for cuts in the salaries of almost everyone paid
by the state, including £13 million of unemployment benefit, were
debated in the House of Commons, they were comfortably
endorsed by the House as a whole and denounced by the rest of
the Labour Party. The problem was that MacDonald's cuts didn't
work. What happened next seems inevitable: the anxieties felt
within the government transmitted themselves to the international
money markets, where dealers began to dump their holdings of
sterling. Under the arrangements governing the gold standard, the
value of the pound was pegged to gold and the Bank of England
was obliged to exchange pounds for gold at the declared rate, in
order to retain the value of the currency. The government was as
unable to fend off the money markets as a mortally wounded ante-
lope can save itself from a pack of hyenas. Gold and foreign
exchange continued to pour out of the Bank of England. There was
a widespread view among authoritative economists – who were as
ready as ever with a theory – that if Britain was forced off the gold
standard, the currencies of much of the continent would collapse
and there would be revolution in central Europe. Up to this point,
the gold-standard value of sterling had been protected with the
help of loans from the US Federal Reserve and the French national
bank. But now, the loans had almost run out. The deputy governor
of the Bank wrote to MacDonald and his Chancellor asking that
the institution be 'relieved of their obligation to sell gold' under the
gold-standard law.[4] There was only ever going to be one outcome
of this crisis, and that the government tried not to see it testifies to
the shadow still cast by the country's days as the world's most
powerful nation.

----

* The next Labour prime minister, Clement Attlee, often thought the most consen-
sual and mild-mannered of Labour leaders, described what MacDonald had done
as 'the greatest betrayal in the political history of this country'.

The Budget announcement was made as the Royal Navy's Atlantic Fleet was steaming north, to gather at Invergordon on the Cromarty Firth for manoeuvres. The money markets were not impressed when, in mid-September, sailors went ashore from their ships at Invergordon, and gathered at the shore canteen and sports field to protest at the public sector pay cut, which bore particularly heavily on young sailors, who were going to find their pay reduced by up to a quarter (admirals, by contrast, would face a cut of 7%). When warships were ordered to put to sea for exercises on 15 September, many ratings refused to work and the vessels were unable to leave. They were on strike, they said. Mutiny had now taken the place of 'belly-aching', and mutiny was an offence punishable by death. But when the mutiny was said to involve 10,000 men, there was safety in numbers, especially when it became known that many of the petty officers and even some of the officer class were sympathetic. (Many naval officers had nothing but contempt for the Admiralty for failing to protect the service.) Official papers relating to the mutiny were destroyed soon afterwards – if records were ever taken – but there seems to have been some panicky talk among the Sea Lords of bombarding the fleet with howitzers from the nearby hills. Mercifully, the idea was stillborn. But the City of London remained deeply nervous and the run on the pound got a great deal worse. What kind of nation had warships that couldn't go to sea because the sailors were in open revolt? The acting commander-in-chief of the Atlantic Fleet, Rear Admiral Wilfred Tompkinson, tried to intercede with the mutineers and with the Admiralty, eventually putting forward his own pay proposals. By now, Cabinet meetings were also feverish. The mutiny fizzled out when the government caved in and limited the pay cuts to a maximum of 10%. The angry sailors agreed to sail the vessels back to their home ports on the promise of an investigation into their grievances. The Admiralty hung Admiral Tompkinson out to dry for not forcing his men to sea, placed him on half-pay and were glad to see the back of him when he retired four years later.

The mutiny was the last straw, and, on 21 September 1931, Ramsay MacDonald threw in the towel and abandoned the gold standard. Winston Churchill, the engineer of the gold-standard mess, had naturally defended it: going off the gold standard would mean the government had as little control over Britain's livelihood as it had over the weather. What would happen, he asked the House of Commons, if France and the United States acquired all the gold in the world? Were we really to assume, that all the rest of the world would be valueless?[5] The question at least showed he was beginning to understand how exchange rates worked. But MacDonald's government had made its mind up and decided to let the value of the pound float. Its value duly sank by over a quarter, which benefitted everyone in an export trade, since it made products cheaper internationally. Sidney Webb moaned that 'Nobody told us we could do this.'[6] He was wrong. Keynes had told the government both that it could and that it should do it seven years earlier.

Five days later, the Labour Party had its revenge on MacDonald and his acolytes who had served in the National Government, by expelling them. One month after that, on 27 October 1931, MacDonald sought a popular mandate in a general election. Luckily for him, he had recently abandoned his Welsh coal-mining seat in Aberavon, partly because he disliked the radical politics of the area. The party knew that Sidney Webb, the MP for the coal port of Seaham, County Durham, was disenchanted with the job, while MacDonald rather liked the idea of representing a different sort of mining town, not least because he had established that he wouldn't be expected to show his face in the place very often.[7] It was also reassuringly close to one of the five houses belonging to his lady-friend, the Marchioness of Londonderry. Edith Vane-Tempest-Stewart, the wife of a hugely wealthy coal magnate, was reputed to have a dragon tattooed on her right leg and a garter snake crawling towards her groin. So Sidney Webb was packed off to the House of Lords as Baron Passfield, leaving MacDonald, as the local MP, free to dance attendance on her ladyship. Webb's wife, Beatrice, sniffed in her diary at the sheer brazenness of what 'amounts almost to a public scandal'.[8] The entertaining spectacle of an illegitimate ploughman's son's infatuation with a marchioness was not lost on fellow Labour MPs. When Edith invited MacDonald to bring any colleagues he chose to a reception she was holding at her London mansion, Arthur Henderson remarked to Willie Adamson, a Scottish coal miner's son, 'Well, Willie, wouldn't you like to go and see the inside of a coal-owner's hovel.'[9]

But Seaham lived up to its reputation for being easy-going and in the new election, MacDonald was re-elected for the seat as a 'National Labour' MP. MacDonald was really campaigning on behalf of the Conservatives and the Liberals who had served in his government. After the rout which followed, a great number of Labour MPs (i.e. not supporters of the National Government) were former mining union agents. The public clearly preferred the National Government to the old-style politics, and MacDonald now had 554 MPs behind him, even though the great majority of them were Conservatives. It meant he was able to take seriously the policies proposed by 'the man from the Pru', George May. He invited the Conservative Neville Chamberlain to take over as Chancellor of the Exchequer from Philip Snowden. Chamberlain was happy to tax imports, but still had to cut government spending, which he wanted to do by, among other things, means-testing benefits. As may be imagined, this also did nothing to enhance MacDonald's popularity among his former colleagues in the Labour Party. He was, anyway, confused and increasingly tired and cranky. In 1932 he had been diagnosed with glaucoma.

In the end, rejected by his party, widowed and sick, his last years were not the culmination of which the country's first Labour prime

minister might have dreamed. He retired as prime minister, handing the job on to the Conservative, Stanley Baldwin. It was almost
all over for him, yet he stood again to be the MP for Seaham in the
general election which fell due in November 1935. But the blood
of the Labour Party was up, and they chose Manny Shinwell, a
pugnacious trade unionist who had served as parliamentary secretary to MacDonald's minister of mines in the first Labour
government, to stand against him. MacDonald suffered a crushing
defeat. They found him a safe seat representing the Scottish universities, but he was confused and feeble, and if he gave a speech, few
of the audience could understand what he was saying. One of his
daughters persuaded him that sea air would do him good, and he
died on board an Atlantic liner in November 1937.

MacDonald is a tragic figure. The first Labour prime minister
ended up reviled and scorned by much of his party. All political
memoirs attempt to justify the author's behaviour, and we can
never be sure how much diaries are written with one eye on future
readers. In December 1932, a year after the formation of
MacDonald's National Government, he had wondered 'Was I wise?
Perhaps not, but it seemed as though everything else was impossible.'[10] If that was really how he felt, he is more to be pitied than
reviled.

A few months before Ramsay MacDonald's death in 1937, the left-
wing publisher Victor Gollancz brought out *The Road to Wigan
Pier*, by the socialist journalist, George Orwell. Wigan being an
inland industrial town on the Leeds and Liverpool Canal there is,
of course, no pier in Wigan, though there once was a coal-loading
jetty. It is a messy, badly edited book. In the first half – an extended
piece of outstanding reporting – Orwell attempts to discover what
daily life is like for those who have to live on very little, and the
effects of unemployment. The reporter came from a privileged
southern background, and the anger he feels at the living and

working conditions of his northern countrymen is never far below the surface.

Coal, he said, was the basis of British civilisation.

The machines that keep us alive, and the machines that make the machines, are all directly or indirectly dependent upon coal. In the metabolism of the Western world the coal miner is second in importance only to the man who ploughs the soil. He is a sort of caryatid upon whose shoulders nearly everything that is not grimy is supported ... Practically everything we do, from eating an ice to crossing the Atlantic, and from baking a loaf to writing a novel, involves the use of coal, directly or indirectly. For all the arts of peace coal is needed; if war breaks out it is needed all the more. In time of revolution the miner must go on working or the revolution must stop, for revolution as much as reaction needs coal. Whatever may be happening on the surface, the hacking and shovelling have got to continue without a pause, or at any rate without pausing for more than a few weeks at the most. In order that Hitler may march the goose-step, that the Pope may denounce Bolshevism, that the cricket crowds may assemble at Lord's, that the Nancy poets may scratch one another's backs, coal has got to be forthcoming. But on the whole we are not aware of it.[11]

Orwell managed to spend a day in a mine. When the machines are in use, he feels the place is like hell:

heat, noise, confusion, darkness, foul air, and, above all, unbearably cramped space ... you crawl through the last line of pit props and see opposite you a shiny black wall three or four feet high. This is the coalface. Overhead is the smooth ceiling made by the rock from which the coal has been cut;

underneath is the rock again, so that the gallery you are in is only as high as the ledge of coal itself, probably not much more than a yard. The first impression of all, overmastering everything else for a while, is the frightful deafening din from the conveyor belt which carries the coal away. You cannot see very far, because the fog of coal dust throws back the beam of your lamp, but you can see on either side of you the line of half-naked kneeling men, one to every four or five yards, driving their shovels under the fallen coal and flinging it swiftly over their left shoulders. They are feeding it onto the conveyor belt, a moving rubber belt a couple of feet wide which runs a yard or two behind them. Down this belt a glittering river of coal races constantly.

Orwell was in a relatively modern mine, in which the proprietors had invested in machinery. In others, there were no conveyor belts to take the coal away and it had to be trundled out in waggons. Soon, the din would be worse, for there would be saw-toothed machines cutting the coal. But the lasting impression made upon Orwell – and the reader – is of the men themselves.

It is impossible to watch the 'fillers' at work without feeling a pang of envy for their toughness. It is a dreadful job that they do, an almost superhuman job by the standards of an ordinary person. For they are not only shifting monstrous quantities of coal, they are also doing it in a position that doubles or trebles the work. They have got to remain kneeling all the while … Shovelling is comparatively easy when you are standing up, because you can use your knee and thigh to drive the shovel along; kneeling down, the whole of the strain is thrown upon your arm and belly muscles. And the other conditions do not exactly make things easier. There is the heat – it varies, but in some mines it is suffocating – and the coal dust that stuffs up your throat and nostrils and collects along your eyelids, and the unending rattle of the conveyor belt, which in that confined space is rather like the rattle of a machine gun. But the fillers look and work as though they were made of iron. They really do look like iron – hammered iron statues – under the smooth coat of coal dust which clings to them from head to foot. It is only when you see the miners down the mine and naked that you realise what splendid men they are. Most of them are small (big men are at a disadvantage in that job) but nearly all of them have the most noble bodies; wide shoulders tapering to slender supple waists, and small pronounced buttocks and sinewy thighs, with not an ounce of waste flesh anywhere … You can hardly tell by the look of them whether they are young or old. They may be any age up to sixty or even sixty-five, but when they are black and naked they all look alike. No one could do their work who had not a young man's body, and a figure fit for a guardsman at that; just a few pounds of extra flesh on the waistline, and the constant bending would be impossible. You can never forget that spectacle once you have seen it – the line of bowed, kneeling figures, sooty black all over, driving their huge shovels under the coal with stupendous force and speed. They are on the job for seven and a half hours, theoretically without a break, for there is no time 'off'. Actually they snatch a quarter of an hour or so at some time during the shift to eat the food they have brought with them, usually a hunk of bread and dripping and a bottle of cold tea. The first time I was watching the 'fillers' at work I put my hand upon some dreadful slimy thing among the coal dust. It was a chewed quid of tobacco. Nearly all the miners chew tobacco, which is said to be good against thirst.

The nakedness necessary in high-temperature mines doubtless came as a shock to many readers. Some men, elsewhere, preferred to wear women's underwear – one ageing ex-miner told me of the Saturday morning shopping trips he used to make to the local Marks & Spencer store with a workmate to buy women's knickers which, being tighter, kept their genitals out of the way more effectively.

Orwell described the miners' 'commute' to work (for which, naturally, they did not get paid). On emerging from the cage which had dropped them into the mine, the men set off to walk to the face where they were to spend the day.

You start off, stooping slightly, down the dim-lit gallery, eight or ten feet wide and about five high, with the walls built up with slabs of shale, like the stone walls in Derbyshire. Every yard or two there are wooden props holding up the beams and girders; some of the girders have buckled into fantastic curves under which you have to duck. Usually it is bad going underfoot – thick dust or jagged chunks of shale, and in some mines where there is water it is as mucky as a farmyard. Also there is the track for the coal tubs, like a miniature railway track with sleepers a foot or two apart, which is tiresome to walk on. Everything is grey with shale dust; there is a dusty fiery smell which seems to be the same in all mines. ... You press yourself against the wall to make way for lines of tubs jolting slowly towards the shaft, drawn by an endless steel cable operated from the surface. You creep through sacking curtains and thick wooden doors which, when they are opened, let out fierce blasts of air ...

At the start to walk stooping is rather a joke, but it is a joke that soon wears off. I am handicapped by being exceptionally tall, but when the roof falls to four feet or less it is a tough job for anybody except a dwarf or a child. You not only have to bend double, you have also got to keep your head up all the while so as to see the beams and girders and dodge them when they come. You have, therefore, a constant crick in the neck, but this is nothing to the pain in your knees and thighs. After half a mile it becomes (I am not exaggerating) an unbearable agony. You begin to wonder whether you will ever get to the end – still more, how on earth you are going to get back. Your pace grows slower and slower. You come to a stretch of a couple of hundred yards where it is all exceptionally low and you have to work yourself along in a squatting position. Then suddenly the roof opens out to a mysterious height – scene of an old fall of rock, probably – and for twenty whole yards you can stand upright. The relief is overwhelming. But after this there is another low stretch of a hundred yards and then a succession of beams which you have to crawl under. You go down on all fours; even this is a relief after the squatting business. But when you come to the end of the beams and try to get up again, you find that your knees have temporarily struck work and refuse to lift you.

At the end of the day, the whole journey must be done in reverse, 'You try walking head down as the miners do, and then you bang your backbone. Even the miners bang their backbones fairly often. This is the reason why in very hot mines, where it is necessary to go about half naked, most of the miners have what they call "buttons down the back" – that is, a permanent scab on each vertebra.' It is painful even to read about.

Photographs of the time show crowds of miners going into the pits wearing cloth caps on their heads. These were not enough to protect from bad bruising or even concussion. Specific groups had worn their own protective helmets for some time: 'sinkers' who drove the first shafts into the ground, tended to wear waterproof, broad-brimmed hats like sou'westers above their shoulder-capes, to keep off cascading water, and by late Victorian days, many 'deputies' – experienced miners employed as supervisors or underground managers – were wearing skullcaps made of leather. In the 1930s some colliery proprietors began to demand that their miners wear hard hats. Initially, these helmets were made of compressed cardboard. So bad were relations between men and bosses, though, that some miners refused to wear the helmets when travelling to the face at which they were to work. Why should they wear special clothing in their own time, since they weren't being paid? Inevitably, helmets – and safety devices generally – became part of wage negotiations. Not least, there was the question of who paid for the things, since at many pits the miners had to supply their own clothes and equipment. By the late 1930s, an estimated two-thirds of miners still chose not to wear protective helmets of one kind or another. Another government intervention, in the form of a Royal Commission on Safety in 1938, suggested owners supply men with helmets. But there was no compulsion.

Towards the end of Orwell's exploration of the miner's life, he thinks about how life might be changed by this thing called 'socialism', which is not, he says, mainly espoused by working men in greasy overalls, but, typically, by prim little secret teetotallers and vegetarians, in white-collar jobs. 'One sometimes gets the impression,' he goes on, 'that the mere words "Socialism" and "Communism" draw towards them with magnetic force every fruit-juice drinker, nudist, sandal-wearer, sex-maniac, Quaker, "Nature Cure" quack, pacifist, and feminist in England.'[12] You couldn't write a sentence like that today, because almost all those categories of person are now accepted as parts of the human quilt. Orwell had recognised that many of the miners had Conservative hearts. It was a realisation that never dawned on many of the leaders of their trade union.

* * *

For proprietors, the 1930s were far short of British coal-mining's finest hour. Export markets which had existed before the First World War were gone and would never come back. Productivity per head had fallen: as economists often pointed out, the number of mouths to be fed by hewing a set amount of coal had risen from six before the war to seven in 1925. By May of that year, two-thirds of coal was being sold for less than it had cost to raise. The solution attempted in 1926, when the government threw taxpayers' money at the problem, allowing the owners to continue making a profit, was clearly not a long-term proposition. From the miners' point of view, the General Strike which followed the subsidy, in May 1926, had been a huge let-down. The seven-month strike in the coal industry of which it was a part – the most drawn-out and bitter industrial dispute in British history – had ended with a miserable settlement which forced them to accept lower pay and longer hours. The Depression had just made matters worse. The mine-owners chased sales by cutting prices, which they could only achieve by reducing wages, along with cutting corners on fripperies like safety. Those who could afford to do so embraced the promise of technology and installed machines to cut the coal, and conveyor belts to transport it to the bottom of the mineshaft.* Apart from the astonishing noise and air pollution produced by the machines – to say nothing of increased anxiety about their bringing on a roof fall – life was made worse for the miners by the new requirement that, instead of working at their own pace, they had to feed the machine at the speed it demanded.

Up to 250,000 miners had lost their jobs in the ten years up to 1934. But wages for those in work had failed to rise. A pamphlet produced by the union in 1933 claimed that miners' output had risen by half since 1920, while their wages had been cut by half.

---

* The machines greatly increased the amount of coal dust in the air. But that wasn't the proprietors' problem.

The whole industry was a shambles. There were 2,000 mines, many of which were unviable. There were about 1,000 proprietors. The majority of the 750,000 railway waggons which shifted the coal spent most of their time standing still. One-third of the 27,000 retail coal merchants handled hardly five tons a week. A lump of coal went through so many stages – with someone making a profit at each point – that when the former chief inspector of mines, Sir Richard Redmayne, tried to explain to the 1925 Royal Commission how the trade worked, he just remarked that 'if you endeavoured to follow a sack of Derby Brights from the colliery to a London cellar you would arrive there a shattered wreck from the number of hands you had gone through'.[13]

Liberal intellectuals argued that the production of coal was about keeping the people warm and illuminated. In which case, there was a strong argument for identifying coal-mining as a service, rather than an industry. That was the basic moral and political argument for the eventual nationalisation of the mines. The miners – as badly led as ever – dreamed about it. But the mine-owners dreamed mainly of making the coal yield up to them a decent profit. The consequences of their beliefs added a practical justification for nationalisation: mine-owners guarded their reserves so zealously that neighbours would stop mining well short of the limits from fear of accusations of trespass, with the result that the coal dug from the ground was not necessarily either the best or the most accessible, just that for which a lease could be shown to exist. Miners trudged great distances underground, coal trucks trundled on unnecessary journeys and drainage systems had to be duplicated, all because, as Herbert Samuel, head of the 1925 inquiry, put it, the owners were 'the fundamentalists of laissez-faire'. They were also utterly mule-like: the following year Churchill's friend, F. E. Smith remarked 'It would be possible to say without exaggeration that the miners' leaders were the stupidest men in England if we had not frequent occasion to meet the owners.'[14] One of the owners had actually told the Samuel Commission investigating the industry that miners blew ten shillings each week going to the cinema. You could hardly have invented a more naturally antagonistic environment.

For most of the time, miners were out of sight and out of mind, which was the way coal consumers liked it. When, occasionally, coal-mining burst into public consciousness, it was almost always bad news. Though it is much less well known than its counterpart in the valleys of South Wales, the North Wales coalfield, which runs in an arc from the most northerly place in mainland Wales – where the estuary of the river Dee debouches into the Irish Sea – east and then south, has the unwanted distinction of becoming in 1934 the scene of one of the worst mining disasters in British history. In 1907, the first sods had been cut for a new mine at Gresford, on the outskirts of Wrexham, the biggest town in North Wales. The downcast shaft was named the 'Dennis', after the family who were the principal local landowners, and the upcast, the 'Martin', after Sir Theodore Martin, the company chairman. Each dropped over 2,000 feet. Three years later, nearly half a mile down, the men sinking the Dennis shaft struck coal. By 1934, the pit was employing almost 2,200 miners. From the bottom of the Dennis shaft men often walked more than a mile to get to the face from which they were to be extracting coal that day. Parts of this section of the pit were horribly hot: men worked almost naked and had bored holes through the soles of their clogs to let the sweat run out. Ventilation was appalling, yet the owners continued to insist it was safer than the average mine, an assessment which perhaps reflects more on the death and injury rate elsewhere than anything else.

In the early hours of Saturday 22 September 1934 almost twice as many men as usual were working in the mine, many having 'doubled up' (working a day shift and then overnight), to be free in the afternoon to watch Wrexham FC play Tranmere Rovers in a

Third Division Northern League match: the fixture was a popular local derby. Double shifts like this were illegal and it is a mark of who called the shots that the company appears to have both tolerated and benefitted from the practice. As it turned out, the match on the Racecourse ground was played between two teams wearing black armbands in front of a crowd of 15,000 people who had just sung 'Abide With Me'.

At just after two that Saturday morning, the entire Dennis section had shaken to a massive explosion. There were 500 men working underground at the time, over half of them in what seemed to be the affected area. Very soon after the explosion, quickly judged to have been caused by 'firedamp' or methane, the manager went into the mine, to try to establish the scale of the damage and casualties. At about 3.30 one of the foremen reported that the underground road to the coalface was on fire, and that there were men trapped behind the flames. Can there be a worse nightmare than to be trapped underground, with a fire between you and safety? A group of six men who had been taking a mid-shift break had by now managed to climb out of the pit. But they were to be the only survivors: John Samuel testified later that when he tried to turn back towards what seemed to be the area of the blast, he was unable to get through the coal dust, which was 'just like a wall'.[15] Another survivor, Robert Andrews, described a smell of burning 'like you have been standing by a bonfire'. Soon before dawn, rescue parties and teams of volunteers were venturing as far as they dared into the mine. One of those who saw the flames remarked that 'the whole level was just one mass of flame, the coal sides of the roadway burning in one white mass'.[16] In the chaos, one of the rescue teams misunderstood their orders and tried to follow what they thought to be a ventilation shaft, despite the fact that in the poisonous air the caged canary they were carrying immediately fell off its perch and died. Only one of the team came back to tell the tale.

By now, Saturday breakfast-time, the forlorn crowds which had become a familiar sight at earlier disasters began to arrive at the pithead – fellow miners, wives, parents and siblings of the men trapped underground: they could not bear to be anywhere but as close as they could get. Like most such crowds, they were numb and quiet.

From deep beneath them they could hear the sound of more underground explosions. The longer the wait went on, the more corrosively certain the crowds became that there would be no happy ending. The president of the Lancashire and Cheshire Miners' Federation, who had been into ten mines after explosions, emerged saying he had never seen anything like it, and there was no chance anyone was still alive. Officials judged that shafts into the affected area would have to be capped. It was over.

Only eleven bodies had been recovered from the mine, and six survivors had staggered out of the pit alive; 265 men and boys had been killed and still lie in their workplace, their families denied the chance even to bury their loved ones: nine Hugheses, eighteen Robertses, nineteen Davieses, and thirty-three Joneses are still in the mine. A heroic miner who said he knew the workings well led three others to try to rescue any survivors. Within a few yards the canary they were carrying with them dropped dead in its cage. All rescuers described an awful smell of burning, and all of the eight victims recovered were believed to have died from carbon monoxide poisoning. Each of their bodies was charred.

The following Monday, 1,100 of the mine's survivors 'signed on' at the local employment exchange. It had been one of the worst tragedies ever to befall British mining, and was inevitably followed by a formal inquiry into what had happened, with union and owners' representatives and expensive lawyers with well-modulated voices bullying people who had not had their advantages in life. It was chaired by the chief inspector of mines, who at least knew about mines, even if he didn't know anything much about how to conduct an inquiry. He sat with a union rep, Joseph Jones, on one side of him and a Yorkshire coal-owner named John Brass on the other. The format was no way to find out anything much – for all three parties were compromised: the chairman because the Mines Inspectorate had failed to monitor the colliery properly, the miners because they had had the opportunity to raise concerns and had not done so, and the proprietors because safety had been compromised for profits. It began in a hopelessly jam-packed Church House,* before being adjourned to the ballroom of a Wrexham hotel, which became just as overcrowded.

The task was to discover how and why the tragedy had happened. That would inevitably mean blaming someone. The future Labour Chancellor of the Exchequer, Stafford Cripps, hired to represent the miners' union, did not hold back and produced a speech so coruscating that, the *Manchester Guardian* remarked, both friends and foes disliked it, though the union later reprinted it as a pamphlet. Cripps suggested that mining was about making a profit at any cost. He thought the behaviour of the Mines Inspectorate at the pit had been 'an absolute farce' and called one of the seams a 'gasometer'. Despite his hyperbole, he was probably on to something – across the industry rates of accidents and fatality had actually been getting worse.[17]

As we have seen, until the catastrophe occurred, Gresford had been touted as a comparatively safe mine, with a lower than average accident rate. Although pretty mechanised, it was not a colliery which promised instant riches. Indeed in three of the past five years, it had made a loss. There was much local chat that the company managing director, Henry Dyke Dennis, who was described even by his friends as 'forceful', had been leaning on the

---

* Church House was demolished by its owner the Duke of Westminster in 1972, and replaced with one of the ugliest shopping centres in Britain. A placard on the site of Church House now advertises 'Skippy's car wash'. The splendid Miners' Institute has been turned into a mosque.

mine manager, a weak-kneed man named William Bonsall, to improve profits. The chain of command was complicated by the survival in North Wales of 'butties', or 'charter masters', middlemen who 'supplied' the miners and divided up the money paid by the bosses as they chose. The chairman of the commission suspected that miners at Gresford were afraid of being victimised if they raised any worries. Cripps, for the miners, plugged away at the suggestion that profits had come before safety – it was discovered, for example, that records of air quality in the mine had simply been forged. With the mine sealed – and most of the bodies still inside it – no one could ever have definitively established the cause of this terrible event. Indeed, after hearing from 185 witnesses, the three men on the commission were unable even to agree on a single report.

In March 1937, forty-two charges were finally laid against individuals and the company. The case fizzled out a few weeks later, with fines totalling £140 being imposed for inadequate record-keeping, plus £350 costs. The following year – four years after the tragedy – inspectors deemed it still too dangerous to re-enter the mine. After the mining industry was nationalised in 1947, the shareholders of the United Westminster and Wrexham Collieries were compensated by the taxpayer for the loss of their pit, and all remaining records destroyed.

What is left of the winding wheel from one of the mineshafts now sits on an industrial estate at the edge of town as a memorial to the men who went to work that September night and never returned. Do the customers of the nearby garden centre ever think of the hundreds of bodies entombed beneath their feet? The corpses, the subterranean road they walked to work and the conveyor belts which they tended are presumably crushed amidst the coal they went to dig. The tragedy's great legacy is 'the miner's hymn', written by a former miner, Robert Saint, as the inquiry attempted to find out what had happened that September night.

'Gresford' is quite simply the most moving piece ever composed for brass band.

True to form, the government of the day established a Royal Commission to investigate safety in mines. In 1954, a Mines and Quarries Act was passed into law. It had been twenty years since the disaster, by which time the colliery had become a byword for the dangers of mining. Still, at every gathering of the Durham Miners' Gala – even after all the mines in the area have been closed – bands from the former colliery villages gather on the racecourse before the political speeches to play the miners' hymn. It still brings tears to the eyes of many.

For all George Orwell's disdain for socialism, the Labour Party at least had a plan, and by the late 1930s, the initiative was clearly with those who believed in nationalisation. Left to its own devices, this brutal industry was in trouble. Between the two world wars, over 1,000 pits were closed, and as coal reserves were exhausted, mining became a much less attractive way of earning a living – the number of men employed in the industry had fallen from 1,227,000 in 1920, to 782,000 in 1938. Miners' wages had been cut so much that instead of coming at or near the top of a pay league, there was nothing particularly attractive about them.[18] By the outbreak of the Second World War in 1939, the coal industry was in crisis.

The essential problem was clear enough to everyone: it cost too much to get British coal out of the ground. The conclusion was by now inescapable that the companies running the country's mines were simply not up to the job of managing such an important part of the national economy. Between 1913 and 1936, the amount of coal produced by one miner in one shift rose 81% in Germany, 117% in Holland, 73% in Poland, yet only 10% in Britain.[19] The best way to improve productivity – as far as an improvement could be effected – would have been for a concerted determination to have seized the industry. But there was too much water under the bridge, there had been too many empty promises and there was simply too much distrust between employers and miners. 'Hate' is a very strong word. But the depths of animosity and distrust between the leaders of the industry and the leaders of the men who made the industry function were profound. Everyone knew that mining was a troubled industry: in 1935, statistics showed that over half of the coal on sale had been hewn from only just over sixty pits, with hundreds which were inefficient and unproductive. The industry had a recruitment problem for the simple reason that wages were too low, the job too unpleasant and the dangers too great. Well-meaning folk from both sides of the fence made suggestions, that miners should be represented in management, that there should be committees drawn from both sides in each mine to talk things through before any confrontation, that similar bipartisan arrangements should exist in each region, and at national level. But between 1929 and 1938, nearly 263 million working days were lost in disputes.[20]

The British government tackled the comparative weakness of the country's coal industry in a familiar fashion. It announced yet another inquiry. The person they chose for the thankless task of trying to find the answer, through a Coal Mines Reorganisation Commission, created in 1930, was Ernest Gowers, a prime example of the ferociously clever young people who at that time entered public service. Gowers had left Cambridge with a first-class degree in classics and rose swiftly through the ranks of the bureaucracy, to be recognised as one of the ablest administrators of his generation. Now he was lured from running the Inland Revenue to be made chairman of the commission. (In retirement he was commissioned by the Treasury to produce a guide to the writing of clear English.* His advice, to 'be short: be simple: be human', has never been bettered.) But restructuring Britain's coal-mining industry

---

* Published as *Plain Words* in 1948, updated many times and still exemplary.

defeated him. A lawyer who saw the whole thing at first hand later wrote to *The Times* that 'Sir Ernest Gowers and his colleagues struggled manfully with their difficulties', but by depriving them of the information on which to base sensible decisions, 'Parliament had inadvertently tied their hands behind their backs'.[21]

But something had to be done. New arrangements gave Gowers more latitude. Crucially, they gave him over £64 million (well over £4 billion in today's values) with which to grease the palms of colliery-owners. So, eventually, at great cost to the public purse, the miners saw something close to what they were after. The owners thundered their distaste for the idea of government interference in their industry and the possibility of having their mines taken away and amalgamated. But they liked being given money and just about every party had run out of ideas. The joint manifesto of the National Government at the previous election (*A Call to the Nation*, 1935) had blathered about 'improved selling arrangements' and had actually proposed that the way forward was to set up yet another Royal Commission.

One after another, members of the House of Lords denounced the 1938 Coal Act. The legislation had been so mucked about with that, even though it was reckoned to be much more effective than the last attempt, eight years earlier, to reshape the industry, it was still a dogs' breakfast, passed by a government under Conservative leadership, implementing a socialist policy. It meant closing pits, at the very time when mining communities were trying to cope with the effects of the Depression. It took money from taxpayers and promised it to the colliery proprietors, and made a Coal Commission the owner of coal reserves, while preventing it from exploiting them. It left plenty of opportunity for obstruction by well-connected proprietors. Those coal-owners who were unsuccessful in preventing reform were more than adequately compensated: the taxpayer was going to give the Church of England's business managers £370,000 a year (about £25 million at today's prices). The Marquess of Bute was to receive £115,000 each year (approximately £8 million today) and the Duke of Hamilton, £113,000. Assorted dukes, earls and lords got much more. It is important to recognise that these payments were not for any activity carried out, but simply for any remaining coal left in the ground. The 1938 Coal Act effectively nationalised the mines, and those owners who wanted to avoid it, were told to get on with their own amalgamations. The *Colliery Guardian*, the voice of the employers, called the policy 'vicious'.[22] The end-of-year *Taunton Courier* had a more sophisticated view, remarking that 'so as not to frighten anyone, this measure of nationalisation is not so-called, but is throughout referred to as one of unification'.[23]

The so-called 'vesting date' when the law would take effect was 1 July 1942. But by then the country had other things on its mind. It was the date on which Rommel launched his first attack on British Empire forces at the little railway halt at El Alamein in North Africa.

12

Workers' Playtime

When Neville Chamberlain made his lugubrious announcement in September 1939 that Hitler had refused to withdraw his troops from Poland, and that 'consequently this country is at war with Germany', the nation's heart sank. The experience of the First World War was still fresh enough in the mind for people to be under no illusions about what might happen. In the corridors of government there ought to have been plenty of people with long-enough memories for there to be a determination not to repeat the mistakes of the previous convulsion, when great numbers of vital workers, including miners, had left their jobs to join up or to find better-paid work elsewhere. Not so. When conscription was brought in, the same day as Chamberlain's sombre news, the National Service Act did not exempt miners, despite naming doctors, engineers and the clergy as essential to survival. The predictable result was a shortage of labour in the coalfields: between 1938 and 1941, 25,000 miners left the Welsh pits alone. When Neville Chamberlain was discarded in favour of Winston Churchill in May 1940, the new prime minister chose as his labour minister Ernest Bevin, general secretary of Britain's biggest trade union, the Transport and General Workers' Union. Bevin's attitude was uncomplicated, believing it was 'a social obligation to defend your own homestead'.[1] The Emergency Powers Act gave him authority to instruct people to work in industries judged essential to the war effort. In April 1941 the mine-owners and the miners' union were told that their industry would become a 'scheduled undertaking', which would mean miners received a guaranteed job and guaranteed wages. Absenteeism was punishable with a £100 fine or a spell in prison. Neither side cared much for the idea, the owners disliking interference and claiming that settled wages would undercut their authority. Seymour Cocks, the long-standing Labour MP for Broxtowe, one of the mining constituencies in Nottinghamshire, told Parliament this was rubbish: 'If you abolished the Essential Work Order, half the men in the pit would leave the industry tomorrow of their own voluntary accord. Discipline, if you call it discipline, is maintained by a system of organised and authorised bullying in an atmosphere of noise, dust, heat, sweat and blasphemy.'[2]

Among the miners, resentment was particularly strong in South Wales, Scotland and the relatively new Kent coalfield, where they disliked not having the right to sell their labour as they chose. Bevin's scheme pleased no one. It was also a flop, and the need for miners was so urgent that worries began to be heard that Bevin would have to pull men out of the fighting, to send them into the mines. It did not happen, but in July 1941 Bevin set about rootling out anyone who had worked as a miner since 1935. Sixty thousand men who had retired or been invalided out of the pits were asked to return.

By comparison with wearing a uniform and chancing your life, mining was not an especially attractive choice and Bevin was not doing well. In July 1943 he told the annual conference of the Miners' Federation that the country needed at least 720,000 miners, and that he was going to launch a recruitment drive. Some ex-miners were lured back from the armed forces and from other industries, but it was nothing like enough. A change to the law had already enabled the government to supplant the owners in the management of the mines, but the Labour Party decided it was time to introduce industrial conscription and proper nationalisation of the collieries.

Bevin liked both these ideas and, though the middle of a war was not felt to be the time for the miners' preferred option of a full state takeover of the mines, he was willing to act to remove the element of choice. In December 1943, he came up with a scheme which attempted to catch the popular imagination: henceforth, one conscript in every ten would spend his war service in a mine instead of in uniform. Every two weeks, a number between zero and nine would be randomly chosen, and those men newly liable for National Service whose registration numbers ended in the digit chosen by lottery would be sent to serve their country underground. In those happy days before legions of government public relations officials, not much was made of the fact that the names were said to have been literally pulled out of a hat. *The Times* merely reported that, under the eyes of three ministers, 'a junior member of the staff of the ministry' had performed the task.[3] The hat in question was later alleged to be Bevin's distinctive homburg. The 'junior staff member' was his secretary. When a rumour ran around the following summer that a slightly more sophisticated method was being used, the industrial correspondent for the *Newcastle Journal* was able to report that 'I can now say on official authority that the ballot is continuing in full operation and is still conducted on exactly the same lines as those in the early days. Mr Bevin is not present at every draw from the hat as he was at the first ballots, but I understand that a senior ministry official is always there and the draw is still made by a junior member of the ministry office staff.'[4] The identity of this staff member (Bevin's secretary) was concealed, said a spokesman, 'lest she should be molested by mothers of boys who were sent to the coal mines'.[5] There is a slight whiff of implausibility to this story. But it was the one the 'Bevin Boys' themselves liked to believe. When you've been picked for an unattractive task which may result in public derision, perceptions – even self-mythologies – matter.

The miners' trade union did not like the sound of the Bevin Boys scheme, which they feared undermined them. But needs must. According to another cherished tale among the Bevin Boys – for which no substantiating evidence can be found – national coal supplies were down to their last three weeks when the first name-drawing took place.

The system turned out to be both wasteful and unpopular. There was no enthusiasm for conscripting only the young men of mining villages, which meant the Bevin Boys had either to be accommodated in hostels and barracks, or billeted on families in mining areas. There were plenty of examples of young men who had undergone naval or aeronautical training in a cadet force who now found themselves sent to labour down the mines. The playwrights and twin brothers Peter and Anthony Shaffer were both sent underground.* Very few exceptions were made: when a BBC engineer asked why an appeals tribunal had rejected his application, the chairman told him 'We never uphold an appeal.' To the inevitable question 'In which case, what's the point of holding a tribunal?', he received the reply 'We live in a democracy.'[6]

The new miners were given a medical examination, issued with travel warrants and despatched for four-week training courses, including much physical exercise (running, boxing, wrestling, judo and so on). It was not until 2008 that the then prime minister, Gordon Brown, bestowed commemorative badges on some of those still alive, and 2013 before a national memorial was erected. Despite their grievances, the scheme's unpopularity and a number of desertions, a Bevin Boys association has in recent times picked up a battered sense of pride in their service, despite the fact that many had to continue in their grimy forced employment until 1947. It was what had been asked of them in wartime and they had done their duty. Though the scheme never achieved even the

* As were the comedian Eric Morecambe and the paedophile Jimmy Savile.

slightest popularity, there were some places, like the colliery in Warwickshire where 400 out of 1,400 underground workers were said to be Bevin Boys, in which they probably saved the industry from collapsing from a shortage of manpower.

Apart from helmets made of compressed cardboard and one pair of hobnailed boots with steel toecaps, the conscripted miner was expected to wear his own clothes in the pit and since these Bevin Boys had no uniform, on the street they were often taken for cowards, deserters, skivers or conscientious objectors. Those who found themselves billeted on mining-village families whose sons were wearing uniform could find themselves in a particularly tricky situation.

The Bevin Boys at Point of Ayr mine composed their own protest song:

> We had to join, we had to join,
> We had to join old Bevin's Army.
> Fifty bob a week, nothing much to eat
> Hobnailed boots and blisters on your feet.
> We had to join, we had to join,
> We had to join old Bevin's Army.
> Bevin [in this, bowdlerised, version] the rascal.[7]

While the ballot became the best-known part of the process for choosing Bevin Boys, fewer than half of them – almost 21,000 – were picked in this way. Another 15,000 men chose to work in the mines instead of serving in the forces. Between 6,000–7,000 more men who were already serving got themselves reassigned to the mines. They were joined by forty-one conscientious objectors. As time went by, a lower proportion of Bevin Boys were chosen by ballot and more 'optants' chose to work as miners instead of wearing military uniform. The Bevin Boys were usually employed as 'colliers' boys' or apprentices, and were therefore paid less than the miners themselves. They were older, though, than peacetime apprentices – many were in their twenties – and complained often that they were given the dullest and worst-paid jobs. As intended, the new labour force was drawn from all social classes. They were often astonished by what they found. 'I never imagined such people existed,' said a son from a wealthy family in Canterbury.[8] Some remarked they found the miners genuine, frank and generous, if – down the mine – crude, sweary and rough. It seems to have been a lonely life for them. Very few decided to continue working in the mines once the moment of demobilisation arrived.

In years to come, many of those who had taken part in the war, whether wearing uniform or not, would remark upon the way that having a common enemy had produced a shared sense of purpose among the British people. The problem had been the Communist Party, whose newspaper, the *Daily Worker*, reacted to Hitler's invasion of France and the Low Countries in 1940 by talking about the response of 'the Anglo-French Imperialist War Machine'. When Hitler invaded Russia in 1941 and Stalin became an ally, politics demanded that British communist sympathies change; from now on, with only small exceptions, all parties supported the Allied war effort.

You might then expect that, whatever the external risk, domestic industrial relations were congenial. You would be mistaken. In 1944, for example, there were over 2,000 strikes, with 3.7 million days of lost production, a total which was not only higher than it had been for a decade, but was greater than would occur for another ten years. The characteristic of most strikes in the early days of the war was that they occurred independently of the relevant trade unions. And they were mainly illegal. During the first few months of the war, there were over 900 strikes, most of them short disputes over piece rates and ending with very few prosecutions. In 1941, engineering apprentices at factories supporting the war machine on Clydeside, in Coventry, in Lancashire and in London, refused to work. Two years later, engineers on Tyneside went out on strike. Although the context of production had changed, the nature of work had not and causes for aggravation were inevitable: the South Wales coalfield was especially restless, with dispute after dispute, over pay and conditions, most of them 'unofficial' (neither endorsed nor organised by the union). The great exception was a strike in Kent.

It was the newest of the British coalfields, the reserves having only been discovered in exploratory diggings for a planned tunnel under the Channel late in the nineteenth century. (That project was designed to use coal-mining technology, and abandoned when the ruling class became obsessed by hysteria about foreign armies using it to invade.) The commercial extraction of coal from beneath the ground of Kent near the straggling village of Betteshanger began in 1928 and had been something of a culture shock for residents of the genteel seaside resorts nearby, for it brought an influx of men from across the country trying to find work. 'No dogs, no miners' signs began to appear in the windows of lodging houses and pubs, though they did nothing to stop the migration. As the colliery became established, Betteshanger was soon adorned with the functional housing and street names characteristic of so many colliery settlements – Circular Road (around which the miners used to race their whippets), Northway and Broad Lane.

The men who came to live on these streets were drawn from Wales, Yorkshire, Scotland and many other coalfields. Often they arrived after being blacklisted for union activities in their previous pits. Inevitably, the Kent coalfield soon acquired its own reputation for militancy, and 'rag-ups' or walkouts over safety, pay or conditions – when, as a widow recalled, miners would regularly be 'suddenly at home'.[9]

Though they were chastised for striking, the Kent miners were of course not unaware there was a war going on – the area was frequently on the receiving end of bombs dropped by enemy aircraft on their way home and great numbers had relatives in uniform. On some days, you could hear German heavy artillery across the Channel. 'Strikes or lockouts cannot be permitted when the enemy are at the gates,' said Ebby Edwards, who had succeeded A. J. Cook as secretary of the Miners' Federation of Great Britain.[10] He was ignored.

In January 1942, miners' wages on a particular coalface were cut without warning. The 1,000 men most closely involved laid down their tools and walked out, soon followed by 3,000 others. This was a clear breach of Order 1305, which had been brought in to make wartime strikes illegal. But the men defied the law's insistence upon compulsory arbitration and stayed out for nineteen days.

The chief constable of Kent bleated that he didn't have enough of the necessary forms to charge them all, and it was decided to take action only against those most directly involved. Eventually, enough extra magistrates were dug out to sign all the paperwork. As colliery bands from other coalfields played in the streets outside Canterbury magistrates' court, wives and children cheered the men into court. A bushy-browed civil servant, Sir Harold Emmerson, watching the case, called the atmosphere 'festive'. Three union officials were sentenced to hard labour, a particularly foolish punishment since it was not something to which they were exactly unaccustomed and they happened, anyway, to be the only people who could call off the strike. Eventually, over a thousand miners were fined £1 each. Finally, at the end of the month, the Secretary for Mines came down to speak to the miners, the officials were released from gaol and everyone went back to work, although the grand total of men who had paid their fines, was only nine: the clerk to the justices had pointed out to officials in London that the county prison would only be able to accommodate the

1,000 defaulters on some sort of shift basis. No one ever did chase them for the fines, for the miners had won. As much as others harrumphed at the miners' victory – one retired colonel and garden-gnome manufacturer in Newcastle-under-Lyme wrote to his local paper suggesting the only reason for releasing the strikers should have been to put them against a wall and shoot them[11] – public opinion seemed much more in tune with the anonymous miner who wrote to the paper two days later. 'Isn't that what Hitler does?' he asked simply. A headline in the *8th Army News* the next spring hit the nail on the head: 'The right to Strike is one of the Freedoms we fight for.'

The curious thing was that so many of the laws of the land ran so counter to this war aim. The entire conflict became known as 'the people's war' for its sheer indiscriminateness – bombing and shelling affected everyone, regardless of their status. Strikes, which almost always sought to benefit a sectional interest, had largely become illegal. A wartime coalition government included most of the mainstream parties and the involvement of the Soviet Union as an ally from 1941 onwards meant that even the Communist Party was committed to avoiding strikes which might jeopardise the war effort. Gestures big and small were made. In February 1944, King George VI and Queen Elizabeth made a visit to the colliery at Elsecar in South Yorkshire, where the attendant press gaggle made much of the fact that they had sat with miners in the canteen to eat a meal of roast beef, sprouts and potatoes, followed by 'golden pudding', washed down with a glass of beer. The queen declared it was a long time since they had had a better meal. 'Yes, that is so,' muttered the king.[12] The checkweighman opined that he felt 'very much at home' with the king, and the local mayor presented him with a safety lamp, pronouncing he was now a Bevin Boy.[13] (Elsecar was one of the collieries which had made the Fitzwilliam family stupendously rich, and the king's father, George V, had been a friend of the seventh earl, 'Billy' Fitzwilliam: during a royal visit in 1912 there had been much incoherent trumpeting about him being 'the first monarch to go down a mine'.*)

It could not last long. The war had brought a temporary truce to most places, but that was all it was. The problems of geology and discontent with ownership structures were unchanged, and periodic confrontations and occasional strikes were inevitable. In the wartime economy, miners were no longer at the top of the tree when it came to wages, as they could discover for themselves by talking to munitions workers. The bad blood between owners and workers was as rancorous as ever. 'Every penny on the wages, every minute off the hours, every improvement in housing conditions, every pithead bath and welfare centre, had to be fought for and won by the miners themselves,' said the president of the Miners' Federation in 1944. 'The owners have never willingly given a single concession.'[14] By the spring of that year, miners were as discontented as ever. Having taken the decision that war-making required planning, it was inevitable that the government would now devise bureaucratic mechanisms to decide who should be paid what. A National Reference Tribunal, intended to keep everyone comfortable about their place in the pecking order, reported in late January 1944. In some places their recommendations meant no wage rise at all. In others they amounted to pay cuts. Two days later, the *Derby Daily Telegraph* reported that 1,400 of the otherwise quite well-paid miners in Lancashire had stopped work in protest. It never formally became a strike, but as weeks passed, the disruption grew sporadically involving more Lancashire miners, then others in Staffordshire, Monmouthshire and South Wales.

By late March, tens of thousands of Yorkshire miners were on strike and within days, Bevin was talking of their action as 'a black

---

* This was untrue, for James I had been down Sir George Bruce's colliery almost 300 years earlier, in 1617. The colliery seams ran out under the estuary of the river Forth, and when he emerged from underground onto one of the mine's man-made islands, the poor booby thought he was being abducted and cried 'Treason!'

spot … What happened this week in Yorkshire is worse than if Hitler had bombed Sheffield and cut our communication.'[15] The minister for fuel and power, David Lloyd George's son Gwilym, let it be known that he was working on a replacement for the payments designed by the tribunal award. It turned out to involve much fudging of allowances, which took average miner's wages from forty-first in the national chart to fourteenth. A rough calculation showed that by the end of April 220,000 miners in South Wales and Yorkshire alone had been out on strike, the government repeatedly suggesting they had been duped by Trotskyite conspirators. The Trades Union Congress pronounced that the miners had 'struck a blow in the back of their comrades fighting in the armed forces', to which militant miners replied that you had more chance of being injured down a mine than at much of the front.

Perhaps the most important thing to notice about these actions is the extent to which they were contained. Everyone knew there was a war on. The miners still did a hard and scary job for not very much pay, but all major parties in Parliament recognised the greater importance of national survival. The miners enjoyed some support from public opinion, but it was compromised by support for those wearing uniform. Trade unions had surrendered their right to disrupt production for the duration of the war and everyone was in the same boat – the moment you emerged from the pit you were in a world of rationing and empty shelves.

But never again would the country produce the amount of coal it had yielded before the First World War. The mechanics of extraction looked feeble. Of course it was true that it was geology which decreed how much harder it was to get coal out of the ground in Britain than it was in, for example, Australia or the United States. But once the fighting had ended the question was, were conditions so much worse in Britain than they were in Germany or the Netherlands, which seemed to be able to dig so much more per shift than the UK? Those who bothered to think about these things saw a progression taking place. In the beginning, humankind had attempted to harness wind and water power. Then it had obtained its energy from vegetation, by burning wood. After that it had burned fossil fuels, beginning with the ones which were easy to reach. Shortly, science would offer nuclear energy which seemed to promise limitless power almost from thin air.

What was wrong with British coal-mining? It wasn't hard to work out, though it was terribly difficult to do much about it. For a start, the mines had often been the consequence of someone having a bright idea and sinking a shaft to see what he could get out of the ground. The result was that they were often awkwardly positioned and inconveniently laid out, and when someone argued that a mine was too small to make anyone's fortune, it was often hard to find another nearby with which it might be easily merged. It didn't help when the proprietors then squabbled among themselves. Mining remained an intensely local industry, with conditions varying from mine to mine. Yet, increasingly everyone recognised that if and when the administration of the mines changed, it would do so nationally, which had been one of the reasons that in 1944, the miners decided to replace their federation of loosely associated local organisations with the National Union of Mineworkers. It would develop into the most feared trade union in the land. The end of the war in 1945 provided an opportunity to take stock, though most of the expertise belonged to those with vested interests. Colliery proprietors produced ludicrously exaggerated estimates of their reserves – in the Bristol and Somerset coalfield, for example, seven of the thirteen collieries claimed they expected still to be producing coal in a century's time (in fact, the last one closed in 1973), while the four Kent mines believed they had reserves to last up to 300 years (the last of them closed in 1989). Productivity figures weren't helped by the fact that the longer coal had been extracted from the seam, the greater the proportion of

each day a miner had to spend trudging the underground 'roads' to
get to his place of work. The Mining Association of Great Britain
claimed their member firms had £100 million available for investment. Oddly, considering their confidence, very few mines seemed
to have embarked upon big spending programmes.

It was a very mixed picture. Enterprising mine-owners had
installed underground machinery to cut coal from the bottom of
the seam, after which deposits above could be blown down with
explosives. But not every proprietor fancied the capital investment
required. In the most mechanised mines, conveyor belts carried
the cut coal away, but conveyors, too, cost money. Though the
number of pit ponies had been steeply reduced, most underground
coal haulage in Britain was by means of awkwardly shaped tubs
attached to an 'endless rope'. A quarter of underground workers in
wartime had been employed hauling coal.

And there was no escaping the fact that relations between the
men who handled the coal and the men who handled the men
were still not good. Until the war, miners and mine-owners were
on opposite sides of the fence. Inside a mine, men often got on well
with their supervisors and 'pit deputies'. Wartime working had
meant new bosses, who perhaps had different priorities from the
old bosses. But the work required was the same. Even the threat of
national extinction during the war had done little or nothing to
improve relations between employers and miners. Mining productivity depended upon translating the work of the man hewing at
the coalface into profits. The industry could not become more
productive by employing more people at the top of the shaft, or in
other ancillary occupations: that would have the reverse effect. In
the end, the health of the industry depended upon the health and
strength of the hewers. It was an intensely physical job, and by the
end of the Second World War, the average age of a miner had
increased, as low wages took a toll on recruitment.[16] Productivity
during the war hadn't improved. In 1939, 766,000 miners had dug

231 million tons of coal. In 1945, the remaining 692,000 raised 174 million tons. Absenteeism had risen continuously during the war.[17] And the series of wartime strikes seemed to demonstrate miners were no less disgruntled than they had ever been. Much of the general public (and many military conscripts) just came to roll their eyes when they heard miners moaning about their bloody 'differentials'.

Time for yet another inquiry. This time, the War Cabinet asked a well-known mining engineer, Charles Reid, to lead six others in finding out what on earth was wrong with the British coal industry. His report was devastating. There were mines which had exhausted their reserves, mines which would never be profitable, many which ought to be merged, yet others where the owners could not afford to sink shafts to reach coal deposits. To make matters worse, there was a shortage of mining engineers to sort things out. Above all, he wrote, 'The problem of securing full cooperation between the employers and the workmen is the most difficult and urgent task the Industry has to face.'[18] Though it would be a political decision, and therefore had to await the result of an election, the report was widely interpreted as suggesting that the only solution was for the industry to be nationalised. By May 1945, the wartime minister for fuel and power, Major Gwilym Lloyd George, had accepted the thrust of Reid's report and was ready to recommend nationalisation. Within weeks of the end of the war, Britain had elected a Labour government, and the nation had a new minister who was publicly committed to the idea.

The ambitions of Clement Attlee's post-war Labour government were breathtaking and dwarfed the plans of any modern government before or since. To slay the 'five giants' – Want, Ignorance, Disease, Squalor and Idleness – identified by William Beveridge as stalking the country, Labour invented the welfare state, to provide care from the cradle to the grave. They believed this noble ambition required government control of the Bank of

England, the steel industry, hospitals, electricity generation, gas supply, the road and rail networks and town and country planning. Attlee sent Ernest Bevin to the Foreign Office, where Frank Giles, later editor of the *Sunday Times*, was one of those working for him. Once, as they stood side by side at a urinal, Bevin remarked, 'This is it, Giles, the socialist dream – the means of production in the hands of the people.'[19]

It was unimaginable that the coal industry might be left out of the sweeping nationalisations of the socialist dream: it had been the foundation of the nation's economy and still employed 700,000 people so, as the biggest civilian employer in the country it would be one of the chief safeguards against Idleness. Bringing the mining industry under government control had been an item of faith for much of the Labour Party since Keir Hardie. Broadly, there were five main arguments advanced. Firstly, at a political level it was simply wrong for a group of individuals to be able to control a public utility for private gain. Secondly, it was morally wrong for them to profit from geological accident. Thirdly, it would be much easier to plan production – and to ensure full employment (both big deals in the new Labour nirvana) – if the industry was controlled by the state. Fourthly, the industry would be more productive and co-ordinated if centrally organised. Fifthly, if the industry was owned by the state there would be better working conditions and relations between workers and management, and so fewer strikes and interruptions to supply. Since unexploited coal reserves in the ground had been the property of the state since the Coal Act of 1938, there was a sense of unfinished business, anyway: to many of the miners' leaders, nationalisation was the promised land. The Second World War had given a good indication of what nationalisation might be like, with the government ordering the workforce about and controlling the price of coal.

A minority of firebrands talked of the state just seizing the mines from the landowners and operators, with no compensation payment of any kind. But, the party decided that, to be trusted, compensation would be made. The 'royalty' paid to landowners for the coal extracted from the ground by the mine operators was a hangover from feudal days. But that was no obstacle. In 1918 the Sankey Commission had discovered that almost half of the nearly £6 million paid by the collieries to landowners in royalties was given to a mere hundred families, including into the very deep pockets of the Marquess of Bute, the Duke of Hamilton and the Duke of Northumberland. Many of these owners could trace their lineage and landholdings back to Tudor times. The two greatest beneficiaries of nationalisation would be the Church of England and the Crown. In 1946, the National Coal Board agreed to pay the landowners almost £81 million (about £3.5 billion at today's values) as compensation for coal left in the ground at exhausted workings. Since there was no way of extracting most of this theoretical coal, the owners must have thought it was Christmas. (Mercifully for the British taxpayer, in 1973, after enormous payments had been made to Church, Crown and other landowners, all outstanding royalties were written off.)

The National Coal Board took over the industry on New Year's Day 1947. By the end of the year the National Coal Board was running almost 1,000 collieries. It discovered it was now also the owner of 140,000 houses; eighty-five brickworks and pipeworks; thirty plants for manufacturing products like coal briquettes; fifty-five coke ovens; numerous railway services (with over 200,000 railway waggons); almost 2,000 farms; assorted offices, schools and village halls. And a holiday camp. The National Coal Board had grand ambitions, creating its own research establishment under the brilliant Jacob Bronowski and employing E. F. Schumacher (later the author of the highly influential 1973 book *Small is Beautiful*) as its chief economic adviser. A film unit turned out more than 900 films.

The miners were thrilled to achieve their ambition. Their trade had never been a way of life in which you could nurture illusions, but many had felt that they had been at the bottom of the heap for far too long. Some could even quote the 1815 Assizes Court judge who'd remarked that it was unusual to bother with a coroner's inquest if the corpse was 'only that of a collier'. They didn't deny there had been some rise in their status since then, but a miner in Durham in the 1940s commented that the prejudice lasted long into the twentieth century: 'You're rats that dig under the earth – that's the way the upper class used to look at you.'[20] They resented the sneers: they did a harsh, unforgiving, dangerous and exhausting job: how dare people look down on them? Now, though, nationalisation conferred status and recognition. It also meant better pay and conditions, more organised and humane management, better housing, improved schools and recreational facilities. When the mines were nationalised in 1947, 326 of them had pithead baths. By 1962 there were 632. Being clean, which so many take and took for granted, is vital not merely to health but to self-esteem. Many had noticed that if a miner had to get on a bus home from work, without the chance to wash, often enough other passengers would move to sit elsewhere. At dances, girls could refuse to partner miners because they spent five days a week in the filthy underground and their weekends getting drunk. After nationalisation, one South Wales miner, Doc Davies, was carried away by the change in their social status. 'If you'd like to compare a miner, I'd say in the old days he was like a mole groping in the dark, burrowing in darkness, but today he is like a peacock, and he is very proud of himself and as proud as that peacock.'[21]

Their housing, too, changed. Instead of the tatty colliery villages thrown up around the mines by the old colliery proprietors, wherever they could the National Coal Board paid a subsidy to local authorities, so that miners were living in public housing among people who held all manner of jobs. There was money set aside to spend on recreational buildings, sports fields, and facilities for old, sick and disabled miners. The first report from the National Coal Board explained the thinking: 'Any organisation must deal honestly with its workpeople, if it is to prosper, but a nationalised industry, existing only to serve public ends, must set an example in the way it treats its employees, enlarges their opportunities and encourages their efforts.'[22]

But the Coal Board's priority remained to get coal out of the ground, as cheaply as possible. There was much talk of making it the most efficient industry of its kind in the world, and there was some early success, increasing output to 197 million tons. The proportion of face-workers was increased, so that by the end of 1948 they made up over 40% of those employed. Finding new miners to cut and haul the coal had not been made easier by the raising of the school-leaving age to fifteen, but by the end of the year, a number of retired miners had been lured back to the pits and, in areas where the union didn't object, some new labour had been hired from 'displaced persons' camps in Germany.

But the abiding memory for most of the public in 1947 was of the one thing from which coal was supposed to protect them. They felt bone-numbingly cold that winter. The National Coal Board had taken over the industry in mild weather. Indeed, mid-January 1947 was almost warm. But then a high pressure system over Scandinavia set off prolonged, extremely low temperatures. Thousands of people were cut off by snowdrifts, some of them over twenty feet deep. Even the Scilly Isles were carpeted in heavy snow. Bitter easterly winds meant teeth chattered everywhere: it snowed someplace in the UK every day for fifty-five days. The Thames froze. Buses and trains were abandoned. Supplies of food ran short and if you could lay your hands on ingredients for a family dinner, it was eaten in overcoats and mittens. Things did not improve in February, when there were only two days in the entire month when the temperature rose above freezing point at the weather station in

Kew Gardens. Indeed, on 25 February, a weather station in Bedfordshire recorded a temperature of minus twenty-five degrees Celsius. Blizzards continued even into March, causing five-metre drifts in the Pennines, with bigger drifts piling up in Scotland.

It was the first test of the new, post-capitalist energy system. And the system failed. The class warrior* Manny Shinwell had been made the new Labour government's minister of fuel and power. He had been warned in October that coal stocks were dangerously low, if it should turn out to be a hard winter. But gambling on the weather was preferable to confrontation with the miners, about whose rate of absenteeism he seems to have been simultaneously baffled, sympathetic and incandescent. Did they not understand how important it was for the nationalised industry to flourish?[23]

Yet, as a man of the left – a 'stormy petrel of trade unionism' he had been called by another left-winger[24] – the unions were telling him not to worry his little head about the industry. They understood Shinwell's prejudices. On taking over as minister of fuel and power he had ordered the gardens of the enormous Yorkshire mansion Wentworth Woodhouse (the biggest privately owned house in Europe) to be dug up, to get at the coal beneath. This had rather put out the owner, the eighth Earl Fitzwilliam, as he'd been assured by Shinwell's predecessor this would only happen in a 'really desperate emergency'.[25] The vast house the family had built on the proceeds of coal-mining stood like a 'jewel in a crown of poverty and grime', as testament to the enormous chasm between the haves and have-nots of the mining world. In the late eighteenth century, it had been one of the most important houses in the land, but no one could quite work out what to do with the place once the army had moved out at the end of the Second World War.

In September 1945, when Manny Shinwell requisitioned the place, he planned to strip the soil from the ground and to begin

---

* He was notorious for declaring the middle class to be 'not worth a tinker's cuss'.

open-cast mining for coal. His Lordship recognised times had changed, but asked the government whether it wasn't possible to get at the coal below the grounds of the house by underground mineshafts instead of by the open-cast mining* being proposed: even the president of the local mineworkers' association had described the gardens as some of the most beautiful in the country and begged for their preservation. Shinwell claimed that the coal which could be extracted from the Wentworth estate was three-quarters of the entire quantity needed to keep the railways of Britain going for a week: needs must. But however he tried to gloss it, his decision to send mechanical diggers into Humphrey Repton's gardens to rip out shrubs, trees and rhododendrons looked an act of vindictive vandalism. Perhaps he justified it by his claim that 'private property must be used for the benefit of the nation … There should be no department of public activity in which Labour has not got to have a finger in the pie.'[26]

The crime of the Fitzwilliam family was to belong to the traditional ruling class. The diggers dropped the waste from their mechanical buckets in front of the baroque west-facing windows. The dowager countess muttered that the diggers were probably owned by one of Shinwell's relatives. The Fitzwilliams had had a good run for their enormous sums of money. But now they said they didn't have the wherewithal to keep the place up any more, held an enormous sale of contents, including George Stubbs's masterpiece, the almost three-metres-tall picture of the Arabian stallion Whistlejacket,† and decided to rent out the Palladian half

---

* Unlike the tunnelling technique, open-cast mining is a surface method, involving digging enormous holes in the ground, and then extracting the coal with mechanical diggers.

† Though he painted dozens of horses, *Whistlejacket*, showing the horse standing on his hind legs – a perfect expression of elegance, power and independence – is generally acknowledged as his masterpiece. It is now in the National Gallery, London.

of the house as a training college for female physical education teachers. As hearty young women vaulted over gym horses, the earl looked out on the advancing bulldozers over a large whisky. When the ninth earl died in 1952, a family squabble over who should inherit titillated the gossip columns for a while as his mother declared one of her sons could be illegitimate. When the tenth earl died without leaving an heir, Sheffield Polytechnic took the place on, and after that the house was bought by a self-made pharmaceuticals magnate and then repossessed by his bank when his cure for herpes turned out to be less permanent than the disease. Other schemes to rescue the house have followed, though it is hard to imagine the place ever reassuming its grandeur.

The miners, though, had got what they wanted. In May that year, a five-day week was introduced, with pay to be the same as for working six days, as long as there was no absenteeism. The Coal Board was unambiguous about its obligations to its workers, stating in its first report that 'a nationalised industry, existing only to serve public ends, must set an example in the way it treats its employees'.[27] The Coal Board spent money improving canteens, and installing and running pithead bathhouses. But there was something not quite right. The chairman of the Coal Board, John (later Viscount) Hyndley, had spent his working life in the industry and seems to have been well regarded and efficient. But he was a remote figure, and in place of the old colliery managers was now a vast and faceless bureaucracy. Over time, industrial relations improved, but initially, morale among the miners does not seem to have got any better. The habit of downing tools to get their way was so deeply ingrained with them that the Coal Board estimated that the amount of production it lost to strikes was doubled from the previous year. Despite increasing the price of coal it made a loss of over £9 million in its first year.

But the writing was on the wall. Though 90% of the energy needs of the country were met by burning coal, the power sources of the future looked to be oil, gas and nuclear fuel. The oil industry calculated that by the mid-1970s, coal would provide less than half of the power used in Britain. Long-term coal was in decline. When a Conservative government was elected in 1955 it did not waste effort attempting to get the industry denationalised.

13

King Coal Coughs

On 8 December 1952 came the event which began to change everything. Cool air from the continent settled over the Thames Valley, trapped by a higher level of warm air. This 'temperature inversion' was not an especially unusual weather event, but it had dramatic consequences in London. It meant that the warm coal smoke discharged from the great number of factories in the capital could not escape, to disperse in the atmosphere. So it cooled and then settled at ground level, where it formed a dense cloud. There had been smogs in London before, but this became the worst of the lot, mainly because coal was now being used everywhere. London had seen the world's first coal-fired power station open at Holborn Viaduct in 1882 and it had been followed by numerous other coal-burning power stations at Barking, Canning Town, Deptford, Enfield, Fulham, Greenwich, Hackney, Lots Road, Neasden, Stepney, Willesden and Woolwich. A new plant was being built among the densely packed streets of Poplar, destined to be proudly opened by the recently ennobled old TUC warhorse, Walter Citrine. Bankside power station in Southwark was being expanded. Most famously there were the four enormous chimneys of Battersea power station in central London, burning a million tons of coal per year, which was delivered by 'flatiron' coasters, with collapsible masts and funnels. That plant, too, was under expansion when the smog swamped the capital's streets.

In addition to the pollution produced from generating electricity, London was still an industrial city, with factory smokestacks all over the skyline. To make matters worse, the National Coal Board had just declared that 'nutty slack' – a particularly filthy type of small coal waste – would no longer be rationed and was available for sale to any householder. Advertisements by the Coal Board promised that 'Nutty slack will help to keep the home fires burning however long and cold the winter.' 'Slack' was the cheapest form of black coal, more like black sand than anything else and burned with a lot of smoke. 'Nutty slack' did have nuggets of coal within it, but four days after it became freely available, the weekly death rate in London had soared to levels last seen at the height of the Blitz. By 13 December, over 4,000 people had coughed and choked to death. Visibility had plunged, making navigation of the city extremely difficult. On the second day of the smog, all five Football League games scheduled to be played in London were cancelled. Children made their way to school with scarves over their mouths, holding hands and feeling their way along the streets. Bus drivers asked their conductors to walk in front of the vehicle, as they followed their torch beams. Even in suburban west London, people could find their way after dark only by following the glint of the occasional light on the trolley-bus wires. Greyhound racing at White City dog track was abandoned because the dogs couldn't see the hare. In some parts of east London, people were unable to see their own feet as they walked along the pavement. They said that if you were lucky enough to be working in the cab of a crane in the docks, you might be able to see above the smog, but down below, the Port of London police were issued with walking sticks, so they could tap their way along the wharves. When it entered buildings, the smog covered everything in slime. A performance of *La Traviata* at Sadler's Wells Theatre had to be suspended after the first act because of incessant coughing from the audience. In cinemas people complained that they couldn't see the screen. To make any progress on the street in a car you needed a companion to walk in front, with a light or flare. Those with the slightest weakness in their chests wheezed with 'fog cough', and anyone with a respiratory condition, and all children, were at serious risk. Hospital oxygen supplies were exhausted. More people were choked to death in Greater London that December than died on the entire country's roads in the whole year.

It was seven months before the government launched a formal investigation into how many people had been killed by the suffocating smoke which had painted the capital murky grey. Later studies showed that there had been at least an additional 7,700 deaths, with some reckonings as high as 12,000 extra fatalities.[1] True to national stereotype, though, what really caught the public attention was the suffering of the prize animals at the Smithfield Agricultural Show being held at Earls Court. Several had to have 'breathing bags' soaked in whisky fitted to their heads. The cow 'Bapton Millie Actress' was treated with an oxygen mask, but before the show began three animals had choked to death and a further eight had had to be slaughtered.[2] The dead included a two-year-old by the unfortunate name of 'Lucky Boy', an Aberdeen Angus crossbred steer valued at £200. His owner, Mr Wishart, was clearly a man inured to suffering, yet gushed to the *Aberdeen Evening Express* that 'Sometimes one or two animals die of exhaustion after travelling … but this year's heavy death toll must be unique.'[3]

The smog was such an astonishing phenomenon that it was an irresistible story. *Reader's Digest* took delight in reprinting a description it claimed to have found in *La Croix*, a Catholic newspaper published in Paris:

You could just see your own feet … As you groped along the pavement, blurred faces without bodies floated past you. Sounds were curiously muffled: motor-car horns, grinding brakes, the alarming cries of pedestrians trying to avoid the traffic and one another ... At London airport a few planes made instrument landings. One pilot, after landing, got lost trying to taxi to the terminal. After an hour a search party went out to look for him. But it too got lost. Soon all air traffic was suspended. As the day went on, the fog changed colour. In the early morning it had been a dirty white. When a million chimneys began to pour coal smoke into the air it became light brown, dark brown, black. By afternoon all London was coughing. On Saturday morning thousands of Londoners began to be frightened. They were those people, mostly over fifty, who had a tendency to bronchitis or asthma. In a long black fog such people are in acute distress. Their lungs burn, their hearts labour, they gasp for breath. They feel as if they are choking to death – and sometimes they do. By Saturday noon all the doctors were on the run. But there wasn't much to suggest – except to try to get to an oxygen tent. All hospitals were overworked ... Workers who couldn't get home slept in their offices or went to police stations and were put up overnight. Members of Parliament were issued blankets and bunked down in lounges of the House ... Police patrolled the docks in life jackets because people who couldn't see the ground walked into the water; a policeman at the Albert Docks pulled out eight. But too often the victims, though their cries were heard, couldn't be found ... On Sunday morning the fog was thicker than ever. At times visibility got down to eleven inches: literally you couldn't see your hand held out in front of your face ... It was cold that day. On the outskirts of town men and women became lost in the murk, sat down – and later were found dead of exposure ... Towards noon on Monday the fog lifted a little, then came down again. Then it rose a little more. Finally it was gone. Londoners rubbed the soot out of their eyes and saw a city covered with

dirt. Every piece of furniture had a slimy, black film. Curtains
were so encrusted with soot that when they were cleaned they
went to pieces. Blonde women became brunettes. It was weeks
before the hairdressers and laundries and cleaners caught up
with their work.[4]

The French reader could scarce resist whistling the 'Marseillaise'
in relief at not being British.

There was no official inquiry into the causes of the London
smog of 1952, which testifies to the fact that it seemed to be
regarded as just one of those things. The portmanteau phenomenon of 'smoke' and 'fog' was not unique to London. But London
had the worst smogs in the world. In complete combustion, all that
is left by a fire is water and carbon dioxide. But the densest collections of unburned particles in urban smoke created smogs so
impenetrable they were known as 'pea-soupers' or 'London
particulars', which crept along the streets like a footpad. People
walked into one another, vessels collided in the Thames. People
drowned in canals they had not seen.

For a good while in the early nineteenth century, some otherwise sensible people had actually believed that pollution was good
for you. The prevailing theory of disease was to attribute illness to
'miasma', an invisible, foul-smelling vapour full of decaying matter.
Smoke, the quacks claimed, acted as a form of disinfectant. That
was not, presumably, how it felt to those who choked as they tried
to breathe.

Coal and its by-product, gas, had already created an entirely
novel way of seeing the world. In place of a gradual lengthening of
shadows and the crepuscular dimming of vision, gas glowed
brightly all night, and human beings took advantage. It turned a
monstrous smoggy mass into an identifiable city of night-time
theatre. The pre-eminent painter of this new world was John
Atkinson Grimshaw, a policeman's son from Leeds. Grimshaw was

beguiled by gaslight as a young man and began to paint night-time scenes he saw in his home city in the late 1850s. By the 1880s he was painting night scenes in Glasgow, Liverpool and London. What is striking about these townscapes is the air of serenity in them, standing as it does in such contrast to the sense of menace you find in so much Victorian fiction about cities at night. 'I considered myself the inventor of nocturns until I saw Grimmy's moonlit pictures', the much more famous artist, James McNeill Whistler, is said to have remarked ruefully, and it is as a moonlight artist that Grimshaw is best known. But most of his paintings include both natural and artificial light, as if he saw a hierarchy in which gaslight outscored its natural counterpart.

Artists themselves were, of course, some of the most obvious beneficiaries of ready artificial light. The diary of the Pre-Raphaelite painter Ford Madox Brown shows the extent to which gaslight had, by the middle years of the century, come to be accepted as an essential supplement to natural light. When trying to finish *The Baptism of Edwin*, the second of his magnificent murals in Manchester Town Hall celebrating the development of that quintessential Victorian metropolis, he found the natural light of the industrial city so poor that 'without the gas on many days I could do nothing'.[5] In the last of the murals, *Dalton Collecting Marsh Fire Gas*, he even celebrated the advance of science and the thrill of artificial light through a bucolic scene in the life of the atomic theorist John Dalton. Like *William Michael Rossetti by Lamplight*, a portrait by Madox Brown of his future son-in-law, the man of letters and co-founder of the Pre-Raphaelite Brotherhood, it is a celebration of science. In the portrait Rossetti is shown hatless, with the gaslight merrily bouncing off his great bald pate.

The warmth of coal allowed artists to paint when their fingers would otherwise be frozen, and the light from gas freed them from the timetable of sunlight. Successful Victorian artists made a great deal of money and gravitated towards west London, where the son of one of the casualties of the railway fever, Henry Fox, fourth Baron Holland, had started flogging off bits of his estate for housing. In the building frenzy which followed, architects, designers, painters, sculptors and writers – and their patrons – snapped up plots and houses in the area. Leighton House, the most famous of these residences-cum-studios, was a carnival of tiles, timbers and Middle Eastern design for one of the most successful of these painters (many of whom should really be classified as producers of mild pornography), Sir Frederic Leighton. Leighton would soon become the holder of the shortest-lived barony in the British peerage, since he died as an unmarried dandy the day after his elevation, having produced numerous paintings, like *The Light of the Harem*, in which the illumination supposed to be falling from a skylight looks remarkably industrial. Leighton had insisted upon gaslight in his studio from the start and had installed an enormous gas-fired 'sunburner' hanging from the ceiling.

But it had been the smog which really changed Britain's capital city. The Japanese artist Yoshio Markino spent most of the first half of the twentieth century in London. When he arrived in 1897 he bought himself a respirator, which he wore whenever he went outside. But within a few years, the London fog had become his 'greatest fascination'.[6] Smog gave the city – whose natural colours he believed to be rather crude – a sombre subtlety he was unable to find anywhere else.

The best-known of the artists to appreciate the unusual appearance of London in its smog was the Impressionist Claude Monet, who loved the opacity it bestowed on the bridges of the Thames and the Houses of Parliament. His letters to his wife describe a feverish enthusiasm as he worked on multiple canvases at once. 'Without fog, London would not be beautiful,' he said.[7] Monet noted that the fogs were less intense on Sundays, which probably indicates the great contribution of industrial smoke to the poor visibility: he was referring not to fog but to smog.

Monet's London paintings belong to the turn of the twentieth century, by which time coal smoke was a fact of life. Charles I had moaned in the early seventeenth century about the smoke of nearby bakeries. But by the turn of the twentieth century, coal was burning in the hearths of most homes in the capital. The faces of the stone lions marking the entrance to York Palace on the Strand – the grandest such edifice of Charles's reign – soon rotted away in the city's sulphurous air. Cleopatra's Needle – given to the British to mark Nelson's victory on the Nile and erected on the Victoria Embankment in 1878 – suffered more damage from the city's filthy air than it had endured in its three and a half millennia in the Egyptian desert. It was inevitable that the world's first industrial nation should have also the world's first man-made environmental crisis. But it took a long time to do anything about it.

The accelerating pace of invention and manufacture brought matters to a head. Industrialists needed technology, power, labour and a market. Inevitably, those who worked in the foundries and factories came to live nearby. Conditions in the cheap housing were harsh. But the distinctive environmental debauchery of the industrial cities was the appalling quality of their air. There was no escape from the filthy atmosphere of the workplace when you went home. And if you had to endure it, so did your family.

In the middle of the nineteenth century there had been anti-smoke organisations formed in industrial towns like Leeds and 'the chimney of the world', Manchester. The campaigners endured the not-entirely-benign tolerance accorded to cranks, but proved the strength of their cause by achieving some by-laws to try to control smoke pollution. Gradually, filthy air became a political issue. A Smoke Nuisance Abatement Act in 1853 was followed about once every ten years to the end of the century by one regulation or another. The problem with all of them was enforcement, since many contained weasel words about restricting emissions 'as

far as possible' or 'as far as practicable'. But the campaigners bashed
on. Francis Albert Rollo Russell, the shy, short-sighted vegetarian
son of former prime minister Lord John Russell, produced a
pamphlet in 1880 claiming that smoke from the vast number of
houses heated by coal was not only fouling the air, but killing
people by the thousand – the death toll in that year's pea-souper
had been 'more fatal than the slaughter of many a great battle', he
said.[8] But his was an isolated voice, and the stock response to those
who complained about the choking atmosphere was that it was the
price of prosperity and progress.

The difficulty in getting anything done about smoke was very
obvious. It was an environmental unpleasantness which affected
everyone, but to control it involved restricting the comfort of individuals. The warmth stayed in the home. The smoke went up the
chimney and elsewhere. Everyone agreed the smoke was a problem. But no one wanted to do without their fire. Because there was
no obvious solution, it was not part of politics: the environment
had yet to become a political issue. As one writer put it, 'smoke
abatement is within that class of subjects sometimes designated as
"non-controversial", not because no controversies are involved, but
because political parties have no definite policies about it'.[9]

Inquiries from select committees and from public health bigwigs
came and went. In 1854, Lord Palmerston had asked the General
Board of Health to examine how to prevent smoke. The committee
at least came up with a thirteen-point checklist which demonstrated that 'black smoke is the result of poor industrial practice,
and it can be fixed'. The only way to get industrialists to behave
differently was to make laws and for the police to enforce them.
The Public Health Act of 1875 gave local authorities the right to
bring charges against industrialists who polluted 'unnecessarily'.
But who was to decide what was unnecessary? The filthy fogs of
industrial cities – and London in particular – were part of life.
Charles Dickens' last completed novel *Our Mutual Friend* (written

in 1864–5) described the effect: 'Animate London, with smarting eyes and irritated lungs, was blinking, wheezing and choking; inanimate London was a sooty spectre, divided in purpose between being visible and invisible, and so being wholly neither ... Even in the surrounding country it was a foggy day, but there, the fog was grey, whereas in London it was, at about the boundary line, dark yellow, and a little within it brown, and then browner, and then browner, until at the heart of the City – which call Saint Mary Axe – it was rusty-black.'[10]

Meantime, public interest in the smoke nuisance seemed to quicken. A London Smoke Abatement exhibition was staged near the Albert Hall in 1881. With its message that, quite apart from anything else, incomplete combustion meant that money was disappearing up the chimney, inevitably it did not draw the crowds a freak show might have achieved. But it received a respectable 13,000 visitors in its first week alone, had to extend its opening hours until 10 p.m., and ran for months. Inside, manufacturers displayed examples of smokeless furnaces, stoves, grates, kitchen ranges and even heavy industrial equipment. A Coal Smoke Abatement Society was formed in 1898. An investigation for the London Meteorological Council discovered that for over two months of the winter, it was impossible to see from a tower in Westminster to St Paul's Cathedral, or vice versa. On 20 December, when wind had blown off much of the fog, it still lay 'flat over the houses like a dirty counterpane'.[11] At a dinner in 1882, the artist Sir Frederic Leighton, president of the Royal Academy and prominent supporter of smoke abatement, had spoken of the misery of having to endure 'interminable hours, days, weeks of enforced idleness spent in the continuous contemplation of the ubiquitous yellow fog, depressing the spirits all the more for recalling the memories of distant lands where the sun shone in the sky'.[12] Whether these thoughts crossed his mind as one of his staff stoked the fire necessary to allow an otherwise naked model to pose in a diaphanous orange chemise for his voyeuristic masterpiece *Flaming June*, is another matter.

Things got no better and in 1905 it was estimated that the canopy hanging over London contained fifty tons of solid carbon and 250 tons of carbon monoxide gas, acids and hydrocarbons. But the language in which it was described was becoming increasingly charged. In 1902, the meteorologist William Napier Shaw had described smoke as 'aerial sewage'. The great evolutionary scientist Alfred Russel Wallace wrote of cities where 'a criminal apathy, an incredible recklessness and inhumanity' forced millions to live among poisonous gases.[13] Admittedly, Wallace had become exceedingly eccentric by this time, but in this, he was right, and the evidence to support this claim about atmospheric pollution (unlike his enthusiasm for spiritualism and anti-vaxing) was all around. Not only was smoke damaging health, making people filthy, and fouling the environment (the leaves of the plants in the garden outside the governor's office in the Bank of England had to be washed with soap and water every week, for example), it was dispiriting. One campaigner even claimed that 'the race is being made weak, bloodless and depressed'.[14] John Tenniel, the chief cartoonist for *Punch* magazine, had depicted Old King Coal as an accomplice of the Angel of Death with a chimney for a hat and a firegrate for a throne. But it was more than a matter of public health: there were discernible social consequences. In *The Destruction of Daylight* (1907), John Graham cited Ruskin's advice to British architects that 'all lovely architecture was designed for cities in cloudless air ... But our cities, built in black air, which by its accumulated foulness first renders all ornament invisible in the distance, and then chokes its interstices with soot ... [in cities] such as this no architecture is possible.'[15] Grand civic buildings, memorials, and art galleries erected to glorify the inventiveness and industry of towns like Birmingham, Manchester and Leeds were soon black as night had been before the arrival of gaslight.

Mine-owners knew the forces of the state would look after their interests. Here, police officers block the streets during the Tonypandy riots in 1910.

During the worst of the riots, the state could – and did – call out the army. The decision to send them was a cause of long-lasting resentment for many Welsh families.

The scene at Senghenydd after the second fire broke out. Fires hampered the rescue effort, and it was said that airborne coal dust exacerbated the explosion.

Rescuers leaving the pit during the Senghenydd colliery disaster in 1913. With over 400 fatalities, it was the worst mining accident in UK history.

A man rollerskates to work with his packed lunch during the General Strike of 1926. Transport workers had joined the strike in sympathy with the miners' cause.

Arthur James Cook, General Secretary of the Miners' Federation of GB, speaks during the General Strike: 'Not a penny off the pay, not a minute on the day.'

An unemployed coal miner in Wigan, England, is photographed in the late 1930s – the reality behind the likes of Orwell's *The Road to Wigan Pier*. 'A sort of caryatid upon whose shoulders nearly everything that is not grimy is supported.'

Young children scrounging for coal fallen from vans at King's Cross during the General Strike.

Hallelujah! Nationalisation, captured at Ty Trist Colliery in Wales, 1947.

A man guides a London bus through thick fog with a flaming torch – the reality of the 1952 smog.

'Bevin Boys', the men conscripted to work in mines during the war, near Canterbury in 1944. They felt neglected by those who spoke of the 'war effort' in terms of military uniforms: soldiers, sailors and airmen.

Miners taking their bath after a day's work in the pits at the New Count Colliery, Leicestershire, in 1943. Cleanliness did wonders for self-esteem – on a bus, people might refuse to sit next to anybody covered in coal dust.

A dying industry deals death. 116 children died in Aberfan when a spoil tip slid down the mountain and engulfed their school in 1966.

Miners left work to dig for their own children.

Picketing miners hurl abuse at those going into work at Thoresby Colliery in Nottinghamshire during the 1984 strike.

Stones are thrown at the police during the same 1984 strikes at Orgreave Coking Plant in Sheffield.

Arthur Scargill, president of the National Union of Mineworkers, gets his heart's desire on 30 May 1984.

'Stand at the window here,' Sherlock Holmes remarks in *The Sign of the Four*. 'Was ever such a dreary, dismal, unprofitable world? See how the yellow fog swirls down the street and drifts across the dun-coloured houses. What could be more hopelessly prosaic and material?'[16] In 'The Adventure of the Bruce-Partington Plans', Holmes sneers at the pedestrian uselessness of the average home-grown criminal for not knowing how to exploit a London pea-souper: 'It is well,' he says, 'they don't have days of fog in the Latin countries – the countries of assassination.'[17]

The social consequence of the capital's filthy air was that those who could afford to do so moved away from the smog, with the poor left to cough their way to work or school. 'Classes are separated in England chiefly by accidental conditions of our fuel combustion,' wrote John Graham.[18] Perhaps if London had burned natural gas, instead of filthy old coal, the west of the city, upwind of the industrial areas, would not have become so much the preserve of the wealthy, and the East End of the deprived.

The problem cried out for government action: who, otherwise, would deprive themselves of warmth for the benefit of everyone? But coal – the fuel of the Industrial Revolution and of the British Empire – seemed secure. In 1913, Londoners burned two tons of coal each per year. It had been so readily available and so abundant that it had acted as a narcotic: long after the point at which they might have imagined an alternative future, the business and technological interests that may have redirected the economy to another source of power could not kick the coal habit. But if anyone had had the wit to see it, the writing was on the wall for coal. In mining areas, they were well aware of the noxious consequences of combustion, since colliery boiler houses were usually run on some of the lowest-quality coal to have been extracted, and the same stuff was given to miners as part of the annual allowance which came with their wage agreement. Inevitably, the imaginative leap necessary to think of the effect of smoke on big conurbations miles away, took a distant second place to the need to make a living.

But one consequence was that the National Smoke Abatement Society began to look a bit less cranky. The next issue of their journal, *Smokeless Air*, in January 1953 printed the results of the society's own health surveys, which they also distributed to politicians and government departments. In May, three representatives of the group were invited to join a government committee investigating air pollution,* and as the next winter approached, the minister for health grudgingly announced that 'smog masks' would be available at public expense. Traditional hearths, of the kind to be found in most homes, were incapable of burning coal fully and cleanly. It hadn't mattered so much when the population was sparsely scattered, but when people were living in densely packed houses, one person's warmth was someone else's wheeze. Clean-burning coal or coke was more expensive than mucky fuel, but both the obvious alternatives to raw coal – gas and electricity – were derived from it. With the benefit of hindsight, it is clear that as soon as cleaner sources of energy were available they would find favour. Parts of the coal industry certainly felt themselves to be immediately threatened. By 1954, the vice president of the Coal Merchants' Federation was urging members to take up the fight to ensure that debates about air pollution and smoke abatement 'are kept in their proper channels',[19] and the next year Mr J. W. Stewart said that it was clear some members were not 'standing up for the open fire quite as they should do'.[20] Soon, the federation had succumbed to the siren promises of a public relations agency.

It wasn't long before all sorts of charlatans were leaping on the clean-air bandwagon. The Conservative MP, Gerald Nabarro, a handlebar-moustached attention-seeker who single-handedly

---

* The committee later claimed that the annual cost of air pollution was £250 million, leaving aside the expense of damage to health and the waste of energy.

justified the belief that politics was mainly about vanity, introduced a Private Member's Bill on clean air, which he withdrew when the Conservative government agreed to bring in its own bill. The Clean Air Act of 1956 was the first piece of legislation of its kind in the world. It banned the creation of certain types of smoke and attempted to establish smoke-free zones. Although most assiduously applied in the south-east of England, the Act applied across the country, and there were reports from mining areas of pitmen objecting to the delivery in their concessionary fuel allowance of coal which had been treated to be 'smokeless'. It made no difference. Even dull old British Railways began a programme to complete a full switch from steam-driven locomotives to diesel power. It was done within twelve years.

The Act did not stop smogs – there was another one in December the very next year, which was reckoned to have taken up to 1,000 lives. And there was yet another in 1962. But the Act had made it clear that the priority from now on was to be public health. The law was followed and amplified by a Clean Air Act in 1968. It was the sort of legislation that was only possible in a well-off society that had risen out of the soot and smoke whence it came.

By now, the industry was facing all sorts of problems. On the one hand, the government insisted upon being able to stick its oar in when it came to setting a price for coal which the citizens might burn in their hearths. On the other, the abandonment of steam power on the railways meant by 1968 they only needed a piffling 60,000 tons. In 1950 they had bought nearly 15 million tons. The people responsible for 'bunkering' naval vessels were also losing interest in the fuel: the 5.5 million tons ordered in 1948 had fallen by 1965 to only 3,000 tons. Admittedly, power stations continued to have a hunger for coal. But there were problems there, too, because the electricity producers were content to burn cheaper coal, wherever it came from. Massive consumption by power stations also meant the coal industry was heavily dependent on the state-run Central Electricity Generating Board and its counterpart in the south of Scotland. Doubtless to some of those planning the economy, this was an example of how managed economies were supposed to work. But it left the industry fearfully exposed.

14

White Heat

By the 1960s the breezy hopes of the early days of nationalisation looked a very poor joke. Coal was a grubby old-fashioned utility, increasingly saddled with slightly comical grandiose propaganda about an entirely different future. Things were made no better by the knowledge that jobs were disappearing fast. If you look at a graph showing the number of collieries in Britain, the line plummets most steeply in the 1960s. The decade belonged to neophiliacs, and they really had little time for something so old-fashioned, smoky, mucky, inconvenient and increasingly uneconomic. The Labour Party was glad of the miners' financial support, but increasingly the future seemed to belong to university graduates in drip-dry shirts and Burton suits. The new generation looked at the former union reps in blazers passing their days in the House of Commons bars getting quietly sloshed on pints of 'Fed' ale in the same way many families regarded embarrassing elderly relatives at Christmas lunch. The miners could put up with being tolerated by the party which had delivered them the nationalisation they had always sought. The National Union of Mineworkers knew only too well how dirty and arduous was the task of extracting coal from the ground, and the steeliness necessary to survive in that environment found an expression in the way they conducted their campaigns for better wages, sick pay and the like. There might, indeed, have been a brief honeymoon in the coal industry, though the marriage was to be short-lived. The NCB stuck to a policy of wage agreements with complicated bonuses and perks applicable to individual mines, which made the chances of another general strike negligible.

Local deals made a sort of sense, since all mines were prisoners of geology, with seams wide or thin, straight or twisted, wet or dry, hot or cold, and so on. Miners had been paid on a piecework basis since time immemorial. The catch was that most of the people employed in the coal industry weren't actually cutting coal, but shovelling it, moving it, washing it, transporting or marketing it. Productivity could only be improved by more coal leaving the face. This productivity problem was the curse of twentieth-century British coal-mining, and by the end of March 1964 the industry was claiming they were modernised and up-to-date – with over three-quarters of their coal being cut and loaded by machines. Piecework could not survive this efficiency drive, and in the summer of 1966 the union agreed to that dream of a planned economy, a national wage deal. It was called the 'National Power-Loading Agreement' (NPLA) to reflect the role of machinery. From now on, the men who cut coal were to be known as 'power-loader men'. They were, in the words of the agreement, to be 'assimilated' and 'interchangeable'.[1]

The new arrangement suited the managers because it meant their wage bill stayed the same whether a man was responsible for thirty tons of coal in a day or 300 tons. It also meant an end to the endless strikes caused when miners were prevented from earning a good wage because of the awkwardness of their working conditions. From the management point of view, the agreement called a spade a spade; the great machines cut the coal with tungsten-tipped picks attached to a revolving drum and fed what they cut onto an armoured conveyor, installing hydraulic roof supports as they went, and the 'interchangeable' two-legged operatives tended to it. The 'power-loader men' would be in a simple team doing a simple job and paid simple wages. As pits began signing up to the NPLA model, they formalised a process that had been ongoing for a few decades: the revered hewers and face-workers began functioning more and more as machine operators. It sounds demeaning, but the notion of a national deal had appealed to the miners because they hated piecework, and, while the new deal would do nothing much for the best-paid miners in places like the Kent coalfield, it would raise wages in the worst-paid areas, like some of the Scottish and Welsh collieries.

The miners were well aware of their reputation, and really didn't much care if it made them unpopular. It is something of a mystery what was going through their minds, as they watched the great promises of the National Coal Board, running their industry 'on behalf of the people', turn out to mean more and more pit closures. Like most of us, probably, their main concerns were with feeding their families and keeping a roof over their heads. And the main business of their bosses was to manage decline. Britain had made its fortune by digging rocks out of the ground and burning them. It was now paying the price of its early enthusiasm: coal was becoming more expensive to extract, while oil was cheap, and nuclear power novel and glamorous.

In 1963, the Labour leader, Harold Wilson, spoke of the country's future being forged in 'the white heat of the technological revolution'. The miners knew there was nothing revolutionary about coal and the expression was typical Wilson, who became prime minister in 1964 and liked to think that the leader of a modern government was a sort of managing director. He behaved throughout his time in Downing Street like the proprietor of a noisy, northern factory which he hoped to turn into a model of efficiency. Wilson was unfortunate in taking over the firm at a time when it could afford neither its commitments nor his ambitions. A National Plan, issued in August 1965 by Labour's deputy leader George Brown, from the corner of Whitehall created for him, the Department of Economic Affairs, proposed that national production be increased by 25% by 1970. It was – of course – unattainable, and alongside it in the National Archives is a confidential letter to Wilson less than a year later in which Brown describes how he proposes to explain away the fact that the National Plan has already failed.[2] Brown was a drunk, but hubris is not a hanging offence. Yet the failure did rather demonstrate the chasm between political promise and reality. Throughout the Labour years of the 1960s, the coal industry shrank – between 1965 and 1969, 200 pits were closed. The bureaucrats in the Coal Board warned of the potential risks of losing a domestic energy supply. But they were no match for the clever talk from the oil company ad men about putting a tiger in your tank. From the suits at the ministry came remarks that if oil prices rose, they would do so less quickly than coal. Then, in 1966, the most memorable tragedy of the decade brought coal and its black history to the front of everyone's mind.

The South Wales coalfield had been extraordinarily productive, making the local ironmasters, the Crawshay family, stupendously rich and enabling them to build an enormous mansion, Cyfarthfa Castle, at Merthyr Tydfil: its seventy-two rooms were between them said to have a window for every day of the year. But the miners' houses that clustered near the first shaft of the Merthyr Vale mine were characteristically mean. The pit had been sunk in 1869, by John Nixon, a veteran of the Marquess of Bute's collieries. The prospect of finding almost smokeless steam coal was what had drawn Nixon to lease land from the marquess and to develop his own pit. After five years of toil, his workers reached the coal and by the turn of the twentieth century there were 2,000 men and boys employed attacking the faces beneath Merthyr mountain. Their houses created the village of Aberfan. In the wave of consolidation which took place in the early decades of the century, the colliery became part of the Powell Duffryn Steam Coal company – the infamous 'Poverty and Death'. The river Taff, a beautiful, tumbling river filled with salmon, trout and sea trout, turned black: local people still recall that the only time they could see the rocks on the bottom of the watercourse was when the mineworkers were on holiday. The Coal Board's streamlining of mining which had killed off other collieries, had been kind to the Merthyr Vale pit. It was modernised and re-engineered for the future.

Although it by now employed many fewer men, it had been a productive mine. By 1966 it had spawned seven vast 'slag' or spoil heaps, where waste rock and unwanted coal fragments were dumped by waggons from the mine. Every colliery had them and local people accepted the slowly changing skyline as part of the price of employment. Over the years, vast spoil heaps had been established on the hills towering over the three little villages of Aberfan, Mount Pleasant and Merthyr Vale where the 800 miners lived in narrow streets of ugly houses. Their wages supported butchers' and barbers' shops, libraries, a post office, a co-op, a garage, a cinema, clothes shops, several pubs and four chapels. The slag heaps were just another fact of life: you mined coal, you lived with the dumps – it was much cheaper for the mine-owners to pile up the waste on the surface than to try to return it whence it came.

The National Coal Board chairman through the 1960s – the effective overall boss of the mine – was Alf Robens, the son of a Manchester cotton salesman who had devoted his life to climbing the Labour Party's greasy pole, becoming a trade union organiser and then MP for the Northumberland mining seat of Blyth. In 1960, approaching fifty and beginning to despair of ever achieving the Labour Party leadership (which he was confident he deserved), the Conservative prime minister of the time, Harold Macmillan, had invited him to become chairman of the National Coal Board. Robens claimed to have no idea why he'd been offered the job.[3] It was, in many ways, a poisoned chalice, since the industry was still uncompetitive and if most of it was ever to be made profitable, the outlook was for more pit closures. But Robens was one of those

men whose endless self-esteem was flattered by being asked to do
a difficult job. He was intellectually nimble and nothing could dent
his self-belief. Macmillan offered him a title with the job (he
became Lord Robens of Woldingham, in the stockbroker belt: the
choice of title was another way of showing that he had arrived),
and few things tickle a political hack more than unelected
eminence. When Robens pointed out to Macmillan that British
mining was in such a mess that it was hard to see how it could ever
again make a profit, the prime minister drawled, as only those who
have attended Eton and Oxford can, 'Don't worry, dear boy. Just
blur the edges – just blur the edges.'[4]

Robens was a clever, arrogant man always convinced he knew
best. He also had fearsome persuasive powers: 'he could charm the
sparrows off the bloody trees' was the way that the miners' union
president Joe Gormley later explained the fact that Robens could
excite standing ovations at mining union conferences, even while
closing pits.[5] (He was additionally blessed in having effectively
neutralised the union through his close friendship with Will
Paynter, a South Wales communist who had been a commander
with the International Brigade in the Spanish Civil War and was
now union general secretary. The two men agreed that the only
way for the industry to survive was to reduce both the number of
pits and the number of miners.) So Robens was able to run the
Coal Board as if it were his personal fiefdom. Nothing was too
good for this tribune of the people, and the apartment in Eaton
Square, the private plane and NCB 1 – his personal Daimler – all
bolstered his not entirely affectionate nickname, Old King Coal.
He did what he wanted and made no effort to hide his disdain for
many politicians: Robens believed that what Britain needed was
fewer speeches and more management.

And so he set about closing mines. When he took over the
industry, Britain had 698 pits, employing 583,000 miners. When
he left for lucrative posts in the boardrooms of the private sector

ten years later, there were 292 pits employing only 283,000 men. Productivity had improved by a claimed 70%. The Merthyr Vale mine had survived Robens' programme of cuts and employed 850 men, among them those nicknamed Dai Fat, Dai Sweat, Dai Shake Hands, Dai Little Engine, Dai Lots of Kids, Dai Gold Watch, Dai Wireless, Dai the Lamproom, Dai Brothers, Dai Electric, Dai the Hole, Dai Stonedust, Dai Pipe, Dai Left Wing, Alan Poisoned Dwarf and Cyril Silent Night. Some of these happily nicknamed men were about to hear the very worst imaginable news.

The morning of Friday 21 October 1966 was misty with autumnal fog: from the bottom of the valley you couldn't see the tops of the surrounding hills. It had been raining for weeks. In the village of Aberfan, at the foot of Merthyr mountain, children had walked across from their houses on the west bank of the Taff to Pantglas Junior School, abuzz with excited talk of the half-term holiday, which was due to begin at lunchtime. On the hillside above the school a 'tipping crew' from the mine had been at work on Tip Number Seven since 7.30 that morning. The heap was the newest spoil tip at the mine – it had had six predecessors – and had been begun in the spring of 1958.

Immediately they started work that morning, the crew realised something was wrong, because part of the tip had moved and broken the rail tracks on which the spoil crane moved. They were unable to raise an immediate alarm, because the wire for their telephone had been stolen. By nine that morning, the rails had slipped another three metres. The crane driver, Gwyn Brown, was standing on the lip of a depression on the hillside when something astonishing happened. 'I couldn't believe my eyes,' he said. The slag was rising like a cobra from a hole. 'It started to rise slowly at first. I still did not believe it, I thought I was seeing things. Then it rose up after pretty fast, at a tremendous speed. Then it sort of came up out of the depression and turned itself into a wave – that is the only way I can describe it – down the mountain ... towards Aberfan

village … into the mist.'[6] Seconds later, the great quantity of water
trapped inside the spoil tip caused the bottom of the hillside to
shoot outwards. The landslide was enormous (it was calculated
later to contain over 100,000 cubic metres of colliery spoil). It
raced downhill, in black waves over twenty feet high, engulfing a
house, tearing trees from the ground, jumping the empty canal by
the village and the railway embankment, destroying everything in
its path. It smashed through the mains pipes carrying water from
the Brecon Beacons to Cardiff, augmenting the torrent.

In Pantglas Junior School below the tip, there was a roar as if 'a
jet plane [was] screaming low over the school in the fog'. The lights
in the school flickered. Then the avalanche struck, smashing
through walls, doors and windows and lifting off much of the roof.
A torrent of black sludge tore through the school, breaking bones,
suffocating and drowning the boys and girls inside. The deputy
head, Dai Beynon, threw himself across three children to try to
protect them. In Mrs Bates's classroom, thirty-three ten- and elev-
en-year-old children perished. In Mrs Rees's room, nineteen
children were killed, another fifteen in Mr Davies's room. The lives
of five children were saved by the school dinner lady Nansi
Williams, who died covering them with her own body. All told,
116 children never came home from school that day.

Mothers who had seen their menfolk off to work at the mine,
unsure of whether they would return, now suddenly had to come
to terms with something they had never foreseen – the death of
their children in a place of safety, killed by a beast their husbands
had loosed from below ground. The emergency whistle sounded
at the mine soon afterwards, and miners raced to the school to
help in the rescue. At the school they found wives, mothers and
teachers digging with their hands in the rubble. The effort had
stripped the skin from some of their hands. The miners formed
disciplined lines, passing along buckets of sludge and wreckage. In
the classrooms, those children who were not terrified were already

dead or dying. Some of those who would survive were trapped behind desks or radiators with dead classmates lying across them. No one was brought out alive after eleven that morning. Bodies of the 116 children and twenty-eight adults were carried to the Bethania, a local chapel which had been set up as a temporary mortuary.

This was a calamity of the most dreadful kind, and demanded the immediate presence of the chairman of the Coal Board. But Lord Robens was nowhere to be seen in Wales. He had insisted upon sticking to his plan to be installed as chancellor of the new University of Surrey in Guildford. There could hardly have been a more embarrassing contrast than that between the river of black sludge which had engulfed a school, killing 116 children, and the well-fed Alf Robens in his blue and gold robes doffing an absurd hat to everyone. He was never forgiven.

Eventually – a day and a half late – Robens arrived in Aberfan, where he merely swanned about with an enormous cigar. He found time to condemn the 'ghoulish' media coverage and after his visit told a television reporter that 'It was impossible to know that there was a spring in the heart of this tip which was turning the centre of the mountain into sludge.'[7] In his own mind, Robens may have been omniscient. But he was no geologist, and his story was simply untrue. It took sixty days for him to correct himself.

A procession of dignitaries soon began arriving in the village, including the prime minister, Harold Wilson, Lord Snowdon who had married the queen's sister, and the queen's husband, the Duke of Edinburgh. Astonishingly, on the advice of Lord Robens, the chairman of the south-west division of the Coal Board – who was attending a conference in Tokyo – was sent a telegram reading 'Everything possible being done. Do not, repeat, do not, return.' The queen laid a wreath after the funeral of the victims. There followed the conventional formalities of mass death. First came the inquest. Feelings were understandably running high and as the names of several of the dead children were read out there came shouts of 'Murderers!' When formal judgement of cause of death of one little girl was given – multiple injuries and asphyxia – her father shouted at the coroner, 'No sir. Buried alive by the National Coal Board.'[8]

Then came the tribunal of inquiry. The government appointed Edmund Davies, a local lad from Nonconformist stock, to lead the investigation.* Two years earlier, he had been the presiding judge at the trial of the Great Train Robbers, where he had declared it would be 'positively evil' to show leniency in sentencing, and handed out a total of 307 years in prison – some of the longest sentences in British criminal history. He now decided the inquiry needed to discover not merely what had happened, but why it had happened and whether it need have happened, which was, effectively, asking whose fault it was. The pursuit of someone to blame is often fruitless and almost always unattractive. But what happened at Aberfan was so shocking, so destructive, so poignant that not to do so would have seemed derelict. The tribunal heard evidence from 136 witnesses and examined 300 exhibits. Squads of lawyers paid their mortgages with work for the Coal Board, unions, councils and trade associations. The tribunal was at the time the longest ever to have heard evidence. But it did not take long to discover what had happened.

The author Laurie Lee later described the tragedy which occurred at Aberfan as one of inertia, 'of a danger which grew slowly for all to see, but which almost no one took steps to prevent.'[9] Anyone who took the trouble to think about it recognised that 'winning' coal from the ground was a dangerous activity. What happened at Aberfan was evidence – like the poison in coal smoke, but much more swift and dramatic – of the terrible price to be paid

---

* He had been born in Mountain Ash, the village in which John Nixon, the man who sank the Merthyr Vale mine, was buried.

for apparently 'free' energy. Since the National Coal Board ran the mine, it was quite obvious where responsibility lay. As the seventh spoil tip had been created eleven years after nationalisation, previous private owners couldn't even be blamed. The local MP – himself a former miner – later commented that the nationalised industry was a form of state capitalism which had 'inherited a beastly and unscientific tradition. It accepted what had been done in the old days.'[10] By the mid-1960s, the spoil tip had grown to a height of over one hundred feet. Now, as the damaged and bewildered community began to try to discover what had happened to it, it was revealed that however much the officials blamed the weather, unusual geology or the quantity of rain, the plain fact was that the tip should never have been established where it was. Ordnance Survey maps of the time of construction demonstrated that the colliery waste was being taken up the hillside to be dumped on top of natural springs. It turned out that local councillors and others had written to the National Coal Board expressing their fears about landslides from the waste tip. In the files of the *Merthyr Express* were the warnings of the late mayor about how the tip might imperil the school. As for Lord Robens, who had belatedly visited the scene of the disaster and then said – wrongly – that the disaster could not have been predicted, tribunal solicitors hadn't even bothered to take a statement from him before the thing began. When – eventually – the investigation invited him to testify Robens admitted that the Coal Board had recognised the potential dangers, but that 'no one ever apprehended a tip slide of this character'.[11]

The children who died in Aberfan are buried alongside each other in two distinctive rows of pillars and arches in the village's steep little graveyard. Many of the graves of children who died at seven, eight, nine or ten now also record the deaths of their parents, who lived their full span, but can never have recovered from the heartbreak of that October day. Often their graves are marked with inscriptions like 'together at last'. The cemetery and the garden of remembrance on the site of the demolished school are quiet, well-meaning attempts to find solace and reconciliation. Decades after the tragedy, people continue to lay flowers on the children's graves.

No one should ever try to minimise the appalling gravity of what happened at Aberfan. But could there almost have been some local complicity? It is a tasteless question – of course no one would toy with the lives of a village's children, and it is true that anxiety had been expressed about the looming slag heap. Was it only the expressionless face of a nationalised industry, legally free from parliamentary scrutiny, which stopped anyone doing anything? Or could it be that background anxiety about the state of the British coal business played a part? Both miners and managers believed the industry was in deep trouble and the National Coal Board was eagerly closing pits and reducing the number of miners to try to improve productivity. Could some people who might have spoken out been cowed by fears that an active spoil heap was at least a sign of life in the mine? How many knew of the potential dangers, and kept silent because without the tip there would be no mine, and with no mine, the village would be likely to die.*

There had been dereliction of duty everywhere. No one from Her Majesty's Inspectorate of Mines and Quarries, for example, had visited the mine or its tips for the previous four years, despite there having been a landslide during the period. On day seventy-four of the inquiry, counsel for the National Coal Board finally admitted 'It need not have happened and should not have happened if proper site investigations had been carried out beforehand. The failure to have any site investigations beforehand must be attributed to lack of instructions from the Coal Board.' That was more

---

* If so, they were wrong. The mine continued operating until the summer of 1989, when it was shut with two days' notice.

than enough for Lord Justice Edmund Davies's tribunal, which produced a report, naming names highly selectively and unfairly.

For fifteen shillings anyone could now read the conclusion of the inquiry that 'blame for this disaster rests upon the National Coal Board ... The Aberfan disaster could and should have been prevented ... our report tells not of wickedness but of ignorance, ineptitude and a failure in communications.'[12] The tribunal's apportioning of blame did not lead to a single prosecution, sacking or even a cut in pay. The Conservative Shadow spokesman on power, Margaret Thatcher, thought 'someone should have resigned', though 'I held back from stating this conclusion with complete clarity.'[13] Plaid Cymru's solitary MP was the only one who thought that both the chairman of the Coal Board, Lord Robens, and the Labour government's minister of power, Richard Marsh, should quit. The law which had created the National Coal Board had granted it freedom from scrutiny by politicians: no Member of Parliament had any right to question officials about the deaths of any constituent. But Lord Robens eventually could see no alternative to the decent thing and offered his resignation. The minister for power refused to accept it. Why? One after another the Labour MPs of South Wales made excuses for the Coal Board and for Lord Robens. There is some evidence that government ministers were afraid of what Robens might say or do if he was a free agent, the senior Labour politician Richard Crossman writing in his diary that 'we should then have all the problems of pit closures being sabotaged by Alf from the outside.'[14] It was more convenient all round – even for the National Union of Mineworkers – to keep on Robens than to take the risk of trying to find someone else.

But this was not the end. The little Welsh village had more pain to suffer.

On the evening of the disaster, the mayor of Merthyr Tydfil had started an appeal for money to help those who were affected. He had no specific purpose to which he wanted to apply the money, but it seemed a way for people to give expression to their shock and sympathy. Because the tragedy was so horrific, the appeal was soon known about across the world and quickly raised far more money than any disaster fund before. By January the following year, nearly 90,000 contributions, including children sending in their pocket money, had raised £1.6 million (nearly £30 million at 2020 values).There were those at the time who said the donations were incoherent, and indeed they were – a natural impulse to want to help people to whom something terrible has happened, using the only obvious means to hand. 'I know that no amount of money can buy these children's lives, but what else can one do?' asked one reasonably typical letter to the disaster fund.[15]

Unedifying rows over the money began early, but it wasn't long after the disaster that local people started to demand that the remaining coal tips be removed. The National Coal Board said there was no danger from other tips, and anyway, they couldn't afford it: if they were to be removed, surely the government could pay?

One of the follies of public ownership was now made plain. Everyone knew that behind the NCB's expensive lawyers was the state. If, in addition to significant legal fees, it now got stuck with the expensive business of removing the coal tips, it would have its hand in the taxpayer's pocket straightaway. The coal industry had been making a loss for years; Lord Robens insisted it simply could not afford a massive unexpected cost. Merthyr Vale was a profitable mine, but who knew what would happen if it had to take on something like this? Miners' familiar fears for their jobs reasserted themselves.

In the end, after much argument, the Labour government forced a deal, which split the cost of removing the pits between the government, the NCB and the disaster fund. There were suggestions that at least everyone could agree on the objective, unlike earlier attempts to put a cash value on a life, and the sordid squab-

bles over whether money might be spent on holidays. But it was a
shameful arrangement which meant that the village would have to
pay to get the tips, which had done it such harm, taken away. S. O.
Davies, the local MP who sat on the fund's management committee, called it 'one of the meanest things I have seen in thirty-four
years in Parliament', and resigned from it.[16] Villagers continued to
argue for decades that the disaster fund should be given its money
back, to be spent on the memorial garden and children's graves,
and in 2007 – forty years after the event – the Welsh Assembly
agreed.

If you go to Aberfan today, the only indication that it once had
a mine is the winding gear sheaves set into the ground. In the old
coal yard, developers have built blocks of detached houses, the
river runs clean, beech trees rustle and the constant thunder of
traffic takes men and women to work in suburban industrial parks.
There is no deep mining in South Wales any longer.

By now, the story of the nationalised coal industry was a deeply
troubled one. The National Coal Board's shiny new metal signs
advertising that they were running the pits 'on behalf of the people'
were soon stained with rust. And the naïve belief that once the
industry was publicly owned, there'd be no more strikes had turned
out to be well off the mark. There was genuine bafflement when
miners would refuse to work. Did they not understand that when
production was lost prices rose, which meant lost customers, and
lost customers meant that pits would close? On top of which it was
an almost impossible industry in which to carry through a plan
consistently. If there ever was a consistent policy, apart from an
attempt to sell more coal while closing more pits.

Everyone knew that coal was burned for heat, but the fact that
most of it was sent to power stations made it invisible. Apart from
the occasional spectacle of a locomotive (increasingly commonly,
a diesel locomotive) pulling waggons to a power station, coal was

out of sight and out of mind. Because the industry was nationalised, it reported to ministers. Being minister of power was either a
job for the clapped-out, or for those who had to be given a job
somewhere or other for political reasons. The post was sometimes
included in the Cabinet and sometimes not, and eventually was
swallowed up in the Ministry of Technology, which had been
created by the Labour government 'to bring advanced technology
and new processes into industry'.[17]

But, although it did open the occasional new pit, the Coal Board
never looked as if it was doing much more than managing decline
– and not even doing that very well. The industry did not look like
an advertisement for a steady, futuristic and visionary occupation.
It was ancient, for one thing, and its management plans juddered,
stopped and started like a teenager behind the controls of a car for
the first time. More pits were closed than was necessary, and once
they were closed, that was usually the end of the story. Though
politicians and policymakers had repeatedly warned in the 1950s
and into the 1960s that it was unwise to become dependent on
imported oil to keep the lights on, oil was often irresistible. For one
thing, if you were building a new power station, you didn't need to
spend nearly as much on the handling equipment necessary for
coal. For another, unlike coal, oil wasn't at the mercy of the mining
and railway unions. During the 1960s, the amount of oil being
burned in power stations doubled.

The Wilson government (1964–70) soon found a shiny and new
love object. There was something about nuclear power that they
simply adored. (The atom had first been split in Manchester so
there was also a sense in sections of the party that the technology
'belonged' to Britain.) Nuclear power chimed with Labour's idea
of all things clean and new: nuclear fission, in which splitting
atoms released heat to produce the steam to drive turbines which
produced power, was a lot more futuristic than using smelly old
coal fires to do so. The key question in this comparison was for

how long a power plant might continue to generate power. Two-thirds of the costs of a nuclear power station were in capital investment and the running costs were correspondingly small, whereas the proportions were inverted with coal and oil. The working assumption was that nuclear plants had an operating life of twenty years, although there was not a single example anywhere in the world of the favoured British design operating commercially. Then the goalposts were suddenly moved and it was claimed that nuclear power stations would be operating not for twenty, but for twenty-five years, thereby giving the nuclear industry a 25% better timescale in which to recoup their costs. What was never taken into account were the financial costs of redundancy in coal communities and the social consequences in places which were now superfluous to the nation's requirements. The Labour Party believed that the tribal loyalty in politics was sufficiently strong that they would suffer no serious political damage, but something of the trust which had previously existed between the Labour Party and the trade unions was damaged by flirting with new technologies. It was impossible to be simultaneously completely behind coal and completely behind nuclear power.

In his inevitably self-serving 1972 memoirs, Lord Robens admitted that he had seen it as part of his duty to be publicly upbeat about the prospects of the coal industry[18] against the enthusiasm for nuclear power which seized so many Labour friends, commenting that 'I can only regret the slum clearances, schools, hospitals, roads and universities that could have been paid for with the money that has been poured down the nuclear drain.'[19] British governments shilly-shallied for years over what ought to be the best energy policy. If such a thing ever existed. In the end, they decided – though it was never anything as positive as a definite decision – that they would muddle through. No politician can produce or restore coal deposits and – posture though they may – deep in their hearts, everybody knew that in the foreseeable

future the days of coal would be over. Natural gas from the North
Sea was a politically convenient alternative. But at the same time,
they allowed the nuclear industry, in which Britain had once been
a world leader, to wither into nothingness. It is not the greatest
advertisement for democracy.

But Britain's nuclear energy programme came to be an object
lesson in the risks inherent in new technology, especially when
coupled to state-planning incompetence. The initial 'Magnox'
power station (the name came from the fact that the uranium fuel
elements were held in magnesium-based alloy containers) had
been built at Calder Hall in Cumberland and opened by the queen
in 1956. It was ballyhooed as the start of the world's first civil
nuclear power programme.* Ten years later, Britain opened
another nuclear power station, at Dounreay in Caithness, on the
north coast of Scotland. But this was of a different type – a 'fast
breeder' reactor, which produced more fissile material than it
consumed. Two months after that, in April 1966, the Labour
minister of power, Richard Marsh, opened a further nuclear power
station at Hinkley Point in the Severn Estuary. It used the previous
Magnox technology. But by the 1970s Magnox had been deemed
inefficient and a set of new gas-cooled reactors were developed.
Another power station in Somerset – Hinkley Point B – was built
to use these 'advanced gas-cooled' plants, and opened in 1976.
Fourteen of these reactors were constructed, but they turned out
to be so tricky to build that by the 1980s Britain was increasingly
interested in using American-designed reactors, which generated
power through the use of pressurised water. Margaret Thatcher's
Conservative government then decided it had overestimated
demand and was anyway more interested in privatising the elec-

---

* Calder Hall produced power until 2003. The plan is to have most of the plant
demolished by 2027, after which the reactor cores 'will enter a period of "care and
maintenance" lasting a number of decades'.

tricity industry, as part of its attempts to dismantle the state-managed regime established after the Second World War. The Labour government which subsequently took office under Tony Blair buried the question of new nuclear power stations under much virtue-signalling about meeting environmental challenges. But then in 2008, Blair's successor, Gordon Brown, finally announced plans for a new generation of nuclear power stations, most of them to be built alongside previous nuclear installations (though in Brown's native Scotland the First Minister declared there was 'no chance' of their being built). By now the electricity industry had been privatised and Margaret Thatcher had so shifted political certainties that the only way to have new nuclear power stations built in Britain – fifty years after the country had constructed the first in the world – was to get state-subsidised French and Chinese companies to do so, having lured them in by promising that British consumers would pay through the nose for the electricity they produced. The French builders of the new nuclear power station under construction at Hinkley Point (Hinkley Point C) have been promised the right to sell their electricity to consumers at twice the normal price of power for thirty-five years.

Coal mines closed steadily throughout the 1960s – once the Labour government had published its fuel policy in 1967 they were shutting at the rate of three each fortnight, and in 1968 alone 25,000 miners were made redundant. If anyone moaned, Labour MPs huffed and puffed and claimed to their constituents that it was all the Coal Board's fault, when in fact the closures were a direct result of government policy which was itself the consequence of the international market. What was to become of men who had put food on the table for their families by this most brutish toil? The 1960s chairman of the Coal Board, Lord Robens, sneered that men who 'had, after all, been producing real wealth, were offered jobs like making one-armed bandits, working in betting shops, and running bingo halls – valuable contributions to the economy indeed ... To remove men from the production of wealth to wasteful servicing or the manufacture of non-essential consumer goods was always the wrong answer.'[20] The echoes of nineteenth-century Methodism reverberate through the old Labour carthorse's words. And the effects of closing mines were not confined to miners who saw their livelihoods vanishing. Robens' sneering was no great incentive to manufacturers whom the government hoped to lure to the abandoned coalfields to build factories.

In a further dozen or so years' time, redundant miners would be glad to be offered jobs like those that Robens sneered at. The nature of what was defined as 'work' was changing. The biggest redefinition was the general acceptance encouraged by the Thatcher government that providing services was quite as important as making things. It was the judgement feasible only in a senescent economy. And such a change would not have been possible without the widespread recognition that the days of the single breadwinner were over: family finances now required two incomes. Not only were former miners now employed as bingo-callers, they also worked in call centres. Assumptions about work had had to change, as had assumptions about gender. A job was a job.

15

'People will always need coal'

(NCB poster, 1974)

Shortly before Christmas 1969, Brendan McKeown, a Belfast-born prospector, took a helicopter back to Aberdeen from an oil exploration rig in the North Sea carrying an old pickle jar he had helped himself to from the rig's canteen. Inside the jar was the first oil to be brought ashore from under the waves.* Tens of billions of barrels of oil were to follow the pickle jar. Oil very quickly became more fashionable than coal.

Drilling for oil and gas out of the rocks under the North Sea was highly dangerous, since it involved working from platforms in some of the roughest seas on earth. Underwater extraction was not entirely novel, since oil had already been extracted from the seabed under the more peaceable waters off the southern coasts of the United States. The North Sea was, though, another proposition: the costs would rival those of putting a man on the moon. Exploring for oil under mountainous seas only became truly worthwhile after the Organisation of Petroleum Exporting Countries (OPEC) cartel hiked the market price of oil in 1973. When the shah of Iran was overthrown in the 1979 revolution, prices went haywire once more, and again, North Sea oil did not appear too expensive to get out of the ground. Within thirty years

---

* It was not the first oil to be extracted in Britain – that had been another achievement of coal-mining, when James Young, a Manchester chemist, had discovered paraffin could be refined from coal, and made himself a fortune.

of the pickle jar arriving on land, the North Sea had become the biggest offshore oilfield in the world.

Offshore exploration offered a vision of buccaneering capitalism at its most adventurous. Early coal miners had perhaps had a similar glamour, but that had been – at best – in the days of black and white. Now, from the warmth of their front room, television viewers could watch in colour as roustabouts wrestled with enormous drills while huge white-crested waves surged around them. Pass the biscuits. Our comfort has been expensively bought!

All those men on oil rigs in hard hats bearing the company logo testified to the new country that had taken shape. Nationalisation of coal-mining had been part of attempts by the Labour government elected in 1945 to build the new Jerusalem. Like a Jenga tower it was now being dismantled. Even though it included the National Health Service, Margaret Thatcher, who was to become prime minister in 1979, loathed the 'post-war settlement' which Labour had imposed on the country. Most of Britain's nationalised industries – like British Leyland, which in 1973 had given the world what was dubbed the worst production car in Western history, the Austin Allegro with its square steering wheel – had become bywords for the second-rate. The label 'the sick man of Europe' had been hung around the country's neck.

Everyone – or at least the sort of know-alls who usually pretend to know these things – had predicted that the Labour leader, Harold Wilson, would win the general election held in June 1970. As prime minister it was he who had decided to call the election, and in the subsequent casting around for excuses for his failure of judgement, the Labour Party blamed everything from the planned introduction of decimal currency to the English football team's defeat by West Germany in the World Cup. After decades of pit closures (even in the infamous Midlands soot-spot, the Black

Country, the last pit had closed in 1968), industrial relations in the mining industry were worsening and the victory of the Conservative leader, Edward Heath, had been, as much as anything, a reflection of the fact that the country had grown heartily sick of the spectacle of trade union leaders sauntering up Downing Street to have 'beer and sandwiches' with the Labour prime minister, in generally doomed attempts to find a cure for the latest symptoms of 'the British disease'. Heath was an unloved politician who never seemed at home in his own skin. But Britain was clearly an unhappy country, and at least he wasn't Harold Wilson.

Edward Heath's first choice to be Chancellor of the Exchequer after his unexpected victory was Iain 'too clever by half' Macleod, a witty, liberal figure in the party who had coined the term 'stagflation' to describe the country's predicament in the 1960s, when the economy refused to grow, despite apparently uncontrollable inflation. But Macleod died within weeks of the election, at which point Heath invited Anthony Barber, a punchy Yorkshireman, to run the country's economy. From the Opposition benches in Parliament, Harold Wilson remarked, with the ineffable intellectual snobbery of an Oxford don, that it was the first evidence he had seen that Heath had a sense of humour. Barber turned out to be one of the worst Chancellors in the history of the job. Public spending was slashed. Taxes were cut. Unemployment rose. Barber had precious little hair to pull out, but eventually, confident an election was in the offing, he gave up. To improve the chances of a Conservative victory, he decided to stoke up a boom and make everyone feel better, by slashing taxes further. Some, like Purchase Tax and the Selective Employment Tax which had been introduced by Labour, were even abolished altogether. The economy roared ahead, the stock market boomed, house prices rose. Unfortunately inflation roared, too. The 'Barber Boom' over which he presided was, predictably, followed by a bust, and Barber felt himself obliged to raise interest rates to their highest level in sixty years.*

But it was not the boom and its aftermath which finally brought down the Heath government. It was the country's coal miners. Leaders of the union had been standing up at the annual conference each year, reassuring members that despite the number of mines they could see being shut down, their trade still had a future. Despite the 'efficiency cuts' of the National Coal Board, the Labour governments of the 1960s had in fact been kind to them, writing off hundreds of millions of pounds accumulated in debts by the industry and sinking millions more into subsidies, while banning imports of cheaper foreign coal. Employment in British coal-mining had meanwhile been falling like a stone. The comfort for those who continued to work as miners was that productivity was shooting up. The union president, Sidney Ford (now Sir Sidney), told them in the summer of 1969 that in the Doncaster area, output per man-shift had risen by no less than 24%.[1] Ford did not trouble to point out that productivity was bound to rise as uneconomic mines were closed.

But even while the national union bosses were talking about the sunlit uplands, miners in Yorkshire were fulminating. The cause of their unhappiness was the pay and conditions of men who worked on the surface – often old or crippled miners judged incapable of labouring underground any longer. The firebrand who led calls for a strike was a young man named Arthur Scargill. Scargill, a weaselly-faced communist with a sharp tongue and nasal voice (and what developed into one of the world's worst comb-overs), considered the established union leaders to be sell-outs. Yorkshire born and bred, Scargill would transform British industrial relations and become a household name. He had had a hard-scrabble

---

* In the familiar British way, Barber's reward for wrecking the economy as Chancellor of the Exchequer was to be given a peerage and to be made chairman of a private sector bank.

childhood and later spoke almost lyrically about the mining village in which he grew up – a place of whippets, racing pigeons, brass bands, choirs and Sunday afternoon bare-knuckle fights for half a crown prize money.[2] He left school at fifteen, to work at a local colliery in Barnsley, and led his first industrial action (against his own union, over when meetings were to be held) at the age of seventeen. To the armour of ideological certainty, Arthur Scargill added a breastplate of rampant egotism.

The hour was his – all across the country the left was on the march. In 1966, the unions had endorsed Harold Wilson's freeze on pay rises: in total there had been 'only' 530,000 days lost to strikes, and most disputes lasted no more than a couple of days – they were 'token strikes' to show the management how fed up the workers were. But by 1972, the number of days lost to strikes had more than trebled to 1,722,000. The trade unions were opposed to any curb on wages and strikes were lasting longer. Scargill's time had come.

All seventy of the Yorkshire mines joined the action in support of the surface workers, a figure that doubled to 140 pits, after they were joined by miners in South Wales, Scotland and Kent. But it was an 'unofficial' strike, not endorsed by the miners' leaders (one of the strikers' demands was that Sidney Ford resign) and only lasted a couple of weeks. It collapsed when the National Union organised a ballot which rolled into one the issue of surface workers' hours and a new pay deal for everyone: unsurprisingly, most miners voted for a pay rise and to leave the issue of surface workers' hours for another day. There had always been communists prominent in the miners' union, but Scargill sensed the betrayal felt by miners. He had persuaded 130,000 men to stop work, and the dispute had been quite enough to establish him as a future leader to watch. He had drawn attention to himself by the use of 'flying pickets', a weapon which would come to inspire awe a few years later.

In the days of flared trousers and hot pants, Brut aftershave and mullet haircuts, the public were pretty familiar with the sight of picket lines when a workforce went on strike. They usually consisted of a group of workers standing around a rudimentary brazier at the entrance to a workplace, advertising the fact that they were in dispute with their employers, and aiming to persuade visitors not to cross their line. Although whether to cross the line was supposed always to be a matter of individual conscience, trade union members were expected to respect a picket line in someone else's industrial dispute.

Disputes were always apparently localised, but the invention of flying pickets made it possible to move strikers about the country from one industrial plant to another. In the miners' strike of 1969, when collieries in Derbyshire and Nottinghamshire were reticent about joining the action to support surface workers, Scargill's trademark flying pickets of Yorkshiremen would be sent to help them make their minds up. The despatch of young men in a vehicle, to strengthen the resolve of weaker brethren elsewhere, was a direct consequence of the new pattern of car-ownership. (Even as a young communist, Arthur Scargill liked to travel in a well-polished Jaguar.) Industrial action in a nationalised industry was made possible by private cars. Flying pickets are now illegal, for the very good reason that the line between picketing and intimidation is very thin. But in the 1960s and 70s, they were a frightening novelty.

Throughout those decades, the pit closures continued, albeit at a slowing rate. And every miner also realised every day that – despite their reputation as 'the aristocracy of the union movement' – they were no longer particularly well off. They had once enjoyed some of the best wages available to manual workers, but inflation had eroded what they could buy with their earnings and they had plunged down the earnings league. In July 1970, the union's annual conference decided they needed a pay rise of 33%.

Left-wing trade unionists had lost their friends in government with Edward Heath's election victory. The Industrial Relations Act brought in by the new Conservative administration in 1971 was hated for its attempt to reduce industrial disruption. Strikes were a fact of British life and the law had been the Tories' response to the frequent cry to be heard in British workplaces of 'Right! Everybody out!' when management attempted to change working practices. The 1971 Act tried to curb some of the unrest by decreeing that only registered trade unions would henceforth be entitled to legal immunity. There could be no more 'unofficial' strikes. By restricting the enjoyment of immunity to what the left considered to be weak-kneed collaborators, the law struck at the heart of collective action – the only weapon manual labourers believed they had against the employers. (It also did nothing much to promote harmony: in 1972 almost 24 million days of work were lost to labour disputes.*)

That year, the National Union of Mineworkers decided they had had enough. The miners' new union president, a Lancastrian named Joe Gormley (he titled his autobiography *Battered Cherub*, which was a pretty accurate description of his appearance), called a strike – the first official national strike since 1926. The demand was for a pay rise of up to 43%. The National Coal Board responded by claiming that to meet the cost of the wage claim, it would have to raise the price of coal by 15%, which would seriously damage demand for the product they all depended upon. The union called out its members on strike and every mine in the country stopped production. The consequence was predictable, and predicted. In 1950 coal had produced about 90% of British energy, and even with the development of new fuels, by 1970 it was still producing nearly half. The coal industry had one, overwhelmingly powerful,

---

* For comparison, there were 273,000 working days lost due to labour disputes in 2018, two-thirds of them in education.

customer. As time passed, electricity generators had tightened their grip as the main consumers of coal. Without coal to fire the steam turbines there would be no electricity.

The consequence was that by February 1972, the Central Electricity Generating Board was issuing public warnings that energy cuts were highly likely. Almost 1.5 million workers were soon idle in Britain's factories. Then on 3 February the *Birmingham Mail* reported that 'lorries formed a mile-long queue in Birmingham today to pick up coke supplies and caused traffic jams on a busy commuter route. The lorries from all over the country waited at Saltley, Britain's last major coke stockpile.' Until the story appeared, the miners had paid no attention to the depot, where an estimated 100,000 tons or so of coke were being stored by the local gas board. The photograph illustrating the article used the proper name of the Birmingham depot and referred to a 'line-up of lorries waiting for coke at Nechells today'.[3] For some reason – was it simply because 'Saltley' sounded more solid than 'Nechells'? – the ensuing confrontation became known as 'the Battle of Saltley Gate': the striking miners redeployed about one hundred pickets from a Midlands open-cast mine, convinced that if their action was to bite, they had to shut the gates and stop the depot functioning. According to a gas company official, it was only after the arrival of 'Arthur Scargill, supported by some 200 or more flying pickets' that things turned nasty.[4] Almost all accounts agree that it was when news camera crews started filming that violence broke out, and that it noticeably persisted in front of journalists. Arthur Scargill – at the time just a union branch delegate – was to be seen standing on the flat roof of a redbrick public-toilet block, commanding his troops through a megaphone. Two days later, the gas official claimed, the number of pickets had risen to between 600 and 1,000. The day after that, the number had grown to between 12,000 and 20,000, with reinforcements pouring in from Yorkshire and South Wales, and there were fears that predictions of a massive punch-up would be fulfilled. The vast majority of the strikers made their point peacefully, but even so great a number was insufficient to stop coke leaving the depot.

The Battle of Saltley Gate had become symbolic of the state of the dispute: neither side could afford to lose. In a brilliant masterstroke, Scargill then appealed for help to shop stewards at Birmingham's myriad engineering factories: all that was wanted, he said, was trade unionists to help with peaceful picketing. At the sound of the word 'solidarity', thousands downed tools and marched on the coke depot. 'The whole of bloody Birmingham's out!' was the joyful exclamation from one of the picketing miners, Charlie McLaren.[5] The local chief constable, Sir Derrick Capper, decided his men were overwhelmed, and the gates were forced closed, which had been the strikers' aim. The government was beaten and began furiously to work out how to eke out the remaining meagre supplies of energy. By the middle of February Edward Heath's government had declared a state of emergency and announced that electricity would soon only be available on a rota basis. A law lord, Richard Wilberforce, was asked to run an inquiry to settle the dispute. He dutifully did what was expected of him and pronounced the miners were a special case and deserved a pay rise of over 20%. Having driven a coach and horses through government pay policy (a limit on pay settlements of 7% or 8%), the public was then treated to the spectacle of all twenty-six committee members of the National Union of Mineworkers processing into 10 Downing Street to drink beer with Ted Heath while they recited to him their shopping list of demands. The law lord's ruling had amply justified their hubristic conviction that they were not like other men.

'The Battle of Saltley Gate' had been the making of Arthur Scargill on national television, and he was keen to consolidate his position in the union leadership. Several decades of closures meant that Yorkshire now stood out as the largest branch of the union by some margin, and by the end of the year, Scargill had been chosen as the NUM compensation agent for the area. He took the time to become well liked there, and acquired a reputation of making public speeches outside the Yorkshire headquarters. As compensation agent he established a tenacious reputation for supporting the interests of his men: when a coal-cutter broke through into Victorian underground workings below Lofthouse Colliery and flooded portions of the mine, killing seven miners, Scargill was there to represent them. He spent six days at the pit, and even guided Edward Heath around when he came to visit the site of the disaster. When the old right-wing area president of Yorkshire died in January 1973, Scargill sailed through the election, racking up almost four times as many votes as either of his competitors. The local presidency guaranteed him a spot on the national council, from which Scargill spoke to an even bigger audience.

Continuing inflation meant that Lord Wilberforce's recommendations on wages would soon be outpaced, and by the summer of the next year, the miners were again complaining that their earnings bought them less – as indeed they did. The union's national conference agreed to demand a 35% pay rise. When it was discovered soon afterwards that the miners' pay was already effectively lower than that recommended by Wilberforce only a year and a half earlier, determination to stage action in support of a pay claim hardened. Arthur Scargill had yet to make it to the very top of the National Union of Mineworkers' greasy pole, but he recognised an ally in the union's vice president, the hard-drinking, gravel-voiced Mick McGahey – so hard-bitten a communist that he had even supported the Russian invasion of Hungary in 1956. (The union president, Joe Gormley, could see the way that the communists were advancing on the top job and made it his business to change the union rules to restrict anyone over the age of fifty-five acceding to the presidency. After McGahey passed this particular milestone, Gormley felt satisfied he'd protected the great office from his bitterest rival.) The leadership's attempt to hold another strike was rejected by a ballot of the members, so instead the union organised a ban on overtime which they hoped would cut coal production by half. To save electricity, Heath tried to spread demand by putting the country on a three-day week, in which most businesses were closed four days in every seven, television stations stopped broadcasting at 10.30 every night, and many pubs didn't open at all. The new rules were to come into effect at midnight on New Year's Eve 1973. Despite the entertaining spectacle of a particularly idiotic Energy Secretary – Patrick Jenkin – publicly advising the citizenry to clean their teeth in the dark, while leaving all the lights blazing at his home, the three-day week did not endear the miners to the general public. But everyone knew the miners did a tough, dangerous job and there was something about the spectacle of the portly Heath – the owner of an ocean-racing yacht – confronting them that was uncomfortably reminiscent of the pre-nationalisation days.

In late January the miners voted by an overwhelming majority to go out on a full strike. On 7 February Edward Heath – not much more loved after his years in office than he had been before – called a general election on the blunt question 'who governs Britain?' By the time the votes had been counted it was clear that, whatever the answer, it was not his Conservative government. Under the British first-past-the-post system, Heath did manage to accumulate more votes than the Labour leader, Harold Wilson. But he fell well short of getting a majority of MPs in the House of Commons. Downing Street reverted to a minority government led by Wilson. The newly installed prime minister immediately more than doubled Heath's offer to the miners and raised their wages by 35%.

Heath had suffered for being simultaneously inept and unlucky. He imagined that by pretending to be an avuncular proprietor, he would gain sympathy. And though Joe Gormley clearly enjoyed being hugger-mugger with the prime minister, ordinary miners, whipped up by Arthur Scargill and his pals, did not. In short,

Heath mishandled the crisis by trying to act tough and then panicking. The country was cold, dejected and rudderless. Heath was also unlucky, in that, however much his Chancellor of the Exchequer mucked about with interest rates, taxes or public spending, the final nail had been hammered into the coffin of his administration by events far away.

Because, by the time Heath called his election, the price of oil had quintupled. A surprise attack by Egypt and Syria on Israel in October 1973 – the Yom Kippur War – had been an attempt to recapture the great areas of land that Israel had taken in the Six-Day War of 1967. It did not go well for the Arabs and the fighting followed its usual course in these confrontations; much breast-beating and shouting, followed by speedy retreat under the weight of superior weapons and tactics. To punish Israel's major ally, the United States, Arab oil-producing nations persuaded the twelve members of OPEC to cut production and to institute an embargo on oil exports. The British position had been that if Israel wanted peace, it should withdraw from the lands it had occupied in 1967, which might have appealed to the oil exporters. But the laws of supply and demand meant the whole world was affected by the sudden oil shortage. The market price rose from $3 a barrel to $12. Even when the cartel's embargo ended in March the following year, the price of oil never went back to what it had been before. At first sight, this might have seemed a great opportunity for the British coal industry. But by the 1970s, oil had acquired such a vital position in the economy that coal could never be a substitute. Vastly higher oil prices just produced inflation and made everything more expensive. The miners felt themselves more disadvantaged than ever.

After the election, the miners were dealing with a Labour government which claimed to have a better approach to the problems in industrial relations caused by rampant inflation. Harold Wilson's demeanour was studiedly workaday. Britain's major trade union leaders – men with no-nonsense first names like Vic, Len, Ray and Jack – became at least as familiar to television viewers as politicians, as they again wandered up Downing Street in bad suits for beer and sandwiches with the prime minister. Union leaders were untroubled by worries about whether their behaviour was strictly democratic (it wasn't) because they had no doubts in their own minds about how integral they were to the country's constitutional well-being. The miners, equally, had no doubts about their pre-eminence among trade unionists. Their tails were up anyway, because the Labour Party claimed to have a coherent energy policy. Wilson had even appointed a former NUM official, Eric Varley, as Energy Secretary. He was the youngest member of the Cabinet – a clever, affable man, whose father had been disabled by the miner's lung condition, pneumoconiosis. The pit-closure programme was bound to continue, as reserves of coal were exhausted, but the future felt brighter.

Soon Wilson gave them even more reasons to be cheerful. A year after the election, while Varley was at Covent Garden watching Verdi's *La Forza del Destino*, Harold Wilson telephoned that he was to switch jobs with the industry minister, Tony Benn. Varley had the tribal affiliations. But Benn had the promise of the future. There was something slightly bonkers about him, but he was definitely a socialist and, as a member of the aristocracy (he had been Viscount Stansgate before he disclaimed his title), he understood the eminence of the National Union of Mineworkers. At the Department for Industry, Benn had drawn up a new Industry Act to plan more nationalisations and had been a tireless promoter of workers' co-operatives (or 'Benn's Follies' as the mandarins in the Treasury liked to call them). In his new role in charge of energy policy, the radical in Benn looked a soft touch for the trade unions. Enthusiasm for modernistic projects married easily with his romantic attachment to colliers in a project said to be sure to secure the future of mining.

The great apostle of this project was the new chairman of the National Coal Board, Derek Ezra. He was a much less bombastic man than Alf Robens, likeable, apparently straightforward and given to determinedly unfashionable tweed coats and hats, instead of Robens' 'look at successful me' pinstripes. He was, though, a classic corporatist of the affable type who had presided over the country's lack of international competitiveness. Ezra had been too long in the industry to question many of its assumptions. Accustomed to the power of the mining unions and comfortable with the leader of the NUM, Joe Gormley, mining came to be known as 'The Derek and Joe Show'. He still had a Tiggerish enthusiasm for his industry and had enthusiastically endorsed the Labour government's bombastic 1974 Plan for Coal. 'The prospects for British coal are bright,' he proclaimed. 'An expanding and prosperous future' lay ahead.[6] As it turned out, he could hardly have been more wrong.

The anvil on which the future of the industry was to be fashioned was Selby, a pleasant market town on the plains of the Vale of York. Exploratory boreholes had disclosed the existence of a bed of coal the size of the Isle of Wight in the ground nearby. The discovery was sensational and seemed to believers in coal to offer a sparkling future. Here, twenty-five miles north of the generous seam at Barnsley, was another, where it looked as though the coal lay in beds a dozen or more feet thick. Under pressure from government, the predicted yield from the 110 square miles of farmland around the town was raised from 2 million tons a year to 10 million, promising to make it the biggest single coal-mining operation in the world. There would be five shafts to extract the coal, connected by underground railways. The engineering work would, said an official of the Coal Board, be like having the Eiffel Tower built underground, with the great benefit for local people that no one would know it was there. The mine would be thoroughly mechanised, the men who worked there technicians, not labourers. The coalfield would, Derek Ezra told the *Yorkshire Post* in July 1973, create no pollution, have no heavy road traffic, no railway sidings, none of the normal winding gear, and no mucky preparation plant.[7] Selby has a stunning medieval abbey. Ezra declared that its elegant Norman nave would be safe. That turned out to be true, but even if he was being as frank as he could be, many of his other promises turned out to be rubbish.

The National Coal Board had recognised how ambivalent local people were about the scheme. No one much looked forward to the prospect of great colliery winding wheels towering over the Vale of York – some of the best agricultural land in the country. Talk of the inevitable subsidence which would follow the scraping out of the mine alarmed others – even with the promise of pillars of coal being left in place below the abbey. A Selby Protection Club was formed by one of the councillors – quite apart from the environmental considerations, there was unease about an influx of colliers arriving to work in the new mine. 'We aren't passing judgement,' said the councillor in the evasive language the English use to pass judgements about class. 'We'll simply be saying "is this for you?"'[8] The Coal Board tried to fight back by being apparently frank about the mine. Senior officials explained the colliery to local people at meeting after meeting. From across the globe, reporters were flown in for visits and told that the coalfield was much more significant than the oilfields under the North Sea.

Of course, the Coal Board won the public relations battle. And their promise at first seemed to be justified, for the mine was soon one of the most productive in the world, providing work for 2,500 people. Locals had been spared the influx of miners living in the area, for most of the men extracting the coal commuted to work, driving from dozens of miles away and sharing the cost of petrol. In many other ways, Selby seemed the way of the future. Instead of five separate pits, there would be five separate entry points, with underground transport to the one exit from which coal would be taken speedily to power stations. Over £1 billion was spent developing the pit, and innovative engineering solutions found for problems like water breaking in – to solve that one, the nearby ground was frozen solid for a year. There would be no slag heaps and much of the ground-level machinery would be hidden from view.

From the coalfield at Selby, you could see the eight cooling towers of the newly built Eggborough power station on the river Aire, which had begun producing electricity only in 1967. With a dedicated railway line, the coal from Selby could be shipped in no time to another nearby power station, at Drax, the biggest power plant in the country. Selby would be plugged into the future. Now that oil prices had overtaken those of coal, it surely made sense to make the best of indigenous production? The government, the National Coal Board and the National Union of Mineworkers, all agreed, and reinforced each other's confidence. There was a public inquiry lasting thirty-eight days, though it was largely a foregone conclusion. The government gave authorisation for the mine 'in the national interest', and in October 1976 the Duchess of Kent stood in a tasselled hat under an umbrella in pouring rain, pulling on a joystick to inaugurate the drilling of the first shaft down to the coal. Joe Gormley, the miners' president, stood on a podium in a sea of mud begging his members to be 'flexible' in forthcoming pay negotiations, because 'We have to prove that nationalisation is not a dirty word.'[9] The eccentric energy minister Tony Benn, standing alongside, delivered himself of the line that King Coal was being restored to his throne and that the Selby coalfield would be the start of Britain's industrial regeneration. The mine would, he claimed, ensure that 'Britain can look forward to ample supplies of energy as far ahead as we can see'.[10]

It turned out to be piffle. The Selby coalfield went from the future to the past with hardly any present. There was only one year when Selby met its target for coal production, and by 2000, the coalfield was losing £30 million a year and closure was inevitable. In October 2004, twenty-one years after opening, it shut. Some of the redundant miners believed there were still coal reserves underground, but the reason given was 'deteriorating geological conditions', which had apparently not been spotted when the mine was being planned. Coal prices had fallen and the contracts to supply coal were worth much less. By 2010, Drax power station was burning imported wood and wood pellets as well as coal to produce the necessary steam. Two years later the private company running the power station began converting the boilers to run on gas. It was the clearest evidence that coal had no place in the twenty-first century.

The February 1974 election had been a humiliation for the Conservative Party under its cold and arrogant leader. No political party is more ruthless than the Conservatives and soon the feeling was widespread that it was time for a new figurehead. There was not time to dump Heath before Harold Wilson decided to call another election – in October 1974 – to consolidate his position. This Heath also lost, though he swore he'd stay on as leader, even though the electorate had clearly had enough of him. In February 1975, Margaret Thatcher challenged him in a ballot of Conservative MPs for the leadership of the party, and won. Thatcher represented an entirely different sort of Conservatism, which detested the corporatist approach of Edward Heath, brilliantly parodied in *Private Eye* as the managing director of 'Heathco', with frequent riffs from him about how the company's Automatic Plastic Beaker Disposal unit had been made to malfunction by inconsiderate members of staff dropping their fag ends into the canteen's plastic cups. Margaret Thatcher's vision of Britain could hardly have been more different. She had no time for malfunctions.

She expected there would be another confrontation between the miners' union and the government sooner or later, but was wise enough only to give battle when she was ready. Two years after

winning the leadership she was presented with a report from one
of her backbench MPs, Nicholas Ridley, on how the government
might avoid another humiliation, like that inflicted by the miners
on Edward Heath. Ridley, the younger son of a Northumberland
coal baron, had determined on a political career as a young man.
(He had been defeated by Alf Robens when, in a kamikaze initiation ritual, he had stood as Conservative candidate in the local
coal port of Blyth.) Disdain was his default setting – as one of his
numerous ways of showing contempt for received wisdom, he
smoked more cigarettes than a beagle in the most deranged animal
experiment.*

Ridley's little group concluded that to win the next battle with
the miners, coal should be stockpiled at power stations, prepara-
tions be made to import coal, and that non-union drivers should
be hired to haul it. All of these tactics were to be used by Mrs
Thatcher's government when, as inevitably happened, there came
another head-to-head with the miners.

Nicholas Ridley's 'plan' – such as it was – had anticipated that a
confrontation between the coal industry and government would
occur a year or two after an election. He was right. Twenty-one
months after the election, plans were announced for the closure of
a further twenty-three 'uneconomic' mines. The National Union
of Mineworkers took the shutdowns as a last straw, and announced
a strike. Joe Gormley talked tough: 'The prime minister should not
make the same mistake as Ted Heath did in 1974, when he thought
he could take us on. The issue about jobs is much more volatile
than pay.'[11] Gormley may have been right, but fighting to retain
jobs by not working was a novel challenge.

---

* A BBC reporter once asked Ridley's opinion about something and got the reply
'That is the most stupid question I've ever been asked.' When the unfortunate inter-
viewer tried again, Ridley responded that his question was 'the second most stupid
question I've ever been asked'.

Industrial unrest was now a familiar feature of British life, as the Labour government led by James Callaghan (an exhausted Harold Wilson had suddenly quit in March 1976) tried to control inflation by limiting pay rises in the public sector to 5%. The unions would have none of it. As the union leadership bent over backwards to hit artificial targets, the pits failed to churn out coal, and Scargill and his supporters constantly agitated for higher general wages. Hard-headedness abounded, and a desperate Joe Gormley put incentive payments and productivity schemes for miners back on the union table at their 1977 conference in order to try and push for the production figures his Plan for Coal was demanding. Many left-wingers feared that incentivising results through bonus schemes would dig a crater in union unity: they were right. Soon divisions were emerging among the miners themselves, between those at profitable pits, largely in the Midlands, who were well placed to attract high bonuses, and those in the populous areas in the North, or in South Wales, who were often working less accessible seams of coal, and were hardest hit by the country's steep inflation rate. Tony Benn, who had spoken so messianically about the wonderful future awaiting the coal industry, had been forced in 1977 to publish another new manifesto with a dull title, *Coal for the Future*, drastically revising down his earlier targets for production figures – though he also earmarked another £200 million of funding for the Selby complex, the price tag for which now stood at an astonishing £3.2 billion. Traditional support for the Labour Party or the NUM among British workers had splintered into more partisan local camps, and – more to the point – the electorate was fed up with what often seemed like a rigged game. Famously, in that 'winter of discontent', there were piles of rubbish which went uncollected, and in Liverpool, corpses which remained unburied. Though few recognised it at the time, the chaos of the Callaghan years represented the death throes of the Britain that the Labour government had tried to build after the Second World War. The most immediately obvious result, however, was Callaghan's defeat by Margaret Thatcher in the election of May 1979.

While Britain was consumed with its own affairs, few remarked on the implications of the fact that the National Coal Board doubled its profits in 1979–80 by selling expensive mining equipment to China. Within a decade, that country was extracting 1 billion tons a year. An enormous amount of cheap coal power pulled China headlong into the new millennium with an effect tantamount to its own industrial revolution. Between 1979 and 2010, the country's GDP increased on average each year by 9%. Since 2011 China has consumed more coal than the rest of the world combined. That arrival of NCB equipment at the end of the 1970s heralded a handover point, as a consequence of which global manufacturing and fossil fuel industry took off in the East and left Britain far behind.

Nationalisation of the coal mines had been a miners' dream. But it had a fatal flaw. Successful public ownership was attractive because the fruits of everybody's labour benefitted everyone. As long as the men and the managers were agreed, it could be immeasurably better than the previous system, in which, when the chips were down, the men and the managers were on opposite sides. But it demanded agreement not merely on how the mine was to be worked, but the nature of the long-term objective.

What happened when the two sides didn't agree? There were formal dispute procedures, which ought to have included worker-directors. The mines had been sunk wherever there seemed a reasonable chance of raising coal, and in the process they had despoiled much previously unblemished land. But once a mine was functioning, it became the place where you slept and ate, visited the doctor, fell in love, had your children and entertained yourself. What these communities lacked in creature comforts, they made up for in social organisations – allotment associations, pigeon and poultry clubs, brass bands, choirs, youth organisations, whippet-racing and eagerly contested giant-vegetable competitions.

What happened when the coal – the reason for the towns' or villages' existence – ran out? At that point, the aims of the managers and the workers diverged. The managers' interest was in making the mines produce profitable coal; the miners' interest was in their life beyond coal. As long as the industry as a whole was growing, there might be hope of being redeployed elsewhere. But pits had been closing for generations. If the whole industry was finished, that was that. And whereas previously, when a private owner decided to close a mine, the pitman had found himself in conflict with shareholders, after nationalisation, he was taking on the state. The colliers could perhaps count on the support of a public who recognised that the miners did a far more wearisome and dangerous job than most of us. A politician of Harold Wilson's sinuousness might talk his way out of confrontation, but when faced with a lacklustre prime minister like Edward Heath, the miners felt they could win. Ominously for them, if it came to a serious confrontation with a tougher enemy, no sensible person would bet their house on a miners' 'knock 'em out and drag 'em away' victory. The government had all the resources of the state to use if necessary, including the police and army, and anyway, no self-respecting democrat could accept defeat for the elected government.

Thatcher and her friends had taken office determined to end the power of the trade unions to make or unmake governments. They had seen enough of the chaos that followed government wage policies to believe that there should be no government control of prices or wages in nationalised industries, and thus no obvious flashpoint. When a stand-off with the miners' trade union loomed, their first action was surprising. Confronted by the prospect of another strike over the closure of the twenty-three uneconomic coal mines, in February 1981, Thatcher blinked. She had her

Energy Secretary, David Howell, stand up in the House of
Commons and declare, without a hint of irony, that 'the long-term
future of the industry, if it can contain its costs and increase its
efficiency, is very bright'.[12] Howell claims he meant every word of
it, but the carefully drafted sentence is an object lesson in the need
to read political small print very closely. Coal seemed at the time
cheaper than gas, oil, nuclear power or renewables. Along with a
promise to cut coal imports and to improve the subsidies being
paid to the nationalised industry, the statement of confidence was
enough for Joe Gormley to call off the strike being threatened by
the miners. The continuing divisions in the union were expressed
by left-wing figures like Mick McGahey, whose Lanarkshire voice
could be heard grumbling that he was 'very far from satisfied'.
McGahey was unhappy at the absence of any clear-cut promise. He
was right to be apprehensive. But everyone knew the NUM was
riven with infighting between left and right and twenty-three pits
had at least been saved. That was the important thing.

It turned out that rather than being a capitulation, this was no
more than a tactical retreat. As Ridley had advocated, stockpiles of
coal continued to be built up at power stations, some of which
were converted so that they could also burn oil. Having seen
Arthur Scargill's flying pickets in action, Ridley's recommendation
of creating a 'flying police force' was also adopted. A new generation was taking charge in both politics and the trade unions. Joe
Gormley retired from the presidency of the miners' union in April
the following year. To no one's great surprise, he was replaced by
Arthur Scargill. In March the following year, the Thatcher government needed to find a new chairman for the National Coal Board.
The man who had succeeded Derek Ezra in the job was a dull,
self-effacing Yorkshireman, Norman Siddall. 'Sid Normal', as he
was quickly known, had been in the coal industry all his working
life and lasted only a year as chairman, before a bad heart forced
him to retire on doctor's advice. In early 1983, government eyes fell

on Ian MacGregor, a pugnacious Scottish-American businessman, to become the next chairman. MacGregor was another proposition to Sid Normal altogether, having previously run the nationalised British Steel Corporation. It employed over 140,000 people and was losing billions of pounds each year. Told to make it profitable, within three years MacGregor had closed steel plants across the country and dispensed with over half the workforce. He was expected to do something very similar with the coal industry and the miners greeted his arrival with an overtime ban, which would in a few months seriously deplete coal supplies. MacGregor was to be the immovable object on which the irresistible force was intended to founder. The stage was set for an enormous showdown.

16

To the Death

By late 1983, Mrs Thatcher was ready. British forces had ejected the Argentine military junta from their occupation of the Falkland Islands. 'Rejoice, rejoice!' she cried. A Conservative government was then re-elected with the biggest majority since 1945. The incoming administration felt triumphant, but embarrassed by the state of much of the country, in which industrial unrest had become a seemingly permanent feature of British life, as a once mighty imperial power struggled to find a place for itself in the world. Now a country written-off as past it had brought off a brilliant feat of arms, and in the eyes of the government restored its international standing. There was, said Mrs Thatcher, much more to do. Britain, she said, had defeated 'the enemy without': now it was time to tackle 'the enemy within'.[1] She was not referring only to miners. But defeating them would have the greatest symbolic impact.

Immediately after the 1979 election, she had told her Home Secretary, Willie Whitelaw, that 'The last Conservative government was destroyed by the miners' strike. We'll have another and we'll win.'[2] Her Energy Secretary, who would be intimately involved in any confrontation, decided he should first pick the brains of Arnold Weinstock of the General Electric Company, generally considered the country's pre-eminent businessman. 'Your first duty,' said the tycoon, 'is to fill the power stations with fuel.'[3] David Howell told Thatcher that they could not be ready for the next miners' strike before it happened. That lack of preparation had been the reason for Thatcher's capitulation when seething miners threatened unrest in early 1981. The message took some time to sink in – 10 Downing Street was still aflame with the election message that the new government was not going to lose any more industrial confrontations. It had been then that Sir Derek Ezra and the miners' leader, Joe Gormley, jointly stomped in to see Howell about the possibility of a coal strike if there were more pit closures, and emerged to tell reporters that not only would the planned pit closures not happen, but that the government had increased their subsidy by £300 million, causing baffled reporters to run to whatever landline telephones they could find, to scream at their news editors 'For "no", read "yes"'.

In retrospect, everyone can see it was just a tactical withdrawal. On 15 September 1983, Mrs Thatcher met in secret at 10 Downing Street with her Chancellor, and newly appointed secretaries for Energy and Employment. The Cabinet Secretary and two senior civil servants were also present. Political sensitivities demanded utter secrecy, but civil service good practice required a record be kept. The result was a document produced under a rubric stating that it was never to be photocopied or circulated outside the prime minister's Private Office. The nature of the discussion made very clear the determination of the Thatcher government to win any future confrontation with the miners. The notes commented that the pit-closure programme had gone further this year than planned: there had been 'one pit closed every three weeks', and that Ian MacGregor planned to close another seventy-five mines in the coming two years, 'sixty-four of which would reduce the workforce by some 55,000'. (When Arthur Scargill became leader, his union had had about 170,000 members.) The memo noted that MacGregor – whom the liberal Bishop of Durham, David Jenkins,[4] called 'an elderly imported American' – then intended to shut down another eleven mines, eliminating a further 9,000 jobs. It was calculated that by the end of the closures he had in mind, two-thirds of Welsh miners would be redundant, half of those in South Yorkshire, nearly half of the miners in the north-east of England, almost half in the south Midlands, and one-third of the miners in Scotland. The whole of the Kent coalfield would be shut down. Had they known about it, miners' leaders would have seen what was being planned as a form of Grand Guignol.

The record of the meeting was made public at the beginning of 2014, under the normal thirty-year declassification rule.[5] Thatcher's new Energy Secretary, Peter Walker, had seemed confident in the meeting that he could achieve the stockpiles of coal which had eluded David Howell.[6] But it is the date of the meeting itself that is significant, for it reveals that the miners' leader Arthur Scargill was right (though disbelieved) that before the miners' strike had even begun, the government had a plan for widespread pit closures and were prepared to fight any ensuing industrial action. The necessary changes to the law were made, requiring trade unions to hold a vote of their members before taking industrial action.

The strike which sealed the fate of an industry which had existed for hundreds of years began six months later, when the new Coal Board chairman, Ian MacGregor, announced in March 1984 that twenty uneconomic mines would be closed, beginning with the pits at Cortonwood and Bullcliffe Wood in Yorkshire, Herrington in County Durham, Snowdown in Kent and Polmaise in the Scottish coalfield. Miners at Cortonwood Colliery were astonished: it had been opened in 1873, but was still reckoned to have generous reserves of good coking coal to be extracted (the National Coal Board had just invested a million in the pit). The Cortonwood miners walked out at midnight on 5 March.

Scargill had been aching for a national strike since his election as president of the National Union of Mineworkers and had balloted his men three times without gaining their support. In the last instance, on 3 March 1983, he lost the vote, with 61% of

Britain's miners opposed to strike action. But now he sensed the wind at his back. The walkout at Cortonwood would begin the longest national strike in British history, and in many of the coalfields there was immediate support for Scargill's finger-stabbing speeches. But the leadership and different districts were divided. Area after area insisted on local ballots, and in every case when they were held – in Cumberland, Lancashire, the Midlands, Northumberland, North Wales, south Derbyshire – the support required for a strike simply failed to materialise. By the end of the week, the fate of the strike was in the balance. In classic barrack-room lawyer fashion, Scargill began arguing that all the rules had been followed to allow regional strikes, which, if taken up everywhere, would, he insisted, amount to a national strike. Scooters, cars, coaches, and minibuses began fanning out from his Yorkshire district in the name of solidarity, enforced or otherwise. In the end, though Arthur Scargill pleaded a multiplicity of reasons for never holding the national ballot of members which would have made the great strike of 1984–5 morally forthright and legally watertight, it never happened. This was a corrosive tactical flaw: evermore, he was vulnerable to the charge that he refused to allow his members to decide for themselves whether they approved of a national action. Numerous union officials still make no secret of their feeling that the reason for there being no national ballot was that 'Arthur was afraid he'd lose it'.

Here was a preening, arrogant union leader made for the television age. Right-wing newspaper columnists, like Paul Johnson, held forth that it was 'the media, and above all the BBC and ITV, by their massive exposure for this glib exponent of political showbiz, who put Scargill where he is'.[7] The description was as overblown as middlebrow newspapers demand, but Johnson had correctly identified the fact that Scargill was a creature of the media age. However much he might, when it suited him, describe the press pack as 'hyenas', the truth was he loved using the mass media, as he adored courtroom histrionics. In Yorkshire he had created his own tabloid newspaper, the *Yorkshire Miner*, in the 1970s and hired Maurice Jones, a communist sub-editor from the *Sheffield Morning Telegraph*, to run it for him. (Unlike the publications of the Coal Board and the NUM it included photographs of Page Three girls, Scargill claiming that objections only came from 'hysterical women', while his editor Maurice Jones was convinced that dungarees were evidence of lesbianism.) In 1977 the two men had managed to get themselves arrested on the picket line at the Grunwick film-processing laboratories in west London, where a largely female, largely Asian, workforce was striking for union recognition. Scargill was freed, emerging with his revolutionary credentials nicely burnished. His absurd journalist friend fled the country and attempted to claim asylum in East Germany, from where he had to be brought home. Since these early shenanigans, Scargill had used the *Yorkshire Miner* as a vehicle to speak directly to his ground troops – and usurp the more moderating influences of the NUM's official magazine published from London, *The Miner*.

Scargill's arrogance ('Remember, you're talking to the inventor of the flying picket'[8] he used to cry) did him no harm, and when *Channel Four News* offered him a producer and crew to make his own report on the strike, he said he found the challenge 'easy'.[9] Austin Mitchell, who had parlayed a career as frontman for Yorkshire Television into being a Labour MP, even claimed that the station 'created' Scargill, as they searched for a left-wing miner's voice. 'It was our Barnsley stringer who put us on to him,' he said, 'but if he hadn't I think we should have had to invent him.'[10] Scargill, who had refined his advocacy skills by being a fearsome compensation agent for injured miners, seized the opportunity television gave him to talk directly to voters, becoming a regular guest on chat shows and radio discussion programmes like *Any Questions?* He instinctively understood the power of simple speech, answered questions succinctly, and dressed the part – in early days in a suit and then in a cap (a baseball cap, rather than an old-fashioned miner's flat cap). He recognised that very often the public had no great regard for his interlocutors and so he treated them with the contempt that much of the audience felt they deserved: plenty of reporters dreaded his sneering ridicule. He could sound aggressive or reasonable, as the occasion demanded, though the strident nasal whine was ever-present.

From the first refusal to come to work in the mine at Cortonwood on 6 March 1984, the strike escalated. It was completely the wrong time of year to stop work: demand for coal falls in the warmer months of the year, whereas, if they had waited, the miners might have had the seasons on their side. Their decision to refuse to work any overtime, which preceded the all-out strike by almost twenty-three weeks, had already had what Scargill himself called 'an extraordinary impact' and there had been no reason why it couldn't have continued until Christmas.[11] Biggest of all blunders, though, was the terrible mistake of not holding a national ballot of members before calling a national strike.

Picketing as such – letting the world know that you were engaged in an industrial dispute – was not illegal, though at the worst of the confrontations peaceful demonstrating could give way to showers of stones, bottles and half-bricks. Inevitably, police were deployed. Many of the miners blamed the storms of missiles on an alliance of communists and hooligans who had joined the protests only half-invited, because they recognised that Scargill detested the whole apparatus of power in the land.

He was very far from being the first communist to become prominent in the miners' unions. According to his biographer, Scargill 'hero-worshipped' another 'King Arthur', A. J. Cook, the leader of the miners in the 1926 General Strike, whom Scargill regarded 'as the sea-green incorruptible'.[12] He certainly made no secret of his eagerness to bring down the government, which cost him the endorsement of the Trades Union Congress and the

Labour Party. By the end of March 1984, an estimated 45,000 miners were holding out against a strike. Many in the very productive Midlands/Nottinghamshire coalfield* went on to join a rival organisation, the Union of Democratic Miners, led by Roy Lynk, which was bankrolled by individuals with deep pockets, many of whom had a cordial loathing for Scargill. It did not prevent mines in the area being mercilessly picketed. (And nor, later, did it save them from closure: in the 1990s the Conservatives repaid the loyalty of the UDM by closing their pits anyway.)

The government fought back with attacks on the union's ability to pay money to members who were on strike, by freezing union assets. New rules on social security benefits meant miners' families were now poorer than they had ever imagined. Margaret Thatcher stuck to her script, publicly protesting that the strike was just an industrial dispute. But the plans she made, including the creation of what was effectively a national police force, show she understood it was much more than that. As ever, it was not the middle classes – let alone the organisers or leaders – who faced each other outside mines and coal dumps. Pickets, scabs and police generally came from the same social class, and – as in most wars – the greatest suffering was borne by the least advantaged. Roy Hattersley, the Labour Party's deputy leader during the strike, had a grandfather who moved directly from the pit to the local police force, and noticed that 'Most miners had a distant relative in the force. During the 1984 dispute, there was at least one inspector who would meet (and greet) his brother on the picket line.'[13]

What were they fighting for? The difference between this strike and most previous ones was in the nature of the objective. In a

---

* Most coal mined in the pits here went to the string of power stations on and around the river Trent – 'Megawatt Valley' as it was called – which produced a quarter of the electricity generated in England and Wales. The coal usually arrived on permanently coupled 'merry-go-round' trains and was unloaded from waggons without their even stopping.

dispute about wages or pensions or holiday entitlement there is a simple calculation for everyone to make. Is the cost of lost production greater than the cost of giving the strikers what they want? It's a pretty straightforward sum. But the miners were not staying away from work because they wanted money. They were withholding their labour because they wanted to 'save' mines from closure. There was more nonsense talked about 'community' in the 1980s than there was about most subjects. But no one in their right mind would claim that 'community' – however you defined it – was capable of a simple arithmetical analysis; it was something felt. The miners may have been incapable of delivering what they sought, but they were definitely not speaking the same language as the other side; the miners were withholding their labour because they and their families wanted to preserve a life they understood. 'Coal not Dole' was the black-on-yellow slogan on the strikers' stickers and lapel badges: they were identifying themselves with the rock. Yet, to the managers, what determined the survival of mining villages was the potential productivity of the mine: if there was nothing to be mined, there was no need for miners. Hence the importance of Scargill's repeated claims that mines were being scheduled for closure despite the existence of exploitable reserves. But the entire history of coal-mining demonstrated that coalfields did not thrive because a bunch of miners happened to have congregated there. Mines existed because some black-hearted capitalist had taken a risk. If it paid off, the miners would arrive and the entrepreneur would get rich. That was how capitalism worked. It followed that the miners' strike could only succeed either if threatened pits had a much longer future than was being predicted, or if the cost of the dispute was intolerable. Neither was the case.

In November 1984 – eight months after the strike had begun, and still with no end in sight – the former Conservative prime minister, Harold Macmillan, delivered his maiden speech in the

House of Lords. He spoke only for himself, but he seemed to capture the soul of a now departed Conservatism. He claimed the strike was breaking his heart. The miners were 'the best men in the world, who beat the kaiser's army and beat Hitler's army, and never gave in'. He claimed the confrontation was both 'endless' and 'pointless'.[14] It was neither, but many felt as distressed as this out-of-touch old man. The strike ground on and eventually came to a hugely consequential conclusion. The miners were not a chance enemy, and neither was the confrontation unanticipated. Margaret Thatcher had decided that the question asked by Edward Heath in February 1974 – 'who governs Britain?' – should receive an unequivocal answer.

In a national strike in many other democracies, the government of the day would have deployed a paramilitary police force answerable to the Interior Ministry; in France, for example, the National Police and their brutish reserve, the CRS, are especially known for riot-control work. In Britain there is no national police force, and no 'riot police'. (Anti-riot operations are left to normal officers with some specialist training.) Almost all policing is local, which is why the country has such an expensive total of police forces, from the City of London police, with under 800 officers, to the Metropolitan Police next door, with well over 30,000. The guiding doctrine of British policing was articulated by the Tory Home Secretary Robert Peel in his 1829 'Principles of Policing': 'the police are the public and the public are the police'.[15] Peel was expressing a long-standing British principle that the only difference between the two categories of citizen is that the police are paid to give full-time attention to duties which are incumbent on everyone. At bottom, whatever authority the police have comes not from the power of the state but the consent of the people.

In the miners' strike, Thatcher came perilously close to destroying this understanding. Nicholas Ridley's plan for winning the next industrial confrontation had envisaged a central mechanism for co-ordinating police deployments. Police officers deployed to a particular spot were always theoretically under the command of the local chief constable. But the 'reporting centre' established at Scotland Yard – where uniformed police officers despatched busloads of West Country police to South Yorkshire or Merseyside officers to Nottinghamshire – certainly looked rather like a national police force. Officers were supplied with helmets and long perspex shields intended to protect them against missiles and charges by massed protesters, and small round shields for when they were to take part in truncheon-wielding 'snatch' arrests. Many police officers were astonished by the powers with which they seemed suddenly to have been endowed: many of them had not dreamed of interfering with free movement by stopping cars carrying flying pickets, arresting the drivers and then releasing them, too late for them to join any picket line. They even seemed to be allowed to put up roadblocks on motorways and to force vehicles with flying pickets off the road.

In theory, every policing operation was under the command of the local force. The cultures of the different forces were apparent in the way they behaved: relations between pickets and police tended to be best where the men on each side belonged to the local community – they understood each other. The most badly behaved police officers were those from forces which had no experience of mining communities. Miners talked of visiting police who were bussed around the coalfields and slept, dozens to a room, in village halls and community centres. They seemed to striking miners to be like 'occupying armies'. The worst of the lot were officers from the Metropolitan Police. People do not starve to death in modern Britain. But they do go hungry, and there was genuine hardship in many of the mining villages, with locally organised soup kitchens providing the only meals available. Yet for the visiting police, the huge amounts of overtime available made it seem like Christmas.

When Metropolitan Police officers sat in their buses and waved five-pound notes at hungry strikers, they made no friends.

The most notorious confrontation – and the turning point of the strike – came at Orgreave, a South Yorkshire plant for making coke, and belonging to British Steel. The miners became fixated on preventing lorries leaving the depot with fuel for the furnaces at Scunthorpe steel plant. Arthur Scargill seems to have thought of Orgreave as a potential 'Second Saltley', the coking depot at which his pickets had defeated the police in the 1972 miners' strike. He was wrong. The confrontation at Saltley Gate had taken place at an urban depot, hedged round by narrow streets. Orgreave was surrounded by fields and approached on a rural road, which the police could open and close when they liked. Thousands of pickets had gathered and were met by great numbers of police, their commanders determined not to go down in history as losers, like the Birmingham chief constable. Had Scargill's bravado led him straight into a trap? As lorry after lorry arrived at the depot to load up with coke Scargill duly appeared at Orgreave, to organise the picketing. Among those arrested in the ensuing donnybrook was the miners' president himself, when he attempted to pass through a police line and was charged with obstruction. Ever quick to make his case that Margaret Thatcher was leading a 'fascist' government, as he was led to a police van he screamed '1984 – Great Britain!'

The pickets had appropriated a couple of songs from the football terraces – 'Here we go, here we go' to the tune of 'The Stars and Stripes Forever', as they waded into the pushing and shoving with the police, and 'There's only one Arthur Scargill' to the tune of 'Guantanamera'. Now they sang the latter. Local magistrates released the miners' leader on unconditional bail, but he had made his gesture. According to his driver and bodyguard Jim Parker, Scargill had 'wanted to be arrested', presumably to make a point to his troops. The arrested miners' leader in open-necked shirt and baseball cap made a good photo, which appeared on the front pages. Even though his refusal to hold a national ballot meant that he was much less likely to enlist public support than the picture of a picket in a novelty policemen's helmet being smiled upon by a genuine copper, there was feeling on the left that Scargill had been victimised. 'Even A. J. Cook, the miners' leader in the lockout in 1926, had not had to endure the violence and the malevolence of the attacks on Arthur Scargill,' thought the Trotskyist journalist, Paul Foot.[16]

The face-off came on 18 June. It was a wonderful sunny day, and by nine in the morning a crowd of pickets estimated at 10,000 had gathered around the plant. Arthur Scargill was among them and was seen, the police claimed, to fall over and tumble down a slope. He was taken to hospital where he said he had been hit by a police riot shield. The confrontation got worse. Convoys of nose-to-tail lorries were still being organised to take coke away from the plant. Some of the pickets attempted to build barricades, with girders, burning vehicles and steel spikes. The police lost control of themselves and behaved shamefully, wading into the pickets, young men eager for a barney with young men from another tribe. Police commanders behaved like medieval army officers, ordering in police dogs and full-scale charges by mounted police. But it was a big field of battle, and in the memory of some of those who were there that Monday morning, everything was peaceful apart from a group of young men shouting insults at the police. Other pickets had taken their shirts off to sunbathe. Some were playing football. Police footage of the day seemed to confirm the impression of peace and relative quiet. Suddenly, the lines of police parted and through the gap rode officers on horseback, gathering speed. They had drawn their batons. The photograph which came to sum up the Battle of Orgreave shows a mounted policeman swinging his baton at a defenceless bystander. Who wasn't even a miner. Who wasn't even a man. Lesley Boulton, an intelligent, reasonable woman, worked as a prop-maker at Sheffield's Crucible Theatre. Her offence was to be left-wing and present. She had moved from north London to Sheffield with her partner, having previously taken part in the anti-nuclear weapon protests at Greenham Common. She was at Orgreave that morning taking photographs as a member of Women Against Pit Closures.

The police said later that there were ninety-three arrests that day, and seventy-two injured policemen. (There were no accurate figures for the number of injured pickets.) The Battle of Orgreave had demonstrated the wisdom of the old saying about being careful what you wish for. Previous generations of miners had believed that if only they could achieve state control of the mines, their problems would be over. Had anyone recognised the compromises it would involve them in, and the price of purity? Although Scargill shouted class war and the left across the country took the miners' side, the strike was really a struggle between small-c conservatives, who wanted to preserve a mining way of life, and a new species of Conservatives, who couldn't stand the old way of doing things and had the forces of the state at their command.[17] What began as a 'fight to defend mining communities' became a struggle for the survival of the union 'your fathers and grandfathers made'. In the course of the strike, 10,000 previously law-abiding miners were arrested – two of them eventually convicted of manslaughter for dropping a concrete block from a footbridge, and killing taxi-driver David Wilkie as he drove a strike-breaking miner to work. The spectacle of helmeted British police officers charging on horseback at unarmed demonstrators with batons flailing – 'medieval' was the word that almost everybody used to describe it – was so astonishing as to be unbelievable. But it was nothing compared to 'Operation Cyclops', a complicated attempt to smear Arthur Scargill with claims that he had taken money from Libya to support strikers and used it to pay off his mortgage. The story was an invention, but gained traction because there was so much untraceable ready cash being passed around in suitcases, holdalls and plastic bags to give money to pickets and to buy food for soup kitchens.

Ninety-three of the pickets were arrested on the day of the big Orgreave confrontation, taken to an old office block and charged with riot and unlawful assembly. All were later acquitted as the prosecution cases collapsed when it emerged that supposedly individual eyewitness statements by police had actually been dictated to them by senior officers. Thirty-four of the police statements, apparently given independently, contained the very same sentence and twenty-two of them the same paragraph. A photograph was produced to show that a miner accused by the police of throwing a stone was almost certainly holding a pork pie. Michael Mansfield, the left-wing QC who defended three of the miners, described South Yorkshire police evidence as 'the biggest frame-up ever'.[18]

'Scandalous' is the only word to describe the behaviour of the police. A month after the Battle of Orgreave, in a speech to her backbenchers, Thatcher described the striking miners as 'the enemy within', a sub-Churchillian choice of words which confirmed her permanent place in the left's bestiary.[19] Soon after the strike was over, she had attended a drinks party at the Home Office to congratulate the chief constables of forces who'd helped defeat the miners. There could hardly have been a greater contrast with the 1947 speech by the Labour fuel and power minister, Manny Shinwell, who had told the miners 'you are public servants upon whose efforts will depend our future as a powerful industrial country'.[20]

In the decades after the cavalry charges, various Home Secretaries refused repeated requests for an inquiry, and over thirty years after the event even rejected an offer by the Bishop of Sheffield to conduct his own independent investigation. When – eventually – the Independent Police Complaints Commission bothered to investigate the police behaviour, sections of their report were only published after the redaction of entire sentences which might have identified the senior police officers who gave the orders. Though South Yorkshire police later paid £425,000 in compensation to thirty-nine miners for assault, false arrest and malicious prosecution, not a single police officer was ever disciplined for any offence. (Five years later, the very same force was held to account for the disaster at Hillsborough football stadium, when ninety-six fans were crushed to death. That earned them a prime-ministerial condemnation for incompetence and dishonesty.) Thus far, this exceptionally ill-favoured force has evaded repeated requests for a full investigation into what it did at Orgreave. In 2016, the then Home Secretary, Amber Rudd, refused an inquiry into what happened on the grounds that no one was killed and it was a long time ago. A previous Conservative Home Secretary, Leon Brittan, had at least admitted to his fear that any inquiry could 'turn into a witch-hunt'. A Freedom of Information Act request in early 2020 to know how many files had yet to be released and whether it was true that some would remain sealed until 2066 was met with the stock promise of a response within twenty working days. When the response eventually arrived – seventy-one days later – it disclosed nothing about why the files had been censored or for how long the redactions would be in force.

Orgreave was the turning point in the strike. Arthur Scargill said the police behaviour was 'reminiscent of a Latin American state'. But it was more than that. The Orgreave confrontation had demonstrated that, whatever the moral worth of their cause, hungry miners in scruffy clothes were destined to lose when pitched against organised, protected and uniformed young men backed by the state. Within weeks, miners had begun drifting back to work. Something had changed in Britain – and it wasn't just that the police had begun to act in ways that had once seemed unimaginable. The strike limped on through Christmas and the new year, costing tens of millions a week. The miners hoped against hope for snow and storms to force the lights out. It didn't happen – there was enough electricity being generated from oil-fuelled power stations, and from the coal of the working mines in the Nottingham coalfield, that the blackouts never came. Just before Christmas the National Coal Board ran an advertising campaign offering bonuses to those willing to go back, and thousands did so. Diehards continued to refuse to work. But by the first week of March 1985, the miners' leadership had decided the strike had run out of steam and the drift back to work was unstoppable. The end came on a Sunday afternoon in pouring rain. Inside Congress House, the spartan Trades Union Congress headquarters near the British Museum in London, the leaders of the National Union of Mineworkers met to make the hardest of decisions. After a year on strike, was it time to throw in the towel? Standing in the rain on the pavement outside the building, a group of miners from Kent kept up a rhythmic chant of 'We're not going back. We're not going back.'

The final vote, when it came, was close, the violence and bitterness of the past year having cemented a certain dogged unity. Ninety-one coalfield delegates wanted to continue the strike. But ninety-eight voted to end it. Arthur Scargill emerged onto the concrete steps of Congress House and announced that the great confrontation with Margaret Thatcher's government was over. He said the miners had been betrayed by the rest of the trade union movement, and 'we face not an employer, but a government, aided and abetted by the judiciary, the police and you people in the media'.[21] (He often spoke like Trump *avant la lettre*, talking about journalists as 'piranhas in a fish tank'.) Scargill may have been given to melodramatic speech but in this he was right, and his list could have included the intelligence services and the miners' previous political allies in the Labour Party for whom they had provided so much – the Labour leader, Neil Kinnock, whose late father had been a miner, had been 'too busy' to turn out on a picket line until the strike was nearly over. He spent much of the conflict denouncing Arthur Scargill as a liar.[22]

The fact was, the miners had had their victory in 1947, and their mistake had been not to discard the language and mindset of the days when their enemies were playing a different game.

Much of the nation was watching an afternoon episode of *Dad's Army* as Arthur Scargill spoke. A BBC text alert suddenly appeared on screen, informing viewers that the miners had voted to return to work. On screen, inside Captain Mainwaring's prototype secret weapon, Corporal Jones, could be heard idiotically murmuring 'gurgle, gurgle, gurgle'.

The strike had lasted for almost a year. The following day, striking miners went back to their institutes and welfare halls, to take down their banners with the pit names and mottoes emblazoned upon them. Colliery bands were convened and crowds of men who had not worked for a year gathered to put a brave face on defeat. On Tuesday 5 March 1985, they returned to work with as much dignity as they could manage amid an atmosphere of reflection and, in some places, almost of carnival. A handful of disappointed Kent miners formed a picket line at one of the Yorkshire pits to try to prevent the return to work (Scargill, who was leading the march back to work, declared 'I never cross a picket line' and led some of the returnees away).[23] In Northumberland there were bizarre scenes as police and management tried to obstruct the return, but in most places, a sense of decency allowed the marches to take place uninterrupted. The miners had been beaten, and everyone knew it: leave them their self-respect. Arthur Scargill had been widely disbelieved (including by me) when he claimed that government plans went much further than the initial announcement, and that the intention was to shut down pits all over the country. But he had turned out to be right. It was the government which was dissembling and the coal industry was to be destroyed. Then, in October 1992, the British coalfields passed the point of no return.

17

Goodnight and Goodbye

The final days of coal are quickly told. Throughout Margaret Thatcher's time in office, government had been setting fire to one state enterprise after another, and then offering it to the private sector as a mildly fire-damaged bargain. The state was divesting itself of aerospace companies, airlines and airports, bus and car companies, electricity, steel and water companies, gas and oil concerns, ports and railway firms. By the time the Conservatives had defenestrated her and installed her palimpsest, John Major, as leader, there was only one great industry waiting to be privatised. The National Coal Board boss, Ian MacGregor, had been handsomely rewarded for his stint with a flamethrower – to the tune of £500,000 a year, and was already turning his hopeless public relations skills* to cooking up his memoirs of the strike with a ghostwriter. But what was to happen to the mines? So far the government hadn't got much further than changing the name of the National Coal Board to 'British Coal' and hiring (at great expense) the bankers Rothschilds to advise on how to get the thing off the books. The industry had been reduced to fifty collieries, employing 54,000 miners. The job of washing the taxpayers' hands of the industry was given to Michael Heseltine, a man whose opinion of his entrepreneurial talents would have made a barrow boy proud.

---

* On one occasion, when surprised by journalists in a hotel, he fled down the back stairs, hiding his face behind a paper bag.

There wasn't much left of coal-mining. Cortonwood mine in South Yorkshire, the flashpoint for the strike, had closed soon after the return to work – the site becoming home to fast-food and cheap clothing outlets, offices and a DIY warehouse, while the pit at Polmaise, near Stirling, where miners had stayed out longest of all the collieries, was buried beneath a commuter town. The pinstriped young men from Rothschilds insisted that if the industry was to be sold successfully – there was a potential buyer in a company called RJB Mining which had had been set up by a businessman called Richard Budge, and named with his initials – it should first be purged of unprofitable mines. Budge, an irrepressible enthusiast, told the government that he could find new markets for British coal. But first, the mines deemed uneconomic had to be shut down. There were thirty-one of them.

Heseltine – the great Nearly Man of late twentieth-century politics – saw a chance to go down in history as the architect of a sale to the private sector previously seen as almost impossible. Once upon a time, Heseltine had imagined that it would be him leading the party – he was cursed by towering ambition, good looks and substantial wealth. But it had been John Major – a man invariably depicted by cartoonists in various shades of grey – who led the Conservatives to victory in the 1992 general election. The new prime minister was determined to abolish the post of Energy Secretary and asked Heseltine if he would give the last rites to the remaining mines as Trade and Industry Secretary. Heseltine consoled himself with the fact that the long-unused title 'president of the Board of Trade' came with the job – he liked to be referred to as 'Mr President' in his new role. It was now October 1992, and Heseltine had no great interest in coal – as a thoroughgoing neophiliac he was more or less devoted to the so-called 'dash for gas', in which electricity generators powered their turbines by burning methane and other gases instead. Gas-fired power stations, he could see, were cheaper to build and more profitable. At the time, there was lots of gas coming into Britain from the drilling fields in the North Sea. The immediate problem was that the electricity industry had already been sold off to the private sector, and the British coal industry's contract to supply them was about to run out. The companies told him they could buy more coal much more cheaply from overseas: did Heseltine really expect them to betray their shareholders? But what was to be done with the remaining fifty deep mines? His department decided that thirty-one of them would be shut down. But the spectacle of the beaten miners returning to work had changed public attitudes.

It was pretty obvious that any sense of fair play in the minds of the public would be appalled that the Midlands miners who had done as asked by the government during the national strike, and continued to mine coal – often at much greater cost than the intimidation and name-calling about being scabs – were to be particularly badly hit. Major's private secretary warned him that there were at least three marginal parliamentary seats which had Union of Democratic Miners pits in them.[1] They were convinced there was little alternative work for them, so Heseltine demanded the Treasury get ready to offer miners redundancy payments equivalent to two years' wages (up to £42,000). Norman Lamont, the singularly hapless Chancellor of the Exchequer (and former Rothschilds banker), had to double the amount set aside for redundancy payments. Heseltine made much of warnings from British Coal that without decent payments there would be 'a collapse in morale, strikes, possible industrial vandalism, and perhaps civil disorder'.[2]

Heseltine was very badly briefed about the extent of public knowledge of the planned pit closures, and assumed everybody knew about the decline, having seen a 'Pits to Close' headline in a local paper when on a visit to Newcastle. But, to his surprise, the end of the strike and the passage of time had changed opinion.

'The trouble didn't come from the miners,' he recalled, 'but from the middle class.'[3]

There was an immediate outcry from within the Conservative Party. The biggest worry was about the Nottinghamshire coalfield, where there had been strong opposition to the miners' strike. Members of the rebel trade union there, the Union of Democratic Miners, felt betrayed: they had saved the country from another three-day week – and saved the Thatcher government. Now they were being rewarded by having the industry's brains beaten out. A lorryload of coal was dumped at the gates of Heseltine's country estate, a 'Coal not Dole' protest from one of the collieries facing closure (when Heseltine decided to give it away to a local old folks' home, the police were adamant that he couldn't dispose of the evidence, since they might 'trace the owners', a feat which eluded them).[4] An estimated (or claimed) 100,000 protesters and miners marched through central London – in contrast to the days of the strike, middle-class bystanders stood and applauded. A photograph on the front page of the *Daily Mirror* showed Arthur Scargill being mobbed by admirers in front of smiling police. The *Sun* reported that 'Sloane Rangers left their tables at swanky eateries' to wave on the marchers.

The government panicked, removed ten of the mines from the closure list and agreed to put off shutting the others. The whole affair had been a shambles. David Poole, a merchant banker attached to the No. 10 Policy Unit, blamed Rothschilds, British Coal, 'mesmerised' ministers and officials, but most witheringly commented that Heseltine had simply not been up to the job, and 'at no point until the crisis broke did he properly engage himself in what was taking place'.

Heseltine was no fool and had by now become well aware of public feeling about the closure of the last pits. Years later, I asked him whether he worried about what had been lost with the eradication of the mining industry. He was unmoved. 'I'll tell you what was lost', he said. 'A dirty, dangerous and unhealthy industry.'[5] So, most of the British coal industry – which the miners had, for so long, been so desperate to see taken away from private owners – was sold back to them. Richard Budge's RJB Mining offered to pay the government £815 million for the English coalfields – £100 million more than anyone else and well beyond what the expensive, incompetent men in well-tailored suits had expected. Within five years, shares in RJB Mining, which had once been valued at over £6 each, had fallen to 33p.

In the twenty-first century, many of the trade union practices of fifty years ago – the calling of strikes by show of hands in some workplace car park, the protection of union assets, the 'closed shop', which required everyone in a workplace to belong to a specified trade union, the free automatic 'check-off' arrangements by which employers deducted union subscriptions from wages – seem scarcely imaginable now. When Margaret Thatcher came to power, 12 million workers belonged to trade unions – more than ever before. By 2018, the number of trade unionists had fallen to fewer than 6.5 million. Teachers were left as one of the few bodies of workers to have a national pay agreement. Nationalisations had been replaced by privatisations and share ownership trebled in the Thatcher years. Once union members had mortgages to pay because they had bought their previously publicly owned houses, they couldn't afford drawn-out strikes, anyway.

Most of the land where the Orgreave plant once stood has been turned over to housing. To obliterate the memory of the clash, the area has been renamed 'Waverley' by some cloth-eared developer, who saw a Walter Scott connection which had eluded everyone else. After a long process of decontamination, the battleground is said to have been cleansed and the nearby river Rother, once proud holder of the title of most polluted watercourse in the land, is said to be teeming with wildlife.

Millions of public money were spent on telling the people who – through the government – already owned the gas industry that they could now buy shares in its newly privatised form, as the country echoed to an advertising campaign with the slogan 'Tell Sid'. Though the ethics may have been questionable, the campaign was successful in promoting popular capitalism. By 2020 gas extracted from the North Sea could meet less than half of the country's needs and the rest was being imported from Russia, Turkey, Europe and assorted unattractive regimes in central Asia and the Middle East.

Across the land, concrete had been poured down mineshaft after mineshaft – often along with all the colliery records. The 187,000 miners of 1984 had fallen to a grand total of 590 by 2018. An increasingly atrabilious Arthur Scargill went on to found the Socialist Labour Party, advocating the abolition of the monarchy, state ownership of industry and withdrawal from the European Union. The party's share of the vote declined in successive elections, riven by the usual doctrinal splits which afflict extreme-left groupings, as the number of letters in the names of breakaway groups threatened to eclipse the number of members. Ian MacGregor had a heart attack and died in Somerset in 1998. Margaret Thatcher lived on until 2013, when she had a stroke and expired while staying at the Ritz. When a fellow miner texted Arthur Scargill with 'THATCHER DEAD', he replied 'SCARGILL ALIVE!' Into his eighties he was still claiming to have been betrayed by other trade unionists and undermined by the secret services. 'I have always said that the greatest victory in the strike was the struggle itself,' he claimed emptily a quarter of a century after the confrontation. It was cold comfort.

Though the death throes of the industry occurred years ago, it is still 'that woman', Margaret Thatcher, who usually gets the blame for the disappearance of coal-mining. When she took office, there had been nearly a quarter of a million men working

in 219 mines. By the time she left Downing Street, both totals had
been halved. But the closures of mines and the handing out of
redundancy notices had begun years before her eminence, and
continued after the Conservative Party had decided it had no
further use for her. Coal-mining had been in decline for one
hundred years before the last deep mine closed. Britain never
again produced as much coal as it had done in 1913, when British
mines had yielded record tons of coal. By 2017, total coal
production had fallen to 3 million tons – a hundred times lower,
and at a rate of extraction not seen for 300 years, all of it scraped
from open-cast mines, where coal deposits lying near the surface
of the ground could be reached by bulldozer. Deep mines had
been closing for generations: nationalisation of the industry
might have been a political victory by the miners, but politics had
no power over nature and, as deposits were worked out, the mines
there had no reason to exist. When you look at the graphs showing
coal production in Britain, you wonder how anyone could have
blinded themselves to the fact that the miners were working in a
dying industry. That was not how they judged their work, of
course, but in the great strike of 1984–5, profit-and-loss
accounting collided with another way of seeing the world. The
bottom-line men and women saw an entire industry with falling
returns, while miners held in their mind an individual mine
which gave life to their community. Once upon a time, miners
had trudged from one hole in the ground to another, in search of
employment, but now the miners were fighting for a settled way
of living around one particular hole.

Of all the pits which were shut down, perhaps the saddest was
Tower Colliery in South Wales, where miners were so keen to
preserve their way of life that in 1995, 239 of them gave £8,000
each from their redundancy payments to buy the pit and to
preserve their jobs. The mine continued to produce coal until,
thirteen years later, with yields diminishing and serious problems

with water in the Bute seam, it was forced to close again. The miners marked the closure with a parade like the one they had staged when they had 'saved' it, after which the pithead buildings were left to weeds and the local vandals.

Margaret Thatcher had done what she had promised she would do: in the years to come, the number of working days lost to industrial disputes plummeted. If even the miners could not win a fight, then who could? Union membership as a whole crashed; and by 2018 only about one-fifth of working men took the trouble to belong.[6] By early 2020 the National Union of Mineworkers had only 311 members: even at the start of the strike of 1984 it had been over 500 times larger.[7] The great political issues of the next thirty years were cultural rather than ideological – about immigration, radical Islam, gender, sexuality, marriage, the European Union and the meaning of family. A few Pollyanna-ish figures on the left said that at least the 1984 strike had generated some low-budget, feel-good movies about mining communities, like *Billy Elliot*, *Brassed Off* and *Pride*. It wasn't much.

So in December 2015, thousands of miners and their families staged a funeral march through the streets of Knottingley near Wakefield in West Yorkshire, accompanied by a brass band and a hooded man dressed as the Grim Reaper. The local Kellingley Colliery, the last of Britain's deep coal mines, had just worked its final shift. Some of the marching miners wept. Children and dogs in the crowd wore 'Coal not Dole' badges. The local MP, Yvette Cooper (the first woman, and the first non-miner, to represent the constituency, and therefore herself a sign of how times had changed), spoke words of outrage to the crowd. It was generally agreed that they had been the victims of a disaster. Reporters usually find what they set out to find and a Reuters correspondent who visited the site of the parade three years later reported that the town had been 'left behind by a global economy that has brought cheaper coal imports from the likes of Colombia and Russia and a push towards generating power from cleaner gas and wind turbines'.[8]

But the sky has not fallen on the old mining communities. Arthur Scargill had predicted an apocalypse if the miners were defeated in what had come to be known as 'the Great Strike'. It is true that many former mining areas still have an air of defeat about them: the men who dug the coal which made Britain great had often been told they had jobs for life, and there is something especially bleak about some of their former communities, with their aimlessness and drug addiction. 'There used to be local policemen – not that we needed them,' one former miner told me in Yorkshire. 'Now it's like the Wild West. There are three cars burned out right now, right outside the police station.' This is politics talking. Inhabitants of what were once miners' homes do their best to keep the places spruce and welcoming, but walk down the streets of many of these areas, and the energy has vanished. It is endlessly repeated by old people in these communities that young men no longer have an adult male whom they can hope to emulate. Keith Gildart, who was once a miner at the Point of Ayr pit in Flintshire, talks of 'a crisis of masculinity', with 'no role' comparable to the days when so many sang in male-voice choirs, played in brass bands, so many wrote, read and discussed pamphlets about their pay and conditions and laid the foundations for a new kind of politics.

The former coalfield towns are still in generally unlovely places. But the number of men registered as unemployed has fallen quite steadily in the years since the strike. Though the number of former miners living there declines each year, they are not prosperous communities. A team of academics who looked at the figures of men claiming benefits as a result of being unemployed concluded that 'The numbers in the coalfields have broadly followed the trend in the UK as a whole, though the rate in the coalfields has always remained a little above the corresponding national figure.'[9]

Some of the old coalfields are popular for warehousing, an appropriate enough activity, given their inner emptiness. (Without a shred of irony, Amazon calls its warehouses, like the one at Coalville, Leicestershire, 'fulfilment centres'. They are scattered all over areas where Victorian industry was strong.) A lot of those who still live in the old mining settlements commute somewhere else to work. The towns remain sickly places: the mining may be gone, but its maladies linger on. Among people living in the former coalfields, a much higher proportion than average claim Disability Living Allowance and hundreds of thousands of working-age people are entitled to incapacity benefit because they've been deemed unable to work due to sickness or disability. Like pockmarks on sallow skin these communities are testament to past sickness, and they do not radiate good health. The population is older than average and tends to die a year earlier than most people in Britain. Jobs are much less easy to find than elsewhere (in 2019 the national average was seventy-three jobs available per hundred people of working age, but in the colliery valleys of South Wales, for example, there were only forty-two).[10] Ideas of what was men's work and what was only suitable for women have had to be abandoned, as brawny males commute to their jobs at call centres. The football clubs, greyhounds, racing pigeons and allotment societies survive in some places, but increasingly they are just hobbies for commuters. In 1920, there had been 1,191,000 miners living in coalfield communities. A century later, in 2020, there were virtually none.

Separate almost entirely from the great wealth, trade union passions, farce and disaster of most British coal-mining, an almost unbroken history of digging coal has survived in a corner of Gloucestershire. Once upon a time, a few thousand men tunnelled into the hills of the Forest of Dean to extract iron ore and coal. This isolated community managed to avoid the political convulsions which overcame most of the rest of coal-mining. It is said that once upon a time several thousand men* held 'freemining' rights among the oak trees and shared grazing for sheep. Perhaps a dozen are still at it. The miners maintain their right was granted by an ancient King Edward for service in war against the Scots, though few can actually recall either which Edward or which war. The few dozen still taking a coal-cutter by the handle appear to choose to do so to live free and are understandably proud to be exercising ancient rights. For how long the pensioners who get their locally sourced coal from the freeminers will be able to continue to defy clean-air laws is anyone's guess. But the Forest of Dean freeminers will perhaps be the last working men to bend double, and descend on foot under the hills.

The men who lived long enough to see their industry closed down around them have not been particularly kindly treated.

First, there were their complicated pension arrangements, under which, in exchange for guaranteeing their pensions, the government took half of any future profit in the fund. At the time, loading the peril on government (making the risk into the taxpayer's problem, not the responsibility of anyone willing to buy the remains of the British coal industry when it was sold off in 1994) had seemed a neat way to make privatisation more attractive to potential investors. The idea worked, and the fact that the government stood behind the scheme meant that the fund could make chancier investments, which had higher returns. But – as per the agreement – in return, the government demanded its 50%. By 2020 it was calculated that the government had been paid over £4 billion by the Mineworkers' Pension Scheme. MPs for former mining areas (including the then leader of the Labour Party, Ed

---

* Since a historic ruling by the Gaveller of the Forest in 2010, the right to become a freeminer has been extended to women who fulfil the other requirements of having been born and living within the Hundred of St Briavels, being over twenty-one, and having already worked for a year and a day in a local mine.

Miliband, who had taken over as MP for Doncaster North from a former miner) periodically got up in the House of Commons to complain at the injustice of an arrangement which had 'taken money out of the pockets of retired miners and their families' and given it to the Treasury.[11] None of them bothered to explain why it was that Miliband's two predecessors as Labour leader had chosen not to do anything about the arrangement when they were prime minister. The average miner's pension is £83 a week.

Some had another indignity to suffer.

In 1998, six miners broken by lung disease had brought a legal compensation case for the damage done to their health by years of labour underground. The year before the miners' case finally fetched up before Mr Justice Turner, the government had dumped the unglamorous and unwanted bits of the industry – like financial liability for subsidence caused by old mine-workings – on a newly created Coal Authority. It was, of course, to be funded by the taxpayer, rather than any of the new private sector owners.

When Mr Justice Turner heard the miners' wheezy stories (one of them, Sam Wells, had died 'after spending the last five years of life in agony' and was represented by his widow, Connie), the High Court judge was angry. He found the British Coal Corporation – the new name for the National Coal Board – had been 'neglectful' about the lung diseases caused by coal dust in its pits. The NCB as was, had, for example, not tried very hard to encourage the miners to wear respirators to protect their lungs. He awarded the men up to £10,000 apiece, which the BBC reported as the 'highest-ever damages bill against a single British employer'.[12] The implications for the taxpayer were momentous. In a spectacular display of incompetence, Whitehall civil servants estimated that there were perhaps 70,000 or so miners who might bring further claims that their breathing had been harmed by coal dust, and another 40,000 former miners who might bring a claim that their health had been damaged by a condition called 'vibration white finger' (nerve and blood-vessel damage to their hands), brought on by operating power tools in the pits. In fact, there were nearly 750,000 claims, and a total payout – from the taxpayer – of over £4 billion. The compensation system enabled them to work out how much they might be entitled to from a simple online calculator and operated on the quaint assumption that lawyers were honourable, requiring injured miners to lodge a claim with their chosen solicitor.

It amounted to an early Christmas for a lucky group of solicitors, who creamed off massive fees. A fixed scale allowed the lawyers to claim £2,023 on each case. As anyone who understood the business could have predicted, lawyers chased ambulances, offering to help miners make claims. Remarkable bills were racked up. A single solicitor, Jim Beresford, was paid £16.7 million in 2006. Two other members of his tiny practice in Doncaster (one of whom was his daughter) pocketed almost £4 million.[13] Most of the miners received less than the cost of administering their claims. As you might expect of the parasites' parasite, the lawyers found multiple ways to take their pound of flesh. Some helped themselves to what they called 'success fees', others sent money the way of 'claims handlers'. Some tried to claim entitlement to part of the compensation itself. Others deducted cash from money due to the miners' union. In contrast, official figures showed that the average payment received by disabled miners was less than £1,000. Nearly 4,000 of the miners received less than £100.

Just before two each afternoon, a French chateau on the edge of Barnard Castle in Teesdale is besieged by visitors. The tourists still flock to see what mining made possible: they have come to this utterly incongruous building to see a silver swan, a remarkable eighteenth-century automaton which once belonged to a local toff. Tourists would far rather gawp at the mansions of the mine-owners than trouble themselves imagining what it must have been like to be one of the grandee's minions deep underground; the Bowes Museum was created to show off some of the fruits of wealth.

The Bowes' fortune came from the enormous quantities of coal their miners dug from beneath the family lands in the area. (The Queen Mother, née Elizabeth Bowes-Lyon, belonged to the family.) The founder of the museum, John Bowes, the illegitimate son of the tenth Earl of Strathmore, was not a fascinating man, being mainly interested in breeding racehorses. But in 1847, this heir to massive estates and coal mines in the north-east of England, did what so many stupendously rich young men had done before him, and took himself to Paris, where he soon settled down with an actress. The two began to amass a great collection of art including Canalettos, an El Greco, a Goya and thousands of *objets d'art*, now housed in the vast French Regency pile they built on the edge of Barnard Castle. (This incongruous building is often described as 'the Wallace Collection of the north'.) Every afternoon at two, one of the ingenious and pointless devices on which they spent the coal fortune performs its party trick. A life-size silver swan, made in 1773 and powered by clockwork, 'swims' upstream amid leaping fish. It has extraordinarily well-observed movements: you can see why it has intrigued its owners. It is a toy with no purpose apart from making spectators gasp at the ingenuity of its eighteenth-century designer. No similar crowds besiege Red Hills, the redbrick pile which houses the headquarters of the Durham Miners' Association, twenty miles away. Red Hills, a solid, squat building with central staircase, rotunda and twenty-eight windows looking out over the courtyard at its front, seems to be saying 'we the men who hew what makes you rich, are quite as grand as you coal-owners'. Inside, laid out in twelve curving rows of battered wooden benches, a meeting room – 'the Pitman's Parliament' – has 298 named places for delegates from each colliery lodge. It is one of the most resonant rooms in Britain, and if you close your eyes you can almost smell the coal and hear the tones – Geordie mainly, but traces too of Sunderland and Wearside accents and migrant voices from Ireland, Wales and Scotland, passionately arguing about rates of pay for a job so few cared to take on but was vital.

The industry has had a strange afterlife. The organisation for senior miners, the National Association of Colliery Overmen, Deputies and Shotfirers (NACODS) is no more, delisted as a trade union in 2016, after confessing that it no longer had any working members. The National Union of Mineworkers moved its head-quarters from London to Sheffield, capital of what was nicknamed at the time the 'Socialist Republic of South Yorkshire', where Arthur Scargill had a great new office building constructed, just in time for the plunge in membership which followed the defeat of his big strike. The national union then moved to Barnsley, to 'squat' in the offices of the Yorkshire branch. The sparkling new head-quarters, with their great marble frieze depicting a pair of miners at work, gathered dust and graffiti and became an eyesore in central Sheffield, until eventually it was rented out for offices, a pub and assorted restaurants. The office from which Scargill once imagined commanding his troops is now used by corporate accountants and the rents are the main income for the union. In 2012 it had emerged that until June 2011 members' subscriptions had been paying the rent and other outgoings of Arthur Scargill, who was by then at the end of his time as 'honorary president' of the union. Meanwhile the union was trying to recover the flat it had rented for him at the 'concrete chic' Barbican development in the City of London, complete with twenty-four-hour concierge service and the rest. Scargill attempted to use 'right to buy' legisla-tion brought in by Margaret Thatcher to achieve ownership of the flat at a discounted price. The legislation had been intended to encourage 'popular capitalism' and the union which had employed him was utterly opposed to the policy. Scargill managed to find time in his busy schedule to appear in court against the trade union which had invented him, in a murky case involving the transfer of union money to an organisation Scargill had established in Paris.

All jobs which depend upon extracting a finite resource must come to an end at some time. But worry about how long the coal boom could last had been growing for a century or more. In 1863 – fifty years before peak production – the brilliant Newcastle inventor and businessman Sir William Armstrong (whom coal power had made into one of the richest men in the world) told the British Association for the Advancement of Science that instead of exporting coal, his city would be importing it. He rather thought the future belonged to renewable energy. Two years later, an iron merchant's son, Stanley Jevons, published a book describing what has become known as the Jevons Paradox: the more efficient the processes in which coal is used, the greater the consumption, and therefore the greater the demand. He considered the problem of 'almost religious importance', because the exhaustion of British coal raised the possibility of the subsequent fall of her empire.[14]

The acres of buildings in Armstrong's Elswick Factory in Newcastle – along with his immense fortune – testified to his ability to see the future. But Jevons was right about the almost insatiable lust for coal power. Britain was fortunate in having such an abundance of coal that the country did not have to import much until 1970. Within just over thirty years, more coal was being imported than was being taken from the ground at home. The takeover by imported coal was the consequence of political decisions, but it is hard to imagine how the coal-mining industry could have survived the early twentieth-century preoccupation with the environment, anyway.

There had been something almost magical about coal: a rock that burns would be a dream. The application of human ingenuity had transformed Britain and made it politically powerful. But very few benefits come at no cost. Complaints about smoke from burning coal had been going on for centuries. In the seventeenth century, John Evelyn had noticed its destructive effects on the classical sculptures plundered and displayed at the Earl of Arundel's palace in the Strand. Those who burned coal tried to offset the effects of smoke by building ever-taller chimneys (some British power stations had chimneys 800 feet tall), but they just ensured that instead of falling on the surrounding area, the acids in the smoke were dispersed over a much larger area. By the 1880s, Norwegians were already complaining that residues from British smoke were falling in their snow, and by the middle of the twentieth century, scientists were examining what lay behind the phenomenon known as 'acid rain'. If you burn coal you get smoke. End of story.

Soon, it was another aspect of smoke which was causing alarm. In 1896 the Swedish scientist Svante Arrhenius suggested that as humanity burned fossil fuels such as coal, the added carbon dioxide gas in the atmosphere would raise the planet's temperature. Back in 1859 John Tyndall, an Irish-born researcher, had had the courage to defy the conventional wisdom that atmospheric gases were permeable to the infrared radiation being thrown back into space from earth, and discovered that the coal gas piped into his laboratory lighting was anything but permeable. The same was true of carbon dioxide. 'As a dam built across a river causes a local deepening of the stream, so our atmosphere, thrown as a barrier across the terrestrial rays, produces a local heightening of the temperature at the earth's surface,' he wrote.[15] Building on Tyndall's research, Arrhenius had made a vital breakthrough in understanding mankind's potential to affect the earth's climate.

By the 1930s, people had realised that the North Atlantic region had warmed significantly during the previous half-century. Scientists initially supposed this was just a phase of some mild natural cycle, with unknown causes. One lone voice, the English engineer Guy Callendar, had the temerity to insist that it was caused by human activity in burning fossil fuels and producing smoke. Callendar was no meteorologist (his job was refining steam power), but by the 1950s, his claims had provoked a few scientists to look into the question with improved techniques and calculations made feasible by Cold War concerns about the weather and the seas. Painstaking measurements by the American Charles Keeling drove home the point in 1960, showing that the level of warming gases in the atmosphere was rising, year by year.[16]

By the 1990s, it had become received wisdom among scientists that the world was one degree Celsius (1.8 degrees Fahrenheit) warmer than it had been at the start of global records in the late nineteenth century. At that rate of progress the Arctic icecap would melt away, weather patterns would change, animal species become extinct, great cities in south Asia and the Middle East become uninhabitable, and entire countries would disappear underwater. The consequence would be vast, unstoppable flows of refugees. Now known as 'greenhouse gases', carbon dioxide and other emissions produced by burning fossil fuels like coal appeared to be raising the temperature of the earth. Drilling down into the ice near the two poles had confirmed that concentrations of these gases in air bubbles preserved in the ice had increased hugely since the Industrial Revolution. It was undeniably also much warmer than it used to be. You couldn't prove that the higher temperatures were caused by human activity. But the warming and the burning of fossil fuels ran in parallel. The quantities of carbon dioxide and the other gases, like methane, water vapour and nitrous oxide were very small (measured in parts per million or billion), so how could they have such an impact? There was a theoretical case made. It argued that the globe was known to be heated by solar radiation. It was also known that the earth reflected back warmth by giving off infrared radiation. Were the additional greenhouse gases bouncing it back to the earth and thus raising the world's temperature? For years, few were prepared to argue causation. But in 2007, the Intergovernmental Panel on Climate Change declared a consensus that 'most of the observed increase in global average temperatures since the mid-twentieth century is very likely due to the observed increase in anthropogenic [human-made] greenhouse gas concentrations ... The observed widespread warming of the atmosphere and ocean, together with ice mass loss, support the conclusion that it is extremely unlikely that global climate change of the past fifty years can be explained without external forcing, and very likely that is not due to known natural causes alone.'[17]

The cautious wording was the language of science, when what the headline-writers wanted was something definite, terrifying, and the more alarming the better. But these were some of the world's most distinguished men and women of science, not some half-naked witch doctors throwing chicken bones into the sand. The scientific consensus became that global warming was real and was caused by human behaviour. From the figures, it was possible to predict that unless there was a drastic – and probably unachievable – drop in emissions, the world would continue to warm up. In December 2015, representatives from 195 nations met in Paris and agreed to keep the increase in global temperatures to lower than two degrees Celsius. They raised a toast to their agreement. But temperatures – and emissions – continued to rise.

The besetting problem with climate change is that it is a worldwide issue, but if it is caused by human activity, it is generated by nation states, whose governments are accountable, if they are accountable at all, only to their citizens. Globally, coal is reckoned to produce two-fifths of the world's energy. So closely is it associated with economic success that in some Asian countries, like Indonesia, South Korea, and India, dependence upon coal has actually increased, despite the discovery of the damage it is said to be doing.[18] As an issue, the climate change question might have been invented for the United Nations, a notoriously inefficient organisation teetering on the brink of bankrupt pointlessness. Climate change was an international problem caused by relatively affluent, industrialised countries, which would hit most profoundly those nations least able to cope. It was almost impossible to apportion blame to individual nations, yet nation states were the only vehicles for change. Cometh the hour, cometh the man.

António Guterres, a well-fed Portuguese former prime minister, had got the job of UN secretary general on the usual Buggins' turn principle and looked as if he'd be hard-pressed to run for a bus in an emergency, even if he could recognise one. In a speech someone had written for him Guterres announced in 2018 that it was 'five minutes to midnight in the global climate emergency', but that there was still time to avert disaster. The clichés fell from his lips and flapped their last gasps like whitebait on a fish-market floor as he went on to suggest that all was not lost if, among other things, no coal-fired power stations were built after 2020. He was followed in his jeremiad by a secular saint. 'If we don't take action,' the television naturalist David Attenborough declared at the start of a United Nations conference in eastern Europe, 'the collapse of our civilisations and the extinction of much of the natural world is on the horizon.'[19] Though the climate change issue was a new sort of challenge, it soon ran into very old-fashioned difficulties. Britain was judged to be producing about 1% of world carbon dioxide emissions, China about 30%.[20] But did it follow that the Chinese were thirty times more responsible for global warming than the British? The Chinese government may have done little to regulate the pollution produced by the country's industries. But it knew how to manufacture an argument. Since greenhouse gases are cumulative, the comparison should, it said, only be made over centuries, which would be a much less attractive prospect for Britain.

By early 2020 the British prime minister, Boris Johnson, was willing to shoulder some of the blame. Because Britain was the first nation to industrialise, the country had a 'responsibility to our planet to lead in this way', he declared in an explosion of Johnsonian pomposity.[21] The amount of electricity being generated by burning coal had already been outstripped by generation from 'renewable' sources. But, after a declaration like that, a revival or expansion of coal burning in Britain was unthinkable. Johnson's predecessors had claimed – a little unconvincingly, many felt – to care about the damage being done by fossil fuels. But the only tax introduced specifically to deter their burning – the Fuel Duty Escalator – did not apply to coal and was anyway abandoned before the millennium.

Boris Johnson claimed to take the issue more seriously, though, as so often, it turned out that the future of the planet mattered a great deal more when illuminated by television lights than it did at other times. And the shadow cast by coal was enormous. *Guilty Chimneys* had been the title of a 1954 Pathé documentary, following a harassed doctor as he tried to find beds for patients unable to breathe because they had committed the folly of trying to fill their lungs. The film was sponsored by the Gas Council. Soon, natural gas was being piped from beneath the North Sea into Britain's cities. Advertisements boasted of how easy it was 'to give up smoking'.

Fashions change. The Labour minister Tony Benn had once talked of a marvellous future in which coal from Selby would drive the nearby Drax power station. He lived long enough (he died in 2014) to see taxpayers' money poured into enabling it to supply Britain with electricity by burning 'biomass' – wood imported from North America. The public money allowed the private company to continue to make a profit, but did diddly squat for what used to be called the balance of trade, and nothing whatsoever for attempts to clean the atmosphere: environmentalists came to believe the plant was the biggest single producer of carbon dioxide in the country.

For the speed of change elsewhere in Britain has been astonishing. In 2013, coal had been the UK's main source of electricity. But it had decisively fallen out of political fashion. Bulletins began to be issued, boasting about how much less coal was being burned in the power stations. By 2015, there was more electricity produced from wind and solar sources than from coal. In 2017 much noise was made about the fact that the nation's power network had not needed to burn coal for twenty-four hours. Two years later came another announcement, that Britain had survived for 125 hours without using electricity from coal, followed soon after by news that carbon emissions were the lowest they had been since 1888. The Conservative government promised it would force all coal power stations to close down by 2025 and was judged in 2020 to be cutting carbon emissions faster than any other major economy.[22]

Coal could probably never have been made into an environmentally clean source of energy. But for years ministers, managers and miners all claimed that Britain 'led the world' in developing technology they said would square that circle. Throughout the 1980s government ministers boasted about how Britain had 'the best clean-coal technology on earth'.[23] It was, they claimed, an area of particular national expertise. Yet dismantling the coal industry has turned out also to mean destroying the research which might have given it a future. Even in the early years of the twenty-first century, the environmental problems of coal were said to have been vanquished by 'carbon capture and storage', in which pollutants were pumped back into holes in the ground, ending atmospheric pollution. A research station had been established at Grimethorpe near Barnsley in South Yorkshire in 1980, where experiments were said to 'show potential' in significantly reducing carbon dioxide emissions when burning coal. But the whole project was razed to the ground in the aftermath of the miners' strike. In the North Wales colliery at Point of Ayr, experimental research had shown it was possible to make oil from coal. But that scheme too was abandoned. The deep-mined coal industry was not merely dead but had had a stake driven through its heart. The colliery was closed, and the only visitors now are bird-watchers at the nature reserve, on the lookout for plovers, warblers and unusual geese. Nature abhors a vacuum. It had taken millennia to form British coal. A few hundred years of mining exhausted the reserves of prehistoric energy laid down in that time. It will take further millennia to replace them: human beings robbed the hydrocarbon bank. Some scientists have speculated that in the event of some humanity-busting apocalypse, there is now simply not enough geological fuel to allow another species to grow and innovate as we have done.

Extracting coal from the ground had made fortunes, cost lives, shaped politics, broken bodies and hearts, enabled scientific genius, provided a playground for egos, created communities and played a great – if unregarded – part in forming a nation. It had driven railway locomotives, lit the streets, powered steamships across oceans and revolutionised the manufacture of almost everything from cloth to chain-making. It had become so integral to the national way of life that its demise was bound to be painful. However unfashionable it may have become since, the British can count themselves lucky to have had great deposits of coal beneath their land. The exploitation of those deposits is an object lesson in entrepreneurism, just as the men, women and children who toiled underground are an object lesson in fortitude.

We seem to have decided that it is a part of our history we no longer need to know about. Apart from a handful of mining museums offering visitors a chance to be lowered into the ground in a miners' cage before they have a nice ice cream, we prefer to knock down the winding wheels above the old mineshafts and to set loose bulldozers to turn spoil tips into something that looks like what they're not. No one now much remembers that it was at

Cramlington that a group of miners dug up the track to derail the *Flying Scotsman* train during the 1926 General Strike. But you cannot avoid 'Slag Alice', the Naked Lady of Cramlington, a group of spoil heaps reconfigured as 'the world's largest human landform' with one-hundred-foot-high breasts. 'Northumberlandia' is a quarter of a mile long and has an oddly contorted lower half. From the air she looks like a badly executed piece of graffiti.

It is no fitting monument to an astonishing history. Much of what went on in the dark beneath our feet is already almost forgotten. One day, it may be impossible to imagine.

Acknowledgements

I owe the greatest of thanks to my fellow digger Jonny Ainslie, whom I met in a café and who turned out to be a superb researcher, willing to put up with any damn-fool query.

David Amos and Natalie Braber volunteered their help in Nottingham; Catherine Bailey; Jon Bailey; Helen Brown and her colleagues at West Cumbria Mining; Mark Carlyle, Jill Clapham and David Cross at the National Coalmining Museum in Wakefield; Robert Colls; Yvette Cooper; Alan Cummings; Rich Daniels and Peg in the Forest of Dean; Paul Darlow, of the National Union of Mineworkers; Jeff Ennis; George Entwistle; Ross Forbes; Keith Gildart; Jonathan Grammond of Wrexham Museum; Lord Heseltine; Jennifer Hillyard and Simon Brooks at the North of England Institute of Mining and Mechanical Engineers; Lord Howell of Guildford; Cai Howells for an intriguing day spent tootling around the valleys (the poor chap had been dropped into the task by his father, Kim Howells, who spent many years as an official of the National Union of Mineworkers in South Wales, before becoming MP for Pontypridd: he spent another day with me in South Wales); my friend Steven Isserlis for enlightening me about Thomas Britton, the small coal man; Dan Jackson; Dan Jarvis MP; Margaret Jones of the Friends of Gresford Colliery Disaster Memorial; Nicholas Jones, Vincent Kane, Keiran-Ann Keilty in Newcastle; Chris Kitchen, General Secretary, National Union of Mineworkers; Ian Lavery MP; Ranald Lawrence at the

University of Sheffield; Tony Lodge; Joyce and George Maitland; Lord Mann; Patrick McLoughlin; Eddie Morgan and his colleagues in The Department; Chris Peace, of the Orgreave Truth and Justice Campaign; Roger Protz; Frank Redmond and friends in the Kent coalfield; my former colleague Jonathan Renouf, who has retained a lifelong affection for the mining communities of the Durham coalfield; Alicia Robinson of the V&A; Marion Shoard; Iain Staffell; Christopher Sylvester; Dave Temple; David Thomas; John Tomaney; Lord Wakeham; Les Wilson; Prof. Tim Wright.

The book was commissioned by Arabella Pike, seen into print by her assistant, Jo Thompson, and tirelessly promoted by Katherine Patrick – they are a great team. My great thanks also to my agent, David Godwin.

Though I approached Arthur Scargill directly and indirectly on several occasions, he declined invitations to talk about the strike he led, or indeed anything else about the industry which gave him a comfortable living for so many years.

None is responsible for any mistakes or misunderstandings. Those are all my own work.

Notes

Prologue

1. See Alan Metcalfe, *Leisure and Recreation in a Victorian Mining Community* (Routledge, 2008), p. 11.
2. Quoted in Duckham and Duckham, *Great Pit Disasters* (David & Charles, 1973), p. 103.
3. Reprinted in T. E. Forster, *Memoir of the Hartley Colliery Accident* (Cornell, 2009), p. 18.
4. Ibid., p. 63.
5. Ibid., p. 65.
6. Ibid., p. 75.
7. Ibid., pp. 79–81.
8. Ibid., p. 91.

Introduction

1. Friedrich Engels, *Die Lage der arbeitenden Klasse in England* (1845). I am indebted to Stanley Williamson's *Gresford: The Anatomy of a Disaster* (Liverpool University Press, 1999) for pointing out the correct translation.

1 Dirty Heat

1. Anonymous pamphlet, published by 'Tyne Pilot', 1842.
2. 'The Case of the Owners and Masters of Ships Imployed in the Coal-Trade' (1730?), in Raymond Turner, 'The English Coal Industry in the Seventeenth and Eighteenth Centuries', *American Historical Review*, vol. 27, no. 1, October 1921.
3. 'Considerations on the Coal Trade' (1748?), in Turner, op. cit.
4. John Wesley, *The Journal of the Rev. John Wesley; enlarged from original mss, Vol. 3*, ed. Nehemiah Curnock (Eaton & Mains, 1909–16), p. 13.
5. See Mark Jenner, 'The Politics of London Air: John Evelyn's *Fumifugium* and the Restoration', *Historical Journal*, September 1995, pp. 535–51.

6. Daniel Defoe, *A Tour Thro the Whole Island of Great Britain divided into Circuits or Journeys* (1724–7), p. 220.

7. 'The New Coal Exchange', *Illustrated London News*, 3 November 1849, p. 303.

8. A. J. Heesom, 'The Third Lord Londonderry and the Coal Trade', *Durham University Journal*, vol. XVI, 1974, p. 238.

9. Anne de Courcy, *Society's Queen: The Life of Edith, Marchioness of Londonderry* (Weidenfeld & Nicolson, 2004), pp. 233–4.

10. Roy W. Sturgess, *Aristocrat in Business: The Third Marquis of Londonderry as Coalowner and Portbuilder* (Durham County Local History Society, 1975), p. 104.

11. H. Montgomery Hyde, *The Londonderrys* (Hamish Hamilton, 1975), p. 57.

12. *The Times*, 13 September 1880.

13. Michael Pollard, *The Hardest Work Under Heaven* (Hutchinson, 1984).

2 Invisible Underground

1. C. Collier, *Gatherings from the Pit Heaps* (1861), p. 17.

2. Quoted in John Benson, *British Coal Miners in the Nineteenth Century* (Gill & Macmillan, 1980), p. 33.

3. Mark Benney, *Charity Main: A Coalfield Chronicle* (Allen & Unwin, 1946), pp. 34–6.

4. Ibid., pp. 38–41.

5. Ibid., p. 42.

6. A. J. Parfitt, *My Life As a Somerset Miner* (1930), p. 12.

7. Robert Williams Buchanan, 'The Cry from the Mine', *The New Rome* (1898).

8. Sarah Gooder, *Children's Employment Commission Report* (1842).

9. J. L. Kennedy, 'Commission report to Parliament', quoted in Ray Devlin, *Children of the Pits* (Friends of Whitehaven Museum, 1988), p. 13.

10. Quoted in ibid., p. 31.

11. Hansard, House of Commons, Deb, 7 June 1842, vol. 63, col. 1320–6.

12. Charles Dickens, *A Review and Other Writings*, reprinted in *Bulletin of the John Rylands Library*, vol. 18, no. 1, January 1934.

13. *The Economist*, 28 September 1844, p. 253.

14. Ibid.

15. Peter Kirby, *Aspects of the employment of children in the British coal-mining industry. 1800–1872*, PhD thesis (1995), p. 207.

16. *Preston Guardian*, 16 January 1847.

17. Hansard, House of Lords, 14 July 1842, vol. 65, cc. 101–24.

18. Jenny Leyland, quoted in Alan Davies, *The Pit Brow Women of the Wigan Coalfield* (History Press, 2002), pp. 86–7.

3 To Those Who Hath Shall Be Given

1. Quoted in Douglas Sutherland, *The Yellow Earl* (Merlin Unwin, 2015), p. 228.
2. *Glasgow Herald*, 7 January 1869.
3. Disraeli probably knew of what he wrote, since he had by now been tolerably happily married for thirty years to Mary Anne Lewis, widow of a South Wales ironmaster and raging right-wing MP. Oddly enough, her first husband, Wyndham Lewis, had a solidly anti-Catholic record. His widow had been born within hailing distance of Castell Coch – then a ruin, but soon to become the third Marquess of Bute's folly of choice.
4. *Merthyr Guardian*, 12 September 1868.
5. Ibid.
6. Joe Mordaunt Crook, *William Burges and the High Victorian Dream* (Frances Lincoln, 2013), p. 234. Lady Bute seemed to adore Burges, too, writing to her sister 'Ugly Burges who designs such beautiful things. Isn't he a duck?' (p. 237).

4 Full Steam Ahead

1. *Monthly Chronicle*, 2 August 1729.
2. Quoted in Jenny Uglow, *The Lunar Men* (Faber & Faber, 2002), p. 223.
3. H. W. Dickinson, *James Watt, Craftsman and Engineer* (Cambridge University Press, 2010), p. 145.
4. James Boswell, *Life of Samuel Johnson*, vol. 2 (Collier & Son, 1925), pp. 204–5.
5. *Monthly Magazine*, 1 June 1802.
6. George Eliot, *The Mill on the Floss*, Chapter Five.
7. From the memorial to James Watt in the Chapel of St Paul, Westminster Abbey.

5 The Right Side of the Tracks

1. See John Owen, *A Short History of the Dowlais Ironworks* (Merthyr Tydfil Borough Corporation, 1972), pp. 13–15.
2. E. K. Harper, *A Cornish Giant* (1913).
3. Charles Cliffe, quoted in Richard Hayman, *Ironmaking, The History and Archaeology of the Iron Industry* (History Press, 2005), p. 7.
4. G. T. Clarke, *Westminster Review*, 1848, quoted in Owen, op. cit., pp. 41–2.

5. Quoted in Raymond Grant, 'Merthyr Tydfil in the Mid-Nineteenth Century: The Struggle for Public Health', *Welsh History Review*, vol. 14, no. 4, 1989, p. 578.
6. Quoted in ibid., p. 582.
7. Quoted in David Rubinstein, *Victorian Homes* (David & Charles, 1974), pp. 127–8.
8. Quoted in Gwynedd Jones, 'Merthyr Tydfil – The Politics of Survival', *Communities: Essays in the Social History of Victorian Wales* (Gomer, 1987), p. 243.
9. E. F. Roberts, quoted in Owen, op. cit., p. 43.
10. Quoted in ibid., p. 42.
11. *Newcastle Courant*, 17 January 1874.
12. Quoted in Michael Freeman, *Railways and the Victorian Imagination* (Yale University Press, 1999), p. 38.
13. Soon, she would be decamping each summer for Balmoral, on the banks of the river Dee, a 500-mile rail journey.
14. Quoted in Andrew Odlyzko, *Collective Hallucinations and Inefficient Markets: The British Railway Mania of the 1840s* (University of Minnesota, 2010), p. 28.
15. *Sun*, 15 October 1845.
16. *The Times*, 24 October 1845.
17. Obituary, *The Times*, 16 December 1871.
18. Figures from Benson, op. cit., p. 9.
19. Charles Dickens, *Hard Times* (Wordsworth Editions, 2000), p. 19. He was conjuring up a northern town full of textile mills, perhaps recalling Preston, which he had visited a few months before writing the book, in 1854.
20. Ibid., p. 18.

6 Smoke on the Water

1. Quoted in Jon Earle, 'Jonathan Hulls and the first patent for steam propulsion', Royal Museums Greenwich Blog, 13 June 2018.
2. Archibald S. Hurd, 'Coal, Trade and the Empire', *The Nineteenth Century*, November 1898, p. 718.
3. Ibid., p. 720.
4. British Parliamentary Papers, 'Minutes of evidence and appendices', *1904 Royal Commission on Coal Supplies*, pp. 143–55.
5. Quoted in Steven Gray, *Steam Power and Sea Power* (Palgrave Macmillan, 2018), p. 74.
6. Hansard, House of Commons, 29 July 1870, vol. 203, col. 1197, 'Coal for the Navy'.

7. Ibid.
8. Quoted in Richard Hallam and Mark Beynon, *Scrimgeour's Small Scribbling Diary 1914–1916: The Truly Astonishing Wartime Diary and Letters of an Edwardian Gentleman, Naval Officer, Boy and Son* (Conway, 2008), pp. 229–30.
9. T. Cooper, RNMN (REC) 018, 'Transcript of Memoirs of Service as a Stoker in the Royal Navy' (University of Leeds, 1975), quoted in Tony Chamberlain, 'Stokers – the lowest of the low? A Social History of Royal Navy Stokers 1850–1950', PhD thesis (Exeter University, 2013).
10. T. B. Dixon, *The Enemy Fought Splendidly* (Blandford Press, 1983), p. 17.
11. Quoted in Steven Gray, 'Coaling Ships With Naval Labour', *The Mariner's Mirror*, April 2015, p. 171.
12. Ibid.
13. W. A. Harding, 'A Report on the Battle of the Falklands', *Falkland Islands Journal*, 2015.
14. A. Novikoff-Priboy, *Tsushima* (Eden and Cedar Paul, 1937), p. 90.
15. Warwick Brown, quoting USNA RG 38 Box 827.
16. *The Times*, 27 June 1897.
17. *The Times*, 3 September 1919.
18. Letter, quoted in Crosbie Smith, 'Dreadnought Science: The Cultural Construction of Efficiency and Effectiveness', *Transactions of the Newcomen Society*, vol. 77, no. 2, pp. 191–215.
19. I am indebted to Chamberlain, op. cit., for this comparison.
20. Ibid., p. 230.

7 All I Want is a Room Somewhere

1. With a population of over 50,000 people.
2. *Morning Advertiser*, 20 December 1807.
3. Quoted in Robert Ellis, *A History of Fire and Flame* (1932), p. 302.
4. Scott, *Letters of 1821–3*, March 1823, p. 347.
5. Quoted in Holland, *A Memoir of the Reverend Sydney Smith*, vol. 2, pp. 222–3.
6. Quoted in Mackenzie, *One Thousand Processes in Manufactures*, p. 264.
7. William Nicholson, *Smoke Abatement: A manual for the Use of Manufacturers, Inspectors, Medical Officers of Health, Engineers and Others* (1905).
8. H. H. Kimball, 'The Meteorological Aspects of the Smoke Problem', *Monthly Weather Review*, 42, 1914, pp. 29–34.
9. In 1906, when he had made a fortune from the coal trade Lewis was the principal founder of an ornate canopied drinking fountain in the centre of Merthyr Tydfil in honour of Lucy Thomas and her husband, Robert.

10. Brace represented the South Wales Miners' Federation at the official inquiry conducted by Richard Redmayne, the chief inspector of mines, the following year.

11. Miners' Federation of Great Britain, 'Coal Mines Eight Hours Bill', second reading, 22 June 1908, p. 40.

12. R. Church, *History of the British Coal Industry*, vol. 3 (Oxford University Press, 1986).

13. Department of Employment, *British Labour Statistics*, Historical Abstract, 1971, table 200.

14. Louise Morgan, *News Chronicle*, 18 February 1936.

8 The People's Flag

1. A 1739 Newcastle pamphlet, *An Inquiry into the Reason for the Advance in Coals*, said 'They pay annual considerations for letting their mines lye unwrought. They rent a great number of Staithes, or Coal Wharfs, of which they make no use at all, save that of debarring others from coming there.' Quoted in Francis Askham, *The Gay Delavals* (Rinehart, 1956), p. 242.

2. Usually involving something to with the genitalia of lads new to the pit.

3. See Thomas Brinley, 'The Migration of Labour into the Glamorganshire Coalfield (1861–1911)', *Economica*, no. 30, November 1930, p. 276.

4. George Dangerfield, *The Strange Death of Liberal England* (1935).

5. Quoted in Gwyn Evans and David Maddox, *The Tonypandy Riots, 1910–1911* (2010), p. 97.

6. *The Times*, 3 February 1912.

7. *British Socialist*, vol. 1, no. 3, March 1912, p. 102.

8. Jack Mitchell, *Robert Tressell and the Ragged-Trousered Philanthropists* (Lawrence & Wishart, 1969), p. 317, quoting Jack Beeching, *Marxist Quarterly*, October 1955.

9 Does Your Country Really Need You?

1. D. H. Lawrence, 'Nottingham and the Mining Country', *New Adelphi*, June–August 1930.

2. D. H. Lawrence, *Sons and Lovers* (1913), p. 155.

3. *Dudley Herald*, 30 January 1915.

4. C. S. Peel, *How We Lived Then 1914–18: A Sketch of Social and Domestic life in England During the War* (Bodley Head, 1929), pp. 57–8.

5. Pauline Bryan, *What Would Keir Hardie Say?* (Luath Press, 2015), p. 179.

6. Figures from Travers Merrill and Lucy Kitson, 'The End of Coal-mining in South Wales: Lessons learned from Industrial Transformation', International Institute for Sustainable Development, 2017.

7. *Porth Gazette*, 3 October 1914.

8. Jeremy Paxman, *Great Britain's Great War* (Viking, 2013), p. 58.

9. Figures from J. F. Martin, 'The government and control of the British coal industry 1914–18', unpublished thesis (Loughborough University, 1981), p. 17.

10. The situation was even worse in Germany, where by March 1916, 282,200 miners had joined up – over one-fifth of the total mining workforce. The German population felt the cold even more acutely than did the British.

11. R. Page Arnot, Lecture, 'The Years of Ordeal: South Wales Miners 1914–1926', *South Wales Miners' Library*, 22 October 1973, https://cymru1914.org/en/view/sound/aaaab00000034

12. Quoted in Chris Wrigley, *David Lloyd George and the British Labour Movement* (Harvester Press, 1976), pp. 123–4.

13. Ibid., p. 125.

14. *Asquith Papers*, vol. 8, fos. 69–70.

15. 'I wonder whether you could induce the owners to be magnanimous for once … the masters are making enormous profits which they are carefully concealing. A hint that the government intended to have their books examined by independent accountants should occasion arise might have a steadying influence', Lord Riddell told Lloyd George (Riddell, LGD/18/7/3).

16. J. R. Raynes, *Coal and Its Conflicts* (1928), p. 146.

17. *Merthyr Pioneer*, 3 March 1917.

18. A. J. Cook, speech in Ynyshir, 20 January 1918.

19. Raynes, op. cit., p. 160.

10 Not Quite What We'd Hoped For

1. The 1907 *Census of Production* showed that coal added more to the net output of the nation than any other industry.

2. *Dundee Courier*, 14 April 1921.

3. Quoted in Paul Foot, 'An Agitator of the Worst Kind': A Portrait of Miners' Leader, A. J. Cook (Bookmarks, 1986), p. 3.

4. Hansard, House of Commons, 'Coal Mines Bill', 5 July 1926, vol. 64, col. 742–802.

5. Herbert Smith, *Buckmaster Proceedings*, 10, quoted in Barry Supple, *The History of the British Coal Industry, Vol. IV, 1913–1946* (Clarendon Press, 1987), p. 426.

6. *Daily Mail*, 25 October 1924.
7. John Maynard Keynes, *The Economic Consequences of Mr Churchill* (1925).
8. *Must The Miners Starve?* (leaflet MC No. 2) 292/252.61/13/18, Warwick Digital Collections.
9. Beatrice Webb, *Diaries*, 10 September 1926.
10. Ibid.
11. David Kirkwood, *My Life of Revolt* (1935), p. 231.
12. Ramsay MacDonald, *Diary*, 3 May 1926.
13. *Daily Mail*, 3 May 1926.
14. Anne Perkins, *A Very British Strike* (Macmillan, 2006), p. 224.
15. Walter Citrine, *Men and Work* (Hutchinson, 1964), p. 194.
16. National Archives, CAB/24/179.
17. Leon Trotsky, *The General Strike* (1926), p. 21.

11 Oops!

1. David Marquand, *Ramsay MacDonald* (Jonathan Cape, 1977), p. 588.
2. Hugh Dalton, *Call Back Yesterday* (Frederick Muller, 1953), p. 290.
3. Hansard, House of Commons, 31 May 1932, fifth series, vol. 266, col. 1015.
4. 'How the Bank of England abandoned the gold standard: Minutes reveal correspondence between Bank and government about removing the pound's peg to bullion in 1931', *Daily Telegraph*, 7 January 2015.
5. Hansard, House of Commons, 'The Standard Rate of Tax for 1931–2 And Consequential Amendments of Law', 15 September 1931, vol. 256, col. 703.
6. A. J. P. Taylor, *English History, 1914–1945* (Clarendon Press, 1965), p. 373.
7. 'They offer me a constituency which I need not visit more than once a year and where, at a general election, three or four speeches at the outside would be all they would ask of me,' he wrote to the chairman of the Aberavon party (quoted in Marquand, *Ramsay MacDonald*, p. 481).
8. De Courcy, op cit.
9. Austen Morgan, *J. Ramsay MacDonald* (Manchester University Press, 1987), p. 145.
10. David Marquand, 'Ramsay MacDonald', *Oxford Dictionary of National Biography*.
11. George Orwell, *The Road to Wigan Pier* (1937), pp. 18ff.
12. Ibid., p. 161.
13. Quoted in Williamson, op. cit., p. 33. I am indebted to Mr Williamson for the figures about the poor health of the coal industry in the 1930s.

14. F. E. Smith, quoted in Frank McLynn, *The Road Not Taken: How Britain Narrowly Missed a Revolution, 1381–1926* (Vintage, 2013), p. 390.
15. *Report of Sir Henry Walker* (Durham Mining Museum), p. 10.
16. Ellis, op. cit.
17. 'Average annual death and injury rates in British coal-mining 1922–1936', in Supple, op. cit., p. 428.
18. Richard B. Simons, 'The British Coal Industry: A Failure of Private Enterprise', *The Historian*, no. 1, Autumn 1953, p. 13.
19. Ibid., p. 12.
20. Harold Wilson, *New Deal for Coal* (1945), p. 34.
21. 'Amalgamation of Collieries', *The Times*, 3 February 1938, p. 8.
22. Quoted in Supple, op. cit., p. 352.
23. *Taunton Courier and Weston Advertiser*, 31 December 1938.

12 Workers' Playtime

1. *Report of Biennial Delegate Conference*, TGWU, August 1941.
2. Hansard, House of Commons, 12 October 1943, vol. 392, col. 761–852.
3. *The Times*, 15 December 1943.
4. *Newcastle Journal*, 15 August 1944.
5. Tom Hickman, *Called Up, Sent Down: The Bevin Boys' War* (History Press, 2010), p. 7.
6. Ibid., pp. 11–12.
7. Einion Evans, 'Nearly A Miner' (unpublished), p. 68, quoted in Keith Gildart, 'Mining memories; reading coalfield autobiographies', *Labor History*, 50:2, pp. 139–61.
8. Ferdynand Zweig, *Men in the Pits* (Gollancz, 1948), p. 33.
9. Di Parkin, *Sixty Years of Struggle: A History of Betteshanger Colliery* (Betteshanger Social Welfare Scheme, 2007), p. 29.
10. Quoted in ibid., p. 42.
11. *Staffordshire Evening Sentinel*, 7 February 1942. George Albert Wade, the letter's author, was the town's answer to Walmington-on-Sea's Captain Mainwaring. He was knighted in 1955 for 'political and public services' and included a rhinoceros on his coat of arms, with the words 'why not'.
12. *Hartlepool Northern Daily Mail*, 10 February 1944.
13. *Yorkshire Post and Leeds Intelligencer*, 10 February 1944.
14. Will Lawther, *Britain's Coal* (Gollancz, 1944), p. 6.
15. *The Times*, 5 April 1944.
16. 'In 1931 only 34.5% of those employed were over 40 years of age, but by 1945 the over-40s had increased to 43.5% of the total, and the industry was forced to rely to an increasing extent upon men who had passed

their prime in physical energy' (H. Townshend-Rose, *The British Coal Industry* (1951), p. 102). The reasons were multiple, including low wages, the rush to join the forces, a drop in the birth rate between 1926 and 1928 and new patterns of transport.

17. Derek Agnew, *Bevin Boy* (Allen & Unwin, 1947), pp. 14–17.
18. Charles Carlow Reid, *Coal-mining: Report of the Technical Advisory Committee* (1945), p. 118.
19. Frank Giles, *Sunday Times*.
20. Zweig, op. cit., pp. 302–3.
21. Quoted in Clinton Jencks, 'Social Status of Coal Miners in Britain Since Nationalization', *American Journal of Economics and Sociology*, vol. 26, no. 3, July 1967.
22. Ibid.
23. 'Any man who absents himself from work without due cause … is rendering a disservice to the whole nation … the production of coal is the most vital consideration that faces the country … We cannot afford to stand any more nonsense. They will have to be dealt with,' said Shinwell to the miners' leaders (*National Union of Mineworkers Annual Conference Report*, 7 July 1947).
24. Catherine Bailey, *Black Diamonds* (Viking, 2007), p. 387.
25. Ibid., p. 390.
26. Speech in Leeds, 6 April 1946.
27. Quoted in Jencks, op. cit.

13 King Coal Coughs

1. Peter Thorsheim. *Inventing Pollution* (Ohio University Press, 2006), p. 165.
2. *Illustrated Sporting and Dramatic News*, 24 December 1952.
3. *Aberdeen Evening Express*, 8 December 1952.
4. *Reader's Digest*, June 1953, pp. 125–30.
5. *The Diary of Ford Madox Brown*, ed. Virginia Surtees (Yale University Press, 1981), p. 336.
6. Yoshio Markino, *A Japanese Artist in London* (1910), p. 4.
7. René Gimpel, *Diary of an Art Dealer* (Farrar, Straus & Giroux, 1966), p. 129.
8. F. A. R. Russell, *London Fogs* (1880), p. 27.
9. J. B. Sanderson, 'The National Smoke Abatement Society and the Clean Air Act (1956)', *Political Studies*, vol. 9, iss. 3, October 1961.
10. Charles Dickens, *Our Mutual Friend* (1865), Book III, Chapter 1, p. 417.
11. Quoted in Nicholson, op. cit., pp. 104–5.
12. *The Times*, 1882.

13. Quoted in Nicholson, op. cit., pp. 248–9.
14. John Graham, *The Destruction of Daylight* (1907), p. 4.
15. Ibid.
16. Arthur Conan Doyle, *The Sign of the Four* (1890), p. 20.
17. Arthur Conan Doyle, 'The Adventure of the Bruce-Partington Plans' (1908), pp. 2–3.
18. Graham, op. cit., pp. 7–8.
19. *Nottingham Evening Post*, 8 April 1954.
20. *Coal Merchant and Shipper*, 4 June 1955.

14 White Heat

1. NCB, 16 November 1966, National Archives COAL 74/6374.
2. PREM 13/827.
3. 'I've never asked him; for me it has always been sufficient that he did so and I accepted', Alf Robens, *Ten Year Stint* (Cassell, 1972), p. 7.
4. Quoted in Gaynor Madgwick, *Aberfan* (Y Lolfa Cyf., 2016), p. 1.
5. Joe Gormley, *Battered Cherub* (Hamish Hamilton, 1982), p. 55.
6. Report of the Tribunal Appointed Under the Tribunals of Inquiry (Evidence) Act, 1921, *Part II: What Happened at Aberfan?*, paragraph 57, 3 August 1967, http://dmm.org.uk/ukreport/553-20.htm
7. Robens, op. cit., p. 251.
8. Madgwick, op. cit., p. 9.
9. Laurie Lee, *I Can't Stay Long* (Andre Deutsch, 1975), p. 74.
10. S. O. Davies, Hansard, House of Commons, Deb, 26 October 1967, vol. 751, col. 1928.
11. Tony Austin, *Aberfan: The Story of a Disaster* (Hutchinson, 1967), p. 195.
12. Ibid., pp. 196–7.
13. Margaret Thatcher, *The Path to Power* (HarperCollins, 1995), p. 143.
14. Richard Crossman, *Diaries, II* (Hamish Hamilton, 1976), p. 453.
15. Quoted in Iain McLean and Martin Johnes, *Aberfan* (Welsh Academic Press, 2020), p. 156.
16. Ibid., p.146.
17. *The New Britain*, Labour party manifesto, 'A Modern Economy, 2: A Plan for Industry', p. 6.
18. 'It was always necessary for me to be optimistic whenever I made a speech about the prospects of the coal industry', Robens, op. cit., p. 128.
19. Ibid., p. 205.
20. Ibid., p. 298.

15 'People will always need coal'

1. Sidney Ford, Presidential Address, 1969.
2. Joan Bakewell, 'Arthur Scargill', *Illustrated London News*, 29 July 1978, pp. 36–7.
3. 'The Long, Long Lorry Queue – To Load With Coke', *Birmingham Mail*, 3 February 1972.
4. Frank Ffoulkes, 'The Saltley Incident', quoted in Paul Routledge, *Scargill* (HarperCollins, 1994), pp. 74–5.
5. Charlie McLaren interviewed in Andy Beckett, *When the Lights Went Out: Britain in the Seventies* (Faber, 2009).
6. Derek Ezra, *Coal: Technology for Britain's Future* (Macmillan, 1976), p. 7.
7. Jeremy Bugler, 'Selby – The Community', *Coal: Technology for Britain's Future*, p. 112.
8. Ibid., p. 110.
9. Joe Gormley speech, Selby, 29 October 1976.
10. Tony Benn speech, Selby, 29 October 1976.
11. Quoted in *Daily Telegraph*, 13 February 1981.
12. Hansard, House of Commons, 17 February 1981, vol. 137, col. 999.

16 To the Death

1. https://www.margaretthatcher.org/document/105563
2. Charles Moore, *Margaret Thatcher: The Authorized Biography, Volume One: Not For Turning* (Allen Lane, 2013), p. 537.
3. Lord Howell, interview.
4. His main problem was that he was an intelligent man who did much of his thinking with his mouth in gear. When he died, the *Church Times* commented that his doubts about whether the virgin birth was strictly accurate 'recalled the storm over Hensley Henson's nomination to the see of Hereford in 1917', as if they thought about little else in Upper Clatford. Jenkins' enthronement in Durham was in March 1985 – Mrs Thatcher commented that 'it wouldn't be spring without the voice of the occasional cuckoo'.
5. When the 1985 Cabinet papers were released a year later, they revealed something of Thatcher's extensive use of the resources of the state to defeat the miners. MI5 had bugged union phones; the prime minister had intervened personally to instruct chief constables to be more aggressive in intercepting flying pickets; the intelligence services had secretly tracked union funds hidden abroad and plans had been made to use the army to move coal supplies.
6. Walker, described on the dustjacket of his memoirs as 'one of Britain's great political survivors', boasted that Thatcher believed 'industrial

unrest in the coal industry was probably the greatest threat to her government and I was the best person to see it did not happen' (Peter Walker, *Staying Power* (Bloomsbury, 1991), p. 166).

7. Quoted in Nicholas Jones, *Strikes and the Media* (Blackwell, 1986), p. 54.

8. *Sunday Times*, 17 November 1974.

9. Nicholas Jones, 'A Piranha Fish Bites Back', *British Journalism Review*, vol. 20, no. 1, March 2009.

10. Routledge, op. cit., p. 67.

11. Arthur Scargill, 'We could surrender – or stand and fight', *Guardian*, 7 March 2009.

12. Routledge, op. cit., p. 9. The phrase had been coined by Thomas Carlyle to describe Robespierre – whom he suggested was as incorruptible as the sea was green.

13. Roy Hattersley, 'Arrogant Met officers soured long friendships during 1984 miners' strike', *Observer*, 1 December 2012.

14. Earl of Stockton, maiden speech, House of Lords, 13 November 1984.

15. 'Sir Robert Peel's Policing Principles', *Definition of Policing by Consent*, gov.uk, 2012 FOI release 25060.

16. Foot, op. cit.

17. As the left-wing historian, Raphael Samuel put it in his introduction to a *History Workshop* book on the topic, the miners were making 'a defence of the known against the unknown, the familiar against the alien, the local and the human against the anonymous and the gigantesque. The miners were fighting against *losing* something.' He claimed that 'the animating spirit of the strike was that of *radical conservatism*', Samuel, *The Enemy Within* (Routledge, 1986), p. 22.

18. See J. Robins, 'Michael Mansfield: Hillsborough, Orgreave & the case for a truth commission', in *The Justice Gap*, 31 October 2012.

19. Margaret Thatcher speech to 1922 Committee, Thatcher Archive: speaking notes, 19 July 1984.

20. Emanuel Shinwell speech, quoted in Martin Adeney and John Lloyd, *The Miners' Strike* (Routledge, 1986), p. 1.

21. Arthur Scargill speech, quoted in '1985: Miners call off year-long strike', BBC On This Day, 3 March.

22. Jonathan and Ruth Winterton, *The Coal Crisis* (Manchester University Press, 1989), p. 300.

23. Peter Wilsher, *Strike: 358 Days that Shook the Nation* (Coronet, 1985), p. 254.

17 Goodnight and Goodbye
1. National Archives PREM 19/3860 (*Financial Position of the Coal Industry 1990*, documents from the Prime Minister's office).
2. National Archives PREM 19/3861 Letter from Michael Heseltine to Norman Lamont, 24 July 1992.
3. Lord Heseltine, interview.
4. Michael Heseltine, *Life in the Jungle* (Hodder & Stoughton, 2000), p. 444.
5. Lord Heseltine, interview.
6. The proportion of working women was slightly higher – 26.2%.
7. TUC figures.
8. Guy Faulconbridge, 'In England's forgotten "rust belt", voters show little sign of Brexit regret', Reuters, 7 August 2018.
9. Christina Beatty, Stephen Fothergill and Ryan Powell, *Twenty Years On: Has the Economy of the UK Coalfields Recovered?*', *Environment and Social Planning A*, vol. 39, 2007, pp. 1667, 1671.
10. All these figures are from Christina Beatty, Stephen Fothergill and Anthony Gore, *The State of the Coalfields, 2019* (Sheffield Hallam University Centre for Regional Economic and Social Research, 2019).
11. Ed Miliband, 'Miners Worked Their Backs Off for This Country – The Least We Owe Them is Fairness and Justice', website, 18 June 2019.
12. BBC, 'UK Miners win historic compensation claim', 23 January 1998.
13. Andrew Norfolk, 'Solicitor Jim Beresford makes £30m from sick miners' compensation scheme', *The Times*, 9 June 2008.
14. William Stanley Jevons, *The Coal Question* (1866), p. 46.
15. John Tyndall, 'On the Absorption and Radiation of Heat by Gases and Vapours, and on the Physical Connexion of Radiation, Absorption, and Conduction', *Philosophical Transactions of the Royal Society of London*, vol. 151, 1861, pp. 1–36.
16. See Spencer Weart, *The Discovery of Global Warming* (Harvard, 2008).
17. IPCC, 2007, p. 39.
18. Powering Past Coal Alliance, 'Phasing out Coal Power', *Energy Revolution: A Global Outlook* (Imperial College, 2018).
19. David Attenborough, UN Summit on Climate Change, Katowice, 3 December 2018.
20. See *Fossil CO2 emissions of all world countries – 2018 Report* (Publications Office, European Union).
21. Boris Johnson speech to 2020 United Nations Climate Change Conference (COP26), 4 February 2020.

22. All these figures should carry a health warning, for they ignored the fact that much of Britain's power was imported from France, where it had been generated in nuclear reactors, and from Germany and the Netherlands, where it had been produced from coal-driven turbines.

23. See 'A Framework for Clean Coal in Britain', TUC, 21 June 2006, and 'Wicks: "All is lost on global warming without clean coal"', *Guardian*, 8 August 2008.

Illustrations

A pithead, c.1775–1825 (*National Museums Liverpool/Bridgeman*)

Illustration of a woman dragging a cart (*Science & Society Picture Library/Getty*)

Illustration of two boys lowered down a mineshaft (*Science & Society Picture Library/Getty*)

J.M.W. Turner's *Keelmen Heaving in Coals by Moonlight* (*Bridgeman Images*)

Yoshio Markino's *Constitution Hill in the Evening* (*Bonhams, London, UK/Bridgeman Images*)

George Childs' *Dowlais Ironworks* (*Bridgeman Images*)

Rescue attempts at Seaham Colliery (*World History Archive/Alamy*)

Engraving of the Watt steam engine (*PRISMA ARCHIVO/Alamy*)

Drawing of Sheffield's rooftops in 1879 (*The Granger Collection/Alamy*)

Statue of Matthew Boulton, James Watt and William Murdock (*Paul Thompson Images/Alamy*)

Statue of the Third Marquess of Londonderry, Charles Vane (*Stuart Lawton/Alamy*)

Photograph of Lord Bute (*TopFoto*)

Portrait of the Earl of Shaftesbury (*Elgar Collection/Bridgeman Images*)

A.J. Munby and Ellen Grounds (*News Dog Media*)

Wigan's pit brow women (*News Dog Media*)

Lancashire's pit brow lasses at Moss Hall (*KGPA Ltd/Alamy*)

The *Turbinia* (*Universal History Archive/Getty*)

A boy with a pit pony and coal trucks (*TopFoto*)

Police officers blocking the streets during the Tonypandy riots (*FLHC 220C/Alamy*)

Soldiers awaiting transport to enforce order on the Tonypandy coal riots (*Pictorial Press Ltd/Alamy*)

The scene at Senghenydd after the second fire broke out (*Bridgeman Images*)

The rescue team leaving the pit during the Senghenydd colliery disaster (*FLHC 1/Alamy*)

A man rollerskates to work with his packed lunch in his hand (*Hulton Deutsch/Getty*)

Arthur James Cook (*World History Archive/Alamy*)

An unemployed coal miner in Wigan (*Granger Historical Picture Archive/Alamy*)

A photograph of young children scrounging for coal (*H. F. Davis/Getty*)

Nationalisation, captured at Ty Trist Colliery in Wales (*Bridgeman Images*)

A man guides a London bus through thick fog in London smog (*Monty Fresco/Hulton Archive/Getty*)

'Bevin Boys' at work in mines during the war (*IWM PD 274*)

Miners taking their bath after a day's work in the pits (*Hulton Archive/Getty*)

Rescue scenes after the mining disaster in Aberfan (*Shutterstock*)

Aberfan (*Bentley Archive/Popperfoto/Getty*)

Picketing miners scream abuse at those going into work at Thoresby Colliery (*Shutterstock*)

Stones are thrown at the police during the strike at Orgreave Coking Plant in Sheffield (*Shutterstock*)

Arthur Scargill arrested on a picket line (*Manchester Daily Express/Getty*)

Index

Introduction

The importance of this black rock cannot be exaggerated. Anything that might be alloyed, armoured, baked, boiled, bolted, brewed, built, canned, caulked, coked, cooked, corrugated, dried, dyed, electrified, fired, forged, fried, frozen, galvanised, gilded, hammered, hasped, illuminated, melted, printed, processed, pulverised, riveted, roasted, salted, scorched, serrated, sharpened, smelted, sugared, tanned, tempered, threshed, tinned, toasted, varnished or welded – to say nothing of countless other processes – depended upon coal. It was midwife to practical genius and without it, we should have nothing much for which to praise the Victorians. Britain dug out its coal more efficiently than anywhere else in Europe, and in time the country has paid the price for its ingenuity and ruthlessness. No one cares about coal any more: the cry now is 'down with fossil fuels' – and nothing is more packed with fossils than a sedimentary rock like coal. Even if you are lucky enough to find the fossils of ferns, or perhaps of insects, inside a lump of coal, in the end, it is just a black rock. By itself, it cannot do anything. So the story is not of a rock, but of human ingenuity. At its heart lies the human urge to break free of the bonds of nature.

Coal has an image problem. Thought of in the abstract it is just a grubby rock, whose extraction from the ground has ruined many a life. Yet individual lumps can look stunning – separate faces reflecting all the colours of a peacock's tail, and the history of its extraction is the story of Britain. In no other business were the political issues so stark. A lucky few owned land, and by some fluke of the law therefore claimed possession of whatever lay beneath it. They needed to do nothing to get even richer – and some became spectacularly wealthy. Most of the rest of humanity might, if they were lucky (or unlucky), be employed to hack the coal out of the ground and bring it to the surface for the owners to take their cut. *Cui bono?* – who benefits? – is the question asked when looking for suspects in a crime. The most obvious beneficiaries of the coal trade were those who could claim a royalty when a shovelful of coal was brought to the surface and carried away. But everyone – including those who worked underground – benefitted, whether they were navvies digging canals or laying railways, 'keel men' loading colliers, brokers who traded the stuff, merchants who sold it, or, indeed, the increasingly comfortable public who could enjoy a warm bath or flick a switch to turn on the lights.

Getting the coal was a murderous, antisocial activity riddled with conundrums. To gather the material that made Britain the first urban nation on earth, the miners often lived in isolated rural communities – meanly laid-out villages of flimsy houses where everyone knew each other's business and interior sanitation was frequently unheard of. The villages had usually been thrown up to service the mine, which might have been sunk in the middle of nowhere. These communities therefore tended to be tight-knit and spawned their own clubs – anything from vegetable gardening to pigeon-fancying. Sometimes these villages had their own meagre arrays of shops, often including 'tommy shops' owned by the mine proprietors. Occasionally, they had churches, more commonly a chapel where Nonconformists worshipped. There was, naturally, no street lighting: you could hear the miners setting off for their shifts in the small hours of the morning from the clatter of their hobnailed boots on the street. Until helmets (initially made of compressed cardboard) became compulsory, many continued to wear their own flat caps below ground well into the 1970s and they ruined their own clothing until the introduction of overalls in January 1979. Each man trooping to the pit carried a cheap metal tin holding their 'snap' or 'bait' for lunch, and usually a flask of cold tea. At work underground, the miners were quite beyond the inclination or ability of their employers to supervise them. When they plunged into the ground inside their metal cage they travelled from a world with rules recognisable to the rest of society, into a nether region in which boys became men very fast. What light they had came from candles, and later from safety lamps, which illuminated very little. Some pits were hot, in which the miners toiled half – or completely – naked. There were no sanitary facilities, so men relieved themselves where they stood or crouched. Many colliers had dark blue scabs running down their backs 'like the buttons on a coat', where their bodies had been cut as they tried to hack with their picks at another face. 'One for all and all for one' was much more than a slogan: the miners organised themselves, knowing that if one of them made a mistake, they could all pay for it with their lives. Because for most of the industry's existence they were paid 'piecework', miners' earnings depended upon how much coal they cut. The 'checkweighman', chosen by the workers to see that no management lackey diddled them, was one of the most respected men in the mine, for in many pits the default setting for relationships between employers and workers was one of naked distrust.

Mining was, then, a naturally fertile ground in which trade unionism might flourish. The evangelising efforts of Nonconformist churches like the Congregationalists, Methodists, and – in particular – the Primitive Methodists bore fruit in early trade union leaders: the Nonconformists chose their leaders not from a separate clergy but from within the congregation, and it was the same with the early trade union leaders. Many adopted communism in much the same way they had heard of the teachings of Jesus. Since their labour was among the most brutish ever expected of otherwise free men, collectively the miners liked to consider themselves an 'aristocracy' of the trade union movement. Even those on the other side of the political fence could sense their power. As the former Conservative prime minister, Harold Macmillan, is repeatedly quoted as saying, 'There are three bodies no sensible man directly challenges: the Roman Catholic Church, the Brigade of Guards and the National Union of Mineworkers.'

There was a home-grown hierarchy within the mines. Despite great variations depending upon terrain and time, the basic formula for working a mine went something like this: the fit young men nearest the coalface were the highest paid, which meant that a miner was at the peak of his earning powers in youth and early middle age. Often he was assisted by one of his children, a brother or family friend working as a 'hurrier', to load and then push away the waggon he had filled with cut coal. Miners might be well paid, but everyone else in the labour movement recognised that they earned it. But by the twentieth century absenteeism was becoming a real problem for mine managers, with the highest rates of unauthorised absence from work among the men with the highest wages: a single man with no dependants who worked at the coalface could often afford not to turn up for work a couple of days a week, whereas a man who worked on the surface wasn't well-enough paid to cope without his wages. The problem for the bosses was that unplanned absences at the coalface affected the entire production line, for it meant less coal was being produced. The employers' answer to the problems posed by absenteeism was usually a bribe: work five shifts and get paid for six. Even so, it was common at some collieries for up to half the workforce to lose the bonus. By the time their industry had been nationalised in the middle of the twentieth century – with taxpayers' money – there were unmarried miners trying to justify their absenteeism by claiming that the levels of income tax required of them made it not worth their while to work.

Old miners, and those whose bodies were broken or worn out, were employed 'bankside' – shovelling, grading and loading the coal that had been brought to the surface. The very infirm cleaned, polished and sharpened the tools of those who cut the coal: in their way the miners looked after their own. Until the 1840s women and children hauled coal waggons underground, while small children sat all day in the dark opening and closing the trapdoors which kept the coalfaces ventilated. But there were very few 'average' mines. To begin with, the quality of the coal extracted varied from one place to another. The miner might be hewing coal a hundred feet underground or thousands of feet down. He might be lying on his side tackling a seam only eighteen inches thick, or be able to stand upright, facing a wall of coal as tall as a house. There were mines where you could get soaked from water seeping in and others in which you got soaked by your own sweat. You shivered in some seams and baked in others. Some pits were plagued by dust, others had good ventilation. The mine might be gassy, or one where a naked candle flame would almost certainly be safe. If he could but see it, above the miner might be moorland, fields, houses or roads. Equally, the miner might be miles out under the sea: what lay above his head was of no interest at all. It wasn't until a new national wage agreement was introduced in 1966 that miners were paid by the shift rather than by the quantity of coal they had cut. The 'power-loading agreement' between management and miners was the first national acknowledgement of the role played by roaring great machines which could be placed alongside a coalface and chew their way through it with tungsten-tipped teeth, a far cry from the old bord and pillar method in which miners cut away coal with a pickaxe, leaving pillars to hold up the roof of the seam.

As almost every primary schoolchild used to be taught, all energy comes originally from the sun, in whatever form it might later be extracted and used. Coal is a fossil fuel made of the remains of trees and plants that grew millions of years ago as a result of photosynthesis, retaining the latent energy within them. In its early stages, the decaying vegetation formed peat, and, as time passed and other layers of rock were laid down above it, the liquid was squeezed from the peat, to form coal. Early coal miners would sometimes have to escape the area fast, when an entire fossilised tree trunk fell from the roof of the seam they were working and even long-established mines could often yield lumps of coal bearing the outlines of prehistoric plants and leaves.

The seams where the black fossils were found lay all over the country. There were significant coalfields in the Scottish Lowlands; in Northumberland and Durham; Cumberland and Lancashire; Yorkshire, Derbyshire and Nottinghamshire; in the Midlands; near Bristol; in Somerset; in North and South Wales and in Kent, to say nothing of smaller deposits, from the northern Highlands to Devon. Not all coal is equal: the worst coal – lignite – burns slowly and smokily, and the best, like the 'black diamonds' of anthracite, have a much higher carbon content and burn hotter and cleaner. It was Britain's good fortune that many of the country's deposits were of better-quality coal. (Germany, by contrast, became the world's biggest producer of low-quality 'brown coal'.) Seams of coal might go on for miles, beneath the surface of the ground (or the sea).

But wherever they were, there has never been any shortage of calamities in coal-mining. As Friedrich Engels put it: 'in the whole British Empire there is no occupation in which a man may meet his end in so many diverse ways as this one'.[1] I sat down one lunchtime with an old Welsh reporter who had spent years in the mining villages of South Wales. He picked up a sheet of A4 paper and began to list on it the colliery disasters he could recall, along with the casualty figures. He had soon covered one side with the total number of dead from accidents between the 1850s and the 1960s. It came to almost 3,000. Then he turned the page and continued his list. The grand total, he claimed, was over 6,000 dead or killed by the Welsh mining industry alone. Thousands more survived to retirement, only to shuffle their way to coughing deaths from one of the respiratory diseases they had contracted underground.

Digging coal out of the ground is a horribly dangerous job. Between 1873 and 1953 85,000 people were killed in mining accidents in Britain. It was the disasters which took hundreds of lives, or dragged on with uncertain outcome which caught the fancy of flibbertigibbet newspapers. But the truth was that death could call at any time, and most of the victims died in ones or twos. Little by little, the numbers added up to enormous totals. It bears repeating that there were a great number of ways to lose your life – crushed, gassed, drowned, burned or even – as happened in at least one accident – being boiled alive in steam cauldrons. There were other less dramatic, but equally remorseless conditions caused by mining, both physical and mental: men who went underground might emerge from the pit one day, but night terrors, laboured breathing and strange eye conditions like nystagmus ('dancing eyes') or photophobia (sensitivity to light) could last for years. Some miners went entirely blind. Other conditions brought on by mining turned the strong, vigorous men who had worked underground into invalids. 'Miners' anaemia' was brought on by the poor – usually non-existent – sanitation in mines, allowing parasitic larvae to enter the body and to develop into hookworms in the stomach, sucking blood from the intestines. 'Beat' hand, knee or elbow – forms of osteoarthritis – were caused by damaged joints. Constant breathing of coal dust brought on 'miners' asthma' or pneumoconiosis, which at its most benign weakened the lung, so that the victim became vulnerable to pneumonia or bronchitis. Local doctors became very familiar with 'miners' phthisis' or 'black spit', a form of silicosis caused by stone dust. One miner who had spent decades down the pit told me what retirement did to former colleagues. 'One day you'd see this brave, brawny man in the pit baths, and, a couple of months later he was just this coughing, shambling wreck. Then, you'd hear he'd died.'

Like the old miners, coal has almost completely disappeared from our lives. We cannot imagine some of our history without it – murky, choking streets are as much a part of Victorian fiction as the characters created by Charles Dickens. Yet even in the old mining communities the enormous winding-gear wheels which once stood at the top of the mineshaft and proclaimed to the world the village's reason for existence, disappeared long ago. Deep mines sunk 1,000 feet or more into the ground are distant memories. Even the great ziggurats of 'slag' – waste or unsaleable coal – have been landscaped into gentler hillocks and grassed over.

Britain has decided that its coal days are over and the future belongs to cleaner energy. A way of life has vanished, and those who might otherwise have had to spend their working lives toiling in the mines, breathing the dust which would send them coughing to their graves, are better off: I never met a miner who wanted the same life for his children. A filthy, dangerous occupation is finished. But a part of our history has gone, and something happens to a people when they lose a sense not only of the origins of the place they live in but of how their politics and identities developed.